Programmed Learning Materials

ARTES LATINAE

LATIN: LEVEL ONE, BOOK ONE

by Waldo E. Sweet

Bolchazy-Carducci Publishers
1000 Brown Street, Unit 101 • Wauconda, Illinois 60084

Copyright © 1966 held currently by Bolchazy-Carducci Publishers. Original Copyright © 1966 by Encyclopaedia Britannica Educational Corporation. All rights reserved. Printed in the United States of America. This work may not be transmitted by television or other devices or processed nor copied, recast, transformed, adapted or utilized in any manner, in whole or in part, without a license. For information regarding a license, write Bolchazy-Carducci Publishers.

ISBN: 0-86516-290-5

Reprint 1996

TABLE OF CONTENTS

Unit 1 Introduction; how to use the program

Unit 2 Pronunciation; Basic Sentence 1

Unit 3 Pronunciation; Basic Sentences 2-4

Unit 4 Distinction between noun and verb, subject and object; meaning of Basic Sentences 1-5

Unit 5 Variant signal for {-s}; new vocabulary; Basic Sentences 6 and 7

Unit 6 Distinction between noun and adjective; Basic Sentences 8-10

Unit 7 Question words **Quis?** and **Quem?**; word order; Basic Sentences 11 and 12

Unit 8 Two-kernel sentences; connector; antonyms; Basic Sentences 13-18

Unit 9 Ablative case; prepositions **cum** and **sine**; the five declensions; characteristic vowel; Basic Sentence 19; derivatives

Unit 10 Ablative of 4th and 5th Declensions; preposition **sub**; Basic Sentences 20-22

Unit 11 Passive voice; Basic Sentences 23 and 24

Unit 12 Neuters; **Quid?**; ambiguity; Basic Sentences 25-29

Unit 13 Gender; agreement of adjectives; Basic Sentences 30-35

Unit 14 Nominative, accusative, and ablative plural of 1st and 2d Declensions; Basic Sentences 36-39

Unit 15 Plural of 3d, 4th, and 5th Declensions; Basic Sentences 40-44

UNIT ONE

Welcome to the study of Latin.

This is a "program," a way of learning which will be new to some of you. Therefore we will spend some time showing you how to proceed properly. You will need a pad of paper to write your answers in, a Reference Notebook to take notes, and two "masks," which can be pieces of cardboard about 4 inches by 5, an old letter, or anything else of that sort. If you are using a tape recorder, you will not need to turn it on until Frame 47.

When you start, you will see that there is a heavy black border across the page. Place your "mask" so that it covers up what is written beneath the border. You will not need the second mask for awhile. All right, arrange your mask as indicated in the picture below.

Frame Number 1. You are now looking at Frame Number 1. You should have your mask arranged so that you can see nothing below the heavy black border. To put it another way, you should be able to see *only* these lines of print above the black border. Now move down to Frame 2; cover everything below Frame 2 with your mask.

▼▼▼▼▼▼▼▼▼▼▼▼▼▼▼▼▼▼

Frame Number 2. In each "frame" you will be asked to perform a small task. Your small task in this frame is to arrange your mask so that you cannot see Frame 3.

When you have done this, go on to Frame Number 3 and arrange your mask so that you can see Frame 3 but not Frame 4.

▼▼▼▼▼▼▼▼▼▼▼▼▼▼▼▼▼▼

VOCABULARY INVENTORY 15-78

Remember that we give only the nominative forms of nouns. Review if necessary.

In this unit you learned two nouns: **dēns** (255), **pēs** (254)

You also learned three new adjectives: **longus -a -um** (251), **multus -a -um** (29), **pie-nus -a -um** (263)

And one new preposition: **ex** (246)

You learned four new verbs: **adjuvat** (183), **fert** (226), **aspicit** (278), **timet** (221)

And you learned that **est** has this irregular plural form: **sunt** (86)

You learned the nominative forms **hic, haec, hoc** (256-262).

TEST INFORMATION

You know how to give six forms of several nouns of each declension. At the present time you are held responsible only for the forms which you have practiced on this program. In other words, the test will ask for the paradigms which you practiced in the program and will not ask you to do *similar* ones.

If you should make an error on the test, be sure that you analyze carefully why you failed to learn that point. Perhaps you should write more, perhaps you should say each answer several times. It is so obvious that it is embarrassing to say, but merely doing the program is a waste of time unless you master the material which is in it, and nobody can do this except you yourself.

1-2

Frame Number 3. The small task which you are to perform in this "frame" is to answer aloud the following question: "What is the number of this frame?" Answer *aloud*, and then pull down your mask to check to see if you were right.

▰▰▰▰▰▰▰▰▰▰▰▰▰▰▰

Answer: "This is Frame Number Three."

Frame Number 4. In many frames you will be asked to complete a word or words. For example, say the following sentence aloud by filling in the missing parts of the last two words.

The first president of the United States was G___ge W_____ton.

▰▰▰▰▰▰▰▰▰▰▰▰▰▰▰

Answer: George Washington.

Frame Number 5. You will notice that the border "breaks up" these lines of type you are now reading and separates them from the rest of the material on this page. The effect is much the same as "breaking up" the individual frames of a film or motion picture. It is for this reason that we call this "Fr___ Number 5."

▰▰▰▰▰▰▰▰▰▰▰▰▰▰▰

Answer: Frame
[Now move on to the next frame. Be sure to slide the mask down only to the bottom of the frame, so that you will not see the answer.]

Frame Number 6. Where you see the dashes, say the answer *aloud*. "How much is two plus two?" "It is _____." [The answer is below the line. Check your answer *after* you have said it aloud.]

▰▰▰▰▰▰▰▰▰▰▰▰▰▰▰

Answer: four.

---

380. St__t t____t F_____m, s_____s f_____t.
℞: Stultī tīment Fortūnam, sapientēs ferunt.

381. P____ D___, n__ pl____s, as_____ m____s.
℞: Pūrās Deus, nōn plēnās, aspicit manūs.

15-77

1-3

7. You may wonder why we ask you to say your answer *aloud*. This program has been tested with hundreds of students, and we have discovered that the students who do the best are those who _____ the questions out l____.

▼▼▼▼▼▼▼▼▼▼▼▼▼▼▼▼

Answer: answer   loud.

8. The first version of this program was written in 1961, which was the one hundredth anniversary of the beginning of the Civil War or the War Between the States. Therefore the Civil War began in the year _____.

▼▼▼▼▼▼▼▼▼▼▼▼▼▼▼▼

Answer: 1861.

9. The first hostile action of the War Between the States was the firing on Fort Sumter. This occurred in the year _____.

▼▼▼▼▼▼▼▼▼▼▼▼▼▼▼▼

Answer: 1861. [Answer aloud.]

10. The last two frames were "teaching frames," designed to teach you the date of a historical event. You will notice that it is difficult not to see Frame 9 and its answer. Therefore we will show you how to use the *second* mask. Place it above the frame you are reading, so the preceding frame and its answer are hidden from sight. Of course, you won't have to use the second mask when working on the first frame at the top of each page. Now perform this task.

The Civil War is also called "The W__ Be_____ the _____s." [If you can't answer, look back.]

▼▼▼▼▼▼▼▼▼▼▼▼▼▼▼▼

Answer: The War Between the States.

11. [Arrange the two masks so that only this frame shows. Try to answer the question. If you can't, then turn back to Frame 8.]

This war began in the year _____.

▼▼▼▼▼▼▼▼▼▼▼▼▼▼▼▼

15-76

376. The signal for the ablative plural of the Third, Fourth, and Fifth Declensions is -----

▼

A: -bus.

377. You also learned five new Basic Sentences. Write them.

F_____ F_____ adj_____.

R: Fortēs Fortūna adjuvat.

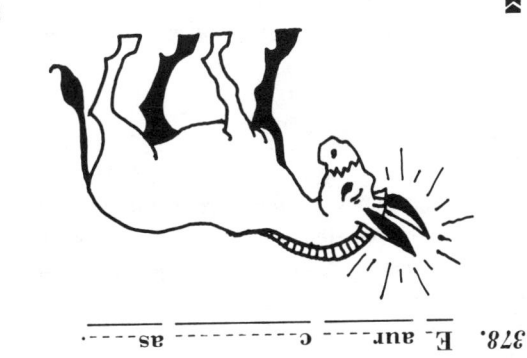

378. E. aur_____ c_____ as_____.

R: Ex auribus cognōscitur asinus.

379. F_____ f_____ m_____, ig_____ pr_____.

R: Fortūna fortēs metuit, ignāvōs premit.

Answer: 1861.
[Did you answer out loud?]

12. You can now see the purpose of the two masks. The purpose of the *lower* mask is to cover the answer until the student has had a chance to _____ the question.

▼▼▼▼▼▼▼▼▼▼▼▼▼▼

Answer: answer

13. The purpose of the *upper* mask is to keep the student from accidentally seeing the answer in one of the earlier _____s.

▼▼▼▼▼▼▼▼▼▼▼▼▼▼

Answer: frames.

14. The theory behind programmed learning is that you will learn faster if you solve many easy problems and know right away whether you are right or wrong. But you would get no practice in *solving* the problems if you were to see the answer ____ (before/after) you replied.

▼▼▼▼▼▼▼▼▼▼▼▼▼▼

Answer: before

15. This program has been tested with hundreds of students. There are no "trick" questions. If you find that you cannot answer a question it means that you have missed a small piece of information in one of the earlier frames. If you cannot solve a problem you should ____ (go back a few frames to try to solve the problem on your own/look for the answer below the line).

▼▼▼▼▼▼▼▼▼▼▼▼▼▼

Answer: go back a few frames to try to solve the problem on your own.

16. We will now talk a little about the strange and wonderful people who spoke and wrote Latin. This section is intended to help you learn how to operate the program. Therefore you will *not* be tested on anything in this Introduction. We are not trying to teach you the date of the beginning of the Civil War but only how to ------- the -------.

▼▼▼▼▼▼▼▼▼▼▼▼▼▼▼

Answer:　　　　　　　operate program.
[You do not have to have exactly the same words as the answer in the program.]

17. The capital city of the people who spoke Latin was Rome. According to legend, in 753 B.C. Romulus, assisted by his brother Remus, founded this city of -----.

▼▼▼▼▼▼▼▼▼▼▼▼▼▼▼

Answer:　　Rome.

18. [Remember that you may look back for the answer if you find that you cannot answer the question; otherwise place the top mask so only this frame is visible.]

The story goes that after the city was founded, an argument arose between the brothers, and Romulus killed his brother -----.

▼▼▼▼▼▼▼▼▼▼▼▼▼▼▼

Answer:　　　　　　　Remus.

19. Romulus and Remus founded Rome in the year --- B.C.

▼▼▼▼▼▼▼▼▼▼▼▼▼▼▼

Answer: 753

20. Now let's stop a minute to find out if you are learning what you are expected to be learning. The date of the founding of Rome was mentioned in an incidental sort of way in Frame 17. If you remembered it, congratulations!

[*Continue on next page.*]

---

365. In English we identify a verb in two ways: it has a special form to show p--- time and it fills a certain ---- in the sentence.

▲

A:　　past
　　　slot (position)

▲

366. In English we identify adjectives by the fact that an adjective has different forms to show m--- and m---.

▲

A: more　most.

▲

367. The forms which show "more" and "most" for the adjective "large" are "-------," and "-------."

▲

A: larger
　　largest.

▲

368. The forms which show "more" and "most" for "ambitious" are "--- ---------," and "--- ---------."

▲

A: more ambitious
　　most ambitious.

▲

369. We also identify English adjectives by the slot they fill in the sentence, but an English adjective must fill --- different slots.

▲

A:　　two

▲

370. To make "happy" modify "boy," in the sentence, "The boy grabbed his lost puppy," we place it between "----," and "----."

▲

A:　　The　boy.

Most students, however, would *not* have remembered the date, but they *would* have remembered that if you can't answer you are supposed to ⸺ ⸺ ⸺ ⸺ ⸺ ⸺ ⸺ ⸺ ⸺ ⸺ ⸺ ⸺ ⸺ ⸺ ⸺ .
[Answer in your own words.]

▼▼▼▼▼▼▼▼▼▼▼▼▼▼▼

Ans: go back a few frames and try to solve the problem on your own.

21. Some students do not do well in school simply because they do not know "how to study." If you follow directions in this program you will *learn* ⸺ ⸺ ⸺ .

▼▼▼▼▼▼▼▼▼▼▼▼▼▼▼

Ans: how to study.

22. If you took the "easy way" and looked at the answer below the border without putting forth *any effort* to solve the problem, you have not yet learned the first point about how to operate the ⸺ ⸺ .

▼▼▼▼▼▼▼▼▼▼▼▼▼▼▼

Ans: program.

23. All right, then, when was Rome founded? It was in the year ⸺ B.C.

▼▼▼▼▼▼▼▼▼▼▼▼▼▼▼

Ans: 753

24. In this program you will learn a lot about Roman gods and goddesses. Chief among them was Jupiter, the supreme god, and his wife Juno. Then there were others, such as Mars, god of war, and Venus, goddess of love and beauty. While Mars and Jupiter are called "gods," Juno and Venus are called "god⸺es."

▼▼▼▼▼▼▼▼▼▼▼▼▼▼▼

Ans: goddesses.

1-7

25. Because the Romans were so warlike, the ancient legend claimed that the father of Romulus and Remus was the war-god M___.

[Look back if you need help.]

▼▼▼▼▼▼▼   ▼▼▼▼▼▼▼

Ans: Mars.

26. In the *Aeneid*, the great poem by Vergil, the hero Aeneas is said to be the son of the goddess of love and beauty, who was named _____.

▼▼▼▼▼▼▼   ▼▼▼▼▼▼▼

A: Venus.

27. For many years Aeneas was prevented from reaching Italy, his destined goal, by the enmity of the queen of the gods, who was named J___.

▼▼▼▼▼▼▼   ▼▼▼▼▼▼▼

A: Juno. [Are you answering aloud?]

15-72

353. If you were asked to define what a noun is, you could not give a definition until you were told wh-- l------ it belonged to.

▲

A: which (what) language

▲

354. In English a noun has the signal {--} to show ------ n------.

▲

A: -s- plural number.

▲

355. An English noun also follows such words as "the," "an," "many," etc., which are the part of speech called "n-----s-----."

▲

A: noun markers.

▲

356. A noun in Latin not only has the singular/plural contrast but it also has three different -----s.

▲

A: cases. (There are five cases, but we have only had three so far.)

▲

357. In English we tell the subject by its ---------------
[In your own words]

▲

A: position (slot, word order).

▲

358. In Latin we tell the subject by its -----, which is ----------.

▲

A: case, which is nominative.

28. Now for a few remarks on the mechanics of the program.

When you first begin you need certain aids which you can soon do without. We say that we "vanish" these aids. For example, at the beginning of the program we completely underlined each frame with a black border. In the last few frames we have v‿‿‿‿ed most of the middle portion of the black border.

A: vanished

29. You no longer need the complete black border to indicate the frame. Therefore we have ‿‿‿‿ed the middle part of it.

A: vanished

30. In the same way, we will give you almost the same frame which we gave you before, but we will vanish some of the aids. While Mars and Jupiter are called "gods," Juno and Venus are called "‿‿‿‿‿‿‿."

A: goddesses.

31. In the earlier frame we gave you a "clue" by furnishing the first three and the last two letters of the word "goddesses." In this last frame we ‿‿‿‿ed this assistance.

A: vanished

32. This kind of assistance to help you solve the problem is called a "cl‿‿‿."

A: clue.

---

347. In Latin, when the subject auctor becomes plural (**auctōrēs**), the verb **laudat** ‿‿‿‿ [In your own words]

A: becomes plural too.

348. In English, when the subject "author" becomes plural ("authors"), the verb phrase "is praising" becomes ‿‿‿‿‿‿‿‿. [In your own words]

A: plural too (are praising).

349. We say that in Latin the subject and verb ag‿‿‿ in number.

A: agree

350. In English do the subject and verb agree in number? That is, when you change the subject "author" to "authors," do you have to make any change in the verb phrase "is praising"? ‿‿‿‿ (Yes/No)

A: Yes

351. Which of these statements is true?
1) English vocabulary has borrowed many words from Latin.
2) English vocabulary has little resemblance to Latin.

A: 1) English vocabulary has borrowed many words from Latin.

352. Which of these statements is true?
1) English structure is much like Latin structure.
2) English structure is almost totally different from Latin structure.

A: 2) English structure is almost totally different from Latin structure. (Although they do both have singular and plural number.)

1-9

33. The number of dashes indicates the number of missing letters. If we ask you for the name of the goddess of love and beauty and leave five dashes, you know that the answer contains ____ letters.

▼▼▼▼▼▼   ▼▼▼▼▼▼

A: five

34. Sometimes we do not wish to clue you with the number of words. In this case we have a long line of dashes. Here is an example. Venus was the goddess of ────────────────── .

▼▼▼▼▼▼   ▼▼▼▼▼▼

A: love and beauty.
[Did you remember to answer aloud?]

35. Sometimes you are asked to make a choice. The signal for a choice is four dashes with the choice in parentheses. Here is an example. The supreme ruler of all the gods was ____ (Mars/Jupiter).

▼▼▼▼▼▼   ▼▼▼▼▼▼

A: Jupiter.

36. Sometimes you will be asked to *write* your answer in your Answer Pad. The signal to write is a *solid* line. Here is an example. Copy down these two names in your Answer Pad: Romulus, Remus. _____, _____.

▼▼▼▼▼▼   ▼▼▼▼▼▼

A: Romulus, Remus.

---

341. portīcus (4) ──── ────

R: portīcus   porticūs
    porticum   portīcūs
    porticū   portibus

▲

342. diēs (5) ──── ────

R: diēs   diēs
    diēs   diem
    diēs   diēbus

▲

343. fūr (3) ──── ────

R: fūr   fūrēs
    fūrem fūrēs
    fūre   fūribus

▲

344. aper (2) ──── ────

R: aper   aprī
    aprum aprōs
    aprō   aprīs

▲

We will have here a short review of the contrast between the structure of English and the structure of Latin.

345. Auctor ōrātiōnem blandam laudat = The ──── is ──── ing ──── .

▲

A: The author is praising smooth (or pleasant) speech.

346. Auctōrēs ōrātiōnem blandam laudant = The ──── are ──── ──── .

▲

A: The authors are praising smooth (or pleasant) speech.

1-10

37. People learn a foreign language in several ways. The first is through *sound*, by h___ing it and sp___ing it.

▼▼▼▼▼▼▼ ▼▼▼▼▼▼▼

A: hearing
   speaking

38. They also learn through seeing it in written form by r___ing and wr___ing.

▼▼▼▼▼▼▼ ▼▼▼▼▼▼▼

A: reading and writing.

39. You all will get plenty of practice in speaking, reading, and writing. A few lucky ones, who have the use of a tape recorder, will also be able to h___ Latin as they take the program.

▼▼▼▼▼▼▼ ▼▼▼▼▼▼▼

A: hear

40. *But* (and this is important) the program is so constructed that whether you have a tape recorder or not you can all do the s___ frames.

▼▼▼▼▼▼▼ ▼▼▼▼▼▼▼

A: same

15-69

336. ✦ ○ •

blanda ōrātiō   blandae ōrātiōnēs
blandam ōrātiōnem   blandās ōrātiōnēs
blandā ōrātiōne   blandīs ōrātiōnibus

▲

337. Habet suum venēnum *blanda ōrātiō.* →

H___ent s___ v___ bl___ or___.

▲

R: Habent suum venēnum blandae ōrātiōnēs.

▲

[If you are not satisfied with your performance, go back and study these noun-plus-adjective paradigms again.]

In this next sequence, write the paradigm of nouns of the five declensions. The number in parentheses tells you what declension the noun is. When "testing frames" like these occur, if you are not sure you can do them, take the opportunity to review, either in the program or in your Notebook. On the other hand, if you are confident that you know these forms, then you may skip to frame 345.

338. musca (1) ——————

[You may say these aloud instead of writing, if you learn better that way.]

▲

R: musca   muscae
   muscam   muscās
   muscā   muscīs

▲

339. taurus (2) ——————

▲

R: taurus   taurī
   taurum   taurōs
   taurō   taurīs

▲

340. orbis (3) ——————

▲

R: orbis   orbēs
   orbem   orbēs
   orbe   orbibus

41. A star in the program [★] means that those who have a tape recorder are to start the tape recorder and l_____ to what is said.

▼ ▼ ▼ ▼   ▼ ▼ ▼ ▼

A: listen

42. However, below each frame where one can listen to the tape recorder there is also a "Visual Check." This means that if you *aren't* using a tape recorder, you can slide your mask down so that you can ___ in written form what people with tape recorders can h____.

▼ ▼ ▼ ▼   ▼ ▼ ▼ ▼

A: see   hear.

43. For those who are using a tape recorder, the signal to *start* the tape recorder is a star in the written program. When you listen to the tape a "Beep!" will mark the end of the frame on tape and will tell you to ___p the tape recorder.

▼ ▼ ▼ ▼   ▼ ▼ ▼ ▼

A: stop

44. You then return to the pr___ed part of the program.

▼ ▼ ▼ ▼   ▼ ▼ ▼ ▼

A: printed

45. A circle following a star means that your "tape teacher," whose voice is on the tape, will say something *once*. Two circles following a star mean that your tape teacher will say the same thing tw____.

▼ ▼ ▼ ▼   ▼ ▼ ▼ ▼

A: twice.

1-12

46. In the next frame you will use a tape recorder if you have one. Those of you who do *not* have a tape recorder should pull down their bottom mask to get the same information in ⸺ form.

▽ ▽ ▽ ▽

A: written

47. Here then is the signal to start the tape recorder. Your tape teacher will say something twice. The "Beep!" will tell you when to stop. ★ ○ ○

▽ ▽ ▽ ▽

Visual Check: The founder of Rome was Romulus, spelled R–O–M–U–L–U–S.
[This is what you would have heard if you had listened to the tape.]

48. (To save time, we will shorten "tape teacher" to "teacher.") As your "teacher" talks, look at this map. ★ ○

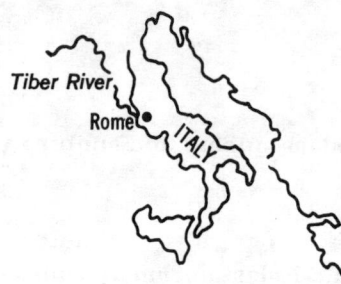

[Listen if you have a tape recorder; read the Visual Check below if you do not.]

▽ ▽ ▽ ▽

[If you used a tape recorder you may skip the Visual Check. If you wish to read it, by all means do so.]

Visual Check: When the Romans first appeared on the stage of history they were a small tribe living in a village called Rome on the Tiber River in Italy. Locate Italy, Tiber River, and Rome on the map.

(The right-hand column is printed upside-down:)

323. Fortēs Fortūna adjuvat. "Ā quō fortēs adjuvantur?" "⸺."

△

R: Ā Fortūnā.

△

324. Fortūna fortēs metuit, ignāvōs premit. "Quid Fortūna premuntur?" "⸺."

△

R: Ignāvī.

△

In this sequence you will first echo the paradigm of noun and adjective phrases. Then you will change a phrase in a Basic Sentence from singular to plural, using one of these forms.

325. We have purposely chosen examples where the noun and adjective do not belong to the same declension and therefore do not rh⸺.

△

A: rhyme.

△

326. ★ ○ • [Repeat until learned.]

medicus ēloquēns
medicum ēloquentem
medicō ēloquentī
medicī ēloquentēs
medicōs ēloquentēs
medicīs ēloquentibus

△

327. Change the italicized phrase from singular to plural.
Nōn quaerit aeger *medicum ēloquentem*. →
N⸺ qu⸺ ae⸺ m⸺ ēl⸺.

△

R: Nōn quaerit aeger medicōs ēloquentēs.

△

328. ★ ○ •

omnis rēs   omnem rem
omnēs rēs   omnem rem
omnēs rēs   omnī rē
omnibus rēbus

△

1-13

49. Sometimes the tape will tell you how to pronounce new names. If you do not have a tape recorder, the pronunciation will be indicated by the V_____ Ch____.

▼ ▼ ▼ ▼   ▼ ▼ ▼ ▼

A: Visual Check.

50. Let us practice this now. Listen to the name of the section of Italy where Rome and the Tiber River were located. ★ ○ ○ Latium [If you have no tape recorder, use the Visual Check below this line.]

▼ ▼ ▼ ▼   ▼ ▼ ▼ ▼

Visual Check: "láy-shum" (This special spelling will indicate how the word is pronounced.)

51. You will often be asked to "echo" your teacher. This means that you are to rep___ what you hear on the tape.

▼ ▼ ▼ ▼   ▼ ▼ ▼ ▼

A: repeat

52. The symbol for "echo" is the black dot, which indicates a blank space on the tape in which you are to e---o what you have just heard.

▼ ▼ ▼ ▼   ▼ ▼ ▼ ▼

A: echo

53. Echo the name of the founder of Rome. ★ ○ • Romulus [If you do not have a tape recorder, look at the Visual Check below this line.]

▼ ▼ ▼ ▼   ▼ ▼ ▼ ▼

Visual Check: "ráw-mew-luss"

54. The echo is usually a double one. The signal is a star ("Start the recorder"), a circle ("Listen"), a dot ("Echo"), a second circle ("Listen again"), and a second dot ("Echo again").

Echo the name of Romulus' brother. ★ ○ • ○ • Remus

▼ ▼ ▼ ▼   ▼ ▼ ▼ ▼

Visual Check: "reé-muss"

315. Fortēs Fortūna adjuvat. (40) ∨ ★ ○ •

▲

316. Pūrās Deus, nōn plēnās, aspicit manūs. (44) ∨ ★ ○ •

▲

317. Fortūna fortēs metuit, ignāvōs premit. (41) ∨ ★ ○ •

▲

318. Stultī timent Fortūnam, sapientēs ferunt. (42) ∨ ★ ○ •

▲

319. Each question will require you to transform a word of the Basic Sentence to another case. Remember that your answer will be in the s--- c--- as the question word.

▲

A: same case

320. Stultī timent Fortūnam, sapientēs ferunt. "Ā quibus Fortūna timētur?" "_____."

▲

R: Ā stultīs.

321. Pūrās Deus, nōn plēnās, aspicit manūs. "Ā quō manūs plēnae nōn aspiciuntur?" "_____."

▲

R: Ā Deō.

322. Ex auribus cognōscitur asinus. "Quantās aurēs habet asinus?" "L_____."

▲

R: Longās.

1-14

55. Now a word of advice, which comes from the experience of hundreds of students who have taken this program. Some students do what they are told and *no more*. If they are asked to echo twice, they will echo only twice. But the students who do well will _____ .
[In your own words]

A: repeat it as many times as they feel necessary to learn.

56. Most of you will not have the use of the tape recorder. When you are asked to echo something you should pull down the mask until you can see the _____ _____ .

A: Visual Check.

57. Then you should _____ . [In your own words]

A: repeat what you see aloud as many times as necessary to learn it.

58. If you do not have the help of a tape recorder you ____ (are excused from knowing these frames/should work just a little harder to make up).

A: should work just a little harder to make up.

59. After all, people have used languages for thousands of years without the use of ____ _____s.

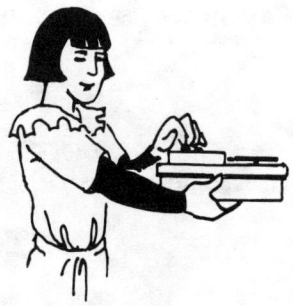

15-65

309. In English the word "clothes," is ____ (singular/plural) number.

A: plural

310. The Latin word **vestis** is ____ (singular/plural) number.

A: singular

311. We mentioned that Basic Sentence 5, **Elephantus nōn capit mūrem**, could either be translated by "An _____ doesn't _____ a _____," or by "_____s don't _____ _____."

A: elephant catch mouse Elephants don't catch mice.

312. In Basic Sentence 18, **Vītam regit Fortūna, nōn Sapientia**, the word **vītam** is singular number in Latin, but we used the plural of the corresponding English word in our translation and said "Fortune, not Wisdom, rules our _____."

A: lives.

313. About seventy-five percent of the time (to make a rough guess) Latin and English will put the same things in the same number. Be on your guard for the other twenty-five percent of the time when Latin uses a singular noun where English would use a _____ noun.

A: plural

Pronounce the following Basic Sentences which you learned in this unit.

314. Ex auribus cognōscitur asinus. (43)
✓ ★ ○ •

A: tape
recorders.

60. Many times you will be asked to give your answer *first* and *then* check with the tape or the Visual Check. The symbol for this is a check mark ("Check your answer"), followed by a star ("Start the tape recorder"), a circle ("Listen to the correct answer"), and a black dot ("Echo the correct answer"). Here is the signal now. Be sure to give the answer aloud *before* you turn on the tape recorder or look at the Visual Check.

Rome was located in the section of Italy called "L_____." √ ★ ○ •

Visual Check: Latium. ("láy-shum")

61. You must be *sure* that your procedure is correct. You should first have _____ed the word "Latium" aloud.

A: pronounced

62. Then you should have t____ed on the tape recorder and l_____ed to the correct answer.

A: turned
   listened

63. Finally, you should have ____ed the correct answer.

A: echoed (repeated)

64. If you are not using a tape recorder, you should have first _____.

A: pronounced the word "Latium" aloud.

---

305. Many languages (Chinese is one) do not make any distinction between singular and plural. If they wish, the speakers of such languages use numerals or words like "many," but the noun itself undergoes no change. To give an example in English (the example will sound funny because English is not Chinese) they say not only "one book," but also "two b____."

A: book.

306. "Two book" sounds funny to us, but that is just the point we are trying to make. The corresponding Chinese expression sounds just right to people who speak _____.

A: Chinese.

307. Both English and Latin have singular and plural number. Can we assume an English plural must be plural in Latin? ____ (Yes/No)

A: **NO!**

308. For example, the noun *vestis* is nominative singular, and yet we translate the Basic Sentence *Vestis virum reddit* as "_____ ____ ___ ____."

A: Clothes make the man.

1-16

65. Then you should have pulled down the mask to ⸺.
[In your own words]

A: see the special spelling which shows how "Latium" is pronounced.

66. Then you should have re⸺ed the word aloud several times.

A: repeated

67. Rome was located in the section of Italy called ⸺.
[Remember, the solid line means to *write* in your answer pad.]

A: Latium.

68. The black border has almost completely disappeared. Now the frames are indicated only by ⸺.
[In your own words]

A: mask indicators on either side of the page.

69. In other words, we have v⸺ed most of the black border.

A.   vanished

70. You will always need to have some indication to tell you how far to pull down the bottom mask, but you no longer need to have the full border. Therefore we have ⸺ed all but two of the mask indicators.

A: vanished

15-63

299. But we could just as easily have described the picture by saying "Here is a ⸺ of students." [In your own words.]

A: class (group, etc.)

300. The word "class" is ⸺ number.

A: singular

301. The word "students" is ⸺ number.

A: plural

302. In the first example ("Here are some students,") we used the concept of ⸺.

A: plural.

303. In the second example ("Here is the class") we used the concept of ⸺ in the same situation.

A: singular

304. Look at the sentence "The rice is good but the potatoes are better." In English, "rice" is a "mass noun," and "potatoes" is a "count noun." In the following sentence, only one of the two words ("rice" or "potatoes") will fit. "On my plate were two ⸺."

A: potatoes.

71. We will now talk a little more about the extraordinary people called the Romans. This will give you further practice in using the program (and the tape recorder, if you are using one).

Listen to your teacher if you have a tape recorder *or* read the visual check if you do not. ★ ○

Visual Check: Modern archaeological research has showed that the site of Rome was occupied somewhat earlier than the legendary date of 753. The evidence also shows that the village of Rome had gained some importance among her neighbors by 600 B.C. Therefore the legendary date of 753 B.C. is not too far off.

72. Therefore, one of the dates of history which you should know, even though it is not precisely accurate, is the legendary founding of Rome in _____ B.C.

A: 753 [Did you *write* the answer?]

73. Let us make sure that you know when to *say* your answer and when to *write* it. Most of the time you will say your answer aloud. The signal to *write* the answer is a ____ (solid/broken) line.

A: solid

74. The signal to *say* your answer aloud is a _____ ____.

A: broken line. (like the one in this frame)

75. ★ ○

Visual Check: By the year 264 B.C. this tiny village on the Tiber had become a world power which had conquered all Italy.

---

295. "¿Quáles datóres Deum violant?"

R: Impúri datóres.

296. Many languages have no singular/plural contrast. To speakers of such languages, it must seem odd that in English we always have to decide whether things are singular or _____.

A: plural.

We said "we have to *decide* whether things are singular or plural" because it is not a question of whether things are really singular or plural. Our language makes us interpret everything in terms of singular and plural, and this is quite independent of the real world. Anything could be described by a singular or a plural noun, as the speaker of the language chooses. Here are some examples.

297. Describe this picture. "Here are some _____." [In your own words.]

A: students (pupils, etc.)

298. "Students" ("pupils," etc.") is _____ (singular/plural) number.

A: plural

76. From now on in the program we will often use symbols rather than written directions. If you should ever forget what these symbols mean, look in the first page of your Reference Notebook, where they are explained.

A star and a circle means that if you have a tape recorder you are to ---------------------------- and --------------------------------.

A: turn on your tape recorder and listen to your teacher say something once.

77. If you do not have a tape recorder, then you are to p--- d--- y--- b---om m--- and r--- the V---al Ch----.

A: pull down your bottom mask and read the Visual Check.

78. Locate Italy on this map. ★ ○

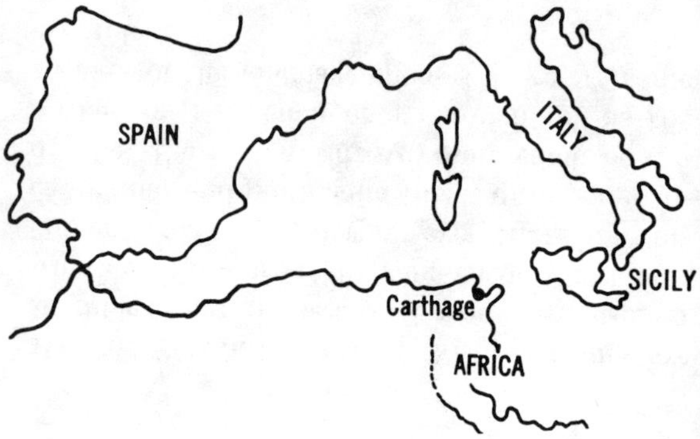

Visual Check: With Italy conquered, Rome turned her eyes to the nations surrounding the Mediterranean Sea and in 264 B.C. became involved in a series of long and bloody wars with a city in Africa named Carthage, C–A–R–T–H–A–G–E.

79. Locate this rival of Rome on the map and write the name in your Answer Pad. _____.

A: Carthage.

288. "Colitne Deum dator pūrus an impūrus?" "_____ _____."

R: Dator pūrus.

289. "Coluntne an violant Deum datōrēs impūrī?" "_____ _____."

R: Violant Deum.

290. "Coliturne Deus ā datōribus pūrīs an impūrīs?" "_____ _____ _____."

R: Ā datōribus pūrīs.

291. "Quālis dator Deum colit?" "_____ _____."

R: Pūrus dator.

292. "Quālis dator Deum violat?" "_____ _____."

R: Impūrus dator.

293. "Quālibus ā datōribus Deus colitur?" "_____."

R: Pūrīs ā datōribus.

294. "Quālibus ā datōribus Deus violātur?" "_____."

R: Impūrīs ā datōribus.

80. ★ ○

Visual Check: Today we use the term "Africa" to designate the entire continent, but as you can see from the map, in ancient times the name "Africa" included only the northern coast of this continent.

81. ★ ○

Visual Check: The soldiers of Rome gradually extended her rule over the entire Mediterranean Basin. This map shows the maximum extent of the Roman Empire, in about the year 100 A.D. At this time Rome was no longer a republic but was ruled by an emperor.

82. The vast territory over which the emperor ruled was called the R___n Em___e.

A: Roman Empire.

83. ★ ○

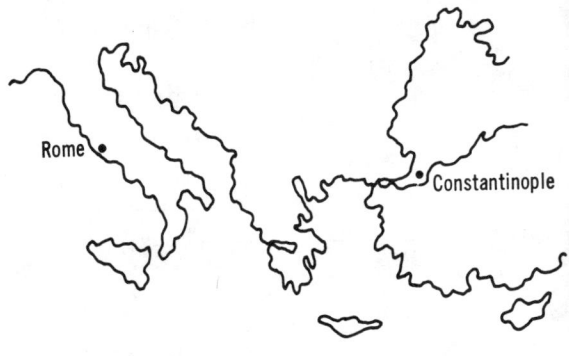

---

283. This reminds us of the story of the "widow's mite" in the New Testament. When she was ridiculed for giving a small gift, Jesus rebuked the critics and said that she should be praised because she had given ——————————. [In your own words]

A: more in proportion to what she had than those who were making fun of her.

284. The picture to illustrate this last Basic Sentence will therefore be the widow offering her small gift. Say the Basic Sentence.

P— D——, n— pl——, as—— m——.

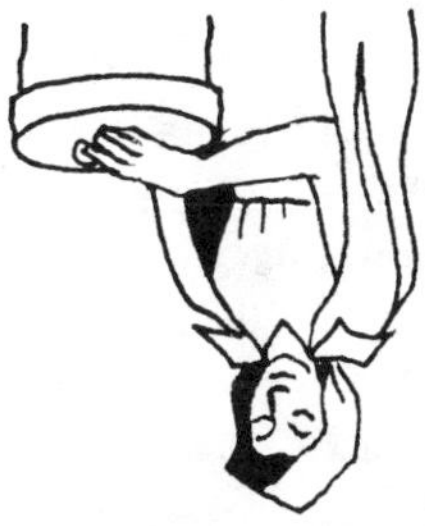

A: Pūrus Deus, nōn plēnās, aspicit manūs. (44)

Question and Answer Drill

285. "Quis pūrās manūs aspicit?" "———."

R: Deus.

286. "Quālēs manūs Deus nōn aspicit?" "———."

R: Plēnās manūs.

287. "Quālem datōrem dīligit Deus, pūrum an impūrum?" "———."

R: Pūrum.

Visual Check: For reasons about which historians do not agree, the western part of the empire slowly decayed. The "fall of Rome" is dated in 476 A.D., when the Emperor at Rome was put to death.

84. Repeat this date several times: 476 A.D.

85. Write in your Answer Pad the date of the "fall of Rome." _____.

A: 476 A.D.

86. The term "fall of Rome" for the events of 476 A.D. is misleading since Rome didn't suddenly fall but rather gradually de_____ed.

A: declined (decayed, deteriorated, etc.)

(The words in parentheses indicated acceptable answers. You may have had still another word or phrase, like "went to pieces." If you are in doubt whether your answer was correct, ask your classroom teacher. "Blew up" would *not* be acceptable.)

87. ★ ○

Visual Check: For generations the barbarians had been pushing in on the Empire from the north and east. It is as misleading to think of 476 A.D. as the sudden end of Rome as it is to think of 753 B.C. as the beginning.

88. However, you should know that the legendary founding of Rome was in ___ B.C. and the so-called "fall of Rome" was in ___ A.D.

A: 753 B.C.
          476 A.D.

1-21

89. ★ ○

Visual Check: For many years before the "fall of Rome" the empire had been split into two sections, the western part with its capital at Rome and the eastern part with its capital at Constantinople.

90. Locate the capital of the eastern part of the Roman Empire on your map in frame 83 and write the name in your Answer Pad. _____.

A: Constantinople.

91. ★ ○

Visual Check: The emperors at Constantinople continued to rule in an unbroken line (although different families held the throne) for a thousand years after the fall of Rome.

92. Constantinople was captured by the Turks in 1453 A.D. This marked the end of the ___tern part of the empire.

A: eastern

93. ★ ○ • ○ • Byzantine

[Look in your Reference Notebook if you have forgotten what the symbols mean.]

Visual Check: "bíz-zun-teen"

[If you do not use a tape recorder, repeat this name several times.]

94. This eastern part of the Roman Empire, which continued to flourish at Constantinople, was called the Byzantine Empire. Write "Byzantine" in your Answer Pad. _____.

A: Byzantine

---

267. ★ ○ ○ P---- D----,

R: **Pūrās Deus,**

268. **Pūrās** ---- (modifies/does not modify) **Deus.**

A: does not modify

269. **Deus** is the {---} of the sentence.

A: {-s}

270. **Pūrās** modifies the {---} of the sentence.

A: {-m}

271. **Pūrās Deus** means that ---- blanks ---- people (or things).

A: God pure

272. ★ ○ ○ **Pūrās Deus, n--- pl----,**

R: **Pūrās Deus, nōn plēnās,**

273. **Pūrās** and **plēnās** both modify the {---} of the sentence.

A: {-m}

274. **Pūrās Deus, nōn plēnās** means that God blanks ---- people (or things) but he ---- ---- blank ---- people (or things).

A: pure does not full

15-38

1-22

95. The capture of Constantinople in 1453 A.D. marked the end of the B_____ne Em____.

A: Byzantine Empire.

96. ★ ○

Visual Check: But even in the west the mighty name of Rome still swayed the hearts and minds of men. Charlemagne was crowned Emperor of the West on Christmas Day in 800 A.D. And of all the cities in his empire, he chose to be crowned in Rome.

97. Charlemagne was crowned Emperor of the West in Rome in the year 800 ____ (B.C./A.D.).

A: A.D.

98. There is a great building in Rome called the Colosseum. In the Middle Ages (after the so-called "fall of Rome") there was a popular saying in Latin, translated as follows:

As long as the Colosseum stands, Rome will stand;/When the Colosseum falls, Rome will fall./ And when Rome f___s, then f___s the world.

A: falls falls

---

264. Echo your teacher's description of this picture. ★ ○ ○ F____ pl____

R: **Fōns plēnus est.**

265. Echo his description of this second picture. ★ ○ ○ M____ pl____ s____

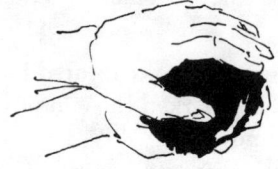

R: **Manūs plēnae sunt.**

266. Your teacher will ask you a question about this picture. Answer using the new adjective. "Quālis lupus est?" "Pl____ ____ ____."

R: **Plēnus lupus est.**

15-57

1-23

99. ★ ○

Visual Check: In 962 A.D. a Saxon lord became Otto I, emperor of a loose political organization which eventually embraced the area now occupied by Germany, Austria, and Northern Italy. This organization was called the Holy Roman Empire. In spite of its weaknesses, the Holy Roman Empire lasted almost a thousand years.

100. It has jokingly been said that this organization received its name from the fact that it was neither h___, R___n, nor an _____.

A: holy, Roman empire.

101. It was called "Roman" because it claimed power over many of the peoples of the world who looked for spiritual leadership to the Pope, who lived in the city of _____.

A: Rome.

102. ★ ○

Visual Check: It is no accident that the Pope still lives in Rome. Although the political Roman Empire had dissolved (or "fallen"), its organization still survived in some measure in the organization of the Church, and the Church preserved many forms of the Roman Empire.

Most striking of all, perhaps, is the fact that the official language of the Roman Catholic Church is Latin.

103. When the Pope issues a message to members of the Roman Catholic Church he writes in the _____ language.

A: Latin

15-56

261. "Ex quibus membris cognōscitur haec fēmina?" "_____." Capillī fēminam reddunt.

R: Ex capillīs cognōscitur haec fēmina. (Haec is feminine nominative singular.)

262. "Ex quibus cognōscitur hoc animal?" "_____." Animal magnōs saltūs facit.

R: Ex saltibus cognōscitur hoc animal. (Hoc is neuter nominative singular.)

263. ★ ○ ● ○ ● *Pūrās Deus, nōn plēnās, aspicit manūs.* (44)

1-24

104. The supreme accomplishment of the Romans was the establishment of law and order. At its height the Roman Empire included most of the continent of _____, and parts of the continents of ____ and _____.

A: Europe
    Asia   Africa.

105. And all this came originally from a tiny town in the section of Italy called L_____. ✓ ★ ○

Visual Check: Latium. ("láy-shum")

106. The *chief* purpose of this introduction is to have you learn ____ (facts and dates about the Romans/how to operate the program).

A: how to operate the program.

107. In the next-to-last frame you should have _____ed "Latium" *before* you ch___ed with the ____ _____ or with the _____ ____.

A: pronounced   checked
   tape recorder   Visual Check.

108. Let us continue.

When we realize what turmoil has existed within these borders since the Romans relaxed their rule upon the land, we can only marvel at the genius of these men from L_____.

A: Latium.

1-25

109. ★ ○

Visual Check: Besides the Romans, the two greatest forces in the life of Western man have been the Hebrews and the Greeks. Both the Christian and the Moslem religions are founded on the writings of the great Hebrew prophets. The Greeks were powerful and original thinkers in almost every field, particularly philosophy, literature, science, history, and art. But neither the Greeks nor the Hebrews passed these ideas directly to the Western world. They gave them to the Romans, and the Romans passed them on to us.

110. The language in which the Europeans of the Middle Ages read about the ideas of the Greeks and the Hebrews was the ----- language.

A: Latin

111. We would now like to clear up a common misconception. The one thing which everyone seems to know about Latin is that it is a "d___ language."

A: dead

15-54

253. "Quem omnis vir ex auribus cognōscit?" "-------."

R: Asinum.

In the next sequence you will be asked how different people and animals are recognized. There will be some outstanding trait (like big ears). Answer on the model of **Ex auribus cognōscitur asinus.** First, however, you will need to practice the forms of two words; one you have met in this Unit, the other is unknown.

254. ★ ○ • **pēs**   pedem   pede
                        pedēs   pedibus

255. ★ ○ • **dēns**   dentem   dente
                        dentēs   dentibus

Read the description of the picture; then answer the question.

256. "Ex quibus membris cognōscitur hic lupus?" "-----------------------------."
Lupus dentēs crūdēlēs habet.

R: Ex dentibus cognōscitur hic lupus. (The form hic is masculine nominative singular.)

257. It seems that you can recognize this wolf by his -----.

A: teeth.

112. ★ ○

Visual Check: Most people who use the term are not sure what it means, but it doesn't sound attractive. Who wants to study a language which is "dead?" Here is what a "dead language" is.

113. A language is officially "dead" when there is no one alive who learned to speak it from his father and mother as a child. There is no one alive today who learned Latin as his native language from his father and mother. Therefore Latin is called a ____ language.

A: dead

114. Countless thousands of languages have disappeared. We have seen this happen in America, where many Indian tribes have disappeared before the on-rush of the Europeans. When there is no one left alive who learned the language of a tribe as a baby, then the language is called "____."

A: dead.

115. But not all languages disappear. Some Indian languages are still spoken in America today. And some languages have spread over large sections of the world. The most widely spread language in the world today is the _____ language.

A: English

---

247. Copy this sentence and its meaning in your Reference Notebook.

248. The donkey, of course, is a symbol of stupidity. The saying Ex auribus cognōscitur asinus means that if you are stupid, no matter how you try to hide it, people will _____ [In your own words]

A: recognize how stupid you are from your actions.

Question and Answer Drill
Say aloud the question and answer.

249. "Ex quibus membris cognōscitur asinus?" "_____."

R: Ex auribus.

250. "Quis ex auribus suis cognōscitur?" "_____."

R: Asinus.

251. "Quis habet aurēs longās?" "_____." (Auxilium sub hāc līneā est.)

Aux: You should be able to guess the new word, longās.

Habetne aurēs longās equus an asinus?

R: Asinus.

252. "Quantās aurēs habet asinus?" "_____."

R: Longās.

1-27

116. The language spoken by the inhabitants of England in the year 1400 A.D. never died out. Children continued to learn this language from their parents. But here is a curious thing. Here is a specimen of "English" from this period, written by a man named Chaucer. Looks strange, doesn't it? And it would *sound* even more strange.

★ ○

Whan that Aprille with his shoures sote
The droghte of Marche hath perced to the rote
And bathed every veyne in swich licour,
Of which vertu engendred is the flour;

(A "translation" of the passage is beneath the mask indicator.)

Translation:

When April with its sweet showers
Has pierced the drouth of March to its roots,
And flooded every vein in such moisture
Of which the result is the awakening power of growing things;

117. ★ ○

Visual Check: English has changed gradually in the last 500 years so that we would not be able to understand Chaucer if he were to appear before us, and we can read what he wrote only with difficulty.

118. The change from the language of Chaucer to our own language was a ---- (gradual/sudden) one.

A: gradual

15-52

243. Say the Basic Sentence which this picture illustrates: St---- t---- F------, s-------- f-----.

R: **Stulti timent Fortūnam, sapientēs ferunt.**

244. ★ ○ • ○ • ○ ★ *Ex auribus cognōscitur asinus.* (43)

245. Write. ★ ○ ○ c------ au----- as-----.

R: **Ex auribus cognōscitur asinus.**

246. The preposition ex often means "from" or "out of." This sentence, however, means, "A ------ is p-------- d by his ---- s."

A: donkey is recognized by his ears.

1-28

119. ★ ○

Visual Check: The English spoken by every generation was just a little bit different from that of the generation before. And the same thing happened in the Roman Empire. In the year 100 A.D., all the Romans in the Roman Empire who spoke Latin (a lot of them in the eastern part spoke Greek instead) could understand each other. But with the breakdown of communications in the years following 476 A.D. the Romans in France did not see or talk with the Romans in Italy very often.

120. The spoken language changed in both countries, but it changed in ____ (the same way/different ways) in each country.

A: different ways

121. Eventually the differences between those who lived in Italy and those who lived in France became so great that those who spoke the French kind of "Latin" could not understand the Italians who spoke the _____ kind of "Latin."

A: Italian

122. The language into which Latin changed in *Italy* is now called "Italian." The Latin which was spoken in Spain changed into the language which we now call "_____."

A: Spanish .

15-31

236. "Ā quibus Fortūna fertur?" "_____."

R: Ā sapientibus.

237. "Quis Fortūnam fert, stultus an sapiēns?" "_____."

R: Sapiēns.

238. "Quis Fortūnam timet?" "_____."

R: Stultus.

239. "Quid agunt stultī?" "_____." (Auxilium sub hāc līneā est.)

Aux: **Quid agunt?** is the plural of **Quid agit?** and means, "What are they doing?" You answer with a plural verb (and the object, if there is one).

240. "Quid agunt sapientēs?" "_____."

R: Timent Fortūnam.

241. "Quālēs virī Fortūnam nōn metuunt?" "_____."

R: Sapientēs virī.

242. The Basic Sentence **Stultī timent Fortūnam, sapientēs ferunt** was written by the Roman playwright P_____ S_____.

A: Pūblilius Syrus.

1-29

123. Italian and Spanish sound very different, but they are both descendants of the _____ language.

A: Latin

124. The English which Chaucer spoke did not die out; it merely _____ed into a different language.

A: changed

125. In the same way, the Latin spoken in Italy, Spain, France, Roumania, and Portugal did not die; it _____.

A: changed into a different language.

126. ★ ○

Visual Check: Latin changed in different ways in different parts of Europe. Gradually certain cities began to increase in importance. One of these cities was Paris, which controlled roughly the area which is now France. The natives of distant parts of France could understand the inhabitants of Paris only with difficulty.

127. Since the city of Paris was so important, people in other parts of France often found it to their advantage to learn to speak the kind of "Latin" (or "French," as we should perhaps now call it) which was spoken in the city of _____.

A: Paris.

15-30

230. Notice that the forms **Quis?**, **Quem?**, and **Quibus?** are like **canis**, **canem**, and **canibus**. The forms **Quo?**, **Qui?**, and **Quos?** are like **tauro**, **tauri**, and **tauros**. The word **Quis?** does not belong to any of the five declensions but is an ir_____ word.

A: irregular

231. Transform to the passive: **Stultī tīment Fortūnam, sapientēs ferunt** → **Ā st_____ is t_____ētur F_____, ā s_____ibus fertur.**

R: **Ā stultīs timētur Fortūna, ā sapientibus fertur.**

Question and Answer Drill

Say both the question and your answer aloud, then write your answer.

232. "Tīmentne an ferunt Fortūnam sapientēs?" "_____."

R: **Ferunt.**

233. "Quem stultī tīment?" "_____."

R: **Fortūnam.**

234. "Tīmeturne Fortūna ā stultīs an ā sapientibus?" "_____ _____."

R: **Ā stultīs.**

235. "Ā quibus Fortūna tīmētur?" "_____."

R: **Ā stultīs.**

1-30

128. ★ ○

Visual Check: The dialect of Paris gradually thus became the most important dialect in France. It became the "standard" form of the language. When a French child from a small village goes to school he has to take classes to learn to speak the standard form of the language, which is the dialect of educated people in the city of Paris.

129. As a *baby* the French child in a small village learns the dialect of _____.

A: the village where he was born.

130. When he goes to school he has to learn the dialect of _____.

A: the city of Paris.

131. The dialect spoken in one village in Europe usually differs slightly from the dialect spoken in the n____ village.

A: next

132. However, after one goes far enough one finds that the natives in village A cannot understand the dialect spoken in village H. If you look at the map you will see that village A is in the country of _____, while village H is in the country of _____.

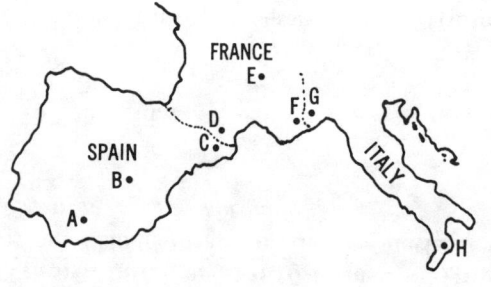

A: Spain
    Italy.

---

225. Stulti timent Fortūnam, sapiéntes ferunt = ____ _____, ____ _____ ___ _____ ___.

A: Stupid people fear Fortune, wise people endure her.

226. Copy this Basic Sentence in your Reference Notebook. (Other words, such as "suffer" or "put up with," are satisfactory for *ferunt*, but put "endure" in your Reference Notebook.)

227. ★ ○ • Quis? Qui? Quem? Quos? Quo? Quibus?

228. Since we ask you to learn these forms perfectly, you may wonder why you are asked to write them in your Reference Notebook. The answer is that no matter how well you know them *now*, you may _____ one of them later.

A: forget

229. If you should wish to check on some forms, you may look them up in _____.

A: Reference Notebook.

133. The dialect spoken in village A is a variety of Spanish, while the dialect spoken in village H is a variety of ———.

A: Italian.

134. ★ ○

Visual Check: It is no surprise to learn that the speakers of Spanish (village A) cannot understand speakers of Italian (village H). However, it is a little surprising to learn that the people in village A cannot understand the people in village C.

135. Even though the people in A cannot understand those in C, both towns are in Spain and both dialects are called a variety of the language we call ———.

A: Spanish.

136. ★ ○

Visual Check: But here is the really surprising part. These dialects change only slightly from village to village; natives of one village can always understand the dialect of the neighboring village, even though it sounds a little different. This is true even when you cross the borders of a country: the villagers of C (in Spain) can understand the villagers of D (in France).

137. They can understand each other even though the dialect of the Spanish village is called a dialect of Spanish and the dialect of the French village is called a dialect of ———.

A: French.

138. Would the French peasants in Village F be able to understand the Italian spoken by the peasants in Village G? ____ (Yes/No)
[Use the map in Frame 132 if you need it]

A: Yes

139. People who speak standard French speak the dialect of the area marked E. People who speak standard Spanish speak the dialect of the area marked B. People who speak only standard French ____ (can/cannot) understand those who speak only standard Spanish.

A: cannot

140. Thus we can see that, far from dying out, the Latin language continued to be spoken over most of southern Europe, although it changed enough in different sections so that _____ _____.

A: _____ people in different sections cannot understand each other. [If you are not sure whether your answer was satisfactory, ask your teacher.]

141. ★ ○

Visual Check: Languages such as French, Roumanian, Portuguese, Italian, and Spanish, are called "Romance" languages.

---

214. The word **fortēs** in the original Basic Sentence, **Fortūna fortēs metuit**, was _____ case; in the answer above it is _____ case.

A: accusative
nominative

215. "Ā quō ignāvī premuntur?" "_____."

R: Ā _____.
Fortūnā.

216. Write this sentence from dictation, paying close attention to the long vowels. ★ ○ ○
F____ f____ m____, ig____ pr____.

R: **Fortūna fortēs metuit, ignāvōs premit.**
[Did you mark five vowels long?]

Here is another Basic Sentence about Fortune and how we should deal with her; this is written by Publilius Syrus.

217. ★ ○ ○ ● ○ ● **Stultī timent Fortūnam, sapientēs ferunt.** (42)

218. The unknown verb **ferunt** is a transitive verb. Which of these statements is true?
1) Both kernels are complete.
2) Neither kernel is complete.
3) The first kernel is complete but not the second.
4) The second kernel is complete but not the first.

A: 3) The first kernel is complete but not the second.

142. They are called "Romance" languages because they are derived from the language spoken by the ancient -----s.

A: Romans.
[Are you remembering to say your answers aloud?]

143. The two main languages of South and Central America are Sp----- and P---------.

A: Spanish   Portuguese.

144. This area is called "Latin America" because the languages spoken there are ---------.
[In your own words]

A: derived from Latin.

145. ★ ○

Visual Check: While *spoken* Latin was changing, another interesting thing was happening. From 50 B.C. to 100 A.D. there was a great burst of literary activity in Rome and many outstanding literary works were written at this time. Most of the material which you will read in this course comes from this period.

146. The Latin which we study is not the *spoken* form of the language but the wr----- form.

A: written

147. ★ ○

Visual Check: As the Roman Empire gradually crumbled, the Romans looked back with reverence to the great days of old. They could see that changes in the political, social, and economic fields were changes for the worse. In their writing, therefore, they tried to imitate the great men of ancient Rome, and they tried to use the kind of Latin that was used in the period of greatest literary activity.

207. On the other hand she is eager to punish the ------s.

A: cowards.

208. We cannot transform the first kernel to the passive, since the verb **metuit** does not have passive forms, but we can transform the second kernel. Fortuna ignāvōs premit ⟶ Ā F------ ig---ī pr--untur.

R: Ā Fortunā ignāvī premuntur.

Question and Answer Drill

Say the question and your answer aloud; then write your answer.

209. "Quis ignāvōs premit?" "_____."

R: Fortūna.

210. "Quōs Fortūna premit?" "_____."

R: Ignāvōs.

211. "Prēmunturne ā Fortūnā fortēs an ignāvī?" "_____."

R: Ignāvī.

212. "Quī ā Fortūnā premuntur?" "_____."

R: Ignāvī.

213. "Quī ā Fortūnā nōn premuntur sed adjuvantur?" "_____."

R: Fortēs.

148. This period was about 150 years, from the year 50 B.C. to ___ A.D.

A: 100

149. But the spoken language had changed so much that a person who spoke the changed form of the language had to learn how to write the older kind. When a boy went to school, he learned how to imitate the writing of the authors who lived in the 150 year period between ___ ___ and ___ ___.

A. 50 B.C. 100 A.D.

150. As models he used the works of the ___er Latin writers.

A: older

151. In the year 500 A.D. was there anyone alive who as a baby had learned to speak Latin the way his parents spoke it? ____ (Yes/No)

A: Yes

152. In the year 500 A.D. was there anyone alive who as a baby had learned to speak Latin the way it was written in the years 50 B.C.-100 A.D.? ____ (Yes/No)

A: No

153. Therefore, by the year 500 A.D. the written standard form of Latin learned in the schools was a "____" language.

A: dead

---

202. This means that the ___ is cr___ing the ___ with his ___t.

A: man is crushing the snake with his foot.

203. Fortūna fortēs metuit, ignāvōs premit (41) = ____ ____s the ____ (and) ____es the c____.

A: Fortune fears the brave and crushes the cowards. [Count yourself right if you said "brave persons," or "cowardly persons."]

204. Copy this sentence and its meaning in your Reference Notebook.

205. This means, "____." [In your own words] **(Auxilium sub hāc lineā est)**

Auxilium: There is a belief (which I have never tested) that while a thistle will sting you if you touch it lightly it will not hurt you if you grasp it firmly.

A: that if you are courageous you will succeed; if you are cowardly you will fail.

206. The author makes the expression vivid by picturing Fortune as a goddess who is frightened by ____ people and therefore helps them because of her fear.

A: brave

15-45

1-34

1-35

154. We therefore have a curious situation. *Spoken* Latin continued to live in changed form in the languages which we call the R_____ languages.

A: Romance

155. Secondly, *written* Latin, as taught in the schools, continued in un_____ed form.

A: unchanged

156. This literary language, which you are going to study, became immortal; that is, it never d___ out and never really ch___ed very much.

A: died   changed

157. Most of the material will come from the period of the greatest writers, that is, from ___ ___ to ___ ___.

A: 50 B.C.   100 A.D.

158. However, we will have some bits from Medieval and Renaissance times so that you can see for yourself how Latin remained a living, vital force through the centuries. Until about 1500 A.D. the language of science, law, medicine, and similar fields was _____.

A: Latin.

159. And the language which they wrote was almost identical with the language used by the Romans in the years ___ B.C. to ___ A.D.

A: 50   100

15-44

198. Which of these statements is correct?
1) Each of these kernels is complete.
2) Neither of these kernels is complete.
3) The first kernel is complete but not the second.
4) The second kernel is complete but not the first.

A: 3) The first kernel is complete but not the second.

199. So far we have had nine sentences which had more than one kernel. Which has been more common, to have both kernels complete or to have one incomplete? _____.

A: There was only one sentence where both kernels were complete and eight where one kernel was incomplete.

200. Supply the missing element in the kernel which is not complete. Fortūna fortēs metuit, _____ ignāvōs premit.

R: Fortūna fortēs metuit,
R: Fortūna ignāvōs premit.

One difficulty in studying any language is that words have many different meanings. Here is a familiar word with a new meaning.

201. Write your teacher's description of this picture. ★ ○ ○ V_____ v_____ p_____ pr_____.

R: Vir vīperam pede premit.

1-36

160. The United States was founded by men who drew their inspiration from Greece and Rome. Here is a small demonstration of this fact. If you happen to have been paid recently, take a dollar bill from your pocketbook and look at the reverse side. Otherwise, look below the mask indicator for the Visual Check.

Visual Check:

161. The first of the two circles is labeled "The Gr___ S___," and the second is labeled, "of ___ _____ _____s."

A: Great Seal
the United States.

162. These two pictures represent the two sides of the _____.

A: Great Seal of the United States

163. Notice that in the first side of the seal there are three *Latin* references. There is the date of 1776, which is written in Roman numerals this way: _____.

A: MDCCLXXVI .

---

193. "Quis fortés adjuvat?" "_____."

R: Fortuna.

194. "Quid agit Fortuna?" "_____."

R: Fortés adjuvat.

195. Write the Basic Sentence which this picture illustrates. F_____ ad_____.

R: Fortés Fortuna adjuvat.

196. ★ ○ • *Fortuna fortés metuit, ignavos premit.* (41)

197. How many kernels are in this sentence?

A: Two

1-37

164. On your bill (or the picture in the last frame), there is a Latin motto at the top of the unfinished pyramid which says, "He (God) looks with favor on our beginnings." The two Latin words which express this thought are _____ _____.

A: **ANNUIT COEPTIS.**

165. You may have been surprised to discover that what we take seven words to express can be said in Latin by only ___ words.

A: two

166. Look at the seal again. Below the pyramid is expressed the thought, "A new system of the ages," meaning that after so many centuries at last a new system of government was being formed. The Latin for this is the three words _____ _____ _____.

A: **NOVUS ORDO SECLORUM.**

167. Look at the other side of the seal. The banner in the eagle's beak contains the words **E PLURIBUS UNUM,** which you may know means "___ ___ of m____."

A: One out of many.

168. Why did these men put these mottoes in *Latin*? The answer probably is that it never occurred to them to do anything else. They were consciously imitating the governments of Gr____ and R____.

A: Greece Rome.

15-42

185.
	Sg.	Pl.
	Quis?	Quī?
	Quem?	Quōs?
	Quō?	Quibus?

186. Copy this paradigm in your Notebook under "Forms."

187. Transform to the passive:
Fortēs Fortūna adjuvat →
F____ēs ā F_____ ad___antur.

R: Fortēs ā Fortūnā adjuvantur.

Question and Answer Drill

The following questions will be on either the original sentence or the passive transformation.

188. "Ā quō fortēs adjuvantur?" "_____."

R: Fortūnā.

189. "Quōs Fortūna adjuvat?" "_____."

R: Fortēs.

190. Fortēs in the above answer is _____ case.

A: accusative

191. "Quī ā Fortūnā adjuvantur?" "_____."

R: Fortēs.

192. Fortēs in this last answer is _____ case.

A: nominative

169. ★ ○ ○ sequence

Visual Check: "seé-kwense"

170. A series of frames which deals with a single subject is called a "sequence." In the last sequence you examined the Latin expressions found on an American d_____ b____.

A: dollar bill.

171. One purpose of this sequence was to illustrate in some measure the intense interest which the founders of the United States had in the countries of _____ and ____.

A: Greece and Rome.

172. However, there was another purpose in this last sequence. Some of you had a dollar bill to look at, others did not. Which would you prefer, to examine the bill for yourselves or to look at the pictures of the Great Seal?_____

A: Since we asked you for your opinion, we can scarcely say that one answer is right and another wrong. Surely most of you, however, would have preferred to examine the original bill.

173. The situation is much the same with the tape recorder. It is *better* to have the use of a tape recorder, but if you do not have one, you can still learn Latin. However, if you do not have a tape recorder, you will not *hear* Latin (except in class), and you must make an extra effort by sp____ing Latin as much as possible.

A: speaking

174. Until the present century it was almost impossible to receive much formal education in America or Europe without studying Latin. To be admitted to most of the well-known colleges, a student had to show that he knew _____.

A: Latin.

---

180. In your Answer Pad, cross out the form of fortés which does not fit into the sentence pattern.

(nom.?) Fortés
(acc.?) Fortés   Fortúna adjuvat.

A: (nom.?) F̶o̶r̶t̶é̶s̶
(acc.?) Fortés   Fortúna adjuvat.

181. Fortés Fortúna adjuvat = _____ blanks _____.

A: Fortune blanks brave people.

182. In English we can use the word "brave" as a noun, so we can say, "Fortune blanks the _____."

A: Fortune blanks the brave.

183. This Basic Sentence is similar to the English saying, "God helps those who help themselves."
Fortés Fortúna adjuvat = _____.

A: Fortune helps the brave.

184. Fortune helps the brave. (40) Copy this sentence and its meaning in your Reference Notebook.

1-39

175. The name "Grammar School" comes from the fact that originally children were sent there mainly to study L____ _____.

A: Latin grammar.

176. In most schools in America today Latin is not a required subject, and yet there are more than a million students in America studying Latin. In a few words, why did *you* choose to study Latin? _____
[Write in your answer pad, using your own words.]

A: Of course there is no "right" or "wrong" answer for this. Perhaps your reason was, "My Dad told me I had to."

Whether you elected Latin on your own, whether your parents wanted you to take it, or whether your school believed that you should study it, the fact remains that somebody decided you would be better in some way for taking Latin.

We would like to point out briefly what seem to *us* to be important reasons for studying Latin. Here is one reason which is easy to see.

Many English words, both common and uncommon, come from Latin. Here, for example, are the opening lines of the Declaration of Independence. The underlined words come from Latin.

> When in the course of human events, it becomes necessary for one people to dissolve the political bands, which have connected them with another, and to assume among the powers of the earth, the separate and equal station to which the laws of nature and of nature's God entitle them, a decent respect to the opinions of mankind requires that they should declare the causes which impel them to the separation.

Notice what happens if we leave out the words borrowed from Latin:

> When in the _____ of ____ _____, it becomes _____ for one _____ to _____ the _____ bands, which have _____ them with another, and to _____ among the powers of the earth, the _____ and ____ _____ to which the laws of _____ and of _____ God _____ them, a _____ to the _____ of mankind _____ that they should _____ the _____ which _____ them to the _____.

15-40

173. And in **Mentēs rēgnum possident** the noun which is plural is _____.

A: **mentēs**.

174. The next Basic Sentence contains the adjective **fortis** which means "_____."

A: brave.

175. When there is no noun for **fortis** to modify, it means a "_____."

A: brave person.

176. ✱ ○ • ○ • **Fortēs Fortūna adjuvat.**
(40)

Write this same Basic Sentence, putting down the first word twice to remind you that it is an ambiguous form.

177. ✱ ○ ○ (nom.?) _____
(acc.?) _____

A: (nom.?) **Fortēs**
     (acc.?) **Fortēs** **Fortūna adjuvat.**

178. Now to decide whether **fortēs** is subject or object of this {-s -m -t} sentence. The word **Fortūna** is _____ case, the {-_-} of the sentence, and _____ of the verb.

A: nominative {-s} subject

179. So **fortēs** must be _____ case, {-_-}, and the _____ of the verb.

A: accusative {-m} object

177. How much information is carried in the message without the words borrowed from Latin? ____

A: Not much

178. ★ ○ ○ derivative

Visual Check: "dur-rív-vuh-tive"

179. Words which are borrowed from other languages are called "derivatives." The English derivative of the Latin word **ēventus** is the word "____."

A: event.

180. And English "course" is a _____ of the Latin word **cursus.**

A: derivative

181. ★ ○ ○ derived

Visual Check: "dee-rýe-vd"

182. English "event" is d____ed from Latin **ēventus.**

A: derived

---

166. When you hear the first two words, **Mentēs rēgnum** you ____ (do/do not) know which is the {-s} and which is the {-m}.

A: do not

167. **Mentēs** and **rēgnum** are both _____ forms.

A: ambiguous

168. When you hear the first three words, **Mentēs rēgnum bonae,** you ____ (do/do not) know what case **mentēs** is.

A: do

169. In the phrase **Mentēs rēgnum bonae** you know that **mentēs** is _____ case.

A: nominative

170. You know that **mentēs** is nominative case here because _____.

A: **bonae,** which agrees with **mentēs,** is nominative plural, feminine gender.

171. Therefore **Mentēs rēgnum bonae** means, "_____ ____ blank a _____."

A: Noble (good) minds blank a kingdom.

172. But there was a *second* signal which showed that **mentēs** was the {-s} of the sentence. Here is the transformed sentence without the modifying adjective: **Mentēs rēgnum possident.** We know that **mentēs** is the {-s} and not **rēgnum** because **possident** is _____ number.

A: plural

1-41

183. Once you begin to study Latin you will discover that you can figure out the meaning of many unfamiliar English words because you know the Latin word from which the English word is _____ed.

A: derived.

184. ★ ○

Visual Check: Improving your knowledge of English is important, but it is not the *main* reason for learning Latin. Some of the advantages cannot be explained to someone who has not gone through the experience of taking a language. For example, you will learn in your study of Latin that languages are different.

185. Is Latin different from English? ____ (Yes/No)

A: Yes

186. ★ ○

Visual Check: Probably everyone answered "Yes" in the last frame, and yet if you have not studied a foreign language before, you cannot possibly understand what we mean by saying that languages are different. They are different in that you have to learn to think in an entirely different way. And what do we mean by "Think in an entirely different way"?

187. You cannot *really* understand until you have _____.
[In your own words]

A: had experience with a foreign language.

15-38

160. Multās jūdicēs fraudēs inveniunt =

A: Judges discover many tricks.

161. Multī jūdicēs fraudēs inveniunt =

A: Many judges discover tricks.

162. Auctor is masculine, ōrātiō is feminine. Auctōrēs laudant blandae ōrātiōnēs =

A: Smooth speeches praise the authors (in other words, favorable reviews of their works).

163. Auctōrēs laudant blandī ōrātiōnēs =

A: Smooth (pleasant) authors praise speeches.

164. Sometimes more than one of these three helps is present (other nouns, the verb, an adjective).

Write Basic Sentence 28 as your teacher makes changes in it. ★ ○ ○ ———.

R: Mentēs rēgnum bonae possident.

165. When you hear the first word, **Mentēs**, you ____ (do/do not) know whether it is the {-s} or the {-m} of the sentence.

A: do not

188. It is fascinating to find out that what may sound to you like funny grunts, snorts, and buzzes can become understandable once you learn the new language.

Listen to speakers in several languages describe this picture. ★ ○

[Of course you can't do this frame without a tape recorder.]

Visual Check: All these speakers said in their language, "The horse is running down the street."

189. Listen to your teacher say this in Latin. ★ ○ ○

Visual Check: "Equus viā currit."

190. Observe that while English uses *seven* words to say this, Latin uses only _____ words.

A: three

191. From these examples you can see that when you hear them, languages sound ____ (alike/different).

A: different.

192. From the Latin example you can see that, for the same idea, languages may use a _____ number of words.

A: different

---

154. **Fūrēs** could not possibly be the subject of **metuit** because _____.

A: **metuit** is singular and the subject will have to be singular, while **fūrēs** is plural.

155. If, however, the sentence began with **Fūrēs metuunt,** then the sentence thus far is ambiguous and could mean either "_____" or "_____."

A: The thieves fear something or Some (plural) people fear the thieves.

156. If you notice the number of the verb, the following sentence is not ambiguous. **Animal pāscunt īnfantēs** = _____.

A: The children are feeding the animal.

157. Finally, adjectives also agree with the nouns they modify in n-----, g-----, and c-----.

A: number, gender, and case.

158. **Jūdex** is masculine gender and **fraus** is feminine gender. Look at this sentence. **Multās jūdicēs fraudēs inveniunt.** **Multās** modifies ---- (jūdicēs/fraudēs).

A: fraudēs

159. Therefore **multās fraudēs** is the {--} of the sentence.

A: {–m}

1-42

1-43

193. An important purpose of this course is to show you the *many* ways in which one language is _____ from another.

A: different

194. In this program you will learn how *two* languages work; these two languages will be _____ and _____.

A: English and Latin.

195. It is a real challenge to learn to th___ in an entirely different way.

A: think

196. ★ ○

Visual Check: Why do we bother to tell you this if you cannot really understand what we mean until you have studied Latin? Perhaps it is like preparing for a trip. Looking at a map would certainly not be a substitute for going there.

197. People are able to find their way around in a new country a little more quickly if first they have seen a ___ of where they are going.

A: map

198. ★ ○

Visual Check: Perhaps the most important reason for studying any subject is that you enjoy it. No matter how important a subject may be to your future career, unless you enjoy what you are doing you will not learn much. Some of you may not have learned to enjoy studying yet; we hope that in this program you will discover that studying a foreign language can be a lot of fun. It will also be hard work.

199. Playing football or running the mile or repairing an antique car is also h___ w____.

A: hard work.

200. We hope that you will learn that working with your mind can be just as exciting as sports or hobbies. Many people find intellectual work even more _____ing than sports or hobbies.

A: exciting

201. Learning Latin will be fun for you, we think, because a whole new world of thought can open to one who learns a _____ language.

A: foreign

202. ★ ○

Visual Check: You will get much pleasure from reading Latin literature. The works which you will read have stood the test of time; they have been read and enjoyed by most of the great minds of the Western world. The literature of Rome is a precious heritage, and by sharing in it you will make yourself richer. You will feel a kinship, not only with the ancient Romans themselves, but with all the writers since who have loved and imitated the classics of Rome.

203. The chief purpose of this course is to give you an acquaintance with Latin l_____.

A: literature.

204. ★ ○

Visual Check: You will find that most of the great writers are saturated with Latin. In your reading in English literature you will begin to discover hundreds of references to Latin. You haven't noticed them much as yet, because you didn't know what to look for.

205. In addition to reading the literature of Rome, one of the important purposes of this course is to open your eyes to the richness of your own l⎯⎯⎯⎯⎯.

A: literature.

206. ★ ○

Visual Check: You have all read or heard about the difficulties caused by the fact that the nations of the world have no common language. There are five official languages in the United Nations: English, French, Russian, Spanish, and Chinese. Countless hours are consumed in translating from one language to another. There is an obvious need for an international language. It is strange to realize that until recently there *was* an international language, the one which you are going to study.

207. Four hundred years ago almost all books were written in the ⎯⎯⎯ language.

A: Latin

208. A hundred years ago the language used in the Parliament of Hungary was ⎯⎯⎯.

A: Latin.

209. The famous mathematician Gauss, who died in 1855, published his mathematical studies in ⎯⎯⎯.

A: Latin.

210. Even today, there are poets who write only in Latin. There have been editions of old favorites translated into Latin, such as *Alicia in Terra Mirabili,* which is the Latin title for A⎯⎯e in W⎯⎯⎯⎯nd.

A: *Alice in Wonderland*.

1-45

137. **Taurus** and **foveās** are ⎯⎯⎯ case and ⎯⎯⎯ number.

A: accusative   plural

138. **Saltūs** and **īnfantēs** however, are either ⎯⎯⎯ or ⎯⎯⎯ forms.

A: nominative or accusative

139. Forms that can be two cases we call ⎯⎯⎯ forms.

A: ambiguous

140. Sometimes you will find a truly ambiguous sentence. For example, **Leōnēs mūrēs metuunt** means either, "⎯⎯⎯ fear ⎯⎯⎯," or "⎯⎯⎯ fear ⎯⎯⎯."

A: Lions fear mice   Mice fear lions.

141. This ambiguity seldom causes trouble. We know that in the real world it is more likely that it is the ⎯⎯⎯ who fear the ⎯⎯⎯ than the other way around.

A: mice   lions

(If, on the other hand, there were mice who were so frightful that they terrified lions, then this fact would be explained.)

142. The ambiguity of such forms as **mūrēs** is almost always solved by other words in the sentence. There are three things specifically which will tell you: another noun, the verb, or an adjective. Let us take the other noun first. If we were to change our sentence so that it began **Leōnēs mūs,** we would know that **leōnēs** was the {⎯⎯} of the sentence because **mūs** is the {⎯⎯}.

A: {⎯m}   {⎯s}

15-34

1-46

211. Latin is used for inscriptions on buildings. Clubs, organizations, and the like use Latin for m_____s.

A: mottoes.

212. When botanists describe a new flower, they are required to write the description in _____.

A: Latin.

213. ★ ○

Visual Check: These are exciting times to live in. Today we are pushing into the future at an enormous rate in many fields. As you well know if you have tried to get some help from your father and mother in physics, chemistry, or math, much of the material which you are studying today was unknown when your parents studied these subjects.

Here lies one of the fascinations of Latin. In an age of change, this is a subject which has remained the same. The *Aeneid* of Vergil which you will read is the same *Aeneid* which your father and mother read.

15-33

[If you made any error in this last sequence, be sure that you learn these paradigms now. On the test for this Unit you will be asked to write the paradigms which you have practiced in this Unit.]

131. We have already given you some practice in noting the difference between certain "look-alikes." **Leō** and **taurō** ____ (are/are not) the same case.

A: are not

132. Leō is ____ case and **taurō** is ____ case.

A: nominative ablative

133. Pick out the nouns in this sequence which are nominative case, like **leō**: **imitātiō, agnō, vitiō, religiō, ōrātiō, oculō, superstitiō, nēmō.**

R: imitātiō ōrātiō religiō superstitiō nēmō

134. Now you must be aware of words which end in **-ās**. **Vēritās** and **similās** ____ (are/are not) the same case.

A: are not

135. Similās is ____ case and **vēritās** is ____ case.

A: accusative nominative

136. Pick out the nouns in this sequence which, like **similās**, are accusative plural: **foveās, vēritās, poenās, fēlīcitās.**

R: foveās poenās

1-47

214. And when your own children go to school, they will read the ___e *Aeneid* which you will read.

A: same

215. You will discover that the *way* in which you learn Latin will be very different from the old way; one difference is this type of learning material, which we call a _____.

A: program.

216. ★ ○

Visual Check: You will, we think, find excitement in traveling back in time to the great days of the mighty Roman Empire. You will read the very words written two thousand years ago by Martial, Phaedrus, Ovid, Vergil, Cicero, and others.

217. The very names are probably unknown to most of you, but Martial, Phaedrus, and the others have been read by millions of people before you who have studied _____.

A: Latin.

15-32

125. Write (or say) the declension of fovea.

R: fovea foveae
 foveam foveās
 foveā foveīs

126. Write (or say) the declension of diēs.

R: diēs diēs
 diem diēs
 diē diēbus

127. Write (or say) the declension of infāns.

R: infāns infantēs
 infantem infantēs
 infante infantibus

128. Write (or say) the declension of agnus.

R: agnus agnī
 agnum agnōs
 agnō agnīs

129. Write (or say) the declension of auctor.

R: auctor auctōrēs
 auctōrem auctōrēs
 auctōre auctōribus

130. Write (or say) the declension of aper.

R: aper aprī
 aprum aprōs
 aprō aprīs

218. ★ ○

Visual Check: Latin often has the reputation of being a hard subject. Some of you may well be wondering just how hard this course will be. We will be frank with you. It takes effort to master any subject or any skill. And the more interesting the subject is, the harder people will work at it. We know that in working with a program like this you will be able to learn faster than in the older way of study. You will also, we hope, find it more interesting. Many of you will be able to proceed at your own rate of progress. If you wish to work harder than your neighbor, that is your privilege.

219. Will this course be hard? We can only say that we hope that you will be interested enough in the subject that you will_____
[In your own words]

A: *want* to work hard.

220. ★ ○

Visual Check: Latin, as a language, is no harder than any other language commonly studied in school. You could learn to say the Latin equivalent of "Hello" and "good-bye" and "Have you two good seats for the show in the Colosseum?" as easily as you could in a modern language. But, although you will speak and hear Latin a lot, our goal is not to be able to converse in Latin.

221. Our goal is rather to r___ L____ l_____.

A: read Latin literature.

---

119. ★ ○ • saltus (4)

Cōnf: saltus saltus
saltum saltus
saltū saltibus

---

120. ★ ○ • agnus (2)

Cōnf: agnus agnī
agnum agnōs
agnō agnīs

---

121. ★ ○ • aper (2)

Cōnf: aper aprī
aprum aprōs
aprō aprīs

---

122. ★ ○ • auctor (3)

Cōnf: auctor auctōrēs
auctōrem auctōrēs
auctōre auctōribus

---

123. ★ ○ • fovea (1)

Cōnf: fovea foveae
foveam foveās
foveā foveīs

---

124. Write the declension of *saltus.* [Or say it, if this is enough for you to learn it.] ——

[If you are completely confident you know these, skip to frame 131.]

R: saltus saltūs
saltum saltūs
saltū saltibus

222. ★ ○

Visual Check: You know from your studies in English that reading literature contains some tough intellectual problems. But it has been frequently observed that many students of high school and college age are eager to grapple with such problems. Most of you want something more challenging than comic books and Western movies. And perhaps the greatest attraction of Latin is its awesome antiquity.

223. Just think, Latin is ___ _____ years old!

A: two thousand

224. Many prominent people have testified to the value of the study of Latin. Here is just a sample, written by a busy man to a high school class in Princeton, New Jersey, who was asked for his views on Latin. The letter is a long one; what follows is just a sample. We have taken the liberty of breaking it up into frames.

"Those who reject the study of Latin on the grounds that it is 'impractical' are to my mind taking the most im_____al position of all.

A: impractical

225. "Far too many of the 'practical' courses (courses that involve training in skills) are teaching people to do things that are obsolete by the time they l___e sch___.

A: leave school.

226. "The true education (that which gives us a feeling of our position in the world and where we came from and where we are going) n___r deserts a person.

A: never

1-49

109-115. Copy these seven paradigms in your Reference Notebook under "Forms." The number shows the declension.

simia (1)	simiam	simiae
	simiam	simiās

lupus	lupī (2)	lupō	lupī
	lupum	virum	virōs
	lupīs	virō	virīs

canis	canēs (3)	leō	leōnēs (3)
canem	canēs	leōnem	leōnēs
cane	canibus	leōne	leōnibus

manus	manūs (4)
manum	manūs
manū	manibus

rēs	rēs (5)
rem	rēs
rē	rēbus

116. Check again to make sure that you have copied these paradigms *exactly* right. Otherwise you will learn them wrong when you review from your Notebook. The next 14 frames give further drill on paradigms. If you do not want it, skip to frame 131.

We will give you practice once more on a sample noun of each of the five declensions. The number indicates the declension. Some of these paradigms will be in the test for this Unit.

117. ★ ○ • diēs (5)

Cōnf: diēs   diēs   diēs
       diem   diēs
       diē   diēbus

118. ★ ○ • īnfāns (3)

Cōnf: īnfāns   īnfantēs
       īnfantem īnfantēs
       īnfante   īnfantibus

1-50

227. "It never becomes 'obsolete' and it never becomes 'out of d____.'

A: date.

228. "To reject the study of Latin because it is a 'dead' language is to reject the study of history because Caesar is ____;

A: dead;

229. "...it is to reject the study of philosophy because Aristotle is ____; it is to reject the study of analytical geometry because Descartes is ____."

A: dead; dead.

230. The man who took the time to express his feelings about Latin works in Washington, D.C. and his name is L____ B____s J_____.

A: Lyndon Baines Johnson.

231. ★ ○

Visual Check: This completes Unit One. When you start the next Unit you will begin the study of Latin. It should be an exciting moment. For two thousand years students have studied this very language which you are to start. What magic is it that today draws *millions* of people all over America and Europe to study this language?

232. We hope that you will discover this magic for yourself and learn why the title "Queen of Languages" has been given to _____.

A: Latin.

---

104. ★ ○ • 2nd decl
vir
virum
virō
virī
virōs
virīs

105. ★ ○ • 3rd decl
canis
can-em
can-e
can-ēs
can-ēs
can-ibus

106. ★ ○ • 3rd decl
leō
leōn-em
leōn-e
leōn-ēs
leōn-ēs
leōn-ibus

Cōnj: leō leōne
leōnēs leōnibus

107. ★ ○ • 4th decl
manus
man-um
man-ū
man-ūs
man-ūs
man-ibus

Cōnj: manus manus
manus manuum
manus manibus

108. ★ ○ • 5th decl
rēs
r-em
r-ē
r-ēs
r-ēs
r-ēbus

Cōnj: rēs rēs
rem rēs
rē rēbus

15-29

15-28

100. ----ūs √---- ★ ○ •

Cōnf: Quercūs sunt.

101. ----ī √---- ★ ○ •

Cōnf: Lupī sunt.

Echo the paradigms of these nouns of all five declensions.

102. ★ ○ • sīmia 1st decl ----a ----ae
　　　　　　　　　　　　　　　　 ----am ----ās
　　　　　　　　　　　　　　　　 ----ā ----īs

Cōnf:　sīmia　sīmiae
　　　　sīmiam　sīmiās
　　　　sīmiā　sīmiīs

103. ★ ○ • lupus 2nd decl ----ī
　　　　　　　　　　　　　　　　　 ----um ----ōs
　　　　　　　　　　　　　　　　　 ----ō ----īs

Cōnf:　lupus　lupī
　　　　lupum　lupōs
　　　　lupō　lupīs

1-51

233. And finally, remember this. Many cities claim to be the world's loveliest or busiest or most famous. Only one city has ever dared to call itself "The Eternal City," and this city is ----.

A: Rome.

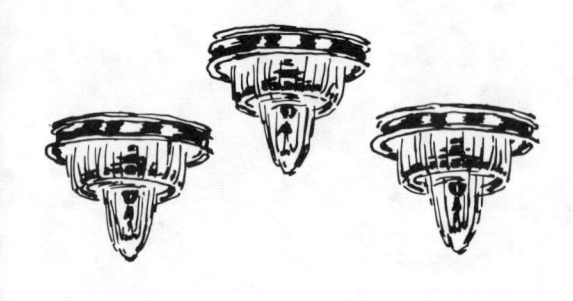

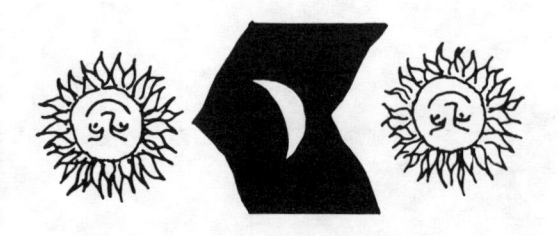

UNIT TWO

We hope that you enjoyed Unit One. You are now ready to start in on Latin itself. This Unit and the next deal entirely with the sounds of Latin. You cannot learn to pronounce sounds without having someone to imitate. Therefore for this Unit and for Unit Three, you must either use a tape recorder or have someone who knows Latin to help you. Most of you will do these two Units in class with your classroom teacher.

Before we start we should explain that we have no way of knowing how far you will get before the class period is over. You may have to stop right in the middle of a series of frames. Therefore, whenever you return to the course, go back a dozen frames or so in order to remind yourself just where you are in the program. Right after a vacation or even after a long weekend, you will probably want to start even farther back. Use your own judgment on this.

1. Listen to your teacher say a Latin sentence. ★ ○ ○ The purpose of this Unit is to have you learn to pronounce this sentence *perfectly*.

2. Languages are made up of sounds. Latin is a language. Like other languages, Latin is made up of _____.

Answer: sounds.

3. The sounds in languages can be divided into two kinds called "vowels" and "consonants." Like other languages, Latin has these two kinds of sounds, _____ and _____.

Answer: vowels   consonants.

4. Listen to your teacher pronounce a Latin vowel. ★ ○ ○

5. A letter in English can sometimes represent *many* different sounds. In Latin, however, a letter represents only ___ sound.

Answer: one

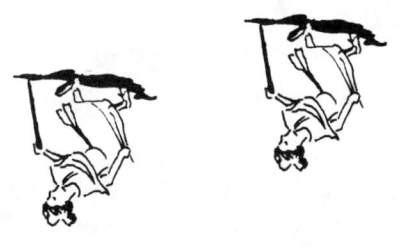

6. In English a sound can sometimes be represented by several different letters or combinations of letters. In Latin, however, a sound is represented by only ___ letter.

Answer: one

7. There are *five* different vowels in Latin. There are therefore ____ different letters to represent these five different vowels.

Answer: five

8. The letters which are used to represent the Latin sounds are the familiar letters that are used to represent English _____.

Answer: sounds.

9. The Romans used the same alphabet as we do. However, some of the letters in Latin do not stand for the same _____ as they do in English.

Answer: sounds

10. The letters which are used in writing Latin are the same as those used in writing English, but the *sounds* for which some of these letters stand are _____ sounds from those for which the same letters stand in English.

Answer: different

11. The alphabet which is used in writing English and most other languages of the Western world is called the "Roman alphabet." It is called this because these letters are the ones used by the ancient _____.

Answer: Romans.

2-3

12. If you ever studied another foreign language, you probably noticed the vowel sounds were shorter and crisper than English vowel sounds. In Latin, too, the vowel sounds are _____ and _____ than the English vowel sounds.

Answer: shorter   crisper

13. Listen to your teacher pronounce another Latin vowel. ★ ○ ○

14. This vowel sound will be represented in Latin ____ (always by the same letter/sometimes by a different letter).

Answer: always by the same letter.

15. When you see a new English word, you may not be sure how to pronounce it. After you have learned the system in Latin, however, when you see any Latin word, even if you don't know what it means, you can _____ it correctly.

Answer: pronounce

16. In learning a new skill you often have to learn technical terms that are used in talking about this skill. "Vowel" and "consonant" are examples of such _____ _____.

Answer: technical terms.

17. Echo a technical term which we will use in the next frame.
     ★ ○ • ○ • syllable

18. We will first show you how to pronounce five Latin vowels. We will then combine these vowels with consonants to form "syllables." Listen to your teacher pronounce a Latin syllable made up of consonant plus vowel. ★ ○ ○

Using the same pattern as **Canēs sunt**, describe the following pictures using Fourth Declension nouns.

89. L_____ sunt. √ ★ ○ •

90. A_____ūs s_____ √ ★ ○ • 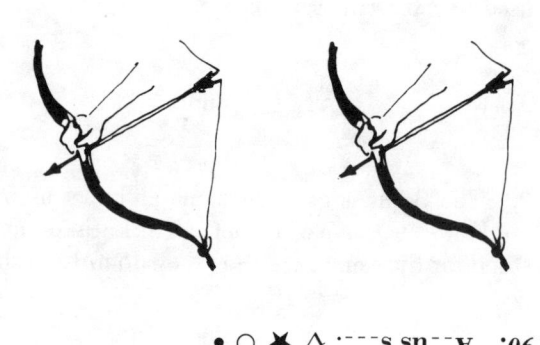
Cōnf: Arcūs sunt.

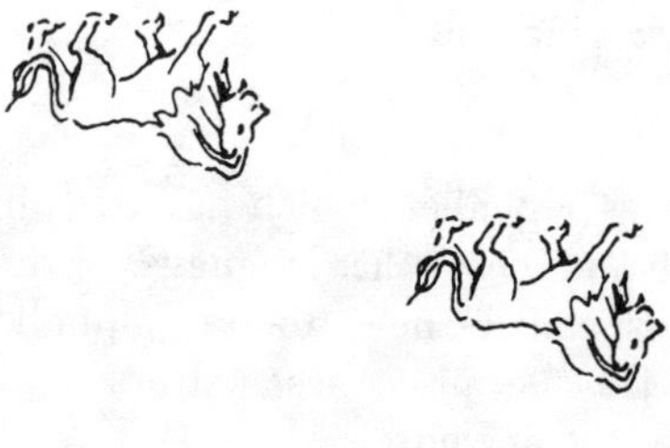

91. M_____ s_____ √ ★ ○ • 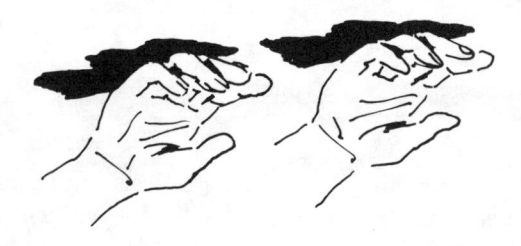
Cōnf: Manūs sunt.

2-4

19. A vowel followed by a consonant is one kind of s_____.

Answer: syllable.

20. Next we will combine these s_____ into words.

Answer: syllables

21. Listen to your teacher pronounce a Latin word. ★ ○ ○

22. We will combine such w___s into sentences.

Answer: words

23. Listen to your teacher pronounce a Latin sentence. ★ ○ ○

You will find out what this sentence means as soon as you have learned how to pronounce it. So now to work!

24. First we will review briefly the meaning of the symbols which give you the instructions about the program. The star means that you are to _____. [Answer in your own words.]

Answer: start the tape player.

25. The large circle means that _____. [Answer in your own words.]

Answer: your teacher will say something on the tape.

26. The large solid dot means that you are to _____. [In your own words.]

Answer: repeat what your teacher said.

85. ★ ○ ○ • M__ae r__j_____ i_____.

86. And rēs, like fīdēs and quercūs, can be not only _____ plural but _____ plural as well.

R: **Multae rēs jūdicem irrītant.**

A: accusative   nominative

The plural of est (which is an irregular verb) is **sunt.** Describe the following pictures which can be described by Third Declension nouns.

87. C__ēs sunt. √ ★ ○ •

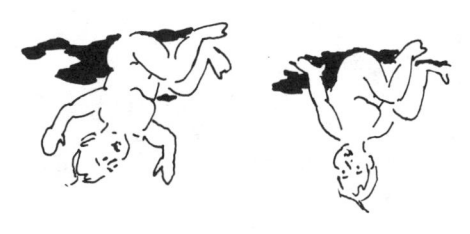

Cōnf: **Canēs sunt.**

88. In____ sunt. √ ★ ○ •

Cōnf: **Īnfantēs sunt.**

15-24

27. The check means, "Ans___ f___t and then ch___ your ___wer."

Answer: "Answer first and then check your answer."

28. Write in your answer pad the combination of three symbols that means, "Start the tape player and listen to your teacher say something twice." _____

Answer: The symbols should be a star and two circles.

29. A solid line in the frame means for you to _____ your answer.

Answer: write [And you should have written this in your answer pad.]

30. A broken line in the frame means that you are to _____ [In your own words.]

Answer: say the answer aloud.

31. We have told you that in programmed instruction the material is broken up into _____ parts.

Answer: small (tiny, etc.)

32. In order to present you with these tiny parts we will work in the next two units on just the sounds. For the present we will not bother with the meaning of either the words or the sentences. When you have reached the point where you can pronounce *four* sentences correctly, then we will help you to discover the _____ of these sentences.

Answer: meaning

2-5

80. This picture describes a slightly different situation. ★ ○ • ○ • M___ēs c____ m____nt.

R: **Mūrēs canem metuunt.**

81. From this example it would seem that the form **mūrēs**, which you have known as accusative plural, is an ambiguous form. In this sentence it is _____ case and _____ number.

A: nominative   plural

82. ★ ○ • ○ • Qu_____ pl_____ st__nt.

R: **Quercūs in plānitiē stant.**

83. **Quercūs**, in this sentence, is _____ case and _____ number.

A: nominative   plural

84. **Quercūs**, like **mūrēs**, is an am_____ form.

A: ambiguous

15-23

2-6

33. Notice that we did not say that we would *tell* you the meaning of these four Latin sentences. Instead we said that we would _____. [In your own words.]

Answer: help you to *discover* the meaning.

34. Your teacher will now say a Latin vowel. Listen carefully. ★ ○ ○

35. Your teacher will say this Latin vowel again. Echo. ★ ○ • ○ •

36. Echo again. ★ ○ • ○ • **a**

37. Say this Latin vowel and check. [Be sure to say it aloud first and *then* check.] a √ ★ ○ •

38. Echo and write in your answer pad the Latin vowel you hear. ★ ○ • ○ • _____

Answer: **a**

39. Your teacher will now say a second Latin vowel. Listen carefully. ★ ○ ○

40. Your teacher will say this Latin vowel again. Echo. ★ ○ • ○ •

41. Echo again. ★ ○ • ○ • **i**

42. Say this Latin vowel and check. i √ ★ ○ •

43. Echo and write the Latin vowel that you hear. ★ ○ • ○ • _____

Answer: **i**

---

75. Júdex únā in rē vincitur → J____ m___ is in r_____ v_____.

R: Júdex multis in rēbus vincitur.

76. Vēritás únā diē aperítur → V_____ m____ is d_____ ap_____.

R: Vēritás multis diēbus aperítur.

77. By adding the adjectives **únā** and **multis** we have changed the meaning of **diē**. Vēritás únā diē aperítur must mean that tr___ is _____ed by one ____.

A: truth is disclosed by one day.

78. Vēritás multis diēbus aperítur = _____

A: Truth is disclosed by many days.

You can probably guess what new form we will take up now.

Echo and write your teacher's description of the following pictures.

79. ★ ○ • ○ •

M___ c___ m____.

R: Mūs canem metuit.

2-7

44. Your teacher will now say both of these Latin vowels. Echo. ★ ○ • ○ • **a, i**

45. Say these Latin vowels and then check. **a, i** ✓ ★ ○ •

46. Your teacher will say one of two Latin vowels. Echo and write the vowel you hear. ★ ○ • ○ • _____

Answer: **a**

47. Your teacher will now say a third Latin vowel. Listen carefully. ★ ○ ○

48. Your teacher will say this Latin vowel again. Echo. ★ ○ • ○ •

49. Echo again. ★ ○ • ○ • **e**

50. Say this Latin vowel and check. **e** ✓ ★ ○ •

51. Echo and write the Latin vowel you hear. ★ ○ • ○ • _____

Answer: **e**

52. Echo the two Latin vowels your teacher says. ★ ○ • ○ • **a, e**

53. Say these Latin vowels and then check. **a, e** ✓ ★ ○ •

Change the following italicized Fifth Declension ablatives from singular to plural, changing the adjective from "one" to "many." (Change the -ē to -ēbus.)

R: Leō multīs saltibus taurum capit.

74. Leō *ūnō saltū* taurum capit → L--- m--- is s------ t------ c------.

R: Rānae multīs lacibus inveniuntur.

73. Rānae *ūnō lacū* inveniuntur → R--- m--- is in l------ inv---------.

R: Simiae multīs in gradibus manent.

72. Simiae *ūnō in gradū* manent → S------ m--- is in gr------ manent.

Change the following italicized Fourth Declension ablatives from singular to plural and change the adjective from "one" to "many." (Change the -ū to -ibus.)

R: Anus multīs cum juvenibus item habet.

71. Anus *ūnō cum juvene* item habet → A--- m--- is c--- j------ l--- h------.

R: Elephantī multīs in orbibus stant.

70. Elephantī *ūnō in orbe* stant → E-------- m--- is in or------ stant.

R: Fūr multīs in lītibus vincitur.

69. Fūr *ūnā in līte* vincitur → F--- multīs in l------ v---------.

2-8

54. Your teacher will say *one* of two Latin vowels. Echo and write the vowel you hear.
★ ○ • ○ • _____

Answer: e

55. Echo the two Latin vowels your teacher says. ★ ○ • ○ • e, i

56. Say these vowels and check. e, i ✓ ★ ○ •

57. Echo and write the vowel you hear.
★ ○ • ○ • _____

Answer: e

58. Your teacher will now say a fourth Latin vowel. Listen. ★ ○ ○

59. Your teacher will say this Latin vowel again. Echo. ★ ○ • ○ •

60. Echo again. ★ ○ • ○ • u

61. Say this Latin vowel and then check. u ✓ ★ ○ •

62. Echo and write the Latin vowel you hear.
★ ○ • ○ • _____

Answer: u

63. Echo the two Latin vowels your teacher says. ★ ○ • ○ • a, u

---

15-20

62. Words like **manus, lacus, morsus, anus** belong to the ------ D---------.

A: Fourth Declension.

63. The characteristic vowel of the Fourth Declension (the vowel which appears in the ablative singular) is short ----.

A: **-u-.** [Remember: the vowel becomes long in the ablative singular in all declensions except Third Declension nouns like **cane.**]

64. However, in the ablative plural **moribus** the characteristic vowel **-u-** has changed to ----.

A: **-i-.**

Echo the ablative plural of the Fifth Declension.

65. ★ ○ • ○ • **in rēbus**

66. ★ ○ • ○ • **sine diēbus**

67. Change from the singular to the plural.
in rē → _____

R: **in rēbus**

68. **sine diē** → _____

R: **sine diēbus**

Change the following italicized Third Declension ablatives from singular to plural and change as well the adjective from "one" to "many." (Change the -e to -ibus.)

64. Pronounce and check. **a, u** √ ★ ○ •

65. Echo and write the vowel you hear.
★ ○ • ○ • ____

Answer: **a**

66. Echo the two Latin vowels your teacher says. ★ ○ • ○ • **u, i**

67. Pronounce and check. **u, i** √ ★ ○ •

68. Echo and write the vowel you hear.
★ ○ • ○ • ____

Answer: **u**

69. Echo the two Latin vowels. ★ ○ • ○ • **e, u**

70. Pronounce and check. **e, u** √ ★ ○ •

71. Echo and write the vowel you hear.
★ ○ • ○ • ____

Answer: **e**

72. Your teacher will now say the fifth (and last) Latin vowel. This one is unlike any vowel in English. Listen very carefully. ★ ○ ○

73. Echo this Latin vowel. ★ ○ • ○ •

74. Echo again. ★ ○ • ○ • **o**

---

58. Fūr ab a__ c__ .... √ ★ ○ • 
Cōnf: **Fūr ab anū cognōscitur.**

59. T__ m__ n__ .... √ ★ ○ • 
Cōnf: **Taurus moribus noscitur.**

60. Fl__ ā l__ dē__ .... √ ★ ○ • 
Cōnf: **Flūmen ā lacibus dēfluit.**

61. F__ ab a__ c__ .... √ ★ ○ • 
Cōnf: **Fūr ab anibus cognōscitur.**

2-10

75. Pronounce and then check. o √ ★ ○ •

76. Echo and write. ★ ○ • ○ • _____

Answer: o

77. Echo the two Latin vowels. ★ ○ • ○ • o, a

78. Pronounce and then check. o, a √ ★ ○ •

79. Echo. ★ ○ • ○ • i, o

80. Pronounce and check. i, o √ ★ ○ •

81. Echo. ★ ○ • ○ • e, o

82. Pronounce and check. e, o √ ★ ○ •

83. Echo. ★ ○ • ○ • u, o

84. Pronounce and check. u, o √ ★ ○ •

85. Echo and write a Latin vowel ★ ○ • ○ • _____

Answer: e

86. Echo and write another Latin vowel ★ ○ • ○ • It was _____.

Answer: i

15-18

55. ★ ○ • ○ •

Describe these pictures, using **-ū** for the ablative singular and **-ibus** for the ablative plural. [Be sure to give your answer *first* and *then* check.]

Fūr ab ? cognōscitur.   Fūr ab ? cognōscitur.

Cōnf: Fūr ab anū cognōscitur.

R: Fūr ab anū cognōscitur.

56. ★ ○ • ○ •

Taurus ? necātur.   Taurus ? necātur.

Cōnf: Taurus morbibus necātur.

R: Taurus morbibus necātur.

57. Fl___ ā l___ dē_____ √ ★ ○ •

Cōnf: Flūmen ā lacū dēfluit.

2-11

87. Echo and write. ★ ○ • ○ • _____ 📧

    Answer: a

88. Echo and write. ★ ○ • ○ • _____ 📧

    Answer: u

89. Echo and write. ★ ○ • ○ • _____ 📧

    Answer: o

90. Echo and write. ★ ○ • ○ • _____ 📧

    Answer: u

91. Echo and write. ★ ○ • ○ • _____ 📧

    Answer: o

92. Echo and write. ★ ○ • ○ • _____ 📧

    Answer: o

93. Echo and write. ★ ○ • ○ • _____ 📧

    Answer: i

94. Echo and write. ★ ○ • ○ • _____ 📧

    Answer: a

95. Echo and write. ★ ○ • ○ • _____ 📧

    Answer: u

15-17

53. ★ ○ • ○ •

Fūr ab __?__ cōgnōscitur.
    Fūr ab __?__ cōgnōscitur.

Cōnf: Fūr ab anibus cōgnōscitur.

R: Fūr ab anibus cōgnōscitur.

54. ★ ○ • ○ •

Flūmen ā __?__ dēfluit. Flūmen ā __?__ dēfluit.

Cōnf: Flūmen ā lacibus dēfluit.

R: Flūmen ā lacibus dēfluit.

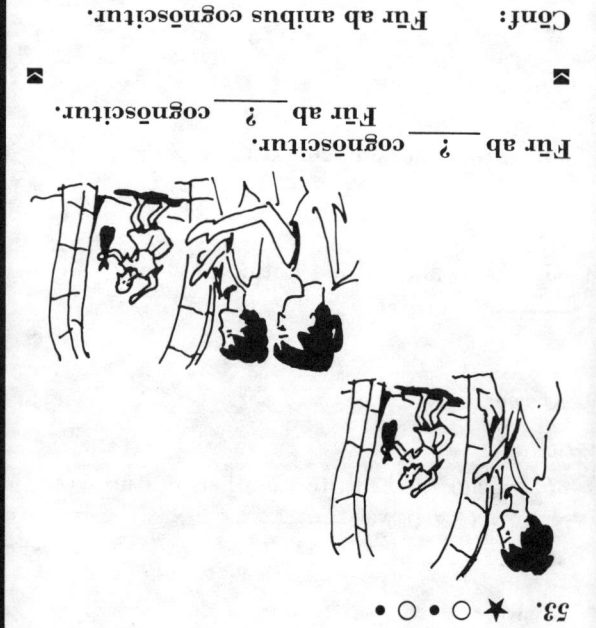

2-12

96. Echo and write. ★ ○ • ○ • _____
📢   ✉

Answer: o

97. Echo and write. ★ ○ • ○ • _____
📢   ✉

Answer: e

98. Echo all five Latin vowels as your teacher says them. ★ ○ • ○ • a, i, e, u, o
📢   ✉

99. Pronounce and check, a, i, e, u, o.
√ ★ ○ •
📢   ✉

100. Your teacher will say one of the five Latin vowels. Echo and write. ★ ○ • ○ • _____
📢   ✉

Answer: e

101. Your teacher will say another one of the Latin vowels. Echo and write. ★ ○ • ○ • _____
📢   ✉

Answer: o

102. Echo and write. ★ ○ • ○ • _____
📢   ✉

Answer: i

103. Echo and write. ★ ○ • ○ • _____
📢   ✉

Answer: a

104. Echo and write. ★ ○ • ○ • _____
📢   ✉

Answer: u

15-16

51. A. ___ ā f ___ dē ___

R: Aqua ā fontibus dēfluit.

52. ★ ○ • ○ •

Echo the description which your teacher gives of one of each pair of pictures, using the ablative of Fourth Declension nouns, with **-ū** for the singular and **-ibus** for the plural. Write the ablative on the right or left side of your Answer Pad according to the position of the picture described.

Flūmen ā ? dēfluit. Flūmen ā ? dēfluit.

Conf: Flūmen ā lacū dēfluit.

R: Flūmen ā lacū dēfluit.

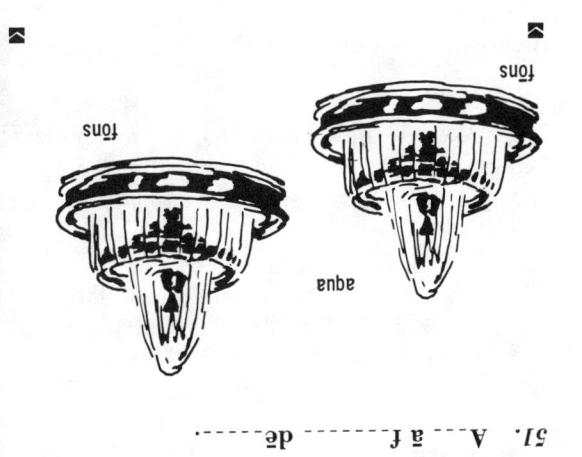

2-13

105. Echo and write. ★ ○ • ○ • _____

Answer: **o**

106. Echo and write. ★ ○ • ○ • _____

Answer: **a**

107. Echo and write. ★ ○ • ○ • _____

Answer: **e**

108. Echo and write. ★ ○ • ○ • _____

Answer: **u**

109. Echo and write. ★ ○ • ○ • _____

Answer: **i**

110. When people sing in a chorus they sing together with other people.

The directions in this program will sometimes ask you to "chorus." This means that you are to say something _____ ____ your teacher.

Answer: together with

111. We will now show you the symbol for "chorusing." (In this frame you will not use the tape player, since we are just *talking* about the symbols.)

The symbol for you to chorus looks like this: [★ ○ ○ ◉ ◉]. The star means that you are to _____ the tape player.

Answer: start

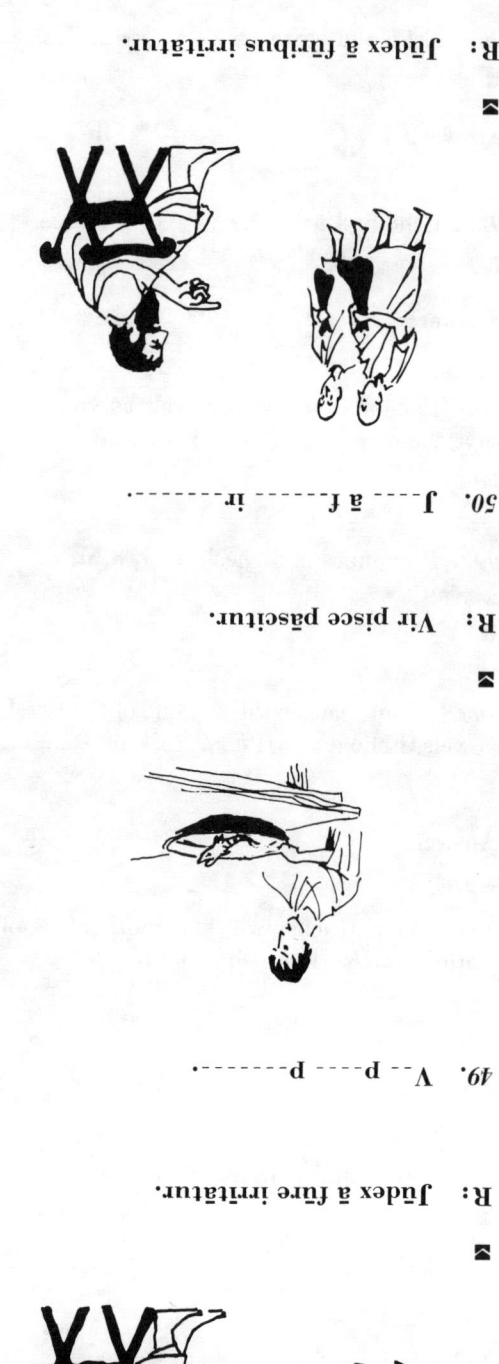

2-14

112. The two circles without the dots mean that your teacher will say something --- times.

Answer: two

113. The two circles with the dots inside mean that you are to answer together with your --------.

Answer: teacher.

114. Listen twice; then chorus five Latin vowels. ★ ○ ○ ◉ ◉ a, o, u, e, i

115. Chorus the vowels again, in a different order. ★ ○ ○ ◉ ◉ e, o, i, u, a

116. Chorus the vowels again, in a different order. ★ ○ ○ ◉ ◉ u, e, o, i, a

117. Pronounce and then check. i √ ★ ○ •

118. Pronounce and check. o √ ★ ○ •

119. Chorus. ★ ○ ○ ◉ ◉ o, i, u, a, e

120. Pronounce and check. u √ ★ ○ •

121. Pronounce and check. a √ ★ ○ •

122. Chorus. ★ ○ ○ ◉ ◉ e, a, u, i, o

123. Pronounce and check. e ✓ ★ ○ •

124. Pronounce and check. a ✓ ★ ○ •

125. Pronounce and check. i ✓ ★ ○ •

126. Pronounce and check. u ✓ ★ ○ •

127. Pronounce and check. o ✓ ★ ○ •

128. Pronounce and check. e ✓ ★ ○ •

129. The sounds used in languages can be divided into v_____ and c_____s.

Answer: vowels   consonants.

130. The Latin sounds which we have been practicing were not consonants but _____s.

Answer: vowels.

131. Consonants do not (usually) occur by themselves, but only with vowels. Your teacher will now say a new Latin word which contains a vowel followed by a consonant. ★ ○ ○

132. Your teacher will say it again. Chorus. ★ ○ ○ • •

133. Echo. ★ ○ • ○ • ab

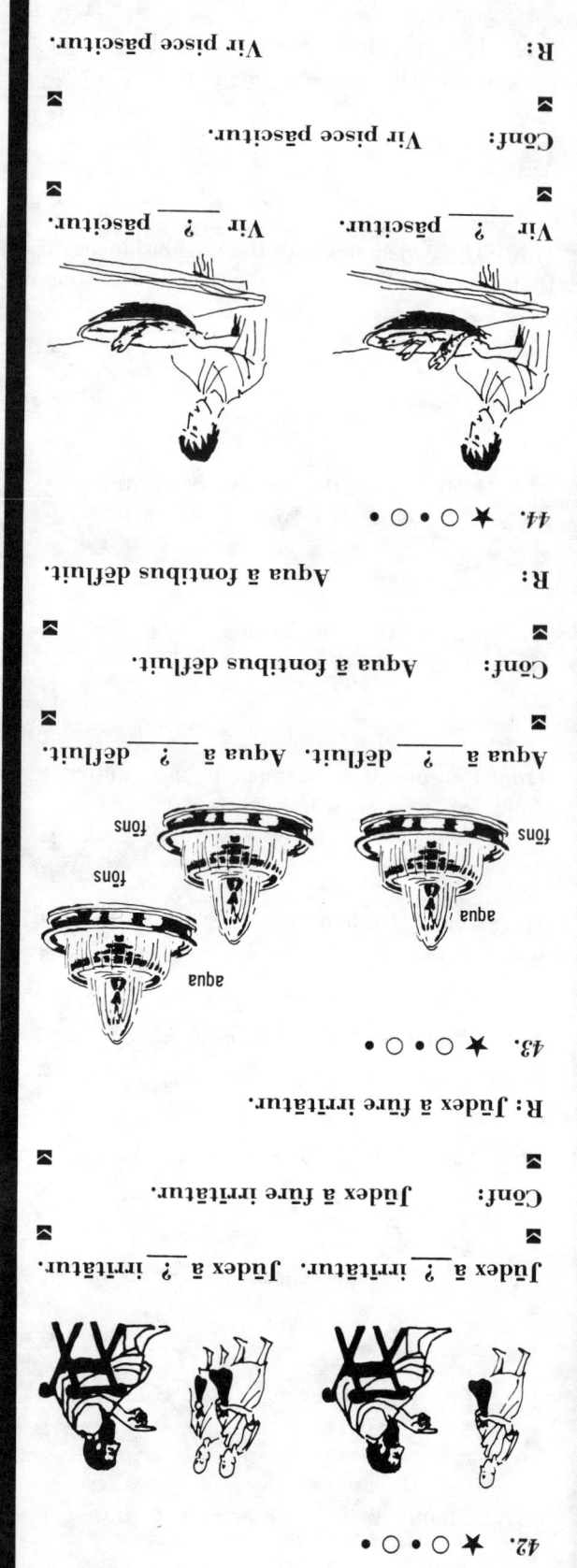

2-16

134. Pronounce and then check. **ab** √ ★ ○ •

135. Echo and write the word you hear.
★ ○ • ○ • ____

Answer: **ab**

136. Your teacher will now say another new Latin word. Listen carefully. ★ ○ ○

137. Your teacher will say it again. Chorus.
★ ○ ○ ◉ ◉

138. Echo. ★ ○ • ○ • **ob**

139. Pronounce and check. **ob** √ ★ ○ •

140. Your teacher will now say one of these two words. Echo. ★ ○ • ○ •

141. Write the Latin word which you just echoed: ____

Answer: **ob**

142. Pronounce and check. **ob** √ ★ ○ •

143. Chorus another new Latin word. ★ ○ ○ ◉ ◉

144. Echo. ★ ○ • ○ • **et**

145. Pronounce and check. **et** √ ★ ○ •

15-12

39. **Agrī ūnam diem metuunt.** ←
Ae___ ūs d___ m_____.

R: **Agrī multās diēs metuunt.**

40. Write down your teacher's description of this picture. ★ ○ ○
A____ c__ c_____ c_____.

Here is a new form of **canis**. Listen carefully.

R: **Asinus cum canibus currit.**

41. The new form **canibus** must be _____ case and _____ number. (**Auxilium sub hāc līneā est**.)

Aux. Remember what case **cum** patterns with.

A: ablative
plural

Echo the description which your teacher gives, and write the ablative on the right or left hand side of your Answer Pad, according to the picture.

2-17

146. Chorus another new Latin word.
★ ○ ● ●

147. The Latin word you just chorused is spelled "at". Echo. ★ ○ • ○ • at

148. Pronounce and check. at √ ★ ○ •

149. Echo. ★ ○ • ○ • at, et

150. Pronounce and check. at, et √ ★ ○ •

151. Your teacher will now say *one* of these two words. Echo and write. ★ ○ • ○ • _____

Answer: at

152. Pronounce and check. at √ ★ ○ •

153. Chorus another new Latin word.
★ ○ ○ ● ●

154. The Latin word you just chorused is spelled "ut". Echo. ★ ○ • ○ • ut

155. Pronounce and check. ut √ ★ ○ •

156. Your teacher will now say *one* of these last three words. Echo and write. ★ ○ • ○ • _____

Answer: at

Change these italicized objects to plural and change the "one" to "many." Say the entire sentence.

32. Anus ūnum *infantem* dīligit. →
A--- multōs in---ēs d-------.

R: Anus multōs infantēs dīligit.

33. Juvenis ūnum *canem* pāscit. →
J------ m--- os c----o p------.

R: Juvenis multōs canēs pāscit.

34. Vulpēs ūnum *mūrem* capit. →
V------ m--- ōs m---- c-----.

R: Vulpēs multōs mūrēs capit.

35. Simiae ūnum *anum* irrītant. →
S------ m--- ās --- ūs ir-------.

R: Simiae multās anūs irrītant.

36. Medicī ūnum *manum* lavant. →
M------ m--- ās m--- l-------.

R: Medicī multās manūs lavant.

37. Virī ūnum *arcum* frangunt. →
V------ --- ōs ar--- fr-------.

R: Virī multōs arcūs frangunt.

38. Fēminae ūnam *rem* quaerunt. →
F------ ---- ās r--- quaerunt.

R: Fēminae multās rēs quaerunt.

2-18

157. Pronounce and then check. **at** ✓ ★ ○ •

158. Chorus a new Latin word. ★ ○ ○ ◉ ◉

159. Echo. ★ ○ • ○ • **id**

160. Pronounce and check. **id** ✓ ★ ○ •

161. Chorus a new Latin word. ★ ○ ○ ◉ ◉

162. Echo. ★ ○ • ○ • **it**

163. Pronounce and check. **it** ✓ ★ ○ •

164. Your teacher will now say one of these two words. Echo. ★ ○ • ○ •

165. The Latin word which you just echoed is spelled _____.

Answer: **id**.

166. Pronounce and check. **id** ✓ ★ ○ •

167. In the examples which you have seen, the consonants all *followed* the vowels. But consonants in Latin may also come *before* vowels. Listen to your teacher say a Latin syllable which is made of consonant plus vowel. ★ ○ ○

168. Your teacher will say this syllable again. Chorus. ★ ○ ○ ◉ ◉

15-10

29. ★ ○ • ○ • **multus, multa, multum**
　　m　　f　　n

A large crowd may be described as a m---itude.

A: multitude.

30. "Quid agit vulpēs?"
"Ūnum m---- pr---- v------."

R: Ūnum mūrem premit vulpēs.

31. Write your teacher's description of this picture. ★ ○ ○ _____.

R: Multōs mūrēs premit vulpēs.

In this sequence, change these italicized Third Declension objects from singular to plural, also changing the adjective from "one," **ūnum**, to "many," **multōs**. If the meaning of any sentence is not clear, ask your classroom teacher for help.

2-19

169. Echo it. ★ ○ • ○ • ve

170. The letter **v** in Latin stands for ____ (the same sound it stands for in English/a different sound from what it stands for in English).

Answer: a different sound from what it stands for in English.

171. The letter **v** in Latin stands for a sound like the sound represented in English by the letter "_ _."

Answer: w.

172. Chorus these three Latin syllables.
★ ○ ○ ◉ ◉ va, ve, vi

173. Pronounce and check. **va** ✓ ★ ○ •

174. Pronounce and check. **ve** ✓ ★ ○ •

175. Pronounce and check. **vi** ✓ ★ ○ •

176. Chorus. ★ ○ ○ ◉ ◉ ve, vi, vu

177. Pronounce and then check. **vu** ✓ ★ ○ •

178. We have had syllables where the order was first a vowel, then a consonant, as in **ab**. We have also had syllables like **vi**, where the order was first a _____, then a _____.

Answer: consonant vowel.

---

26. "Quid agit anus?" "Etiam ūnam r____ met____."

R: Etiam ūnam rānam metuit anus.

27. Write your teacher's description of this picture. ★ ○ ○ M____ r____ m____ a____.

R: Multās rānās metuit anus.

28. ★ ○ • ○ • **Multōs mūrēs metuit anus.**

Here the old lady is afraid of m____ mice.

A: many

15-9

2-20

179. Listen to another kind of syllable. ★ ○ ○

180. Your teacher will say it again. Echo. ★ ○ • ○ • ves

181. Pronounce and check. ves √ ★ ○ •

182. The order of sounds in the syllable you just pronounced was the consonant v, the _____ e, and the _____ s.

Answer: vowel   consonant

183. Write the syllable which you hear. ★ ○ ○ _____

Answer: ves

184. Ves is the first _____ of your first Latin word.

Answer: syllable

185. Your teacher will now say a second Latin syllable. ★ ○ ○

186. Echo. ★ ○ • ○ • tis

187. Say this syllable and check. tis √ ★ ○ •

188. Your teacher will now say a Latin word made up of two syllables. ★ ○ ○ vestis

---

21. M ____ m ____ l ____

R: Medicus manūs lavat.

The only Fifth Declension nouns which have all the plural forms are the two most common ones, rēs and diēs. Echo your teacher as he changes the italicized objects from singular to plural.

22. ★ ○ • ○ • Fēminae *rem* quaerunt. → _____ ___ _____.

Conf: Fēminae rēs quaerunt.

23. ★ ○ • ○ • Aegrī *diem* metuunt. → _____ ____ _____.

Conf: Aegrī diēs metuunt.

Now make this same change of the italicized word from singular to plural, changing the -em to -ēs.

24. Auctor *diem* laudat. → Auctor _____ laudat.

R: Auctor diēs laudat.

25. Jūdex *rem* cognōscit. → Jūdex _____ cognōscit.

R: Jūdex rēs cognōscit.

2-21

189. Echo. ★ ○ • ○ • **vestis**

190. Pronounce and check. **vestis** √ ★ ○ •

191. Echo and write the word you hear.
★ ○ • ○ • _____

Answer: **vestis**

192. This word **vestis** is the first word of your first Latin s_____.

Answer: sentence.

193. Chorus the first syllable of another word.
★ ○ ○ ◉ ◉

194. Echo. ★ ○ • ○ • **vi**

195. Pronounce and check. **vi** √ ★ ○ •

196. Chorus another Latin syllable, being careful to imitate the roll of the **r** sound, so different from English. ★ ○ ○ ◉ ◉

197. Echo. ★ ○ • ○ • **rum**

198. Pronounce and check. **rum** √ ★ ○ •

199. Echo. ★ ○ • ○ • **virum**

R: **Simia anus irritat.**

20. S____ an__ ir____.

R: **Medicus manum lavat.**

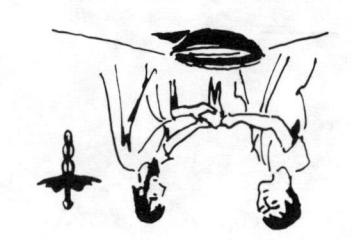

19. M____ m____ l____.

R: **Vir arcus frangit.**

18. V__ ar___ fr___.

15-7

2-22

200. Pronounce and check. **virum** √ ★ ○ •

201. Echo and write. ★ ○ • ○ • ———.

Answer: **virum**

202. Echo. ★ ○ • ○ • **vestis virum**

203. Pronounce and then check. **vestis virum** √ ★ ○ •

204. Echo and write the two words you hear. ★ ○ • ○ • ——— ———.

Answer: **vestis virum**

205. Chorus another syllable. ★ ○ ○ ◉ ◉

206. Echo. ★ ○ • ○ • **red**

207. Pronounce and check. **red** √ ★ ○ •

208. Chorus another syllable. ★ ○ ○ ◉ ◉

209. Echo. ★ ○ • ○ • **dit**

210. Pronounce and check. **dit** √ ★ ○ •

211. Your teacher will now say a word made up of **red** and **dit**. Listen *carefully* to the unusual **dd** sound. ★ ○ ○ **reddit**

212. Echo. ★ ○ • ○ • **reddit**

15-6

15. ★ ○ • ○ •

Simia ? irritat.   Simia ? irritat.

Conf: **Simia anus irritat.**

R: **Simia anus irritat.**

16. ★ ○ • ○ •

Medicus ? lavat.   Medicus ? lavat.

Conf: **Medicus manūs lavat.**

R: **Medicus manūs lavat.**

Describe these pictures, using -**um** for the singular and -**ūs** for the plural.

17. S——— a——ir———.

R: **Simia anum irritat.**

2-23

213. Pronounce and then check. **reddit**
✓ ★ ○ •

214. You have been chorusing syllables and words; in the next frame we apply this ch____ing technique to a sentence.

Answer: chorusing

215. Chorus, trying to imitate the sounds of the **r** and **dd**. ★ ○ ○ ⊙ ⊙ **Vestis virum reddit**.

216. In the last frame you should have spoken along with your teacher the last ___ times he said the Basic Sentence.

Answer: two

217. Echo. ★ ○ • ○ • **Vestis virum reddit**.

218. Pronounce and check. **Vestis virum reddit**. ✓ ★ ○ •

219. Write this sentence from dictation.
★ ○ ○

_____ _____ _____.

Answer: **Vestis virum reddit.**

220. We know that you are impatient to understand the meaning of **Vestis virum reddit**. But you will have to wait a little longer. By presenting you with tiny bits of information that you can use to make further discoveries, programmed instruction helps you to discover things for yourself. You can't yet discover the meaning of **Vestis virum reddit** because you do not yet have enough such ___s of _____.

Answer: bits of information.

2-24

221. This course is built around a number of sentences like **Vestis virum reddit**. Because they are *basic* to the course we call them "Basic Sentences." **Vestis virum reddit** is one of the four _____ _____ you will study in the next Unit.

Answer: Basic Sentences

222. But before you learn the meaning of this sentence, you must learn to pronounce ____ (1/2/3/4) *more* Basic Sentences.

Answer: 3

SUMMARY

223. In this Unit you worked entirely on the sounds of Latin. First of all you learned that there are two kinds of sounds, vowels and _____.

Answer: consonants.

224. You learned to pronounce the five Latin _____s.

Answer: vowels.

225. You then learned to combine consonants and vowels to form s_____.

Answer: syllables.

226. You then combined these syllables into ____s.

Answer: words.

---

9. L---- a--- in------.

R: **Lavat anus infantem.**

10. C---- an-- m-----.

R: **Capit animal mūrēs.**

11. L---- a--- in------.

R: **Lavat anus infantēs.**

12. The Fourth Declension also has the signal length of vowel plus -s. Therefore the plural of manum is m-----.

R: **manūs.**

15-4

227. And finally you pronounced a complete B____ S_____.

Answer: Basic Sentence.

228. Now that you have had a little experience with the program, here is some more advice on how to proceed. Remember: the purpose of this program is to help you *learn*. Move through the program rapidly, but do not *race* through it. If you go *too* fast, making rash guesses, then you may not _____ the material.

Answer: learn

229. We therefore suggest that you think the entire frame through _____ you answer.

Answer: before

230. The next bit of advice is similar. If you make a wrong answer, study the frame carefully to see where you made your mistake. If you still do not understand, then ask your classroom teacher for help. Every *right* answer is a small step forward; every wrong answer is a big step back. An occasional mistake is inevitable, but if you make a mistake you cannot see the reason for, you should _____. [In your own words.]

Answer: ask your classroom teacher for help.

231. If you make a mistake, the next frame or two will help you "unlearn" the mistake. If, however, you miss several frames in a row, then you should either go back in the program or ask for help. There are no real "rules" to the program. Together we have a single purpose: for you to *learn* Latin by whatever means seems _____. [In your own words.]

Answer: the most efficient, best, etc.

R: Pāscit juvenis canēs.

8. P_____ j_____ c_____·

R: Capit animal mūrem.

7. C_____ a_____ m_____·

Describe these pictures, using -em for the singular and -ēs for the plural. Be sure to speak aloud.

R: Capit animal mūrem.

Cōnf: Capit animal mūrem.

Capit animal ? .   Capit animal ? .

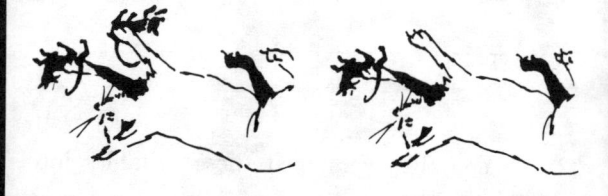

6. ★ ● ○ ● ○ •

2-26

TEST INFORMATION

At the end of every Unit there will be a test. You will be tested, naturally, on what you supposedly learned in this Unit.

One of the chief differences between good students and poor students is that the good student analyzes what the book, lecture, or program was about and reviews any points that are still not clear.

The purpose of the summary which you have just read was to remind you what it was that you had learned. We assumed earlier that from this summary the student would be able to figure out what the tests would examine. To our surprise we found out that certain students did poorly because they did not know what was going to be on the test.

We have therefore decided to give you this additional information: for awhile we will outline for you the test item by item, along with the frame numbers where you can review any points about which you feel unsure. We will not continue to do this throughout the program: it will eventually become *your* responsibility to figure out what the Unit was about and what the tests will cover.

You might ask yourself this question: what did you practice in this unit? First you practiced vowels. Therefore the first thing which you will be asked to do will be to write down some Latin vowels from dictation.

Secondly, you learned to pronounce syllables. You will be asked to write down some syllables from dictation.

But the main purpose was to teach you to pronounce a Latin sentence correctly. Therefore you will be asked to read correctly the sentence **Vestis virum reddit.**

But what does "correctly" mean? Remember what was stressed on the program. Your teacher will listen to see how you pronounce the sound represented by the letter **v**. He will listen to hear whether you trill the sound /**r**/. And finally he will listen for the double /**dd**/.

So now you know what the test for Unit Two will be like. Your teacher may of course add some items which were covered in class.

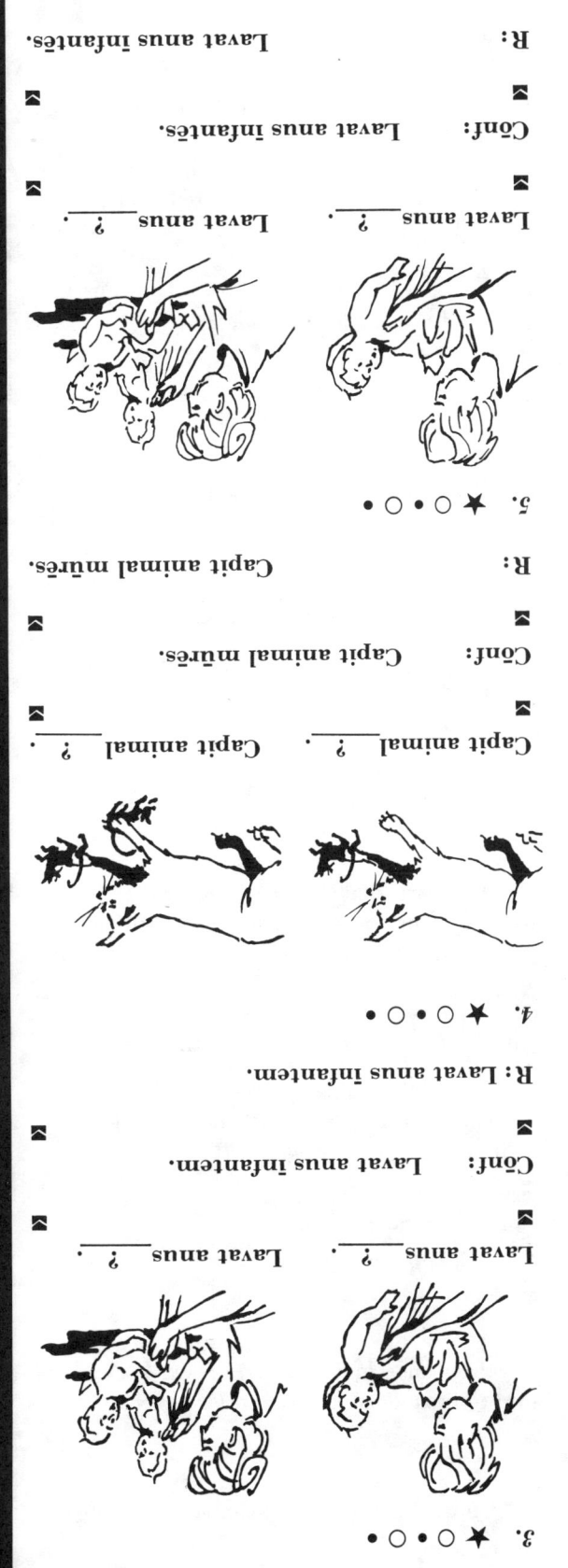

UNIT THREE

1. We will now continue with the Latin sounds. In this Unit you will learn to pronounce three more Basic Sentences. But first let us review the meaning of the symbols that tell you how to proceed.

If you use a tape recorder, the star means that you are to ───── the tape player.

Ans:　　start

2. If you do not have a tape recorder, the star means that your teacher will ─── something.

Ans:　　　　　say

3. In the answer above, *Ans* is an abbreviation for the word ──────.

Ans:　　answer.

4. The direction "chorus" means that you listen to your teacher say something twice, then you say the same thing twice ──── your teacher.

Ans:　　　　　with

5. Chorus the first syllable of a second Basic Sentence. ★ ○ ○ ◉ ◉

6. Echo. ★ ○ • ○ • **ma**

7. Pronounce and check. **ma** √ ★ ○ • [Be sure to pronounce it first and *then* check.]

8. Chorus another Latin syllable. ★ ○ ○ ◉ ◉

UNIT FIFTEEN

The accusative plural of the Third, Fourth, and Fifth Declensions also have the signal of length of vowel and -**s**. This means that to form an accusative plural of a Third Declension noun you change the -**em** of the singular to -**ēs**.

1. As before, your teacher will describe one of the two pictures. Echo and write the accusative form on the right or left hand side of your answer pad according to the position of the picture described. Remember, the singular ends in -**em**, the plural in -**ēs**. Therefore the plural of canem is ──**ēs**.

R:　canēs.

2. ★ ○ • ○ •

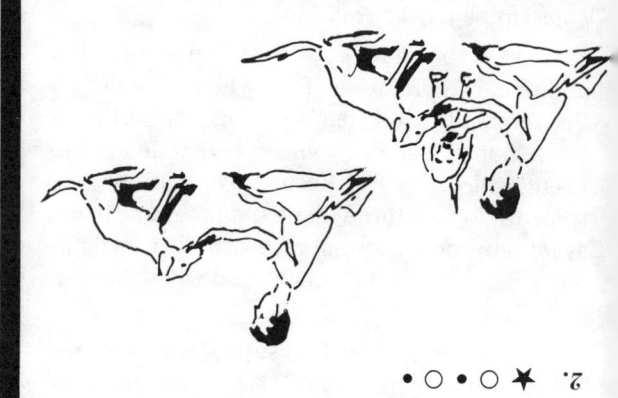

R:　**Pāscit juvenis canēs.**

[Did you remember to say your answer aloud as well as write?]

Conf:　**Pāscit juvenis canēs.**

Pāscit juvenis ─?─ . **Pāscit juvenis** ─?─ .

3-2

9. Echo. ★ ○ • ○ • **nus**

10. Pronounce and then check. **nus** √ ★ ○ •

11. Echo a word. ★ ○ • ○ • **manus**

12. Pronounce and check. **manus** √ ★ ○ •

13. Echo and write the word you hear.
    ★ ○ • ○ • _____

    Ans: **manus**

14. Your teacher will now say a new two-syllable word, very similar to **manus** except for the last sound. ★ ○ ○

15. Your teacher will say this word again. Chorus. ★ ○ ○ ● ●

16. Echo. ★ ○ • ○ • **manum**

17. Pronounce and then check. **manum** √ ★ ○ •

18. Echo and write. ★ ○ • ○ • _____

    Ans: **manum**

19. Echo. ★ ○ • ○ • **manus manum**

VOCABULARY INVENTORY

In this Unit you learned two nouns that are antonyms: **religiō** (147) **superstitiō** (151)

You also learned two verbs that are antonyms: **colit** (156) **violat** (158)

You learned two other verbs: **pāscit** (262) **frangit** (264)

And two other nouns: **cōnsilium** (221) **lacrima** (261)

Finally, you learned two new forms of the question word **Quis?** **Quī?** (174) **Quōs?** (169)

TEST INFORMATION

You will be asked to produce only forms which you have seen or heard. However, the questions will not necessarily be the exact frames as in the Unit. You may be asked to use in a sentence a word which you practiced in a paradigm.

The number of the frame where the word occurred is given in parenthesis. Review if necessary.

305. In this next list some of the nouns which end in -ās are nominative like **vēritās**, while others are accusative plural like **rānas**. Which of the following nouns are accusative plural?
fēminās, fēlīcitās, rēgīnās, lacrimās, vēritās

R: **fēminās   rēgīnās,   lacrimās,**

14-67

3-3

20. Pronounce and then check.
manus manum √ ★ ○ •

21. Echo and write. ★ ○ • ○ •
_____ _____

Ans: **manus manum**

22. Chorus another Latin syllable.
★ ○ ○ ◉ ◉

23. Echo. ★ ○ • ○ • **la**

24. First pronounce and then check. **la**
√ ★ ○ •

25. Chorus another Latin syllable.
★ ○ ○ ◉ ◉

26. The Latin syllable you just chorused is spelled **vat**. Echo. ★ ○ • ○ • **vat**

27. Pronounce and check. **vat** √ ★ ○ •

28. Echo a new word. ★ ○ • ○ • **lavat**

29. Pronounce and check. **lavat** √ ★ ○ •

30. Chorus the entire sentence. ★ ○ ○ ◉ ◉
Manus manum lavat.

---

300. When asked a **Quem?** question you answered with a noun in the _____ case and _____ number.

A: accusative
singular

301. When you were asked a **Quī?** question, you answered with a noun in the _____ case and in the _____ number.

A: nominative
plural

302. **Quem?** and **Quōs?** questions are answered by nouns in the _____ case. However, **Quem?** asks for the _____ number and **Quōs?** asks for the _____ number.

A: accusative
singular
plural

303. **Quō?** asks for a noun in the _____ case of the _____ number.

A: ablative
singular

304. As you learn more and more forms, you are discovering more and more words which, although they rhyme, are not actually the same form. In this list all the words end in long –ō. Which of them are *ablative* case? **religiō, cōnsilio, ōrātiō, superstitiō, membrō, nēmō, pūrō, venēnō, imitātiō, leō, medio, cōnfirmātiō.**

R: cōnsilio   membrō
        pūrō   venēnō
                     medio

14-66

3-4

31. Echo. ★ ○ • ○ • **Manus manum lavat.**

32. Pronounce and check.
Manus manum lavat. ✓ ★ ○ •

33. Write. ★ ○ ○ ──── ──── ────. [In the answer pad write out the whole sentence.]

Ans: **Manus manum lavat.**

34. Echo. ★ ○ • ○ • **Vestis virum reddit.**

35. Echo. ★ ○ • ○ • **Manus manum lavat.**

36. So far in the program it has been necessary for you only to follow directions. From this point on we are going to ask you to do more than follow directions. You know that these two sentences are called "Basic Sentences," because they are a ────── part of the course.

Ans: basic, important, etc.

37. Therefore you should learn them as soon as possible. In the next frame we will *ask* you to echo a Basic Sentence only once. But if you have any doubt about the sentence, repeat it *again*, and, if necessary, again and again until you have l────ed the sentence.

Ans: learned

38. Echo. ★ ○ **Manus manum lavat.** [Repeat as many times as necessary in order to learn it.]

39. Echo. ★ ○ **Vestis virum reddit.** [Repeat as many times as necessary.]

14-65

296. The third one stated that the intelligence of women was inferior to that of men. M──ō c────ō f────ae v────nt v────s.

R: **cōnsiliō fēminae vincunt virōs.**

Malō in

297. The last Basic Sentence said that when dealing with a person of a cruel nature it will do no good to weep. C────s l────s p────tur, n────n f────tur.

R: **Crūdēlis lacrimīs pāscitur, nōn frangitur.**

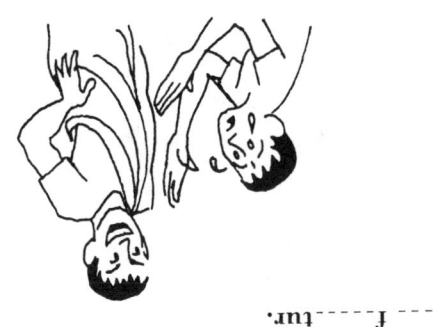

298. This last Basic Sentence, as well as the one about women, was written by ────────.

A: **Publilius Syrus.**

299. In this Unit you were asked a number of questions on Basic Sentences. When asked a **Quis?** question you answered with a noun in the ────── case and ──────── number.

A: nominative singular

3-5

40. Two more sentences to go! Then you will start to discover their meanings.

The five Latin vowels which you have been pronouncing are called "short" vowels. For each "short" vowel there is a corresponding "long" vowel. Your teacher will now say a familiar Latin vowel which will be "short;" it will be followed by the corresponding long vowel. Notice how much *longer* the second vowel is than the first. ★ ○ ○

41. We call them "long" vowels because, compared with the "short" vowels, they take about twice as ____ to pronounce.

Ans: long

42. Your teacher will say this pair again. Chorus, being careful to make the second vowel twice as *long* as the first. ★ ○ ○ ● ●

43. Compared with the short vowel the long vowel takes about _____ as long to say.

Ans: twice

44. To show that a Latin vowel is long we place a line over the letter. The letter a stands for the short vowel, but the letter ā (with the line over it) stands for the ____ vowel.

Ans: long

45. Listen again. ★ ○ ○ a, ā

46. Echo. ★ ○ ● ○ ● a, ā

47. First pronounce and then check. a, ā
✓ ★ ○ ●

R: Religiō deōs colit, superstitiō violat.

295. The next sentence contrasted religion and superstition. R____ō d____ c____t, s_____ō v____t.

R: Aquila nōn capit muscās.

294. Basic Sentence 36 said that eagles had more important things to chase than flies. Aq____ ____ c____t m____s.

You can now see if you have mastered these all important Basic Sentences.

Cōnf: Crūdēlis lacrimīs pāscitur, nōn frangitur.

293. ★ ○ ● Cr____ l____ p____ fr____. (39)

14-64

3-6

48. There is a technical term for this line that we place over the letter. Echo as your teacher says this technical term. ★ ○ • ○ • macron

Visual Check: "máy-cron"

49. This technical term for the mark over a long Latin vowel is spelled "macron." Pronounce and then check. macron √ ★ ○ •

Visual Check: "máy-cron"

50. The letter ā has a macron over it to show that the vowel it stands for is not short but _____.

Ans: long.

51. We can see that the letter ā is a long vowel because of the _____ over the letter.

Ans: macron [Did you remember to *write* the answer?]

52. The word "macron" is a _____ term.

Ans: technical

Copy this in your Reference Notebook. "A long vowel in Latin is marked by a macron over the vowel."

53. Your teacher will now say another short vowel followed by the corresponding long vowel. ★ ○ ○

54. Your teacher will say this pair again. Chorus. ★ ○ ○ ● ●

---

287. You should be able to decline all First or Second Declension nouns which we have had in this Unit. To test yourself, write the paradigm of vir. _____ _____

R: vir   virī
    virum virōs
    virō   virīs

288. See if you can write the paradigm of poena. _____ _____

R: poena   poenae
    poenam poenās
    poenā   poenīs

[If you had any trouble, go back to frame 181 and study the paradigms carefully.]

289. The signal for the plural of the *active* verb is -nt, as in vincunt, while the signal for the plural passive is _____.

R: -ntur.

Echo the four Basic Sentences which you learned in this Unit. If you have any trouble, study them in your Reference Notebook.

290. ★ ○ • Aqu----- c---- m----- (36)

Cōnf: Aquila nōn capit muscās.

291. ★ ○ • R---- d---- c----, s---- (37)

Cōnf: Religiō deōs colit, superstitiō violat.

292. ★ ○ • M--- c------ f------ v------ (38)

Cōnf: Malō in cōnsiliō fēminae vincunt virōs.

14-63

3-7

55. Echo the Latin vowels you just chorused.
★ ○ • ○ • **e, ē** [Remember to repeat *several times* if necessary.]

56. Pronounce and check. **e, ē** √ ★ ○ •

57. Your teacher will now say another pair of long and short vowels. ★ ○ ○

58. Here is this pair again. Chorus.
★ ○ ○ ◉ ◉

59. Echo. ★ ○ • ○ • **i, ī**

60. Pronounce and then check. **i, ī** √ ★ ○ •

61. Your teacher will now say another pair of long and short vowels. ★ ○ ○

62. Here is this pair again. Chorus. ★ ○ ○ ◉ ◉

63. Echo. ★ ○ • ○ • **o, ō**

64. Pronounce and check. **o, ō** √ ★ ○ •

65. Your teacher will now say another pair of long and short vowels. ★ ○ ○

66. Here is this pair again. Chorus. ★ ○ ○ ◉ ◉

67. Echo. ★ ○ • ○ • **u, ū**

---

281. While **pāscit** means "feeds," there is an adjectival form of the verb, **pāstus**, which means "fed." There is a Latin word **pāstūra** which is formed from this adjectival stem. **pāstus**. So the English "pasture" comes from **pāstūra**, which is connected with the **pāstus** stem of the verb ――――.

R: **pāscit**.

282. Another stem of **frangit** is **frāctus**. From it comes a Latin noun **frāctūra**. From **frāctūra** comes the English word "――――."

A: fracture.

[You will learn more about the different stems of the verb later in the course.]

SUMMARY

283. In this Unit you learned the ―――― number of First and Second Declension nouns.

A: plural

284. The characteristic vowel of the First Declension is ――.

R: **a**.

285. The characteristic vowel of the Second Declension is ――.

R: **o**.

286. Before the ablative ending **-is** these characteristic vowels d――――.

A: disappear.

14-62

3-8

68. Pronounce and check. **u, ū** √ ★ ○ •

69. The sound **u** is a _____ vowel and **ū** is a _____ vowel.

Ans: short
long

70. You will now hear *one* of these two vowels. Echo and write the one you hear, being sure to write the macron if the vowel was long. ★ ○ • ○ • a ? ā ? It was _____.

Ans: ā.

71. Echo and write. ★ ○ • ○ • i ? ī ? _____

Ans: i

72. ★ ○ • ○ • [The symbols tell you to echo and write.] e ? ē ? _____

Ans: ē [The answer is right *only* if it has the macron over the letter.]

73. ★ ○ • ○ • o ? ō ? _____

Ans: o

74. ★ ○ • ○ • u ? ū ? _____

Ans: u

75. ★ ○ • ○ • a ? ā ? _____

Ans: e

14-61

274. "Quis lacrimīs pāscitur?" "_____."

R: Crūdēlis.

275. "Quem lacrimae nōn frangunt?" "_____."

R: Crūdēlem.

276. "Quid agunt lacrimae?" "_____."

R: Crūdēlem pāscunt.

277. "Quid nōn agunt lacrimae?" "_____."

R: Crūdēlem nōn frangunt.

278. "Quis lacrimīs nōn frangitur?" "_____."

R: Crūdēlis.

279. The English word "pasture" comes from the Latin **pāstūra**, which is in turn connected with the Latin verb p---it.

R: pāscit.

280. You may think that the resemblance of "pasture" to **pāscit** is not very clear. Here is the connection. Latin verbs usually have three different stems. A number of common English verbs, like "sing/sang/sung" also have three different ----s.

A: stems.

76. ★ ○ • ○ • a ꭇ ā ꭇ ____

Ans: ā

77. ★ ○ • ○ • i ꭇ ī ꭇ ____

Ans: ī

78. ★ ○ • ○ • o ꭇ ō ꭇ ____

Ans: o

79. ★ ○ • ○ • u ꭇ ū ꭇ ____

Ans: ū

80. ★ ○ • ○ • o ꭇ ō ꭇ ____

Ans: o

81. ★ ○ • ○ • e ꭇ ē ꭇ ____

Ans: ē

82. ★ ○ • ○ • a ꭇ ā ꭇ ____

Ans: a

83. ★ ○ • ○ • o ꭇ ō ꭇ ____

Ans: ō

84. Now there is a four-way choice. (If you are not clear about what the symbols mean, check on their meaning in your Reference Notebook. If you still have trouble, ask for help.) ★ ○ • ○ • a ꭇ ā ꭇ i ꭇ ī ꭇ ____

Ans: a

---

269. Echo a new technical term. ★ ○ • ○ •

metaphorical

VCh: "met-uh-for-rick-cull"

270. Tears would be an unsubstantial diet. Therefore we assume that the expression "is fed by tears" is what we call a "metaphorical" meaning; that is, it is not to be taken in the ordinary sense of the word "feed," which means to give food. "A cruel person is fed by tears" means then that a cruel person is _____ [In your own words]

A: pleased by other person's tears.

271. People don't break the way statues or dishes do. Therefore we conclude that the expression Crūdēlis lacrimīs nōn frangitur also has a m_____al meaning.

A: metaphorical

272. This sentence was written by the same author as the sentence we learned previously, the one about women. Both sentences were written by the Roman author P_____ S____.

A: Publilius Syrus.

Question and Answer Drill

The following questions will be on the new Basic Sentence Crūdēlis lacrimīs pāscitur, nōn frangitur, or on its active transformation, Crūdēlem lacrimae pāscunt, nōn frangunt.

273. "Pāsciturne an frangitur crūdēlis lacrimīs?" "____."

R: Pāscitur.

3-10

85. ★ ○ • ○ • e ̆ ĕ ē ĭ ī ĭ ī ̆ _____

Ans: i

86. ★ ○ • ○ • i ̆ ī ̆ ō ŏ ō ̆ _____

Ans: ō

87. ★ ○ • ○ • u ̆ ū ̆ ĕ ē ̆ _____

Ans: ū

88. ★ ○ • ○ • a ̆ ā ̆ ŏ ō ̆ _____

Ans: a

89. Now a six-way choice. ★ ○ • ○ • i ̆ ī ̆ ĕ ē ̆ a ̆ ā ̆ _____

Ans: ī

90. ★ ○ • ○ • a ̆ ā ̆ ŏ ō ̆ ĕ ē ̆ _____

Ans: ā

91. ★ ○ • ○ • • ĕ ē ̆ ĭ ī ̆ u ̆ ū ̆ _____

Ans: u

92. ★ ○ • ○ • • ŏ ō ̆ ĕ ē ̆ ĭ ī ̆ _____

Ans: ē

93. ★ ○ • ○ • • a ̆ ā ̆ ĕ ē ̆ ŏ ō ̆ _____

Ans: o

---

264. Read the description of this picture and check. **Insānus effigiem frangit.** √ ★ ○ •

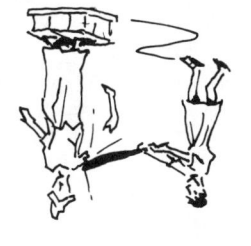

265. Insānus effigiem frangit means that the cr----- p-----ing is br---ing the -------

A: crazy person is breaking the statue.

266. Pronounce and check. **Crūdēlis lacrimīs pāscitur, nōn frangitur.** (39) √ ★ ○ •

267. Crūdēlis lacrimīs pāscitur, nōn frangitur means, "A ----- ----- is f--- by t-----, not ----en by them."

A: A cruel person is fed by tears, not broken by them.

268. Copy this Basic Sentence and its English meaning in your Reference Notebook.

14-59

3-11

94. ★○•○•a⌐ā⌐u⌐ū⌐o⌐ō⌐____

Ans: a

95. ★○•○•i⌐ī⌐o⌐ō⌐u⌐ū⌐____

Ans: u

96. ★○•○•e⌐ē⌐u⌐ū⌐i⌐ī⌐____

Ans: ū

97. Echo a *long* Latin vowel and write.
★○•○•____

Ans: ō

98. Echo a *short* Latin vowel and write.
★○•○•____

Ans: u

99. Echo and write ★○•○•____

Ans: ā

100. Echo and write. ★○•○•____

Ans: i

101. Echo and write. ★○•○•____

Ans: ē

102. Echo and write. ★○•○•____

Ans: i

14-58

259. Echo your teacher's description of this picture. ★○•○• **Ex o------ l------ d------.**

260. **Ex oculīs lacrimae dēfluunt** means that t----s are ----ing from the ---s.

Cōnf: Ex oculīs lacrimae dēfluunt.

A: tears are flowing from the eyes.

261. Echo the paradigm of the word "tear." ★○•○•
lacrimae   lacrima
lacrimās   lacrimam
lacrimīs   lacrimā

262. Read the description of this picture and check. **Juvenis simiās pāscit.** √ ★○•○•

263. "**Juvenis simiās pāscit**" means that the ---- is f------ the m------.

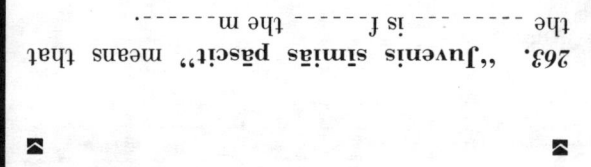

A: young man is feeding the monkeys.

3-12

103. ★ ○ • ○ • ____

Ans: o

104. ★ ○ • ○ • ____

Ans: e

105. ★ ○ • ○ • ____

Ans: ū

106. ★ ○ • ○ • ____

Ans: o

107. ★ ○ • ○ • ____

Ans: a

108. ★ ○ • ○ • ____

Ans: ā

109. Whether the vowel is long or short is very important in Latin. There are thousands of pairs of words where the two words have entirely different meanings even though the *only* difference to be seen between them is the "length" of the vowel. For example, here are two words that differ only in the length of the vowel. ★ ○ ○ est, ēst

110. The word **est** (with the short vowel) means "is." The word **ēst** means "eats." Listen. ★ ○ ○ Are the two words **est** and **ēst** *pronounced* alike? ____ Yes/No

Ans: No

14-57

254. This frame is just for the ladies. Gentlemen should skip to frame 255.

The original Basic Sentence is not kind to women. Change it to say that *men* are better than women at making a bad plan. Malō in cōnsiliō fēminae vincunt virōs. Malō in cōnsiliō f_____ vincunt v_____.

R: Malō in cōnsiliō fēminās vincunt virī.

255. ★ ○ • ○ • *Crūdēlis lacrimīs pāscitur, nōn frangitur.* (39)

256. ★ ○ ○ Cr____ l____ p____, n____ fr____. [Mark five vowels with macrons]

R: Crūdēlis lacrimīs pāscitur, nōn frangitur.

257. Crūdēlis is an adjective. If it modifies a noun, draw an arrow to the noun it modifies; if it does not modify any noun, say so.

A: It doesn't modify any noun.

258. Therefore in this sentence it is used as a noun and means "cr--- p-----."

A: cruel person.

3-13

111. Are **est** and **ēst** *spelled* alike? ____ Yes/No

Ans: No

112. The difference in spelling between **est** ("is") and **ēst** ("eats") is the m_____ over the Latin word for "eats."

Ans: macron

113. Copy the Latin word for "eats." _____ [Look back if you wish.]

Ans: ēst

114. In order for the preceding answer to be correct, there must have been a _____ over the vowel.

Ans: macron

115. Echo your teacher as he pronounces two more words that differ only in the length of one of the vowels. ★ ○ • ○ • **liber, līber**

116. Your teacher will say one of these two words. Echo and write. ★ ○ • ○ • **liber? līber?**

Ans: **līber**

117. **Liber** (without the macron) means "book" and **līber** (with the macron) means "free." Say the Latin word for "book" and then check. √ ★ ○ •

Visual Check: **liber**

---

248. "Quōs malō in cōnsiliō fēminae vincunt?" "_____."

R: **Virōs.**

249. "Malō in cōnsiliō quī fēminās vincuntur?" "_____."

R: **Virī.**

250. "Quī virōs vincunt malō in cōnsiliō?" "_____."

R: **Fēminae.**

251. "Bonō in cōnsiliō quī fēminās vincunt?" "_____."

R: **Virī.**

The expression **cōnsilium capiunt** means "(some people) make a plan." Answer the next question according to the sense of this last Basic Sentence—even though you may not agree with the idea.

252. "Quāle cōnsilium capiunt fēminae?" "_____."

R: **Malum cōnsilium.**

253. "Quāle cōnsilium capiunt virī?" "_____."

R: **Bonum cōnsilium.**

14-56

3-14

118. Even the Latin long vowels are shorter and crisper than English sounds which they resemble. We will give you practice now in telling the difference between these Latin and English sounds. Remember that the Latin sounds will be _____ and _____ than the English ones.

Ans: shorter   crisper

119. In this frame you will hear two words. One of them will be a familiar English word; the other will be a Latin word. Echo. ★ ○ • ○ • English "day," Latin dē

120. Now echo just the Latin. ★ ○ • ○ • dē

121. Now pronounce Latin dē and check. √ ★ ○ • [Remember, say it first yourself and then check.]

122. Which word ends in a "yuh" sound, English "day" or Latin dē? ★ ○ ○ "day," dē

Ans: English "day"

123. Which word is shorter and crisper, English "day" or Latin dē?

Ans: Latin dē

124. ★ ○ • ○ • "day" ¿dē? _____

Ans: dē

125. ★ ○ • ○ • English "Dee" (the girl's nickname), Latin dī

14-55

244. Publilius Syrus lived in the first century before Christ, when women had obtained a great deal of freedom in personal and legal matters, although they never did achieve political equality. Divorce was easy to obtain for both men and women. The first century before Christ marked the decline of the Republic and the establishment of the Empire. It was a time of great turmoil. Not unnaturally, there were men who were inclined to believe that women should not have been granted so much _____

A: freedom.

245. But why, you may ask, did we include such a saying in our Latin program? _____ [In your own words]

A: Of course we don't know what you think, but it seems to us that the hostility shown to women by some men during Roman times is of some interest, particularly at a time like the present when the position of women has changed so much in the last fifty years.

246. As you know, there are still plenty of men who firmly believe that a woman's place is in the _____

A: cave.

247. Here is the original sentence but without the macrons. Copy it in your answer pad. Then listen to your teacher read it and mark the five long vowels with macrons. ★ ○ ○ Malō in cōnsiliō fēminae vincunt virōs.

R: Malō in cōnsiliō fēminae vincunt virōs.

Question and Answer Drill

The passive transformation of this sentence is Malō in cōnsiliō ā fēminīs vincuntur virī.

3-15

126. ★ ○ • ○ • "Dee"? dī? _____

Ans: "Dee"

127. ★ ○ • ○ • English "two," Latin tū

128. ★ ○ • ○ • "two"? tū? _____

Ans: tū

129. ★ ○ • ○ • English "dough," Latin dō

130. ★ ○ • ○ • "dough"? dō? _____

Ans: dō

131. Chorus the first syllable of a new Basic Sentence. ★ ○ ○ ● ●

132. ★ ○ • ○ • hi

133. Pronounce and then check. hi √ ★ ○ •

134. Chorus the second syllable. ★ ○ ○ ● ●

135. ★ ○ • ○ • la

136. Pronounce and check. la √ ★ ○ •

137. Chorus the third syllable, being careful to roll the r. ★ ○ ○ ● ●

---

239. This is a mean thing to say about women. Of course we mustn't blame Publilius Syrus, since we can't tell how he used this line in his play. For example, someone may have immediately contradicted the character who said this line and proved that women were smarter than men. But we want to take this opportunity to explain the position of women in Roman times. (When we say "Roman times," you must remember that this covers a period of over a thousand years.) During the early days, the children were subjected to the authority of the f----- of the family.

A: father

240. In fact, in early times the father had the power of life and ----- over his children.

A: death

241. The children were said to be in manū with respect to the father, which means that they were under the legal au-----ty of the father.

A: authority

242. When a girl married, she ceased to be in manū to her father; but instead she became ----- with respect to her husband.

R: in manū

243. But as the primitive civilization of the early Romans came in contact with other cultures, the women began to obtain more fr-----

A: freedom

3-16

138. ★ ○ • ○ • rem

139. Pronounce and then check. rem √ ★ ○ •

140. These three syllables form a word. Your teacher will now say the whole word. Chorus. ★ ○ ○ ◉ ◉

141. ★ ○ • ○ • hilarem

142. Pronounce and check. hilarem √ ★ ○ •

143. Echo and write. ★ ○ • ○ • _____

Ans: hilarem

144. Chorus the first syllable of the next word. ★ ○ ○ ◉ ◉

145. Echo. ★ ○ • ○ • da

146. Pronounce and then check. da √ ★ ○ •

147. Chorus the second syllable. ★ ○ ○ ◉ ◉

148. ★ ○ • ○ • tō

149. Pronounce and then check. tō √ ★ ○ •

150. Chorus the last syllable. ★ ○ ○ ◉ ◉

14-53

232-236. Chorus these five other sayings from the plays of Publilius Syrus. ★ ◉

232. Etiam capillus ūnus habet umbram suam. (11)

233. Crūdēlem medicum intemperāns aeger facit. (12)

234. Lēx videt īrātum, īrātus lēgem nōn videt. (13)

235. Numquam perīc'lum sine perīc'lō vincitur. (25)

236. Habet suum venēnum blanda ōrātiō. (34)

237. These sayings were written by _____

A: Pūblilius Syrus.

238. The last Basic Sentence we learned was also written by Publilius Syrus. Say it aloud and write it.

M_____ in cōn_____ f_____ vincunt v_____. (38) (There are five long vowels.)

R: Malō in cōnsiliō fēminae vincunt virōs.

3-17

151. ★ ○ • ○ • **rem**

152. Pronounce and check. **rem** √ ★ ○ •

153. Your teacher will now say the whole word. Chorus. ★ ○ ○ ● ●

154. ★ ○ • ○ • **datōrem**

155. Pronounce and check. **datōrem** √ ★ ○ •

156. Echo and write. [Remember, this word has a macron.] ★ ○ • ○ • _____

Ans: **datōrem**

157. Your teacher will now say the first two words of the Basic Sentence. Listen carefully. ★ ○ ○

158. Your teacher will say them again. Chorus. ★ ○ ○ ● ●

159. Echo. ★ ○ • ○ • **hilarem datōrem**

160. Pronounce and check. **hilarem datōrem** √ ★ ○ •

161. Echo and write. ★ ○ • ○ • _____ _____
[Remember, this phrase has a macron.]

Ans. **hilarem datōrem**

---

226. Write Basic Sentence 38 and its English translation in your Reference Notebook.

227. The author implies that women are superior to men in just one respect: women are better at _____ bad _____s.

A: making bad plans.

228. Women surpass men in making a bad plan = M_ō in c_____ō f_____ae v_____nt v_____ōs.

R: **Malō in cōnsiliō fēminae vincunt virōs.**

229. Echo the English pronunciation of the name of the author of this saying, "**Publius Syrus.**" ★ ○ • ○ •

VCh: "**pooh-blili-lee-yuss sir-russ.**"

230. While many of our Basic Sentences come from famous writers like Cicero, Ovid, and Horace, some of the sentences are from people who are little known today. Pronounce the name "**Publilius Syrus.**" √ ★ ○ •

231. Publilius Syrus is a good example of an author who is not known to the general public. He wrote a number of plays which were extremely popular, but none of them have survived. What is left of his work is a collection of over 700 lines of sayings like the following: **Nōn semper autem facilem habet Fēlīcitās.** This was written by _____ _____.

A: Publilius Syrus.

14-52

3-18

162. Chorus the first syllable of the third word.
★ ○ ● ●

163. ★ ○ • ○ • dī

164. dī ✓ ★ ○ • [First say it and *then* check.]

165. Chorus the second syllable. ★ ○ ○ ● ●

166. ★ ○ • ○ • li

167. li ✓ ★ ○ •

168. Chorus the last syllable of this word.
★ ○ ○ ● ●

169. ★ ○ • ○ • git

170. git ✓ ★ ○ •

171. Chorus the whole word. ★ ○ ○ ● ●

172. Echo. ★ ○ • ○ • dīligit

173. Pronounce and check. dīligit ✓ ★ ○ •

174. Echo and write. [Don't forget the macron.]
★ ○ • ○ • _____

Ans: dīligit

14-51

220. "Quid nōn agit aquila?" "_____
_____."

R: capit muscās.

221. ★ ○ • cōnsilium
cōnsilium
cōnsiliō

("plan") 2d Declension neuter.

222. Malō in cōnsiliō fēminae vincunt
virōs. (38) ★ ○ ○ •

223. ★ ○ ○ M_____ = c_____
= _____

Cōnf: Malō in cōnsiliō

224. ★ ○ ○ Malō in cōnsiliō _____.

Cōnf: Malō in cōnsiliō fēminae
vincunt virōs.

225. Malō in cōnsiliō fēminae vincunt
virōs means that _____ surpass _____ in (making)
a _____.

A: women surpass men in making
a bad plan.

3-19

175. Your teacher will now say the first three words of this Basic Sentence. Listen. ★ ○ ○

176. ★ ○ ○ ◉ ◉ hilarem datōrem dīligit

177. ★ ○ • ○ • hilarem datōrem dīligit

178. hilarem datōrem dīligit √ ★ ○ •

179. ★ ○ • ○ • _____ ____ ____ [In these frames, be careful not to look back.]

Ans: hilarem datōrem dīligit

180. Echo the first syllable of the last word. ★ ○ • ○ •

181. ★ ○ • ○ • De

182. De √ ★ ○ •

183. Chorus the last syllable of the last word. ★ ○ ○ ◉ ◉

184. ★ ○ • ○ • us

185. us √ ★ ○ •

186. Chorus the whole word. ★ ○ ○ ◉ ◉

---

214. Echo the transformation of Aquila nōn capit muscās. (36) ★ ○ • ○ • **Ab aquila nōn capiuntur muscae.**

215. Notice that because the subject of the passive verb **capiuntur** is the plural noun **muscae**, the signal on the end of the verb is -----.

R: -ntur.

Question and Answer Drill

The following questions are based on the Basic Sentence **Aquila nōn capit muscās** or on its transformation **Ab aquila nōn capiuntur muscae.**

216. "Quōs nōn capit aquila?" "_____."

R: Muscās.

217. "Quis muscās nōn capit?" "_____."

R: Aquila.

218. "Ā quō muscae nōn capiuntur?" "_____."

R: Ab aquilā.

219. "Quī ab aquilā nōn capiuntur?" "_____."

R: Muscae.

14-50

3-20

187. ★ ○ • ○ • Deus

188. Deus ✓ ★ ○ •

189. ★ ○ • ○ • _____

Ans: **Deus**
[Did you remember to both echo and write?]

190. ★ ○ ○ ◉ ◉ H_____ d_____ d_____ D____. [If you are not sure of what to do, ask your teacher.]

191. ★ ○ • ○ •

Visual Check: **Hilarem datōrem dīligit Deus.**

192. Hilarem datōrem dīligit Deus. Pronounce and check. ✓ ★ ○ • [Check *after* you have said it.]

193. ★ ○ ○ _____ _____ _____
[Remember this sentence has two macrons.]

Ans: **Hilarem datōrem dīligit Deus.**

194–196. Echo the three Basic Sentences which we have had. [Repeat as many times as you feel necessary to learn them.]

194. ★ ○ • *Vestis virum reddit.*

195. ★ ○ • *Manus manum lavat.*

196. ★ ○ • *Hilarem datōrem dīligit Deus.*

14-49

209. **Quem?** asks for a noun in the _____ case of the ____ (singular/plural).

A: accusative
singular.

210. **Quōs?** asks for a noun in the _____ case of the ____ (singular/plural).

A: accusative
plural.

211. Like **Quis?** the new form **Quī?** asks for a noun in the _____ case, but in the plural number.

A: nominative

212. Answer a question on this familiar picture. "Quis leōnem metuit?" "_____."

R: Aper.

213. Answer another question on this similar picture. "Quī leōnem metuunt?" "_____."

R: Aprī.

3-21

197. We will take up the meaning of these sentences when we have learned just one more _____ Sentence.

Ans: Basic

198. This next Basic Sentence we will take up as we did the other three, first syllable by _____, then word by ____, until finally you are given the entire _____.

Ans: syllable   word   sentence.

199. Chorus the first syllable of the fourth Basic Sentence. ★ ○ ○ ◉ ◉

200. ★ ○ • ○ • vē

201. vē √ ★ ○ •

202. Chorus the second syllable. It contains an **r**, which you know is different from the English sound. ★ ○ ○ ◉ ◉

203. ★ ○ • ○ • ri

204. ri √ ★ ○ •

205. Chorus the third syllable. ★ ○ ○ ◉ ◉

206. ★ ○ • ○ • tā

---

202. *Agnus lupum metuit* → Ag--- l--- m---unt. √ ★ ○ •

Conf: Agni lupum metuunt.

203. *Simia rānam videt* → S----- r----- v.-ent. √ ★ ○ •

Conf: Simiae rānam vident.

204. *Fēmina laudem quaerit* → F----- l----- qu---unt. √ ★ ○ •

Conf: Fēminae laudem quaerunt.

205. *Lupum fovea tenet* → L--- f----- t----- . √ ★ ○ •

Conf: Lupōs fovea tenet.

206. *Viperam taurus premit* → V----- t----- pr----- . √ ★ ○ •

Conf: Viperās taurus premit.

207. *Cum aprō canis est* → Cum ap--- c--- --- . √ ★ ○ •

Conf: Cum apris canis est.

208. The question word **Quis?** asks for a noun in the _____ case of the ____ (singular/plural).

A: nominative   singular.

3-22

207. tā √ ★ ○ •

208. Chorus the last syllable of this word.
★ ○ ○ ◉ ◉

209. ★ ○ • ○ • tem

210. tem √ ★ ○ •

211. Chorus. ★ ○ ○ ◉ ◉ vēritātem

212. Echo. ★ ○ • ○ • vēritātem

213. Pronounce and then check. vēritātem
√ ★ ○ •

214. Echo and write. ★ ○ • ○ • _____ [This word has two macrons.]

Ans: vēritātem

215. Chorus the first syllable of the second word. ★ ○ ○ ◉ ◉

216. ★ ○ • ○ • di

217. di √ ★ ○ •

218. Chorus the last syllable of this word.
★ ○ ○ ◉ ◉

---

195. *Lupum agnus metuit* → L----- ag----- m----- √ ★ ○ •

Cōnf: Lupōs agnus metuit.

196. *Aquila agnum capit* → Aqu----- ag----- c--iunt. √ ★ ○ •

Cōnf: Aquilae agnum capiunt.

197. *Cum equō fēmina est* → Cum equ----- f----- √ ★ ○ •

Cōnf: Cum equīs fēmina est.

198. *Fovea lupum tenet* → F----- l----- t--ent. √ ★ ○ •

Cōnf: Foveae lupum tenent.

199. *Fēminam vir dīligit* → F----- v----- d----- √ ★ ○ •

Cōnf: Fēminās vir dīligit.

200. *Agnum aquila capit* → Ag----- aqu----- c----- √ ★ ○ •

Cōnf: Agnōs aquila capit.

201. *Rēgīnam jūdex metuit* → R----- j----- m----- √ ★ ○ •

Cōnf: Rēgīnās jūdex metuit.

14-47

3-23

219. ★ ○ • ○ • ēs

220. ēs √ ★ ○ •

221. Chorus the whole word. ★ ○ ○ ◉ ◉

222. ★ ○ • ○ • diēs

223. diēs √ ★ ○ •

224. Your teacher will now say the first two words of this Basic Sentence. ★ ○ ○ [If you need help on the symbols, ask your teacher.]

225. ★ ○ ○ ◉ ◉ vēritātem diēs

226. ★ ○ • ○ • vēritātem diēs

227. √ ★ ○ •

228. ★ ○ • ○ • ____ ____ [Remember, this phrase has three macrons.]

Ans: **vēritātem diēs**

229. Chorus the first syllable of the last word in this sentence. ★ ○ ○ ◉ ◉

230. ★ ○ • ○ • a

231. a √ ★ ○ •

232. Chorus the second syllable. ★ ○ ○ ◉ ◉

---

189. Write the paradigm of aper. ____

R: aper aprī aprō aprum aprōs aprīs

190. Write the paradigm of rēgīna. ____

R: rēgīna rēgīnae rēgīnam rēgīnās rēgīnīs

191. Write the paradigm of fovea. ____

R: fovea foveae foveam foveās fovea foveīs

Change the first noun (which is italicized) from singular to plural in these 16 sentences. Say the whole sentence.

192. Cum fēminā equus est → Cum f____ eq____ ____ √ ★ ○ •

Conf: Cum fēminīs equus est.

193. Asinum vir premit → As____ v____ pr____ ____ √ ★ ○ •

Conf: Asinōs vir premit.

194. Rānam simia videt → R____ s____ v____ ____ √ ★ ○ •

Conf: Rānās simia videt.

14-46

3-24

233. Echo. ★ ○ • ○ • pe

234. Pronounce and check. pe ✓ ★ ○ •

235. Chorus the last syllable of this word. ★ ○ ○ ● ●

236. ★ ○ • ○ • rit

237. rit ✓ ★ ○ •

238. Your teacher will now say the whole word. ★ ○ ○

239. Your teacher will say it again. Chorus, trying to roll the **r**. ★ ○ ○ ● ●

240. ★ ○ • ○ • aperit

241. aperit ✓ ★ ○ •

242. ★ ○ • ○ • _____

Ans: aperit

243. Your teacher will now say the whole sentence. Listen particularly to the r's. ★ ○ ○

244. Chorus again. Notice how the **-s** of **diēs** is pronounced with **aperit**. ★ ○ ○ ● ●
V_____ d___ ap____.

245. ★ ○ • ○ • V_____ d___ ap____.

14-45

If you were able to do the last four frames perfectly without using the extra help under the line, skip to frame 192. Otherwise continue until you are making no errors. Then if you like, you may skip to frame 192. Or you may give the answers orally. It makes no difference as long as you are able to do similar frames perfectly on the test for this Unit.

184. Write the paradigm of rāna. _____

R: rāna rānae
    rānam rānās
    rānā rānīs

185. Write the paradigm of vipera. _____

R: vipera viperae
    viperam viperās
    viperā viperīs

186. Write the paradigm of equus. _____

R: equus equī
    equum equōs
    equō equīs

187. Write the paradigm of vir. _____

R: vir virī
    virum virōs
    virō virīs

188. Write the paradigm of simia. _____

R: simia simiae
    simiam simiās
    simiā simiīs

3-25

246. **Vēritātem diēs aperit.** Pronounce and check. ✓ ★ ○ •

247. ★ ○ • ○ • ____ ____ ____ [Remember, this sentence has three macrons.]

Ans: **Vēritātem diēs aperit.**

248–251. Echo the four Basic Sentences we have had. Pay particular attention to the trill of the **r**'s. Repeat as often as needed.

248. ★ ○ • *Vestis virum reddit.*

249. ★ ○ • *Manus manum lavat.*

250. ★ ○ • *Hilarem datōrem dīligit Deus.*

251. ★ ○ • *Vēritātem diēs aperit.*

SUMMARY

252. In this unit you learned that in Latin the long mark, or macron, distinguishes l___ vowels from _____ vowels.

Ans: long
short

253. You also learned to pronounce three more B____ Sentences.

Ans: Basic

TEST INFORMATION

In this unit you learned to distinguish between long and short vowels. Therefore you will be asked to write down both long and short vowels as your teacher reads them.

You learned to pronounce three more Basic Sentences. Therefore a second part of the test will be to read correctly one of these Basic Sentences. Be sure to make the distinction between long and short vowels.

You are now ready for the test for Unit Three.

---

180. The signal on the plural *passive* verb is _____.

R: -ntur.

For the next twelve frames we will practice the paradigms of First and Second Declension nouns. If you feel that you can already do them, skip to frame 192.

181. Write the paradigm of **taurus**. _____ (Auxilium sub hāc lineā est.)

Auxilium: taurus -ī
-um -ō
-ō -īs

R: taurus taurī
taurum taurōs
taurō taurīs

182. Write the paradigm of **fēmina**. _____ (Auxilium sub hāc lineā est.)

Auxilium: -a -ae
-am -ās
-ā -īs

R: fēmina fēminae
fēminam fēminās
fēminā fēminīs

183. Write the paradigm of **lupus**. _____

R: lupus lupī
lupum lupōs
lupō lupīs

14-44

4-1

UNIT FOUR

1. It was necessary to do Units Two and Three either with your teacher or with a tape recorder, because in order to pronounce the Latin correctly you had to have someone to im_____.

Ans: imitate.

2. The *best* way to do this program would be to be able to have a teacher or tape recorder to listen to at all times. But this is seldom possible. Therefore we have arranged the program so that you can work either *with* a teacher or tape recorder or _____ a teacher or tape recorder.

Ans: without

3. When working by yourself it is most important that you should _____ aloud.

Ans: speak (talk, etc.)

4. When you have a teacher or a tape recorder, you are able to *hear* Latin as well as *see* it. You will learn faster if you can both ___ and ____ what you are learning.

Ans: see   hear

5. Therefore, when working by yourself take particular care to ___ the Latin al____.

Ans: say   aloud.

6. If you don't have the use of a tape recorder, don't feel too badly. People have learned foreign languages for centuries *without* the aid of a ____ _____.

Ans: tape recorder.

14-43

172. "Quōs superstitiō violat?" "_____."

R: Deōs.

173. ★ ○ •   Deus   dī
                Deum   deōs
                Deō   dīs

[Although the regular forms deī and deīs do occur in the nominative and ablative plural, the forms dī and dīs are far more common.]

174. Echo the nominative plural form of Quis? ★ ○ • ○ Quī?

175. The passive transformation of our Basic Sentence is Religiōne dī coluntur, superstitiōne violantur. Answer the following questions. "Quō dī coluntur?" "_____."

R: Religiōne.

176. "Quī religiōne coluntur?" "_____."

R: Dī.

177. "Quī superstitiōne violantur?" "_____."

R: Dī.

178. "Quō dī violantur?" "_____."

R: Superstitiōne.

179. In looking at such forms as quaerunt and violantur, we can see that the signal on the plural *active* verb is ---.

R: -nt.

4-2

7. In the next six frames we will review the meaning of the different symbols; you will not use the tape player until Frame 94. The star [★] means that you are to _____. [In your own words.]

Ans: start the tape player.

8. The symbol [○] means that _____. [In your own words.]

Ans: your teacher will say something.

9. The symbol [●] means that you are to repeat _____. [In your own words.]

Ans: what your teacher said.

10. The symbol [√] means that you are to _____ your answer.

Ans: check

11. The combination [√ ★] means:
   "Ans___ f___t and then ch___ your ___wer."

Ans: Answer first and then check your answer. (This answer should have been spoken aloud.)

12. The symbols for "Start the tape player and listen twice" are _____.

Ans: ★ ○ ○

13. A broken line means to ___ your answer.

Ans: say

Question and Answer Drill

R: **Religio deōs colit, superstitiō violat.**

164. Religion honors the gods, superstition violates them = R____ d___ c___t, s_____ v____t.

165. "Quid deōs violat?" "_____."

R: Superstitiō.

166. "Quid deōs colit?" "_____."

R: Religiō.

167. "Quid agit religiō?" "_____."

R: Deōs colit.

168. "Quid agit superstitiō?" "_____."

R: Deōs violat.

169. Echo a new form of the question word.
★ ○ ● ○ ● Quōs?

170. The signal -ōs on the new question word Quōs? indicates that this word asks for the accusative of the _____ number.

A: plural

171. "Quōs religiō colit?" "_____."

R: Deōs.

14. Now we will help you to discover what the Basic Sentences mean. To do this you must first learn a new "distinction." A distinction is a significant difference of some sort. You have for example learned the distinction between vowels and ----------.

Ans: consonants.

15. You learned the distinction between the different vowels, such as the ---------- between **a** and **o**.

Ans: distinction

16. You also learned the ---------- between **a** and **ā**.

Ans: distinction

17. If you were to hear the sentence, "The boy bit the dog," you would know at once who bit and who was bitten. Every language has a system of signals which tells us these things. But just as the *sounds* of English are different from the *sounds* of Latin, just so the *signals* of English are different from the ------s of -----.

Ans: signals of Latin.

18. At this point we will take a quick look at the way English works. We are assuming that you know *nothing* about the signals that are used in English. First of all, let us see how we identify nouns and verbs in English.

Classes of words are different "parts of speech." A verb is one part of speech and a noun is another ---- of ------.

Ans: part of speech.

159. If you "violate" the law, you break the law. If one country "violates" the rights of another country, it injures those rights. **Superstitio deōs violat** means, "S---------- v-------- the ---s."

A: Superstition violates the gods.

160. We learned that **superstitiō** and **religiō** are antonyms. The verbs **colit** and **violat** are also antonyms. When we say that a country must honor the rights of another country, we mean that those rights must not be v------ed.

A: violated.

161. **Religiō deōs colit, superstitiō violat** = ----- ----- h---rs -------------- ---- --------.

A: Religion honors the gods, superstition violates them.

162. Write Basic Sentence 37 and its English translation in your Reference Notebook.

163. The Latin sentence omitted the object in the second kernel. We do not omit the object in English; instead we say, "Religion honors the gods, superstition violates ---m."

A: them.

19. One mark of identification of an English noun is the signal {-s} to show "more than one." For example, we say "one overcoat" but "many overc____."

Ans: overcoats.

20. Can we add this signal {-s} to "book" and say "many books"? ____ (Yes/No)

Ans: Yes

21. Since we can add this signal {-s} (which means "more than one") to the word "book," then "book" (like "overcoat") is the part of speech called a ____.

Ans: noun.

22. Can we add this "more than one" signal {-s} to "could" and say "many coulds"? ____ (Yes/No)

Ans: No
[Well, you could *do* it, but it wouldn't mean much, except "There are too many 'could's' in this sentence."]

23. Therefore "could" ____ (is/is not) a noun like "book."

Ans: is not (Except that in the expression "too many 'could's' " it *would* be a noun.)

24. A different version of a signal is called a "variant." We say "one ox" but "many oxen." Therefore the ending "-en" is a ____ of the {-s} signal to show more-than-one.

Ans: variant

---

152. Pronounce English "superstition," Latin **superstitio.** ∨ ★ ○ •

153. Pronounce: **Religiō deōs colit, superstitio violat.** ∨ ★ ○ •

154. This is a ___ kernel type of {-s -m -t} sentence.

A: two kernel type

155. Expand as indicated: **Religiō deōs colit, superstitio ____ violat.**

R: **Religiō deōs colit, superstitio deōs violat.**

156. ★ ○ ○ R——d c———— ———v————s (37)

R: **Religiō deōs colit, superstitio violat.** (37)

157. Religiō and **superstitio** are antonyms: "_____" is something good and "_____" is something bad.

A: religion
superstition

158. Pronounce English "violate," Latin **violat.** ∨ ★ ○ •

25. We do not say "two foots," but we say "two ____."

Ans: feet.

26. The variant signal for "more than one" in "feet" is a change inside the word, the change from "oo" to "__."

Ans: ee

27. But here is an unusual situation: we do not say "two sheeps" but rather "two _____."

Ans: sheep.

28. In the case of the "two sheep" we borrow a term from mathematics and say that the signal which shows "more than one" in "two sheep" is the variant "zero."

When we use the expression "He shot two deer," the signal on "deer" that shows "more than one" is the variant ____.

Ans: zero.

29. In English we also identify nouns by the "slot" they can fill; that is, by their position in the sentence. Any word that can fill the slot occupied by "dog" in the sentence "I see the *dog*" is a noun. Can we replace "dog" by "book" and say "I see the *book*"? ____ (Yes/No)

Ans: Yes

30. In other words, "dog" and "book" can fill the same ____ in the sentence.

Ans: slot

---

145. By *producing* the forms now, you will be able to r_____ these forms instantly when you meet them later.

A: recognize

146. • *Religiō deōs colit, super-stitiō violat.* (37)

147. *Religiō* looks like the English word "_____."

A: religion.

148. Pronounce English "religion," Latin re-ligiō. ∨ ○ ★ • •

149. English words ending in "-ion-," (such as "imitation") come from Latin words whose nominative form ends in the two letters ____-iō.

R: -iō.

150. Therefore the unknown word **religiō** must be _____ case.

A: nominative

151. **Superstitio** resembles the English word "_____," and it must be _____ case.

A: superstition; nominative

4-5

14-39

4-6

31. Because "book" can fill the same slot as "dog," it is the same p____ of sp____ as "dog."

Ans: part of speech

32. "Dog" is a noun. Because "book" fills the same slot as "dog," the word "book" is the part of speech called a ____.

Ans: noun.

33. Say the words that can normally fill the slot in the sentence "I see the ____."

I see the { ship. / slowly. / hammer. / is. / pretty. / difficulty. / an.

Ans: ship. hammer. difficulty.

34. Therefore "ship," "hammer," and "difficulty" are all ____s.

Ans: nouns.

35. "Slowly," because it cannot fit into the slot after "I see the . . . ," is *not* a ____.

Ans: noun.

36. The word "book" works like the word "dog" in two ways: it takes the signal {-s} to mean "more than one," and it fits in the same ____ as "dog."

Ans: slot

14-38

140. angulus ------
      ------ ------
      ------ ------ ∨ ★ ○ •

Conj: angulus angulō
      angulum angulōs
      angulī angulīs

Now try First and Second Declension nouns mixed.

141. Write the paradigm of poena. ____

R: poena poenae
   poenam poenās
   poenā poenīs

142. Write the paradigm of oculus. ____

R: oculus oculī
   oculum oculōs
   oculō oculīs

143. The reciting or writing of the paradigm of a noun is an excellent way to have a quick review, for in a minimum of time you can give all possible forms of the word. It is a useful way of helping you to learn the different c____s of the Latin noun.

A: cases

144. The purpose of this course is to teach you to read Latin literature. You cannot do this unless you can *instantly* recognize the different ____s of the nouns.

A: cases

37. "Dog" and "book" are therefore ____ (the same part of speech/different parts of speech).

Ans: the same part of speech.

38. "Dog" and "book" are both ____s.

Ans: nouns.

39. We could also say, "I see the writing." In this sentence "writing" is the part of speech we call a ____.

Ans: noun.

40. There are two nouns in the sentence, "The dog killed the snake." They are "___" and "___."

Ans: dog snake.

41. "Snake" can fill all the slots that "dog" can fill. "Dog" and "snake" are therefore the
_____.

Ans: same part of speech.

42. Say the words that can normally fill the slot in the sentence, "The ____ is here."

The $\begin{Bmatrix} \text{boy} \\ \text{is} \\ \text{goes} \\ \text{quickly} \\ \text{dog} \\ \text{paper} \\ \text{action} \end{Bmatrix}$ is here.

Ans: boy
dog
paper
action

4-8

43. The word "the" in English is called a "noun marker" because it comes before ____s.

Ans: nouns.

44. The words "boy," "dog," "paper," and "action" can all be preceded by this noun marker "____."

Ans: the.

45. Therefore all four words ("boy," "dog," "paper," and "action") are ____s.

Ans: nouns.

46. In the sentence, "The boy is here," we know that "boy" is a noun for two reasons:
   (1) It has the form "boys,"
and (2) _____ [In your own words]

Ans: It fits into a noun slot; that is, it comes after a noun marker.

47. In English there are other noun markers besides "the." "A," "an," "many," and "some" are followed by nouns and are therefore the part of speech we call a ____ _____.

Ans: noun marker.

48. Sometimes another word (or several words) can come between the noun marker and the noun.

In the expression "the tall tree," the noun is the word "____."

Ans: tree.

---

131. _____ cognōscit.

R: Asinus lupum cognōscit.

132. _____ metuunt.

R: Aprī leōnem metuunt.

133. _____ cernunt.

R: Elephantī mūrem cernunt.

134. _____ cognōscunt.

R: Asinī lupum cognōscunt.

14-36

49. So the *two* clues which identify an English noun are the signal {-s} that means "____ ____ ___," and the ____ it fills in the sentence.

Ans: more than one ... slot

50. Like an English noun, an English *verb* is identified by changes in the form of the word and by the ____ it fills in the sentence.

Ans: slot

51. In English, verbs may be recognized by the fact that they can take the signal {-ed} to mean "happened in the past." We say, for example, "This month I *walk* to school every day," but "Last month I w___ed to school just once."

Ans: walked

52. "Today I am going to watch only one TV program, but yesterday I w_____ three."

Ans: watched

53. There are also variant signals to show "happened in the past." For example, we can say, "This month I drive to school every day, but last month I drove just once." The variant here of "drive" is "_____."

Ans: drove.

54. We say, "Today I bring home only one package, but yesterday I br_____ home three."

Ans: brought

Describe these pictures, remembering that if the subject is plural the signal will be -i. Remember also that the verb changes number to "agree" with the subject.

R: **Elephantus mūrem cernit.**

Cōnf: **Elephantus mūrem cernit.**

? mūrem cernit. ? mūrem cernunt.

130. ✶ ○ • ○ •

Cōnf: **Taurī viperam inveniunt.**

R: **Taurī viperam inveniunt.**

? viperam invenit. ? viperam inveniunt.

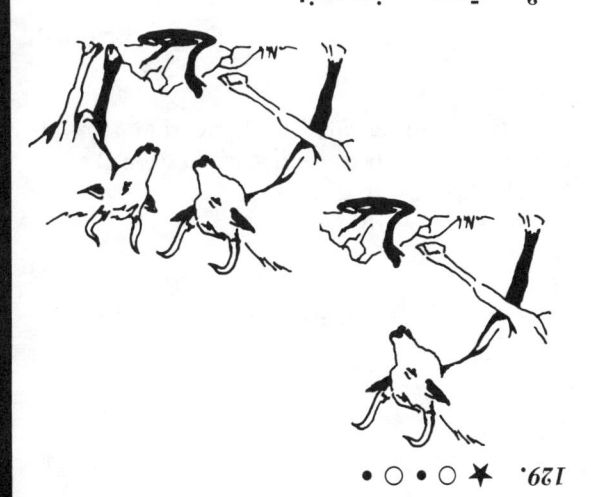

129. ✶ ○ • ○ •

4-10

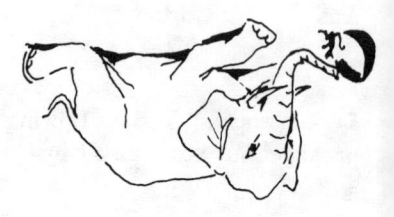

55. Like nouns, verbs in English may also be recognized by the s___ they fill in the _____.

Ans:　　　　slot　　　　　　sentence.

56. Say the words that can normally fill the slot in the sentence, "I ____ quickly."

$$I \begin{Bmatrix} \text{the} \\ \text{run} \\ \text{look} \\ \text{boy} \\ \text{jump} \\ \text{walk} \\ \text{action} \end{Bmatrix} \text{quickly.}$$

Ans:　　　　run
　　　　　　look
　　　　　　jump
　　　　　　walk

57. Those four words are all ____s.

Ans:　　　　　　　　verbs.

58. We can recognize "walk" in "I walked quickly" as a verb not only because it has the form "walked," but because it fits in the v_____.

Ans:　　　　　　　verb slot.

59. In "I ran quickly" we know that "run" is a verb not only because it has the form "ran," but also because _____.
[In your own words.]

Ans:　　　　it fits in the verb slot.

60. In English, verbs may be recognized by two signals:

(1) _____.
     [In your own words.]

(2) _____.
     [In your own words.]

Ans: (1) They have a form that means "happened in the past,"
(2) They fit into the verb slot in the sentence.

61. One of the most common slots for an English verb to fill is between two nouns. Say the words that can normally fill the slot in "The man ____ the bear."

"The man ⎧fears⎫ the bear."
        ⎪red⎪
        ⎪ceiling⎪
        ⎨action⎬
        ⎪calls⎪
        ⎪kills⎪
        ⎩quickly⎭

Ans: fears
         calls
         kills

62. Because the words "fears," "calls," and "kills" can fill the slot between "The man" and "the bear," you know these words are ____s.

Ans: verbs.

63. You will now learn a technical term, "subject," the name given to words that fill the slot occupied by "The woman" in the sentence, "*The woman* washed the clothes."
In this sentence, "The woman" is the _____ of the sentence.

Ans: subject

---

125. Now describe this picture. Notice that there is only one boar. A ---- l---- m---it.

R: Aper leõnem metuit.

Your teacher will say either **Aper leõnem metuit** or **Aprī leõnem metuunt**. Echo and write the subject on the right or left side of your answer pad.

126. ✱ ○ ○ •

? leõnem metuit.   ? leõnem metuunt.

Conf: Aprī leõnem metuunt.

R: Aprī leõnem metuunt.

64. The subject of the sentence, "*The girl* washed the clothes" is "--- ----."

Ans: The girl.

65. In the sentence "The boy broke the window," the phrase "The boy" is the ------ of the sentence.

Ans: subject

66. In the sentence "The cow kicked the pail," the subject is "--- ---."

Ans: The cow.

67. The subject in English fills the slot that comes ------ the verb.

Ans: before

68. The subject of "The man was bitten" is "--- ---."

Ans: The man.

69. The subject of "The man was bitten by the snake" is "--- ---."

Ans: The man.

70. The subject of "The snake bit the man" is "--- -----."

Ans: The snake.

121. **umbra** ------
------ ------
----- ------ √ ★ ○ •

Cōnf: **umbra** **umbrae**
umbram **umbrās**
umbrā **umbrīs**

122. **aqua** -----
----- -----
---- ----- √ ★ ○ •

Cōnf: **aqua** **aquae**
aquam **aquās**
aquā **aquīs**

We will now learn the nominative plural of the Second Declension. The signal is **-ī**. Echo your teacher as he describes this picture.

123. ★ ○ • ○ • **A__ī l_____ m____nt.**

Cōnf: **Aprī leōnem metuunt.**

124. **Aprī leōnem metuunt** means, "--- b___s f___ ___ l___."

A: The boars fear the lion.

4-13

71. You will now learn a technical term, "object," the name given to words that fill the slot occupied by "the clothes" in the sentence "The woman washed *the clothes*."
In this sentence, "the clothes" is the ------ of the sentence.

Ans: object

72. The object of the sentence "The woman washed *the floor*" is "--- -----."

Ans: the floor.

73. In the sentence "The boy broke the window," the phrase "the window" is the ------ of the sentence.

Ans: object

74. In the sentence "The cow kicked the pail," the object is "--- ----."

Ans: the pail.

75. While the subject in English fills the slot that comes before the verb, the *object* fills the slot that comes ----- the verb.

Ans: after

76. In a sentence like "The cat caught the mouse," the subject "cat" comes ------ the verb and the object "mouse" comes ----- the verb.

Ans: before
after

14-31

116. Echo the forms of the First Declension that you now. Echo the singular, then the plural.

★ ○ •   fēmina   fēminae
        fēminam   fēminās
        fēminā   fēminīs

[After echoing, remember to repeat the paradigm aloud several times.]

117. The characteristic vowel of fēmina (although it disappears in the ablative plural) is ----.

R: a

118. Write the paradigm of fēmina. ------ ------. (Sub hāc līneā est auxilium)

Auxilium: a-----   a-----
            am-----   as-----
            ā-----   īs-----

R: fēmina   fēminae
   fēminam   fēminās
   fēminā   fēminīs

[You probably do not need this reminder, but if you have been writing the paradigms on 3x5 cards, you can add the plural at this point for all the nouns.]

119. In the form fēminīs the characteristic vowel of the First Declension, a, has ---------ed.

A: disappeared.

120. In the next three frames you will be asked to say the paradigms of First Declension nouns.

∧ ○ ★ • ⊙   a-----   ae-----
            am-----   as-----
            ā-----   īs-----

Conf: nia is   fēminae
      niam   fēminās
      nia is   fēminīs

77. We said a few frames ago that one of the common slots for an English verb to fill was between two nouns. The noun that comes *before* the verb ("The man saw the snake") we call the _____ of the verb.

Ans: subject

78. And the noun that comes *after* the verb, as in "The man saw the snake," we call the _____ of the verb.

Ans: object

79. In the sentence "The boy sees the dog," the subject is "___ ___," and the object is "___ ___."

Ans: the boy
the dog.

80. In "The teacher spoke," no noun comes directly after the verb. Therefore you can see there is no ____ (subject/object) of this verb.

Ans: object

81. "Spoke" is the part of speech we call a _____.

Ans: verb.

82. Some verbs are made up of more than one word. For example, the verb in "The firemen put out the fire" is the two words "___ ___."

Ans: put out.

---

112. _____ irritant.

Cōnf: Simiae leōnem irritant.

113. _____ ab _____ currit.

Cōnf: Vīpera ab aquilā currit.

114. _____ cernunt.

Cōnf: Fēminae fūrem cernunt.

115. You can now predict the nominative plural of First Declension nouns. Say in Latin, "Queens give both family and beauty."

Et g____ et f____ r_____ dōnant.

R: Et genus et fōrmam rēgīnae dōnant.

4-15

83. "Firemen" and "fire" are both the part of speech we call ____s.

Ans: nouns.

84. In "The firemen put out the fire," "the fire" is the _____ of the verb.

Ans: object

85. We do *not* need to know the meaning of a word in order to identify its part of speech. Look at the sentence, "The queeks disappeared over the winter." What part of speech is the nonsense word "queeks?" ____ (noun/verb).

Ans: noun.

86. We know that "queeks" is a noun because it has the noun more-than-one signal {-_} and follows a noun _____.

Ans: {-s} marker.

87. In order to get the meaning of our Basic Sentences you must learn the distinction between Latin "nouns" and Latin "verbs."

Latin nouns are a class of words that are signalled by an {-s} or an {-m} at the end of the word. Because there is an {-s} at the end of **Deus** you know that **Deus** is a ____ (noun/verb).

Ans: noun.

88. Latin *nouns* are signalled by {-s} or {-m} at the end of the word. Latin *verbs* are signalled by {-t} at the end of the word. If you see a Latin word that ends in {-t} you know that it is a ____.

Ans: verb.

4-16

89. If you see a Latin word that ends in {-s} you know that it is a ____.

Ans: noun.

90. If you see a Latin word that ends in {-m} you know that it is a ____.

Ans: noun.

91. Because there is an {-m} at the end of **vēritātem**, you know this word is a ____.

Ans: noun.

92. You know that **vestis** is also a noun, because it has an {__} at the end of the word.

Ans: {-s}

93. **Datōrem** is a ____ (noun/verb).

Ans: noun.

94-95. ★ ○ • **Hilarem datōrem dīligit Deus.**

[If you have a tape recorder, echo. If you do not have a tape recorder, say the sentence aloud several times.]

The verb in **HilareM datōreM dīligiT DeuS** is the Latin word _____T.

Ans: dīligiT

96-97. ★ ○ • **VestiS viruM reddiT.** The verb is the word _____T.

Ans: reddiT.

---

105. ★ ○ • ○ •

? vīperam laudant.

? vīperam laudat.

Cōnf: Rāna vīperam laudat.

R: Rāna vīperam laudat.

106. ★ ○ • ○ •

? fūrem cernit.   ? fūrem cērunt.

Cōnf: Fēminae fūrem cērunt.

R: Fēminae fūrem cērunt.

107. ★ ○ • ○ •

? ab aquilā currunt.

? ab aquilā currit.

Cōnf: Vīperae ab aquilā currunt.

R: Vīperae ab aquilā currunt.

14-28

4-17

98-99. ★ ○ • **ManuS manuM lavaT.** The verb is the word _____.

Ans: lavaT.

100-101. ★ ○ • **VēritāteM diēS aperiT.** The verb is _____.

Ans: aperiT.

102. **Dīligit** is a verb because it has the signal {--}.

Ans: {-t}.

103. **Vēritātem** is a noun because it has {--}.

Ans: {-m}.

104. **Aperit** is a verb because it has {--}.

Ans: {-t}.

105. **Vestis** is a ____ because it has {--}.

Ans: noun {-s}.

106. In the Basic Sentence **ManuS manuM lavaT** there are two nouns, m___s and m___m.

Ans: manus manum.

107. In the sentence **ManuS manuM lavaT**, the same word has both the {-s} signal and the {-m} signal.
The form with the {-s} signal is the word _____, and the form with the {-m} signal is the word _____.

Ans: manuS manuM.

101. In addition, the verb **necat** changes to _____.

R: necant.

102. When the subject is singular, we use the form **necat** with the signal **-t**, but when the subject is plural, instead of **necat** we use the form **necant** with the signal ____.

R: -nt.

In this sequence your teacher will say either **Fēmina fūrem cernit.** ("The lady discovers the thief.") or **Fēminae fūrem cernunt.** ("The ladies discover the thief.") Echo and write the subject on the side of your answer pad corresponding to the position of the picture your teacher describes.

103. ★ ○ ● ○ ●

? fūrem cernit.   ? fūrem cernunt.

Cónf: **Fēmina fūrem cernit.**

R: **Fēmina fūrem cernit.**

104. ● ○ ● ○ ★

? leōnem irrītat.   ? leōnem irrītant.

Cónf: **Simiae leōnem irrītant.**

R: **Simiae leōnem irrītant.**

4-18

108. Since **manus** has an {-s}, you know it is a _____ (noun/verb).

Ans: noun.

109. Since **manum** has an {-m}, you know it is also a _____.

Ans: noun.

110. ManuS and manuM are d_____ forms of the s___ word.

Ans: same   different

111. Echo a new form of the word **vēritātem**.
★ ○ • ○ • **vēritās**

112. VēritāS and vēritāteM are _____ forms of the same word.

Ans: different

113. THE CONTRAST IN FORM between **manuS** and **manuM** and between **vēritāS** and **vēritāteM** is THE CHIEF DIFFERENCE between English and _____.

Ans: Latin.

114. Copy this frame down in your Reference Notebook under the section labeled "Facts About Latin."

14-26

96. Describe and check, using familiar forms.
V_____ t_____ n_____ ∧ _____ ★ ○ •

A. The snake is killing the bull.

97. Vipera taurum necat = _____

Cōn: Vipera taurum necat.

98. ★ ○ • ○ • Here is a new situation.

V_____ ae t_____ n_____nt.

Cōn: Viperae taurum necant.

99. Viperae taurum necant = _____

A: The snakes are killing the bull.

100. In changing from singular to plural, the word **vipera** changes to _____.

R: **viperae**.

4-19

115. Latin nouns have the signal {-˽} or {-˽}; Latin verbs have the signal {-˽}.

Ans: {-s} {-m}
{-t}

116. Remembering the signals which tell whether a Latin word is a noun or a verb, identify the following forms as nouns or verbs. **DeuS** is a ____.

Ans: noun.

117. DiēS is a ____.

Ans: noun.

118. AperiT is a ____.

Ans: verb.

119. LavaT is a ____.

Ans: verb.

120. ManuS is a ____.

Ans: noun.

121. As you might expect, we are simplifying the situation. You will later learn that there are other signals for nouns and other signals for verbs. But *for the present*, nouns can be identified by the signals {-˽} and {-˽}, and verbs by {-˽}.

Ans: {-s} {-m} {-t}.

Next you will learn the nominative plural.

R: Saccus ā similis aperītur.

95. ——— aperītur.

R: Aqua ab equīs bibitur.

94. ——— bibitur.

R: Canis ab asinīs premitur.

93. ——— ab ——— premitur.

14-25

4-20

122. Is it necessary to know the *meaning* of a Latin word in order to tell whether it is a noun or a verb? ____ (Yes/No)

Ans: No

123. We did not tell you the meaning of the four Basic Sentences before this, because we wished you to see that we can identify parts of speech as subject, object, and verb, *without* reference to the _____ of the words in these sentences.

Ans: meaning

124. We will now tell you how to identify Latin subjects and Latin objects. As you know, Latin nouns have the signal {-s} or {-m}. The nouns that have the signal {-s} are the *subjects*. You can probably guess that the nouns that end in {-m} are the _____s.

Ans: objects.

125-128. Echo the four Basic Sentences which we have had.

125. ★ ○ • VestiS viruM reddiT.

126. ★ ○ • ManuS manuM lavaT.

127. ★ ○ • VēritāteM diēS aperiT.

128. ★ ○ • HilareM datōreM dīligiT DeuS.

129. The words that have the subject signal {-s} in these four sentences are _____, _____, _____, and _____.

Ans: vestiS manuS diēS DeuS.

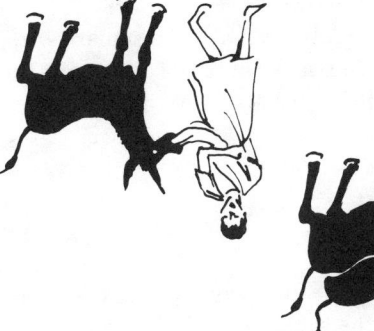

130. Therefore **vestiS**, **manuS**, **diēS**, and **DeuS** are the _____s of their sentences.

Ans: subjects

131. From looking at the position of **vestiS**, **diēS**, **manuS**, and **DeuS** in their sentences, it is apparent that Latin subjects ____ (come first in the sentence as in English/may occur anywhere in the sentence).

Ans: may occur anywhere in the sentence.

132. In English we identify the subject by its *position* in the sentence; in Latin we identify the subject by the signal {__}.

Ans: {-s}.

133. *For the present*, at least, all Latin subjects have the signal {__}.

Ans: {-s}.

134. In English we identify the object by its *position;* in Latin we identify the object by the signal {__}.

Ans: {-m}.

135. In which language do we signal subject and object by position, Latin or English? ____

Ans: English.

136. In which language do we identify subject and object by the signals {-s} and {-m}? _____

Ans: Latin.

4-22

137. Pay close attention now, for this is the most important frame in the entire course.

LATIN *NEVER* SIGNALS SUBJECT OR OBJECT BY POSITION BUT BY THE SIGNALS {-S} AND {-M}.

Copy this sentence in your Reference Notebook under "Facts About Latin."

▼   ▼

138. In Latin the subject, object, and verb can occur in *any* order; we identify the subject not by position, but by the signal {--}.

▼   ▼

Ans: {-s}.

139. In Latin the subject, object, and verb can occur in ___ order; we identify a Latin *verb* by the signal {--}.

▼   ▼

Ans: any
       {-t}.

140. In Latin the subject, object, and verb can occur in ___ _____; we identify the *object* by _____.

▼   ▼

Ans: any order
the signal {-m}.

     ★ ○ • VēritāteM diēS aperiT.
141. Since Latin objects have the signal {-m}, you know that the object in this sentence is the word _____. [Print the signal in a big letter.]

▼   ▼

Ans: **vēritāteM**.

142. The verb in this sentence is the word _____. [Print the signal in a big letter.]

▼   ▼

Ans: **aperiT**.

R: Simia cum equō currit.

▲

Conf: Simia cum equō currit.

▲

Simia cum ?̄ currit.   Simia cum ?̄ currit.

★ ○ • ○ •   *84.*

R: Juvenis ab asinō tenētur.

▲

Conf: Juvenis ab asinō tenētur.

▲

Juvenis ab ?̄ tenētur.   Juvenis ab ?̄ tenētur.

★ ○ • ○ •   *83.*

14-22

4-23

143. The subject of this sentence is the word _____. [Print the signal in a big letter.]

Ans: diēS.

144. In this sentence **VēritāteM diēS aperiT**, the subject is the ____ (first/second/third) word in the sentence.

Ans: second

145. In **HilareM datōreM dīligiT DeuS**, the subject is the ____ (first/second/third/fourth) word in the sentence.

Ans: fourth

146. In English, because the word order carries much of the structural meaning, word order is "fixed." Which is an English sentence? "The man stands still," "Stands man still the."

Ans: The man stands still.

147. In Latin the word order is ____ (fixed/not fixed).

Ans: not fixed. (Roman writers took advantage of this flexibility of word order, by using word order for *emphasis*. In Latin, important words are frequently postponed so that they come as a surprise.)

148-149. ★ ○ • **VestiS viruM reddiT.** Here the verb is the ____ (first/second/third) word in the sentence.

Ans: third

14-21

78. The signal on the First Declension noun **fēminīs** that shows ablative plural is ____.

R: -īs.

79. The plural of **lupō** is **lupīs**. The signal for the ablative plural of the Second Declension nouns is therefore ____.

R: -īs. (just like the First Declension)

80. In the First Declension noun **fēminīs** the characteristic vowel a (that appears in **fēmina**, **fēminam**, **fēminā**, and **fēminās**) _____ s before the signal -īs.

A: disappears

81. In the Second Declension noun **lupīs** the characteristic vowel o (that appears in **lupō** and **lupō** and is changed to u in **lupus** and **lupum**) _____ s before the signal -īs.

A: disappears

82. ★ ○ ○ •

Echo your teacher as he describes one picture of each pair and write the ablative form on the left or right side of your answer pad, according to the picture it describes.

Simia cum ? currit.   Simia cum ? currit.

Cōnf: Simia cum equīs currit.

R: Simia cum equīs currit.

150. In the kind of *English* sentence we have been discussing, the verb comes between the s_____ and the o_____.

Ans: subject and the object.

151-152. Now for the meaning of the Latin sentence. The word **vestiS** means "clothes." From the ending, we know that **vestiS** is the _____ of the sentence.

Ans: subject

153. In order to show in English that "clothes" is the subject, we place the word "clothes" in the slot that comes _____ the verb.

Ans: before

154. But since no verb has yet appeared, we will use the colorless made-up verb "blank" and say that **vestiS** means, "Cl_____ blank."

Ans: Clothes blank.

155. **VestiS** means not just "Clothes" but "Clothes _____."

Ans: Clothes blank.

156. The word **viruM** means "the man." But in order to show the meaning of the Latin ending {-m}, in English we must place the corresponding English word "the man" in the object slot _____ the verb "blank."

Ans: after

4-25

157. **VestiS viruM** therefore means "_____ blank the ____."

Ans: Clothes blank the man.

158. We use the colorless verb "blank" in English so we can show that "clothes" is the subject by putting it _____ a ____.

Ans: before a verb.

159. We show that "man" is the object in English by putting it _____ the ____.

Ans: after the verb.

160. Let us go through this just once more. **VestiS** means not just "Clothes," but "_____."

Ans. Clothes blank.

161. And **VestiS viruM** means, "_____ _____ the ___."

Ans: Clothes blank the man.

162. The verb **reddiT** means "make." In order to show that it is a verb, we drop it into the slot previously occupied by the colorless verb "blank." **VestiS viruM reddiT** therefore means, "Clothes ____ the man."

Ans: Clothes make the man. That is, people will judge you (rightly or wrongly) by the way you dress. (Now you know a Latin sentence!)

---

69. V__ cum f_____ stat.

R: **Vir cum fēminā stat.**

70. C____ cum r____ lītem habet.

R: **Canis cum rānā lītem habet.**

71. J_____ ā s_____ quaeritur.

R: **Juvenis ā simiā quaeritur.**

72. _____ ____ qu_____.

R: **Juvenis ā simiā quaeritur.**

163. Copy (accurately!) both the Latin sentence and the English meaning in a part of your Reference Notebook labeled "Basic Text." This is Basic Sentence number 1.

164. Clothes make the man = V_____ v____ r_____. [The equal sign [=] stands for "means in Latin."] Write out the whole sentence. Print the signals in big letters.

Ans: **VestiS viruM reddiT**.

165. **VestiS viruM reddiT** means, "Clothes make the man." The word that means "the man" is _____. [Print the signal in a big letter.]

Ans: **viruM**.

166. The word that means "make" is _____.

Ans: **reddiT**.

167. And the word that means "clothes" is _____.

Ans: **vestiS**.

168. We know that **vestiS** is the subject because it has the signal {--}.

Ans: {**-S**}.

169. In English it is position that identifies the subject and object; in Latin it is the signals {**-S**} and {**-M**}. If we leave the *signal* {**-S**} on **vestiS**, but change its position in the Latin sentence and say **ReddiT vestiS viruM**, will **vestiS** still be the subject? ____ (Yes/No)

Ans: Yes

Now describe these pictures. The last letter will be -ā if the person or animal is standing (quarreling, etc.) with one animal or person. The last two letters will be -is if he is standing with more than one person or animal.

R: Juvenis ā simiīs quaeritur.

Conf: Juvenis ā simiīs quaeritur.

Juvenis ā ? quaeritur. Juvenis ā ? quaeritur.

68. ★ ○ • ○ •

R: Rāna ā vīperis premitur.

Conf: Rāna ā vīperis premitur.

Rāna ā ? premitur. Rāna ā ? premitur.

67. ★ ○ • ○ •

14-18

170. Will **viruM** still be the object? ____
(Yes/No)

Ans: Yes

171. Since the words still have the same signals, does **ReddiT vestiS viruM** still mean "Clothes make the man" or will it mean "The man makes clothes"? _____.

Ans: It *still* means "Clothes make the man."

172-175. Echo the following sentences. [If you have no tape recorder, say them aloud several times.]

172. ★ ○ • **Hilarem datōrem dīligit DeuS.**

173. ★ ○ • **VestiS virum reddit.**

174. ★ ○ • **ManuS manum lavat.**

175. ★ ○ • **Vēritātem diēS aperit.**

176. You have seen that in English the subject comes *before* the verb. Examine the sentences above to see where the subject comes in Latin.

In Latin the subject comes _____
(before the verb/after the verb/anywhere in the sentence).

Ans: anywhere in the sentence.

177. In English the object comes *after* the verb. In Latin the object comes _____.

Ans: anywhere in the sentence.

4-28

178. In English the verb comes *between* the subject and the object; in Latin _____ _____.

Ans: _____ the verb comes anywhere in the sentence.

179. All your life you have been responding to the position of the words in sentences, an English signal. You must now learn to *ignore* the position of the words in Latin and respond instead to the Latin signals {-s} and {-m}.

In this sequence we are going to tempt you. We are going to leave the signals {-s} and {-m} unchanged, but we are going to change the position of the words to an order that will tempt you to think that the former subject is now the object. Resist the temptation!

Notice that **vestiS** still has the signal {-S} and **viruM** still has the signal {-M}.

      ViruM reddiT vestiS.
      IGNORE the signal of position!

Is **viruM,** in its new position, *still* the object of this sentence? ____ (Yes/No)

Ans: Yes

180. Ignore the signal of position; look at the Latin signals. **ViruM reddiT vestiS** means, "_____."

Ans: Clothes make the man.

(Changing the order of words as we have done changes the *emphasis* of the words, but we are not concerned with that right now.)

Here is a second Basic Sentence.

181-182. **VēritāteM diēS aperiT.** The subject is ____.

Ans: **diēS**.

---

61. ★ ○ • ○ •

Vir cum __?__ stat.   Vir cum __?__ stat.

Cōnf: Vir cum fēminā stat.

R: Vir cum fēminā stat.

62. Vir cum fēminā stat means, "_____."

A: The man is standing with the woman.

63. ★ ○ • ○ •

Canis cum __?__ lītem habet.   Canis cum __?__ lītem habet.

Cōnf: Canis cum rānīs lītem habet.

R: Canis cum rānīs lītem habet.

64. "Canis cum rānīs lītem habet." means, "_____."

A: The dog is quarreling with the frogs.

14-16

4-29

183. The object is _____.

Ans: **vēritāteM**.

184. The verb is _____.

Ans: **aperiT**.

185. The word **vēritāteM** means "the truth." But in order to show the meaning of the signal **{-M}** in English we must put the word "truth" ____ (before/after) the verb "blanks."

Ans: after

186. So **vēritāteM** means, "Something (or somebody) _____ the truth."

Ans: blanks

187. **DiēS** is the _____ of the sentence.

Ans: subject

188. **DiēS** means "time." Therefore **VēritāteM diēS** means "____ blanks the _____."

Ans: Time blanks the truth.

189. The verb **aperiT** means "discloses." **VēritāteM diēS aperiT** means, "_____."

Ans: Time discloses the truth.

---

57. A. _____ videt.

R: Anus viperās videt.

58. F. _____ videt.

R: Für elephantōs videt.

59. As. _____ videt.

R: Asinus lupōs videt.

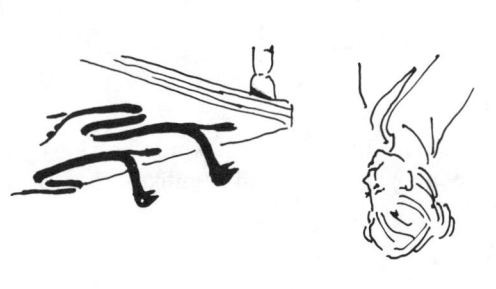

60. Now the ablative plural. Echo the plural of **cum fēminā**. ★ ○ • ○ • **Cum fēminīs**

As before, your teacher will describe one of two pictures. Echo and write the ablative form on the left or right hand side of your answer pad.

14-15

4-30

190. This is the second Basic Sentence. Copy both the Latin sentence and the English meaning in the part of your Reference Notebook labeled "Basic Text." Need we warn you to be careful? If you copy it incorrectly, you will learn it incorrectly.

191. "Time discloses the truth" = V_____ d___ ap____. [This sentence has three macrons. Print the signals in big letters.]

Ans: **VēritāteM diēS aperiT.**

192. VēritāteM diēS aperiT. The word that means "discloses" is _____.

Ans: **aperiT.**

193. The word that means "time" is _____.

Ans: **diēS.**

194. The word meaning "truth" is _____.

Ans: **vēritāteM.**

195. The order of the words in **VestiS viruM reddiT** is ____ (like/unlike) English word order.

Ans: unlike

196. The order of the words in **VēritāteM diēS aperiT** is ____ (like/unlike) English word order.

Ans: unlike

14-14

53. Quaerit aeger medicum → **Quaerit aeger** _____.

R: **Quaerit aeger medicōs.**

54. Quaerit aeger medicōs means, "_____."

A: A sick person seeks doctors.

Write your description of the following pictures. Say that one person or animal sees other persons or animals, using the accusative plurals of both the First and Second Declensions, that is, either -ās or -ōs.

55. V____ r____ videt.

R: **Vir rānās videt.**

56. _____ eq___ videt.

R: **Infāns equōs videt.**

4-31

197. We will tempt you again by putting the Latin object in the place filled by the English subject and the Latin subject in the place filled by the English object. You must therefore resist the temptation to respond to the English position signal in a Latin sentence. Instead, look at the Latin signals {-S} and {-M}:

VēritāteM aperiT diēS.

Ignore the position signal. Does this sentence still mean "Time discloses the truth," or does it now mean, "Truth discloses the time"? It means "_____."

▼

Ans: Time discloses the truth.

198. Now for the meaning of the third Basic Sentence. ★ ○ • **HilareM datōreM dīligiT DeuS.**

▼

199. Ignore the English position signal and observe the Latin signals instead. If we tell you that

hilareM datōreM means "a cheerful giver,"
   dīligiT means "loves," and
   DeuS means "God,"

then the sentence **HilareM datōreM dīligiT DeuS** means _____.
(A cheerful giver loves God/God loves a cheerful giver).

▼

Ans: God loves a cheerful giver. [If you missed this, go back to frame 137 and work up to here again. You do not need to use the tape however.]

---

48. • ○ ★ ∧ _____ in _____ •

Cōnf: **Lupōs juvenis invenit.**

49. _____ ∧ ○ ★ •

Cōnf: **Equōs anus tenet.**

50. In the last sequence the abbreviation "Cōnf:" stood for the Latin word _____.

R: **Cōnfirmātiō**

51. You can now predict the accusative plural of the Second Declension. Change the italicized accusative singular to accusative plural.
Vestis *virum* reddit. → **Vestis ___ōs reddit.**

R: **Vestis virōs reddit.**

52. **Vestis virōs reddit** means, "_____."

A: Clothes make men.

4-32

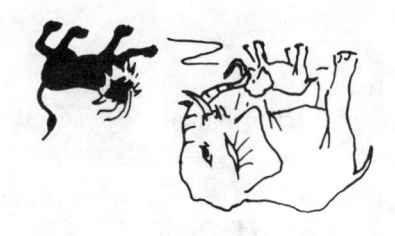

200. **Hilarem datōrem dīligit Deus** comes from a Latin translation of the New Testament. The New Testament was originally written in Greek, but it was translated into the _____ language.

Ans: Latin

201. The word order in **HilareM datōreM dīligiT DeuS** is ____ (like/unlike) English word order.

Ans: unlike

202. **HilareM datōreM dīligiT DeuS.** The two words that mean "cheerful giver" in this sentence are _____ _____.

Ans: **hilareM datōreM**.

203. The word that means "God" is _____.

Ans: **DeuS**.

204. And the word that means "loves" is _____.

Ans: **dīligiT**.

205. Let us now show you how to react to this Latin sentence word by word. First we have the object **HilareM datōreM** ("cheerful giver"). We indicate that this is an object by placing its English equivalent in the object slot after the verb "blanks." So **HilareM datōreM** means: "S_____ (or something) _____s a _____ _____."

Ans: Somebody (or something) blanks a cheerful giver.

4-33

206. The next word in the sentence is the verb **dīligiT** (loves). We now drop "loves" in the slot occupied by the verb "blanks." In place of "Somebody blanks a cheerful giver" we now have "_____."

▼

Ans: Somebody loves a cheerful giver.

207. **DeuS** ("God") completes the sentence. Substitute "God" for "somebody" in the subject slot. **HilareM datōreM dīligiT DeuS** means, "_____."

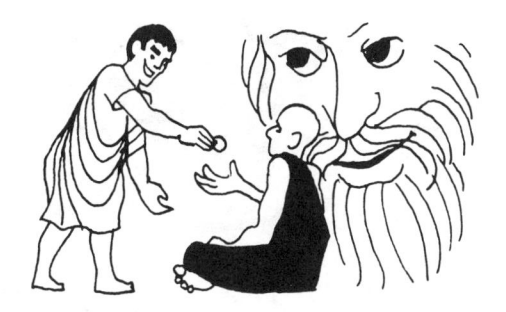

▼

Ans: God loves a cheerful giver.

208. Copy this Basic Sentence and its English meaning in your Reference Notebook under "Basic Text."

209. Echo and write. ★ ○ • H_____ d_____ d_____ D___. (Be careful not to look at this frame when you do the next frame.)

▼

Ans: HilareM datōreM dīligiT DeuS.

210. God loves a cheerful giver = H_____ d_____ d_____ D___. [Print the signals in big letters.]

▼

Ans: HilareM datōreM dīligiT DeuS.

Now describe these pictures. The accusative will be **-um** if the person or animal catches (discovers, etc.) only *one* animal; it will be **-ōs** if he catches *more than one*.

R: **Equōs anus tenet.**

▲

Conf: **Equōs anus tenet.**

▲

? anus tenet.   ? anus tenet.

44. ★ ○ • ○ •

R: **Lupum juvenis invēnit.**

▲

Conf: **Lupum juvenis invēnit.**

▲

? juvenis invēnit.   ? juvenis invēnit.

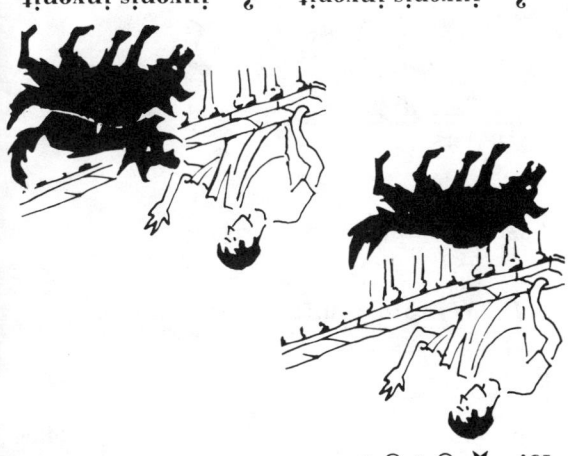

43. ★ ○ • ○ •

14-11

4-34

211. Write a review sentence from dictation. ★ ○ ○ [If you have no tape recorder, try to write from memory.]

V____ v____ r____. [Print the signals in big letters.]

▼ ▼

Ans: VestiS viruM reddiT. [If you missed this, study the three Basic Sentences in your Reference Notebook.]

212. VestiS viruM reddiT means, "_____ _____."

▼ ▼

Ans: Clothes make the man.

213. Write another review sentence from dictation. ★ ○ ○

V_____ d___ ap____. [Print the signals in big letters.]

▼ ▼

Ans: VēritāteM diēS aperiT.

214. VēritāteM diēS aperiT means, "____ _____."

▼ ▼

Ans: Time discloses the truth.

14-10

Do the same for the next sequence of pictures. Echo what your teacher says and write the accusative on the appropriate side of your answer pad, according to the picture.

41. ★ ○ ● ○ ●

? leō irritat.   ? leō irritat.

▲ ▲

Cōnf: **Elephantōs leō irritat.**

▲

R: **Elephantōs leō irritat.**

42. ★ ○ ● ○ ●

? anus tenet.   ? anus tenet.

▲ ▲

Cōnf: **Equum anus tenet.**

▲

R: **Equum anus tenet.**

215. Here is the fourth Basic Sentence. ★ ○ •
ManuS manuM lavaT.

216. In this sentence the same word occurs twice, once with the signal {--} and once with the signal {--}.

Ans: {-s} {-m}.

217. So the same thing is both the ------ and the ------ of the sentence.

Ans: subject object

218. When this happens in Latin, it means that one of these things acts upon another one of the same kind. Here is a picture of what this word stands for.

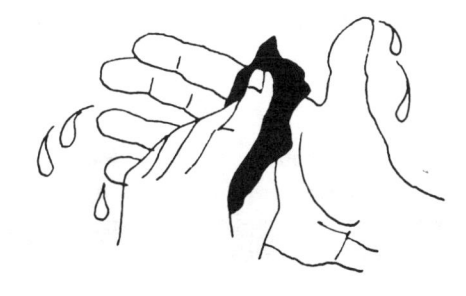

ManuS is the ------ form, and **ManuM** is the ------ form.

Ans: subject object

219. The meaning of **manuS manuM** is that (one) h--- blanks (another) h----. [The parentheses show that there is no corresponding Latin word present for "one" and "another."]

Ans: hand hand.

---

37. *Lupōs juvenis invenit* = The ------ ------ the ------.

★ ○ ○ •

38. In this frame your teacher will say either *Lupum juvenis invenit* or the phrase containing the new form, *Lupōs juvenis invenit*. Echo what he says and write the accusative form on the left or right side of your answer pad, according to the position of the picture described.

A: The young man discovers the wolves.

? juvenis invenit.   *? juvenis invenit.*

Cōnfirmātiō: *Lupōs juvenis invenit.*

R: *Lupōs juvenis invenit.*

39. The characteristic vowel of Second Declension nouns like **lupus/lupum/lupō** is ----.

R: -o- (not -u-).

40. The signal for the accusative plural **lupōs** is length of the ch---------- v---------- and the sound -s-.

A: characteristic vowel

4-35

220. The verb **lavaT** means "washes." The meaning of **ManuS manuM lavaT** is, "(One) ____ _____ (another) ____."

Ans: (One) hand washes (another) hand.

221. "(One) hand washes (another) hand" =

M____ m____ l____.

Ans: **ManuS manuM lavaT.**

222. Copy this Basic Sentence and its meaning in your Reference Notebook.

223. The word order in **ManuS manuM lavaT** is ____ (like/unlike) English word order.

Ans: unlike

224. The word order of all the Basic Sentences so far has been _____ English word order.

Ans: unlike

225. The word order of a Latin sentence will *occasionally* be like English word order, but this will be only a coinc_____.

Ans: coincidence.

4-36

A: The young man discovers the wolf.

36. **Lupum juvenit invenit** = The _____ d_____ s the _____.

★ ○ ● ○ **lupōs**

35. Echo a new form of the word for "wolf."

A: Eagles don't catch flies.

34. In giving the English translation we do not necessarily have to give an English singular where Latin uses the singular. Another good way of translating **Aquila nōn capit muscās** would be to say "_____ don't _____ s."

A: plural

number.

of the new Basic Sentence is in the _____

33. **Aquila nōn capit muscās** differs from **Elephantus nōn capit mūrem** in two ways: not only are the animals different but the object

R: **Elephantus nōn capit mūrem.**

32. Instead of flies, an eagle hunts something more important. This is the same thought that was expressed in Basic Sentence 5, which was E_____ c____ m____ nōn m____.

14-8

4-37

226. "One hand washes another hand" is what we call the "plain meaning" of this Basic Sentence. No one would ever quote **ManuS manuM lavaT** if there were not a deeper meaning, which we will call the "poetical meaning."

Did you ever try to wash just *one* hand? When you wash your hands, your right hand washes the left hand, but in return _____ _____. [Answer in your own words.]

Ans: the left hand washes the right hand.

227. In other words, the help we give someone else cannot always be considered unselfish, because _____. [In your own words.]

Ans: we also receive help from the other person.

228. Many Basic Sentences have both a plain and a poetical meaning. "One hand washes another" is the _____ meaning of **Manus manum lavat.**

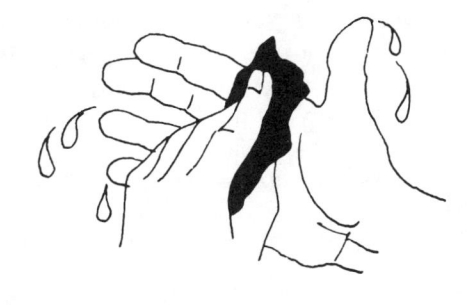

Ans: plain

---

26. The characteristic vowel of a First Declension word like **femina** is ____.

R: a.

27. The signal for the accusative plural **feminās** is length of the characteristic ____ and the sound -s-.

A: vowel

28. ✱ ○ • ○ •

Aquila nōn capit muscās. (36)

29. ✱ ○ ○ Aqu___ n___ c___ m___.
[Did you mark the two long vowels?]

R: **Aquila nōn capit muscās.** (36)

30. This means that an ____ doesn't ____.

A: an eagle doesn't catch flies.

31. Write Basic Sentence 36 and its meaning in your Reference Notebook.

229. "Working together is often profitable to both sides" is the _____ meaning of **Manus manum lavat.**

Ans: poetical

230-231. Since the Basic Sentences are an essential part of the course, we will give you constant review on them. In the following frames, echo the Basic Sentence. Then repeat it as many times as is necessary for you to learn it. Next give the English meaning. [The equals sign here indicates "Give the English for this Latin."]
★ ○ • **HilareM datōreM dīligiT DeuS** = _____. [If you are not using a tape recorder, pronounce the sentence by yourself a number of times.]

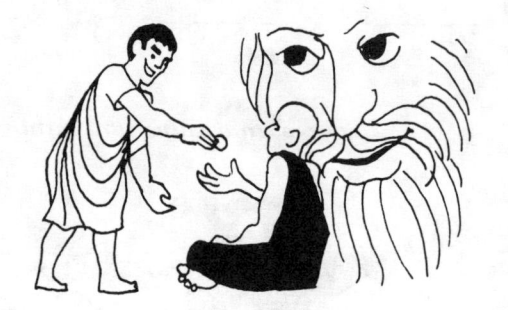

Ans: God loves a cheerful giver.

232. Now say these sentences aloud, supplying the missing signals that indicate subject {-s}, object {-m}, and verb {-t}. **Vesti_ viru_ reddi_.**

Ans: VestiS viruM reddiT.

---

19. In this last sequence, the abbreviation "R:" stood for the Latin word _____.

A: **Respōnsum.**

Now that you have learned the system, you can *predict* what the accusative plural of other First Declension nouns will be. Change the italicized objects from singular ("one") to plural ("more than one") by changing from **-am** to **-ās**. Read the whole of your transformed sentence aloud, then write the word that you have transformed from singular to plural.

20. *Cautus metuit foveam lupus* → Cautus _____ lupus.

R: metuit

21. *Cautus metuit foveās lupus* = "_____."

R: foveās

A: The cautious wolf fears pitfalls.

22. *Vītam regit Fortūna, nōn Sapientia* → _____ regit Fortūna, nōn Sapientia.

R: Vītās regit Fortūna, nōn Sapientia.

A: Fortune, not Wisdom, rules lives.

23. This means, "_____."

24. *Sapiēns rēgīnam laudat* → Sapiēns _____ laudat.

R: Sapiēns rēgīnās laudat.

25. This means, "_____."

A: The wise man praises queens.

4-39

233. Manu_ manu_ lava_.

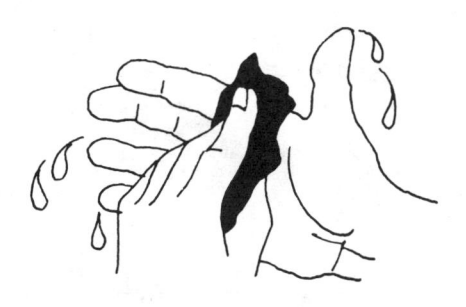

Ans: ManuS manuM lavaT.

234. Vēritāte_ diē_ aperi_.

Ans: VēritāteM diēS aperiT.

235. Hilar_ datōr_ dīligi_ Deu_.

Ans: HilareM datōreM dīligiT DeuS.

15. ____ ās l__ vidēt.
R: Sīmiās leō vidēt.

16. ____ v____ premit. 
R: Rānās vīpera premit.

17. ____ ____ metuit. 
R: Vīperam aper metuit.

18. ____. 
R: Fēminās canis premit.

14-5

236. In constructing this program we have tried to guarantee your success in learning Latin. However, it is impossible to predict *all* the problems which *all* the students will have. Suppose that you find one particular Basic Sentence hard to remember. You must then take it upon yourself to do a little *extra* work on this point that to you seems difficult. For example, you might ___ the Basic Sentence aloud several times from your Reference Notebook.

Ans: say (read, etc.)

237. In addition, you might _____ it down several times on a piece of scrap paper.

Ans: write (copy, etc.)

238. You may have noticed that there is a great deal of review in this program. But individuals differ, of course, and you may wish to _____ some point that no one else does.

Ans: review

239. If you wish to review any point, therefore, feel free to go b___ in the program.

Ans: back

240. A convenient place to review Basic Sentences is in your R_____ N_____.

Ans: Reference Notebook.

241. Take upon yourself the responsibility of using this program in the way that is most efficient for *you*. After all, whether or not you learn is your own _____.

Ans: responsibility.

4-41

242. Now a little further practice in ignoring your lifelong habits of English, where *position* identifies subject. In **HilareM datōreM dīligiT DeuS**, the Latin subject is the ____ (first/second/third/fourth) word in the sentence.

Ans: fourth

243. In **VestiS viruM reddiT** the Latin subject is the ____ (first/second/third) word in the sentence.

Ans: first

244. In **ManuS manuM lavaT** the Latin subject is the ____ (first/second/third) word in the sentence.

Ans: first

245. In **VēritāteM diēS aperiT** the Latin subject is the ____ (first/second/third) word in the sentence.

Ans: second

246. In the English translations of these sentences the English subject has always come b_____ the verb.

Ans: before

247. The English words "the" and "a" are the part of speech called ____ _____s.

Ans: noun markers.

---

9. ★ • ○ • ○ •

? vipera premit. ? vipera premit.

Cōnfirmātiō: Rānās vipera premit.

Respōnsum: Rānās vipera premit.

10. ★ • ○ • ○ •

? aper metuit. ? aper metuit.

Cōnfirmātiō: Vīperam aper metuit.

Respōnsum: Vīperam aper metuit.

11. ★ • ○ • ○ •

? canis quaerit. ? canis quaerit.

Cōnfirmātiō: Fēminās canis quaerit.

Respōnsum: Fēminās canis quaerit.

4-42

248. In the Latin sentences you have seen there ____ (were some/weren't any) words which served as noun markers.

Ans: weren't any

249. The system by which a language signals its meanings (using parts of speech, subject, object, etc.) is called its "structure." English signals are different from Latin signals. So we say that English and Latin have _____ structures.

Ans: different

[If you do not have a tape recorder, skip to frame 279. Your teacher will cover this material in class later.]

250. We will now return briefly to Latin pronunciation. There is a Latin word **redit** (with one "d") that means "goes back." Listen carefully now to the contrast between two Latin words. ★ ○ ○ **reddit, redit.**

251. Echo these two words. ★ ○ • ○ • **reddit, redit.**

252. Your teacher will say either **reddit** or **redit.** Echo and write down the one you hear. ★ ○ • ○ • _____.

Ans: reddit

253. In Latin there are some "double consonants." There is a single **d** in **redit** but a _____ **d** in **reddit.**

Ans: double

254. Pronounce the English words "latter" and "later" and check with the tape. _____, _____. √ ★ ○ •

14-2

5. The sentence **Simiās juvenis videt** described a situation in which the young man saw _____.

A: several (two) monkeys.

6. We call the form "monkey," the "singular" number of this noun, and the form "monkeys" is the "plural" n_____.

A: number.

7. Since you know that the form **simiam** is *accusative case* and *singular number,* it is apparent that the new form **simiās** is _____ case and _____ number.

A: accusative case and plural number.

8. In the following sequence, an animal will be chasing (seeing, etc.) either *one animal* or *several animals.* If you hear the familiar form in **-am** you will know that the animal is chasing just one animal. But if you hear the new form **-ās** you will know that he is chasing _____.

A: several animals. (more than one animal).

Echo what your teacher says and write the accusative form on the *left hand* side of the page in your answer notebook if it describes the left hand picture, and on the *right hand* side of the page if it describes the right hand picture.

4-43

255. Although we find many English words spelled with pairs of identical *letters*, this English spelling convention does *not* indicate the kind of double consonant sound which we have in Latin. The two "t's" in "latter," for example, show that the letter "a" has ____ (the same sound as/a different sound from) the "a" in "later."

A: a different sound from

256-257. Echo. ★ ○ • ○ • English "redder," Latin **reddit**. The pronunciation of the "dd" is ____ (the same/different) in English and in Latin.

Ans: different

258. Your teacher will say two more Latin words, where the second word has a double consonant. ★ ○ ○ **sumus, summus.**

259. ★ ○ • ○ • **sumus, summus**

260. Your teacher will say one of these two words. Write down the one that you hear. ★ ○ ○ **sumus? summus?** _____.

Ans: **summus**

261. Pronounce **sumus, summus** and check. ✓ ★ ○ •

262. Now a brief review on the importance of the contrast between long and short vowels. We are only practicing the pronunciation. Do not bother to learn these words. Echo. ★ ○ • ○ • **fugit, fūgit.**

UNIT FOURTEEN

14-1

1. Read this description of the picture and check. **Fēminam canis premit.** ✓ ★ ○ •

2. Echo the description of this picture in which your teacher uses a new form of **fēmina**. ★ ○ • ○ • **Fēminās canis premit.**

3. The difference between the two pictures is that in the first the dog is chasing just one woman, while in the second he is _____ . [In your own words]

A: chasing more than one (two).

4. Write your teacher's description of this picture, using a new form of the word **simia**, similar to **fēminās**. ★ ○ ○ S_____ j_____ v_____ .

Respōnsum: **Simiās juvenis videt.**

4-44

263. The Latin word for "he runs away" is **fugit**, while the word for "he *ran* away" is **fūgit**. Echo and write the Latin word you hear. ★ ○ • ○ • _____.

Ans: **fūgit** [Without a macron your answer is *wrong*.]

264. You will hear these two Latin words again. Echo and write them in the order in which your teacher says them. ★ ○ • ○ • _____, _____

Ans: **fugit, fūgit**

265. **Fugit** means "he runs away," but **fūgit** means "he ___ away."

Ans: ran

266. Say the Latin for "he ran away" and then check **fūgit** ✓ ★ ○ •

267. In addition to five short Latin vowels there are five corresponding ____ vowels.

Ans: long

268. A long vowel is signalled in writing by a _____.

Ans: macron.

269. Say the technical term that signals a long vowel and then check. _____ ✓ ★ ○ •

Visual Check: Macron (máy-cron)

270. Echo a new pair of Latin words. ★ ○ • ○ • **notus, nōtus**

TEST INFORMATION

13-77

The Summary will serve to remind you of what you learned in this Unit, and you will naturally be questioned on what you learned. One piece of advice. The noun-plus-adjective combinations are difficult. You were given your choice, to say them or to write them. If you know them perfectly, then you are all set. But if you tried to "save time" by saying them, rather than writing, and do not have these paradigms under control, take the time now to go back and learn them. Learning is your responsibility; the program and your teacher can only help you; you must do the work—all of it.

The paradigms will be only those which you have practiced in this Unit. The questions on pictures will be like those in this Unit, but the pictures may be different; there may be kind and cruel donkeys, for example.

Use the Vocabulary Inventory above to check your knowledge of these words. The number indicates the frame where the word was explained. Turn to that frame and study it again if you are unsure.

4-45

271. Echo and write the Latin word you hear.
★ ○ • ○ • _____

Ans: **notus**

272. Echo another pair of Latin words, which contrast **o** and **ō**. ★ ○ • ○ • **modo, modō**

273. Echo and write the Latin word you hear.
★ ○ • ○ • _____

Ans: **modō** [Did you remember the macron?]

274. The *only difference* in sound between the different words **modo** and **modō** is the _____ of the final v_____.

Ans: length vowel.

275. In Latin we indicate the length of a long vowel by the mark called a _____.

Ans: macron.

276. Echo. ★ ○ • ○ • **utī, ūtī**

277. Echo and write the Latin word you hear.
★ ○ • ○ • _____

Ans: **utī**

278. Here are two forms of the same word. One is a familiar form, the other is not. Echo and write them in the order in which your teacher says them. ★ ○ • ○ • _____, _____

Ans: **manūs, manus**

VOCABULARY INVENTORY 13-76

In this Unit you learned eight neuter nouns: corpus (61-62), genus (76), flūmen (102), factum (183), dictum (185), venēnum (214), animal (337), membrum (393).

You learned seven nouns of different declensions: rēgīna (87), forma (91), aqua (122), spēs (191), ōrātiō (212), fōns (242), salūs (290), and a new meaning for rēs (192-193).

You learned eight adjectives:
   m   f   n
sānus, sāna, sānum (67-69),
   m   f   n
medius, media, medium (108-112),
   m   f   n
īnsānus, īnsāna, īnsānum (128-129),
   m   f   n
pūrus, pūra, pūrum (243-248),
   m   f   n
impūrus, impūra, impūrum (252),
   m & f   n
fortis, forte (276),
   m   f   n
blandus, blanda, blandum (229),
   m   f   n
quantus, quanta, quantum (291),
   m   f   n
ignāvus, ignāva, ignāvum (277).

You learned four verbs: invēnit (142), dōnat (88), dēfluit (238), bibit (122).

You learned that a familiar connector can occur in pairs: et . . . et (78).

You also learned an expression which means "not at all:" minimē (340).

You are now ready to take the Test for Unit Thirteen.

279. Language is speech. In learning a language, you must do a lot of sp___ing.

Ans: speaking.

280. And in doing this program, speak up in a loud, clear voice. We think that you will do better if you read *all* the Latin al___.

Ans: aloud.

281. We will now take up a new Latin sentence. It contains some new vocabulary. Echo a new word. ★ ○ • ○ • nōn

282. The Latin word **nōn** does not have any other forms. **ManuS** and **manuM** are different forms of the same word, but not all Latin words change form as **manuS** does. **Nōn** is a word that does ___ _____ form.

Ans: not change

283. **Nōn** is used to make a statement negative; that is, it says that something is ___ so.

Ans: not

284. **ManuS manuM nōn lavaT** therefore would mean that one hand does ___ wash another hand.

Ans: not

285. **VēritāteM diēS nōn aperiT** = Time does ___ _____ the truth.

Ans: Time does not disclose the truth.

---

407. Ā f____ p___ p___ dēflī___ aq___. (35)

Respōnsum: Ā fonte pūrō pūra dēfluit aqua. (35)

408. The hardest thing about this Unit was the neuter of Third Declension adjectives. See if you can write the paradigm of hilare dictum.

Respōnsum: hilare dictum
hilare dictum
hilarī dictō

409. You will also be tested on such noun-and-adjective combinations as **blanda ōrātiō**. See if you can write the paradigm. _____

Respōnsum: blanda ōrātiō
blandam ōrātiōnem
blandā ōrātiōne

410. You now know ten Second Declension neuter nouns. Remember them! ★ ○ • mem- brum, venēnum, dictum, factum, re- spōnsum, rēgnum, auxilium, vitium, vīnum, perīclum

411. You also know five Third Declension neuter nouns. Remember these, too! ★ ○ • opus, animal, flūmen, genus, corpus

You must know how to decline all fifteen of these. In addition, you will be responsible for all the paradigms which you were required to write out. If you are unsure of any, study them from your Notebook (but make sure that your notebook is accurate).

4-47

286. A Latin noun changes form. Its subject form has {--}; its object form has {--}.

Ans: {-s}   {-m}.

287. Nōn is different from all the other Latin words we have met so far, because it _____ _____.

Ans: does not change form.

288. One hand washes another hand = Man__ m____ lav__. [The dashes show the number of missing letters.]

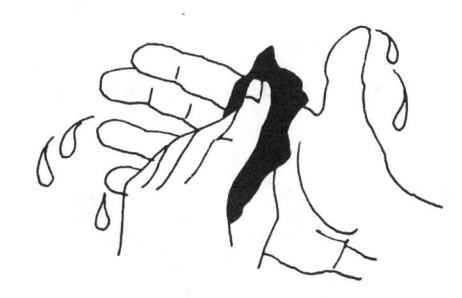

Ans: **Manus manum lavat.**

289. One hand *doesn't* wash another hand = M____ m____ n__ l____.

Ans: **Manus manum nōn lavat.**

---

403. This was written by the poet H_____.

A: Horace.

404. Īn_ m___ fl___ qu____ aqu___. (32) [Pronounce and listen for the long vowels.]

Respōnsum: **Īnsānus mediō flūmine quaerit aquam.** (32)

405. R___ nōn sp___ f_____ n___ d_____ qu____ am____. (33)

Respōnsum: **Rem nōn spem, factum nōn dictum, quaerit amīcus.** (33)

406. H___ s___ v_____ bl_____ ōr_____. (34)

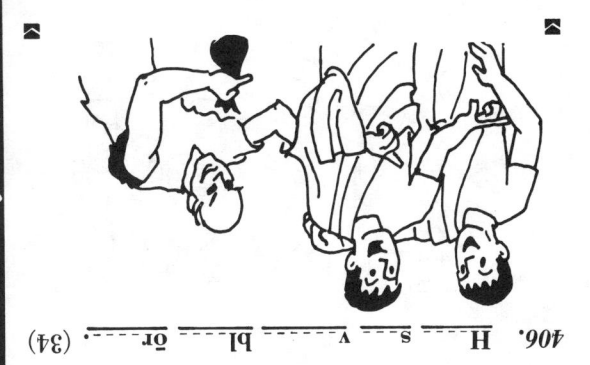

Respōnsum: **Habet suum venēnum blanda ōrātiō.** (34)

13-74

4-48

290. Describe the following pictures.
Vest___ vir___ redd___.

Ans: **Vestis virum reddit.**

291. V_____ v____ n___ r_____.

Ans: **Vestis virum nōn reddit.**

292. Vēritāt___ di___ aper___.

Ans: **Vēritātem diēs aperit.**

293. V_____ d____ ___ ap____.

Ans: **Vēritātem diēs nōn aperit.**

---

399. Nouns do not have these three genders. However, we say that the word **fōns** is masculine because it is modified by a _____.

A: masculine adjective.

You learned six new Basic Sentences. Review them in your Reference Notebook, if you like, before doing this next sequence.

400. M___ s___ c_____ s_____. (30) [Don't forget the four macrons in this sentence]

Respōnsum: **Mēns sāna in corpore sānō.** (30)

401. This sentence was written by J_____.

A: Juvenal.

402. Et g___ et f___ R___ P_____ d_____ (31) [Four macrons.]

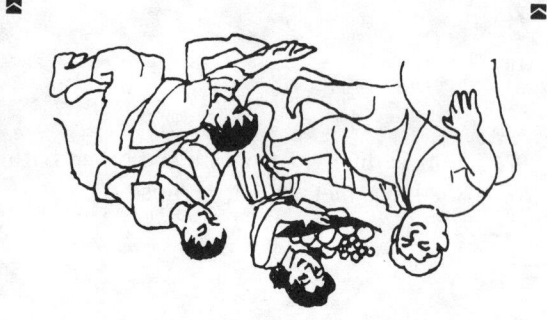

Respōnsum: **Et genus et formam Rēgīna Pecūnia dōnat.** (31)

13-73

4-49

294. Now we will take up some more of the vocabulary necessary to understand our new Basic Sentence. Listen carefully to a new word, noticing that the combination **ph** in Latin sounds like an English "p," but with a stronger puff of air. ★ ○ • ○ • **elephantuS**

295-296. Echo the subject and object of a sentence. ★ ○ • ○ • **ElephantuS mūreM**

ElephantuS mūreM = The _____ blanks the m___e.

Ans: The elephant blanks the mouse.

297-298. We now know that an elephant does something to a mouse. Echo your teacher as he completes this sentence. ★ ○ • ○ • **ElephantuS mūreM dīligiT.**

This sentence means, "The el_____ ____s the _____."

Ans: The elephant loves the mouse.

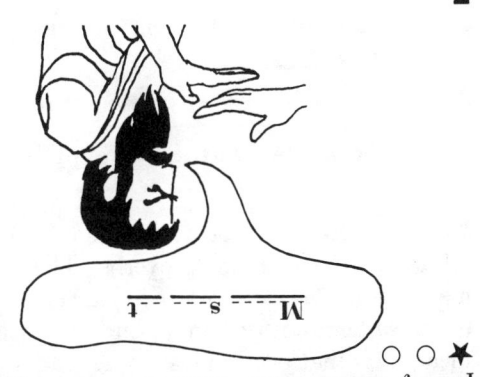

13-72

394. In this picture the patient has been having trouble with his hand. This is the final visit, and the doctor is telling him that his hand is completely cured. Write what he tells the patient. ★ ○ ○

M____ s___ __t

Cōnfirmātiō: **Manus sāna est.**

395. Here is the same information using the new noun as a synonym for **manus.** ★ ○ ○

Mem____ s____ __t.

Cōnfirmātiō: **Membrum sānum est.**

396. We said ____ manus, but _____ membrum.

Respōnsum: sāna sānum

397. The change in the adjective from **sāna** to **sānum** is a difference in the _____.

A: gender (**Manus** is one of the few feminine Fourth Declension nouns.)

SUMMARY

398. In this Unit you learned that adjectives not only have different cases but they have three different _____s.

A: genders.

4-50

299. Chorus a new Basic Sentence. ★ ○ ○ ◉ ◉
ElephantuS nōn capiT mūreM.

300. ★ ○ • *ElephantuS nōn capiT mūreM.*
[Repeat as often as you need.]

301. Write this same sentence from dictation.
★ ○ ○ <u>El_____</u> <u>n__</u> <u>c____</u> <u>m____</u>. [If you have no tape recorder, try to remember.]

Ans: **ElephantuS nōn capiT mūreM.**

302. **ElephantuS nōn capiT mūreM** = An _____ doesn't catch a _____.

Ans: An elephant doesn't catch a mouse.

303. Echo and write the sentence again.
★ ○ • ○ • _____

Visual Check: **ElephantuS nōn capiT mūreM.**

304. The five Basic Sentences we have had are all famous sayings or proverbs. The "plain" meaning of **ManuS manuM lavaT** is "One hand washes another hand," but the "poetical" meaning is that people must coo_____ with one another.

Ans: cooperate

---

387. ★ ○ ○ L____ c____ _____.

388. Write your teacher's description of the last picture. _____.

Respōnsum: **Lupus cautus est.**

389. ★ ○ ○ _____ _____.

Confirmātiō: **Animal cautum est.**

390. Write his second description of the same picture. _____.

Respōnsum: **Animal cautum est.**

391. In the first description we used the form *cautus*, because **lupus** is _____ gender.

A: masculine

392. In the second description we used the form *cautum*, because _____.

A: animal is neuter gender.

393. ★ ○ • **membrum** ("part of the body")
membrum
membrī
membrō

4-51

305. The "poetical" meaning of **ElephantuS nōn capiT mūreM** is that an elephant is too _____ to bother with a tiny mouse.

Ans: important, etc.

306. Let us take this sentence word by word and try to interpret it as a Roman would (although we will still have to talk about it in English for a while longer).

307. **ElephantuS** = An _____ _____s.

Ans: An elephant blanks.

308. **ElephantuS nōn** = An _____ doesn't _____.

Ans: An elephant doesn't blank.

309. **ElephantuS nōn capiT** = "An _____ ____n't _____ (something)."

Ans: An elephant doesn't catch (something).

310. **ElephantuS nōn capiT mūreM** = _____.

Ans: An elephant doesn't catch a mouse.

---

381. ✶ ○ • ir____ f__

Cōnfirmātiō: īrātus fūr īrātum fūrem īrātō fūre

382. Write the paradigm you just echoed.

īr____ f__

Respōnsum: īrātus fūr īrātum fūrem īrātō fūre

383. ✶ ○ • f____ g____

Cōnfirmātiō: facile genus facile genus facilī genere

384. Write the paradigm you just echoed.

f____ g__

Respōnsum: facile genus facile genus facilī genere

385. ✶ ○ • cr_____ sp__

Cōnfirmātiō: crūdēlis spēs crūdēlem spem crūdēlī spē

386. Write the paradigm you just echoed.

cr_____ sp__

Respōnsum: crūdēlis spēs crūdēlem spem crūdēlī spē

13-70

4-52

311. Copy into your Reference Notebook this fifth Basic Sentence.

312. Does this Basic Sentence make a statement which is true about just one specific elephant, or does it describe the behavior of elephants in general? _____.

Ans: It describes the behavior of elephants in general.

313. Since it makes a general statement that is true about almost all elephants, we translate it; "An elephant doesn't catch _ mouse."

Ans: a

314. To express such general statements in English, we can also use the "more than one" form. Instead of saying, "An elephant doesn't catch a mouse," we might say: "_____s don't catch ____."

Ans: Elephants   mice.

315. Now for a new point of structure. Echo a technical term. ★ ○ • ○ • {-s -m -t} sentence

316. The most common type of Latin sentence is the kind we have been studying, with a s_____, an _____, and a v____.

Ans: subject   object   verb.

317. Because Latin signals its subjects with {-s}, objects with {-m}, and verbs with {-t}, we have called this common type of sentence an {-s -m -t} sentence, although in Latin the subject, object, and verb can be in ___ order.

Ans: any

---

376. Decline the Latin for "big jump."

m ----- s ------

Respōnsum: magnus saltus
magnum saltum
magnō saltū

In this sequence echo your teacher as he declines five different noun-plus-adjective phrases. Repeat them several times. You will then be asked to write the paradigm of these same phrases. [Again, you may *say* them if you think you can learn them better that way.]

377. ★ ○ • m ----- op---

Confirmātiō: magnum opus
magnum opus
magnō opere   [Don't look at this answer when you do the next frame.]

378. Write the paradigm you just echoed. [Or say it.]

m ----- op---

Respōnsum: magnum opus
magnum opus
magnō opere   [If you said it, learn it.]

379. ★ ○ • h ----- d-----

Confirmātiō: hilāre dictum
hilāre dictum
hilārī dictō

380. Write the paradigm you just echoed.

h ----- d-----

Respōnsum: hilāre dictum
hilāre dictum
hilārī dictō

4-53

318. VestiS viruM reddiT is an {-- -- --} sentence.

Ans: {-s -m -t}

319. Instead of using the word "verb" we will often use the symbol {-t}. The {-t} in this sentence is the Latin word _____

Ans: reddiT.

320. The {-s} in this sentence is the word _____

Ans: vestiS.

321. And viruM is the {--} of the sentence.

Ans: {-m}

322. ManuS manuM lavaT is an {-- -- --} sentence.

Ans: {-s -m -t}

323. The {-m} in this sentence is the word _____

Ans: manuM.

324. HilareM datōreM dīligiT DeuS is also an {-s -m -t} sentence but the order is {--}, {--}, {--}.

Ans: {-m} {-t} {-s}.

325. The {-s} in this sentence is the word _____

Ans: DeuS.

---

369. Write the Latin paradigm for "one lion."

l.... ū....

Respōnsum: leō ūnus
leōnem ūnum
leōne ūnō

370. Write the Latin paradigm for "smooth speech."

bl.... or....

Respōnsum: blanda ōrātiō
blandam ōrātiōnem
blandā ōrātiōne

Echo these paradigms.

371. ★ ○ • genus ignāvum ("cowardly family.")
genus ignāvum
genere ignāvō

372. ★ ○ • medium flūmen ("middle of the river.")
medium flūmen
mediō flūmine

373. ★ ○ • magnus saltus ("big jump.")
magnum saltum
magnō saltū

Either say or write these as you prefer. But *learn them!*

374. Decline the Latin for "cowardly family."

g.... ign....

Respōnsum: genus ignāvum
genus ignāvum
genere ignāvō

375. Decline the Latin for "middle of the river."

m...... fl......

Respōnsum: medium flūmen
medium flūmen
mediō flūmine

13-68

326. You will find out later why there are *two* {--}'s.

Ans: {-m}

327. **VēritāteM diēS aperiT** is an {-- -- --} sentence.

Ans: {-t -s -m}

328. The order here is {--}, {--}, {--}.

Ans: {-m} {-s} {-t}.

329. The {-t} in this sentence is the word _____

Ans: **aperiT**.

330. The {-s} is the word _____.

Ans: **diēS**.

331. **ElephantuS nōn capiT mūreM** is an {-- -- --} sentence.

Ans: {-s -m -t}.

332. The order here is {--}, {--}, {--}.

Ans: {-s} {-t} {-m}.

333. You will find many Latin words easy to remember because they have an English derivative. On the other hand, the English derivative may mislead you in the pronunciation of the _____ word.

Ans: Latin
[If you have no tape recorder, skip to frame 346. Your teacher will cover frames 334-345 in class.]

Echo these paradigms.

365. ★ ○ ● **canis magnus** ("large dog") canem magnum cane magnō

366. ★ ○ ● **leō ūnus** ("one lion") leōnem ūnum leōne ūnō

367. ★ ○ ● **blanda ōrātiō** ("smooth speech") blandam ōrātiōnem blandā ōrātiōne

368. Write the Latin paradigm for "large dog." c_____ m_____

Respōnsum: canis magnus canem magnum cane magnō

362. Write the Latin paradigm for "talkative doctor." m_____ el_____

Respōnsum: medicus ēloquēns medicum ēloquentem medicō ēloquentī

363. Write the Latin paradigm for "intemperate sick person." int_____ ae_____

Respōnsum: intemperāns aeger intemperantem aegrum intemperantī aegrō

364. Write the Latin paradigm for "every word." om_____ d_____

Respōnsum: omne dictum omne dictum omnī dictō

4-55

334-340. A Latin word is often pronounced very differently from its English derivative. Here is a list of English words with the Latin words from which they are derived. Your teacher will pronounce the Latin word. Echo him.

ENGLISH   LATIN

334. ★ ○ • ○ • hilarious—**hilarem**

335. ★ ○ • ○ • deity—**Deus**

336. ★ ○ • ○ • vest—**vestis**

337. ★ ○ • ○ • virile—**virum**

338. ★ ○ • ○ • elephant—**elephantus**

339. ★ ○ • ○ • lavatory—**lavat**

340. ★ ○ • ○ • verity—**vēritās**

Pronounce and check the following sentences.

341. **HilareM datōreM dīligiT DeuS.** √ ★ ○ •

342. **VestiS viruM reddiT.** √ ★ ○ •

343. **ManuS manuM lavaT.** √ ★ ○ •

344. **VēritāteM diēS aperiT.** √ ★ ○ •

345. **ElephantuS nōn capiT mūreM.** √ ★ ○ •

SUMMARY

346. In this unit you learned to distinguish between Latin nouns and Latin _____.

Ans: verbs.

347. You also learned that Latin nouns have both a _____ form and an _____ form.

Ans: subject   object

4-56

348. Latin subjects have the signal {˗˗}.

Ans: {-s}.

349. And Latin objects have the signal {˗˗}.

Ans: {-m}.

350. The most important frame in the entire course says that Latin *never* signals subject or object by position but by the signals {˗˗} and {˗˗}.

Ans: {-s} {-m}.

351. You also learned five Basic Sentences. Write down the Basic Sentence which fits each picture.

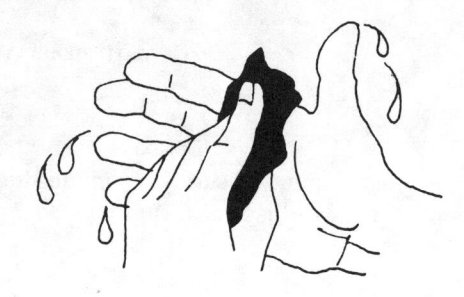

M____ m____ la___.

Ans: **Manus manum lavat.**

352. Ve____ vi___ red___.

Ans: **Vestis virum reddit.**

13-65

352. Write your teacher's answer in one word.

★ ○ ○ "_____."

Confirmātiō: Stultus asinus est.

Respōnsum: Stultus.

353. Ask what kind of woman this is. "_____ ?" ∧ ★ ○ •

Confirmātiō: Quālis fēmina est?

354. "_____," ★ ○ ○

Confirmātiō: Incerta fēmina est.

Respōnsum: Incerta.

355. Ask what kind of wine this is. "_____ ?" ∧ ★ ○ •

Confirmātiō: Quāle vīnum est?

4-57

353. Vēr_____ d___ ap____.

Ans: Vēritātem diēs aperit.

354. Ele_____ n__ cap__ mūr__.

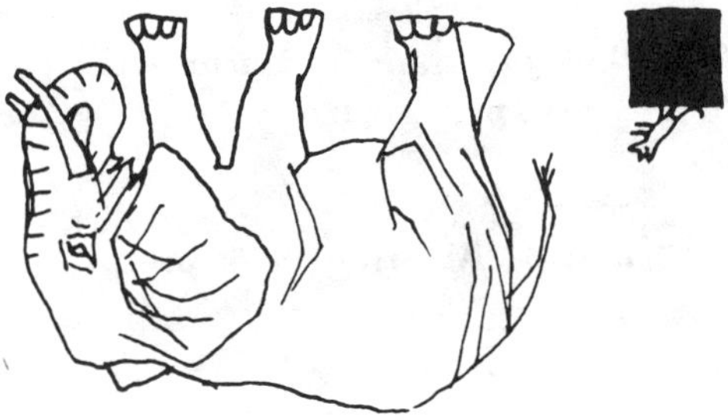

Ans: Elephantus nōn capit mūrem.

355. Hil____ dat____ dī_____ D___.

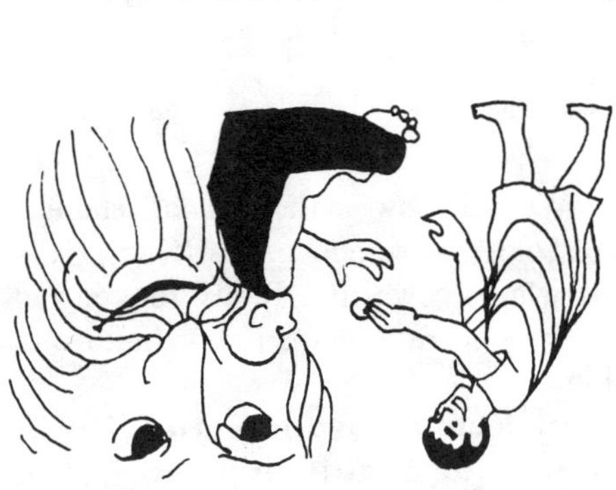

Ans: Hilarem datōrem dīligit Deus.

13-64

349. In the following sequence, ask your teacher what kind of (**Quālis?**, **Quāle?**) person, animal, or thing is there. Check with the tape, then write your teacher's answer.

Ask him what kind of monkey this is. "Qu____ s____?" ∨ ✱ ○ • (Auxilium sub hāc līneā est.)

Auxilium: **Simia** is feminine, so use the feminine form **quālis?**.

Cōnfirmātiō: Quālis simia est?

350. Write the one word of your teacher's answer that is important. [If you don't have a tape recorder, then guess.] ✱ ○ ○ "_____."

Cōnfirmātiō: **Ignāva** simia est.

Respōnsum: **Ignāva**.

351. Ask him what kind of donkey this is. "_____?" ∨ ✱ ○ •

Cōnfirmātiō: Quālis asinus est?

TEST INFORMATION

You will be asked to perform the following tasks:
1) to read aloud one of the five Basic Sentences.
2) to produce one of these five Basic Sentences in writing when given a picture and the clue of the first letter of each word, as in frames 351–355. Notice, however, that your task on the test is just a little bit harder because you will be given only the *first* letter of each word.
3) to identify subject, object, and verb, as in frames 181–184.
4) to identify English nouns, verbs, subjects, and objects, as in frames 17–87. However, the sentences and words will be new.

---

344. "Vīpera mūrem ignāvum premit."

"M⎯⎯ ; v⎯⎯ p⎯⎯ a⎯⎯ f⎯⎯."
∨ ★ ○ •

Cōnfirmātiō: Minimē; vīpera premit animal forte.

345. We will now make a small change. You will be told that someone sees (fears, etc.) some *person* who is cowardly. Reply that in fact this person sees a brave man. Echo the first contradiction.
"Fūr jūdicem ignāvum metuit."
"Minimē; fūr metuit vir⎯⎯ fort⎯⎯."
★ ○ • ○ •

Cōnfirmātiō: Minimē; fūr metuit virum fortem.

346. "Leō juvenem ignāvum premit."

"M⎯⎯ ; l⎯⎯ pr⎯⎯ virum f⎯⎯." ∨ ★ ○ •

Cōnfirmātiō: Minimē; leō premit virum fortem.

347. "Canis fūrem ignāvum mordet."

"M⎯⎯ ; c⎯⎯ m⎯⎯ vir⎯⎯ f⎯⎯." ∨ ★ ○ •

Cōnfirmātiō: Minimē; canis mordet virum fortem.

348. "Anus medicum ignāvum dīligit."

"M⎯⎯ ; an⎯⎯ d⎯⎯ v⎯⎯ f⎯⎯." ∨ ★ ○ •

Cōnfirmātiō: Minimē; anus dīligit virum fortem.

UNIT FIVE

1. We will now review briefly the meanings of the different symbols which give you your instructions. The star [★] means that you are to _____. [In your own words]

A: start the tape player.

2. The large circle [○] means that _____. [In your own words]

A: _____ your teacher will say something.

3. The solid dot [●] means that you are to _____. [In your own words]

A: repeat (or *echo*) what your teacher says.

4. The check sign [√] means that you are to _____. [In your own words]

A: Say your answer *first* and then check your answer with the tape.

5. The solid lines [_____] mean to _____ your answer in your answer pad.

A: _____ write

6. The broken lines mean to ___ your answer _____.

A: _____ say aloud.

7. We would like you to work as efficiently as possible. It may well be that by now you can work without the top mask. This will speed you up somewhat. But if you do stop using the top mask you must be careful not to look accidentally at the previous _____.

A: _____ frame.

5-1

Cōnfirmātiō: Minimē; jūdex capit animal forte.

★ √ • ○ •

343. "Jūdex equum ignāvum capit."
"M____; j____ c____ an____ f____."

Cōnfirmātiō: Minimē; anus metuit animal forte.

★ √ • ○ •

342. "Anus aprum ignāvum metuit."
"M____; anus m____ animal f____e."

Now try these yourself. Answer first, then check.

Cōnfirmātiō: Minimē; anus videt animal forte.

★ ○ ○ •

"Anus taurum ignāvum videt."
"Minimē; anus videt ani____ fort____."

341. When your teacher says, "The old lady sees a cowardly bull," correct him by saying, "Not at all, she sees a brave animal." Echo your teacher as he does the first contradiction.

★ ○ ○ • Minimē

340. Echo the word for "Not at all."

In case you are wondering, there is some variation between -e and -ī in the ablative of the Third Declension. In general, however, you can count on nouns ending in -e and adjectives ending in -ī as in cane (noun) and fortī (adjective).

Respōnsum: omne.

339. The form forte is the same case as ____ (cane/aure/mūre/omne).

13-62

5-2

8. You should be careful not to look *accidentally* at the previous frame, because you need practice in recalling the information just given you. But if you *wish* to look back, you may do so. For example, suppose that you cannot recall the information that you need but remember that it is in the frame above. In this case ____ (you should make a mistake rather than look back/ you may look back).

A: you may look back.

9. Remember: you do not learn skills by doing things in the wrong way but by practicing them in the _____ way.

A: right

10. You will be judged *not* by the score you make on this program, but rather by your performance in class and your scores on the _____ after each unit.

A: tests

11-16. Echo the subject and object forms. Repeat until learned. We have marked the syllable which is accented to help those who are not using a tape recorder.

11. ★ ○ • ○ • véritās
              vēritátem

12. ★ ○ • ○ • véstis
              véstem

13. ★ ○ • ○ • mánus
              mánum

14. ★ ○ • ○ • Déus
              Déum

15. ★ ○ • ○ • elephántus
              elephántum

16. ★ ○ • ○ • díēs
              díem

---

333. Cautious imitation blanks = _____.

Respōnsum: Cauta imitātiō.

334. Gender in Latin is a distinction which we must make if we wish to have an adjective modify a noun. Does English compel us to make this kind of distinction? ____ (Yes/No)

A: No

In English grammar the term "gender" is sometimes used in a way quite different from that in Latin grammar. In English, all males are referred to as "he," all females are referred to as "she," and all things that do not have biological sex are referred to as "it." (When in English we call a boat "she," we are regarding it as a living female thing.)

335. Does English have grammatical gender (change of adjective form according to the noun it modifies) of the kind which Latin has? ____ (Yes/No)

A: No

336. We will give you extra practice here on the neuter adjectives like omne. Echo these *many times.* ★ ○ •
  omneØ corpusØ
  omneØ corpusØ ("every body")
  omnī corpore

337. ★ ○ • animalØ forteØ Animal is a new
  animalØ forteØ   noun.
  animālī fortī   ("brave animal")

338. Note that the ablative of the new noun animal ends in _____.

Respōnsum: -ī

13-61

5-3

17. Earlier we spoke of "variant signals" in English for the form which indicates "more than one." We pointed out that we do not say "two foots" but rather "two f__t."

A: feet.

18. The change from "oo" to "ee" in the middle of the word to show "more than one" is in English a v_____ signal.

A: variant

19. These different signals for "more than one" are called _____ _____s.

A: variant signals.

20-21. In the same way, Latin nouns have two different signals for subject. Echo the subject and object forms of these words.

20. ★ ○ • ○ • **vír**
                    vírum

21. ★ ○ • ○ • **dátor**
                    datórem

22. Since you know only the subject and object forms, for the present *any* noun form which does not have the signal {-m} is the _____ form.

A: subject

23. Since you know that **viruM** is the object form, then **vir** must be the _____ form.

A: subject

24. You know that the object form is signalled by {-_}.

A: {-m}.

Respōnsum: **Bona ōrātiō.**

Good speech blanks = B____ ōrā____
332. Third Declension nouns ending in **-iō**, like **ōrātiō**, are also feminine gender.

Respōnsum: **Certa**
                           félicitās.

331. Sure prosperity blanks = C____ fēli____.

Respōnsum: **Certa vēritās.**

330. Sure truth blanks = Cert. vēr____.

Respōnsum: **vēritās**

329. There are aids to help you identify the gender of some nouns of the Third Declension. For example, Third Declension nouns ending in **-tās**, like v__tās, are feminine gender.

A: any of the three.

328. Non-personal nouns (like **Iis, auris, opus, vestis, orbis**) will be ____ (masculine/feminine/neuter/any of the three).

Respōnsum: **corpus, genus, flūmen,** and **opus.**

Auxilium: The meanings of these words are "body," "family," "river," and "work."

327. Now for Third Declension nouns. You know four neuter nouns of the Third Declension, c____, g____, fl____, and o____. (**Auxilium sub hāc lineā est.**)

13-60

5-4

25. Since you know that **datōreM** ("giver") is the object form, then **dator** _____. [In your own words.]

A: _____ must be the subject form.

26-33. Give both the subject and object forms of these words and check. [If you do not have a tape recorder, a visual check is given below. Be *sure* to give your answer aloud.]

26. dátor, _____ ✓ ★ ○ •

Visual Check: **dátor, datṓrem**

27. elephántus, _____ ✓ ★ ○ •

Visual Check: **elephántus, elephántum**

28. vír, _____ ✓ ★ ○ •

Visual Check: **vír, vírum**

29. mánus, _____ ✓ ★ ○ •

Visual Check: **mánus, mánum**

30. véstis, _____ ✓ ★ ○ •

Visual Check: **véstis, véstem**

31. vḗritās, _____ ✓ ★ ○ •

Visual Check: **vḗritās, vēritā́tem**

32. Déus, ____ ✓ ★ ○ •

Visual Check: **Déus, Déum**

33. díēs, ____ ✓ ★ ○ •

Visual Check: **díēs, díem**

---

321. Here is the second "rule" that will help you to tell the gender of Latin nouns. *Most* (but not all) male animals or persons have Latin names that are masculine gender. In the same way, *most* (but not all) females have Latin names that are _____ gender.

A: feminine (This is the reason for the names "masculine" and "feminine" gender.)

322. You have learned that *most* Fourth Declension nouns are _____ gender.

A: masculine

323. But the Fourth Declension noun **anus** is a feminine noun because it refers to a _____ person.

A: female

324. With the names of animals there is considerable variation from this "rule." For example, **vulpēs** is always feminine gender, whether it refers to a female fox or a ____ fox.

A: male

325. A fish, even a female one, is a **magnus piscis** and is therefore _____ gender.

A: masculine

326. But those are exceptions; the "rule" is that males of all declensions are _____ gender, and *most* females of all declensions are _____ gender.

A: masculine feminine

13-59

5-5

34. The subject form of **datóreM** is _____.

A: **dator**.

35. The subject form of **viruM** is _____.

A: **vir**.

36-43. Give the subject and object forms of these words and check. Notice that the order of the words has been changed. Remember about the new subject forms **vir** and **dator**.

36. _____s, véstem √ ★ ○ •

Visual check: **véstis, véstem**

37. _____, datórem √ ★ ○ •

Visual Check: **dátor, datórem**

38. ___s, Déum √ ★ ○ •

Visual Check: **Déus, Déum**

39. _____s, vēritátem √ ★ ○ •

Visual Check: **vēritās, vēritátem**

40. ___, vírum √ ★ ○ •

Visual Check: **vír, vírum**

41. _____s, elephántum √ ★ ○ •

Visual Check: **elephántus, elephántum**

42. ___s, díem √ ★ ○ •

Visual Check: **díes, díem**

43. ma__s, mánum √ ★ ○ •

Visual Check: **mánus, mánum**

44. Here are the nouns lined up in column form with the signals {-s} and {-m} set off by a vertical line:

Dictionary Meaning	Structural Meaning
diē	S
die	M
Deu	S
Deu	M
manu	S
manu	M
vesti	S
veste	M
elephántu	S
elephántu	M

[We will mark where the accent falls only when we think you might be in doubt.]

To the *left* of the line we have the "stem" of the word, the part that carries the "dictionary meaning" of the word. To the *right* of the line we have the sounds **-s** and **-m**, which are the structural signals which tell whether the word is _____ or _____.

A: subject   object.

45. Let us now arrange two other words in column form in the same way:

vir	
viru	M
dátor	
datóre	M

To the *left* of the line we have the stem of the word that carries the _____ meaning of the word.

A: dictionary

---

310. "Quālem faciem habet fēmina?" (blandus) "Bland__ faci__ h_____." √ ★ ○ •

Cōnfirmātiō: **Blandam faciem habet.**

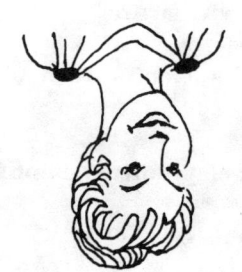

311. Write the paradigm of **blanda faciēs**.

Respōnsum: **blanda faciēs**
blandam faciem
blandā faciē

312. "Quālis spēs in faciē est?" (bonus) "_____ in _____." √ ★ ○ •

Cōnfirmātiō: **Bona spēs in faciē est.**

313. Diēs is a word of wide meaning. It means the light of day, light itself, and the 24-hour period that we call "day." In Vēritātem diēs aperit it means "_____."

A: time.

314. We will use diēs now in the sense of "day"; with this meaning it is feminine gender. "Quālis diēs est?" "Inc___ d___." √ ★ ○ •

Cōnfirmātiō: **Incerta diēs est.**

5-7

46. To the *right* of the line we have the signal of the "structural meaning" that tells whether the words are _____ or _____.

A: subject   object.

47. In the word **datōreM**, the *first* part of the word (**datōre-**) indicates the _____ meaning of the word, which is "giver."

A: dictionary

48. In the word **datōreM**, the *last* part of the word, the {**-m**}, indicates the _____ meaning of the word.

A: structural

49. The structural meaning of the {**-m**} is "_____ of the sentence."

A: object

50. In the word **virum**, the **viru-** part shows the _____ meaning of the word, and the {**-m**} part shows the _____ meaning.

A: dictionary
            structural

51. Let us look at our last two words again.

vir	
viru	M
dator	
datōre	M

It is clear that the sound that shows object form is the same as in all the words we have had before; it is the sound ___.

A: **-m**.

---

306. And to agree in case with the question word **quālem?**, both **bonus** and **effigiēs** must be _____ case.

A: accusative (The nouns in this sequence are all feminine gender.)

307. "Quālem effigiem videt vir?" (bonus)
"Bo____ eff____ v____ v____."
● ○ ★ ∧

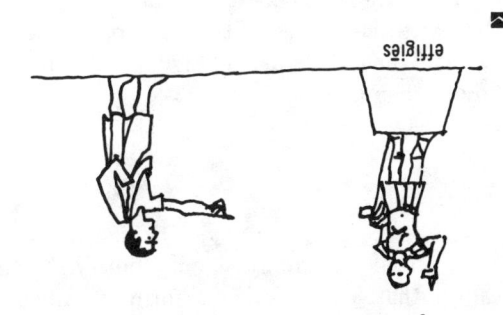

Cōnfirmātiō: Bonam effigiem videt vir.

308. "Quō locō est quercus?" (medius)
"Me____ pl____."
● ○ ★ ∧

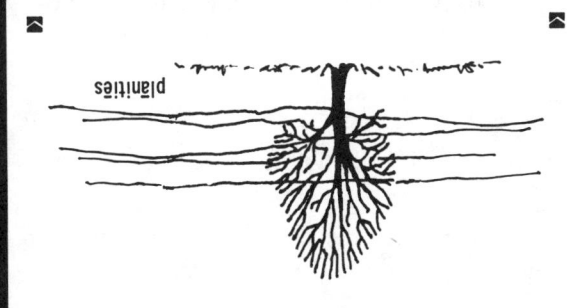

Cōnfirmātiō: Mediā plānitiē est.

309. "Quō locō est elephantus?" (medius)
"M____."
● ○ ★ ∧

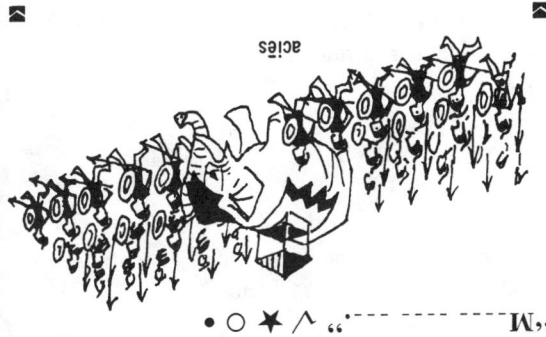

Cōnfirmātiō: Mediā aciē est.

13-56

5-8

52. But what is the signal on the *right hand* side of the line to show subject form in the forms **vir** and **dator**? There is _____ on the right hand side of the line.

A: nothing

53. Therefore, "nothing" on the right hand side of the line is the new variant signal that shows that **vir** is the _____ form.

A: subject

54. And the signal that shows that **dator** is the subject form is "_____" on the right hand side of the line.

A: nothing

55. To express the concept of "nothing" in mathematics we use the term z____.

A: zero.

56. In English we use the signal {-s} on most nouns to mean "more than one." However, in the sentence "I saw two sheep," the word "sheep" has the variant signal ____ to show "more than one."

A: zero

57. The new variant signal "nothing" which shows that **vir** is subject form is called the variant signal ____.

A: zero.

58. The signal which shows that **dator** is subject form is also the variant signal ____.

A: zero.

---

301. This picture illustrates the saying, "head over heels in love." But look at the picture. His ____ are over his ____.

A: heels head.

302. ★ ○ ● **bona spēs**
bonam spem
bonā spē

303. Write the paradigm of **bona spēs**.

Respōnsum: **bona spēs**
bonam spem
bonā spē

304. ★ ○ ● **magna aciēs**
magn-- aci--
magn-- aci--

Cōnfirmātiō: **magna aciēs**
magnam aciem
magnā aciē

Now for **quālis**? questions on feminine Fifth Declension nouns. Answer with the adjective that is given in parenthesis, and the appropriate Fifth Declension noun. The frames will look like this:

"Quālem effigiem videt vir?" (**bonus**)

305. Note that we give the masculine nominative form (**bonus**) of the adjective; to make it agree in gender with **effigiēs**, you must transform it to _____ gender.

A: feminine

5-9

59. The *old* variant signal for subject, as in **diēs**, was the sound ___.

A: -s.

60. In other words, Latin nouns may have either of *two* signals to show subject form: they have either the old variant -s or they have the new v_____ s_____ z____.

A: variant signal zero.

61. Therefore the signal for subject, which we represent by the symbol {-s}, may either have the old variant __, or it may have the new variant signal ____.

A: -s
         zero.

62. The symbol {-s} therefore stands for *any* form that indicates the _____ of the sentence.

A: subject

63. The subject may end either in the sound __ or in the _____ _____ ____.

A: -s   variant signal zero.

64. Therefore the *symbol* {-s} stands either for the sound __ or for _____.

A: -s   the variant signal zero.

65. You must not make the mistake of assuming that the sound -s is the "real" signal for {-s} simply because they happen to use the same letter. Since you have learned the -s signal for the Latin subject, we have referred to zero as a _____ signal.

A: variant

---

297. "Quantō morsū mūs quaeritur?"
"_____" ^ ★ ○ •

298. Fifth Declension nouns are all feminine, except that *diēs* is sometimes feminine and sometimes masculine. We agree that this seems silly, but there are a *few* Latin nouns which are sometimes one gender and sometimes another _____.

A: gender.

Cōnfirmātiō: **Magnō morsū quaeritur.**

299. One of the greatest mistakes that the beginner can make is to assume that a foreign language will be "logical." He believes his own language to be "logical" because he has grown up with it. He is quite unaware of the l____ of logic and consistency in his own language.

A: lack

300. English isn't "logical" either. For example, we say, "I put on my shoes and stockings." As a matter of fact you don't put on your shoes first and *then* your stockings; you put on first your _____ and then your _____.

A: stockings   shoes.

13-54

66. However, perhaps it will be clearer if we refer to -s as being the *old* variant signal and zero as being the ___ variant signal.

A: new

67. The only two words which you know at present that have the new variant signal zero instead of the old signal -s to show subject form are the words ___ and _____.

A: vir   dator.

68. The {-s} which shows that **vir** is subject form is not the sound -s but the new _____.

A: signal zero.

69. The {-s} which shows that **dator** is subject form is _____.

A: zero.

70. When we look at the contrasting pair **vir** and **viruM**, we see that the vowel _ has disappeared in the subject form.

A: u

71. When we look at the contrasting pair **dator** and **datōreM**, we see that in the subject form the vowel **e** has also _____ed.

A: disappeared.

72. The first signal for subject you learned, as in **vestis** was the sound ___.

A: -s.

73. In the subject form **vir**, zero is the ___ signal for {-s}.

A: new

74. In **vestis** the signal {-s} is __, but in **vir** the signal {-s} is ____.

A: -s
   zero.

75-76. To remind you that the signal for subject in **vir** and **dator** is not the sound -s but the new signal zero, for a while we will write the zero signal using the symbol [Ø]. Echo your teacher as he pronounces these subject forms.

75. ★ ○ • ○ • virØ   76. ★ ○ • ○ • datorØ
    [The zero, of course, is not pronounced.]

77. Pronounce the subject and object forms of the word for "man" and check. virØ
    viruM √ ★ ○ •

78. The signal for subject in **virØ** is _____. [In your own words.]

A: Ø (or zero variant).

79. The signal for object in **viruM** is ___.

A: -m.

80. The {-s} (signal for subject) in **datorØ** is _____. [Print the signal]

A: Ø.

5-11

Leave the {-s} out of the answer. As usual, if you do not understand both the question and the answer, ask your classroom teacher for help.

In this sequence your teacher will ask you about a step (**gradus**), a lake (**lacus**), a bite (**morsus**), or a jump (**saltus**). You are to answer that it is BIG, using some form of the paradigm of
         m
         f
         n
magnus, magna, magnum.

A: big (large, etc.)

291. The question word adjective **Quantus?**
     f
     n
     m
Quanta?, Quantum? means "how ___?"

290. Echo the forms of a new Fourth Declension noun meaning "jump."
★ ○ • **saltus**
         saltum
         saltū

Respōnsum: magnus lacus
               magnum lacum
               magnō lacū

[If you made an error it means you did not repeat the paradigm often enough in the frame before.]

289. Write the paradigm of **magnus lacus**.

★ ○ • magnus lacus
      magnum lacum
      magnō lacū

288. *Almost* all Fourth Declension nouns are masculine. They are therefore modified by masculine adjectives like **magnus**, which belongs to the Second Declension. Notice that noun and adjective do *not* rhyme in the ablative.

13-52

5-12

81. The signal for {-s} in **vestis** is ___.

A: -s.

82. The signal {-s} in the form **datorØ**, however, is _____.

A: Ø (or zero).

83. **Elephantus** has the subject signal ___.

A: -s.

84. ★ ○ • **datorØ**
    datōrem
Write the symbol which shows that **datorØ** is subject form. _____

A: Ø

85. ★ ○ • **virØ**
    virum
The symbol which shows that **vir** is subject is _____.

A: Ø.

86. From now on, in an {-s -m -t} sentence, an {-s} may either stand for a word which ends in the sound -s (like **DeuS**, **vestiS**, **vēritāS**), or for a word which has zero, like ___Ø, or _____Ø.

A: virØ
datorØ.

87. When we wish to show "any subject form" (whether signalled by the variant -s or the variant Ø) we will use -s surrounded by braces like this: {-s}. Copy this symbol. _____

A: {-s}

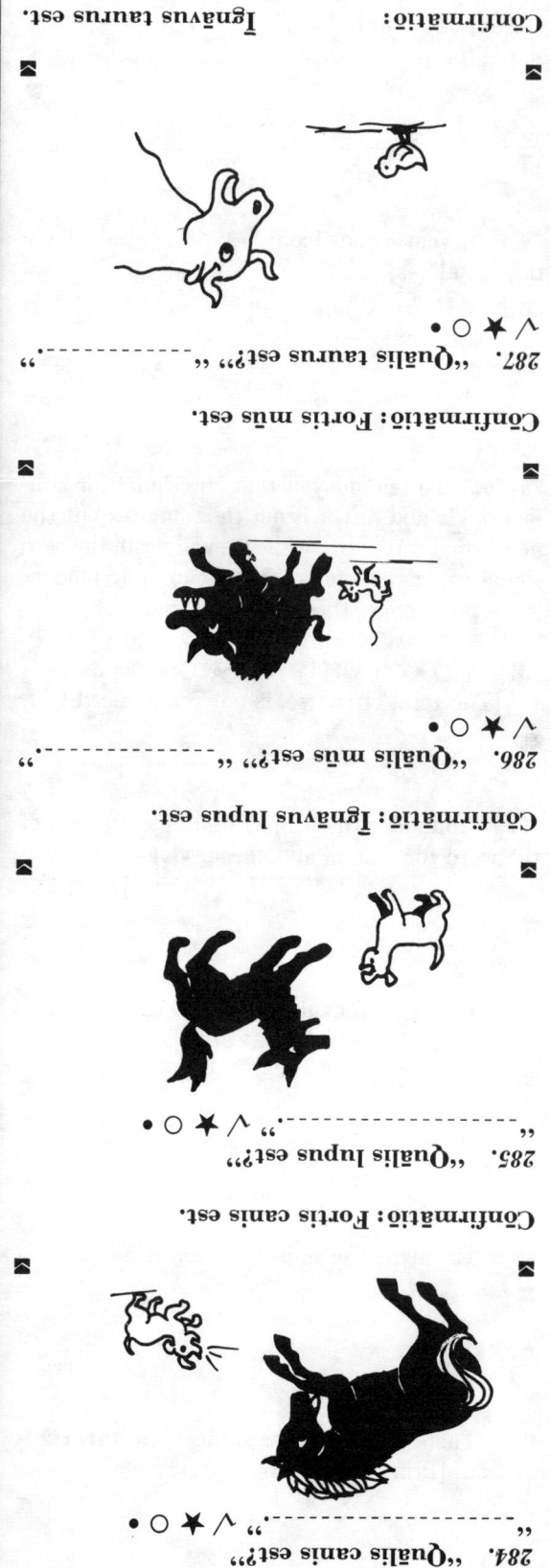

---

284. "Quālis canis est?" ∨ ★ ○ • "_____."
Cōnfirmātiō: Fortis canis est.

285. "Quālis lupus est?" ∨ ★ ○ • "_____."
Cōnfirmātiō: Ignāvus lupus est.

286. "Quālis mūs est?" ∨ ★ ○ • "_____."
Cōnfirmātiō: Fortis mūs est.

287. "Quālis taurus est?" ∨ ★ ○ • "_____."
Cōnfirmātiō: Ignāvus taurus est.

13-51

88. The symbol {-s} stands for "any _____."

A: subject form.

89. Rewrite **vir** by adding the special symbol that stands for zero: **vir_**.

A: virØ.

90. Rewrite **dator** by adding the special symbol that shows it is the {-s} form: _____.

A: datorØ.

91. In **Deus**, the signal is __; in **dator** the signal is the ____.

A: -s Ø.

92. Note that not only does **datorØ** have the new signal zero, but the vowel **-e-** which appeared in **datōrem** has _____ed in the subject form.

A: disappeared

93. Write the subject forms of **datōrem** and **virum**, using the symbol that shows the subject form. _____ _____

A: virØ datorØ

94. Echo the subject and object of the word for "mouse." ★ ○ • ○ • mūsØ
    mūreM
The signal at the end of the word **mūsØ** which shows you it is subject form is ____.

A: Ø (zero).

Describe these animals as brave or cowardly, according to the picture. Check your answer with the tape.

280. "Estne aper fortis an ignāvus?"
"_____ ap__ est." ∨ ★ ○ •

Cōnfirmātiō: Ignāvus aper est.

281. Ignāvus aper est =
It's a _____.

A: It's a cowardly boar.

282. "Estne vir fortis an ignāvus?"
"_____." ∨ ★ ○ •

Cōnfirmātiō: Ignāvus vir est.

283. "Quālis equus est?"
"_____." ∨ ★ ○ •

Cōnfirmātiō: Ignāvus equus est.

5-13

13-50

95. All languages have restrictions on where sounds may occur. One restriction in Latin is that the sound s does not occur as a single consonant between two vowels in any native Latin word. Where we would expect s we find r instead. We would expect that the object form of mūsØ would be *mūsem (the asterisk shows that this is an imaginary form), but because Latin s between vowels changes to r, we find that the object form of mūsØ is actually _____.

A: mūrem.

96. The sound s does not occur as a single consonant in Latin between v____s.

A: vowels.

97. Where we would expect an s, as in *mūsem, a single s between vowels changes to the sound ____.

A: r.

98. Because the subject form is mūsØ, we would have expected that the object form would have been *mūsem, but the object form of mūs is actually m____m.

A: mūrem.

99. The asterisk [*] means that *mūseM is an _____ form.

A: imaginary

---

274. "Quālis simia est?" "____s." ∧ "____" ★ ○ •

Cōnfirmātiō: Simia blanda est.

275. Except for the neuter nouns (like vitium), *almost* all Second Declension nouns are modified in the nominative by bonus, in the accusative by bonum, and in the ablative by bonō. Therefore *almost* all Second Declension nouns except neuters are _____ gender.

A: masculine

276. Echo the nominative forms of the adjective "brave." m & f n fortis forte ★ ○ • ○ •

277. Echo the nominative forms of the adjective "cowardly." m f n ignāvus ignāva ignāvum ★ ○ • ○ •

278. The adjective fortis, forte belongs to the ____ (1/2/3/4/5) Declension.

A: 3

279. The adjective ignāvus, ignāva, ignāvum belongs to the ____ (1/2/3/4/5) Declensions.

A: 1 and 2

100. The combination -ts *never* occurs at the end of a Latin word. Therefore the subject form of vēritāteM is not *vēritātS but _____.

A: vēritāS.

101. Because of the asterisk you know that *vēritāts is an _____-y word.

A: imaginary

102. Back to some review. In English the position of the words in a sentence is one of the most important structural signals in the language. As speakers of English you have all learned to respond to the signals of position. Signals of position are ____ (English/Latin) signals.

A: English

103. Because you are used to responding to the position of words in English, the position of words in Latin will mislead you at first. In learning Latin you must therefore learn to _____ the signals of position.

A: ignore (disregard, etc.)

104. To identify the subject and object of a Latin sentence you must _____ the position of the words and observe the Latin signals of {__} and {__}.

A: ignore
{-s} {-m}.

105. We will give you practice on this now.
    ElephantuM mūsØ =
The _____ blanks the _____.

A: The mouse blanks the elephant.

106. **Mūs∅ elephantuM =**
....

A: The mouse blanks the elephant.

107. **Elephantus mūrem =**
....

A: The elephant blanks the mouse.

108. **Elephantum mūs∅ =**
....

A: The mouse blanks the elephant.

109. **Mūrem elephantus =**
....

A: The elephant blanks the mouse.

110. Pronounce and check. **Elephantus nōn capit mūrem.** √ ★ ○ •

111. We will now make two changes in this Basic Sentence, but we will leave the word order the same. We will change **elephantuS** to **elephantuM**. **ElephantuM** will now be the _____ of the sentence.

A: object

112. We will change **mūreM** to **mūs∅**. **Mūs∅** will now be the _____ of this changed sentence.

A: subject

---

267. "Estne simia crūdēlis an blanda?" "S_____." √ ★ ○ •

Cōnfirmātiō: Simia blanda est.

268. "Estne rāna crūdēlis an blanda?" "R_____." √ ★ ○ •

Cōnfirmātiō: Rāna crūdēlis est.

269. "Estne simia crūdēlis an blanda?" "S_____." √ ★ ○ •

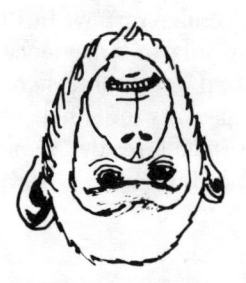

Cōnfirmātiō: Simia crūdēlis est.

270. "Estne rāna crūdēlis an blanda?" "R_____." √ ★ ○ •

Cōnfirmātiō: Rāna blanda est.

5-17

113. However, we will leave the *order* of the words in the sentence unchanged. Our new sentence (with a different subject and a different object) now looks like this: **ElephantuM nōn capiT mūsØ**. Does the sentence still mean, "An elephant doesn't catch a mouse," or does it now mean, "A mouse doesn't catch an elephant"?

A: A mouse doesn't catch an elephant. (And it's true, too.)

114. Give both the dictionary meaning and the structural meaning. Pronounce the Latin.
HilariS datorØ = The ch_____ g____ blanks.

A: The cheerful giver blanks.

115. MūsØ = The m____ blanks.

A: The mouse blanks.

116. VēritāS = Tr___ blanks.

A: Truth blanks.

117. DeuM = Somebody blanks ____.

A: Somebody blanks God.

118. Lavat = Somebody w____es something.

A: Somebody washes something.

119. Manum = Somebody _____s a h____.

A: Somebody blanks a hand.

13-46

There are some general rules which enable you to predict probably ninety per cent of the genders. There are about 30 neuter nouns in this first year, and you will be drilled on them until you know them. But how do you tell which nouns are masculine and which are feminine? There are two ways to tell.

First, you can usually predict the gender of a noun by the declension to which it belongs.

264. Almost all First Declension and all Fifth Declension nouns (with one exception) are feminine gender. Almost all Second Declension nouns (except the neuters of course) and almost all Fourth Declension nouns are masculine gender. Therefore the only declension which offers any problem is the _____ Declension.

A: Third

The next sequence will give you practice in using the right adjective with First Declension nouns.

In this sequence you will be asked whether certain people and animals are kind **(blanda)** or cruel **(crūdēlis)**. To decide, observe their actions or their expressions.

265. We have chosen these antonyms because **crūdēlis** is a ____ (1st/2d/3d) Declension adjective, while **blanda** is a ____ (1st/2d/3d) Declension adjective.

A: 3d 1st

266. "Estne fēmina crūdēlis an blanda?"

"F_____t." ∧ ✱ ○ •

Cōnfirmātiō: Fēmina crūdēlis est.

5-18

120. **Diem** = Somebody _____ _____.

A: Somebody blanks time.

121. **Elephantum** =
_____ blanks an _____.

A: Somebody blanks an elephant.

122. **Aperit** = S_____ dis____s _____.

A: Somebody (or something) discloses somebody (or something).

123. **Capit** = _____ c____s _____.

A: Somebody catches somebody.

124. **VirØ** = The ___ _____.

A: The man blanks.

125. **Dīligit** = _____ l__s _____.

A: Somebody loves somebody.

126. **Reddit** = _____ m___s _____.

A: Somebody makes something.

127. **VesteM** = _____ _____ the _____.

A: Somebody blanks the clothes.

The question which has surely been in the back of your mind is how to know *which one* of the three forms of **pūrus** to use to modify a noun.

Cōnfirmātiō: Ā fonte pūrō pūra dēfluit aqua. (35)

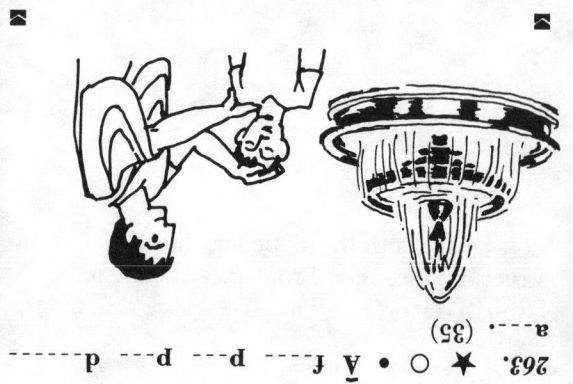

263. ✱ ○ • Ā f_____ p_____ p_____ p_____ a____. (35)

Cōnfirmātiō: Habet suum venēnum blanda ōrātiō. (34)

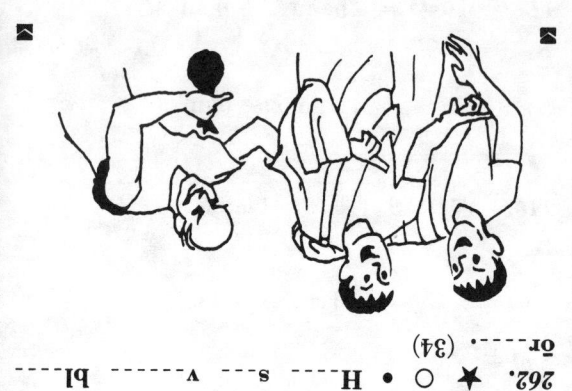

262. ✱ ○ • H_____ s____ v_____ bl_____ or____. (34)

Cōnfirmātiō: Rem nōn spem, factum nōn dictum, quaerit amīcus. (33)

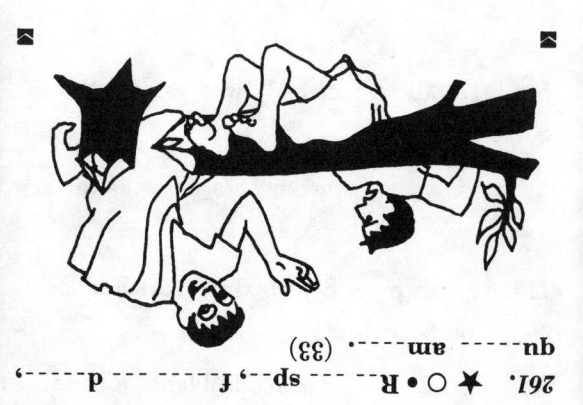

261. ✱ ○ • R_____ sp____, f_____ d_____, qu_____ am____. (33)

13-45

5-19

128-135. In your Reference Notebook, in the section marked "Latin Forms," copy these eight pairs of words in the space marked "Item #1." Print the signals in big letters.

128.	129.	130.	131.
virØ	manuS	mūsØ	vestiS
viruM	manuM	mūreM	vesteM

132.	133.	134.	135.
datorØ	vēritāS	diēS	DeuS
datōreM	vēritāteM	dieM	DeuM

We will now practice combining these words into three word sentences. We will build up these sentences one word at a time. In giving the English equivalents, show subject and object by position, using the colorless verb "blanks." Pronounce the Latin aloud.

136. Vēritātem = _____ s the _____.

A. Somebody blanks the truth.

137. Vēritātem Deus = ___ _____ ___ _____.

A: God blanks the truth.

138. Pronounce and check. Vēritātem Deus aperit. √ ★ ○ •

139. Vēritātem Deus aperit = _____ _____.

A: God discloses the truth.

140. Now for a second {-s -m -t} sentence. Lavat = S_____y w____s s_____g.

A: Somebody washes something (or somebody).

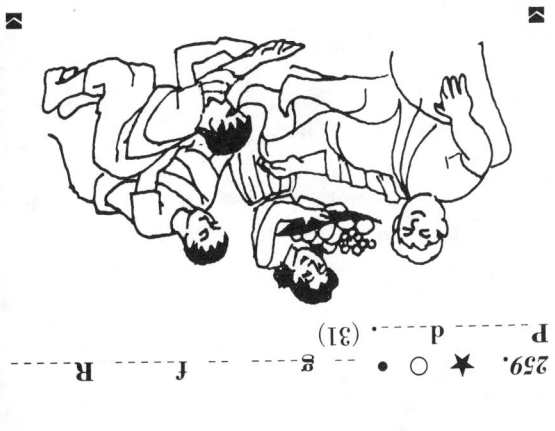

5-20

141. Since you have been told that this is a three-word {-s -m -t} sentence, the next word must be either the _____ or the _____ of **lavat**.

A: subject   object

142. **Lavat virØ** = The ___ ___s _____.

A: The man washes something.

143. Pronounce and check. **Lavat virØ vestem.** ✓ ★ ○ •

144. **Lavat virØ vestem.** = _____ _____.

A: The man washes the clothes.

145. Here is another three-word sentence presented one word at a time. **VirØ** = _____ _____.

A: The man blanks.

146. **VirØ mūrem** = _____ _____.

A: The man blanks a mouse.

147. Pronounce and check. **VirØ mūrem capit.** ✓ ★ ○ •

148. **VirØ mūrem capit** = _____ _____.

A: The man catches a mouse.

13-43

252. From a pure spring flows pure water = Ā f____ p____ p____ d____ a____.

Respōnsum: Ā fonte pūrō pūra dēfluit aqua.

[You should be able to guess the meaning of the new adjective, impūrus, impūra, impūrum.]

Question and Answer Drill

253. "Quālis aqua dēfluit ā fonte impūrō?" "_____ _____."
(Auxilium sub hāc līneā est.)

Auxilium: Quālis aqua dēfluit ā fonte impūrō, pūra an impūra?

Respōnsum: Impūra aqua.

254. "Quālī ā fonte dēfluit aqua impūra?" "_____ - _____."

Respōnsum: Impūrō ā fonte.

255. "Quālem aquam habet fōns pūrus?" "_____ _____."

Respōnsum: Pūram.

256. "Quālis fōns aquam pūram habet?" "_____ _____."

Respōnsum: Pūrus fōns.

257. "Quālem aquam habet fōns impūrus?" "_____ _____."

Respōnsum: Impūram aquam.

5-21

149. Now give an English meaning when you see *two* nouns. **VirØ manum** = The ___ ___s the ___.

A: The man blanks the hand.

150. **VirØ manum capit.** √ ★ ○ •

151. **VirØ manum capit** = _____ .

A: The man catches the hand.

152. **Elephantum mūsØ** = _____ .

A: The mouse blanks the elephant.

153. **ElephantuM mūsØ dīligiT.** √ ★ ○ • = _____ .

A: The mouse loves the elephant. Why not? Elephants are lovable animals.

154. Now *write* the Latin for these same {-s -m -t} sentences. Check to make sure there is a subject and object in each sentence. The man catches the mouse = **V__Ø m____ c____.** [Write the signals in large letters.]

A: **VirØ mūrem capit.**

155. The man washes the clothes = **L____ v__Ø v_____ .**

A: **Lavat virØ vestem.**

---

247. Or, from a good school come ___ .

A: ___ graduates.

248. • **fōns pūrus** ★ ○ • fontem pūrum fonte pūrō

249. • **aqua pūra** ★ ○ • aquam pūram aquā pūrā

[Repeat until you have learned these paradigms]

250. It is obvious from the adjectives that the words **fōns** and **aqua** belong to different ___ .

A: genders.

251. Say the paradigm of **vīnum pūrum**. √ ★ ○ •

___ ___
___ ___
___ ___

Cōnfirmātiō: vīnum pūrum
vīnum pūrum
vīnō pūrō

13-42

5-22

156. God discloses the truth = V_____
D___ a_____.

A: **Vēritātem
Deus aperit.**

157. The mouse loves the elephant =
E_____ m__Ø d_____.

A: **Elephantum mūsØ dīligit.**

158. The man catches the hand = V__Ø
m____ c_____.

A: **VirØ
manum capit.**

159. Describe the next three pictures, which show new situations, and check your answers with the tape. [Visual checks below the line.]

MūsØ v_____ lavaT. √ ★ ○ •

Visual Check: **MūsØ vesteM lavaT.**

160. El_____ lavaT virØ. √ ★ ○ •

Visual Check: **ElephantuM lavaT virØ.**

---

241. Write your teacher's description of this picture. ★ ○ ○ **Ā f_____ d_____ a__.**

fōns

Cōnfirmātiō: **Ā fonte dēfluit aqua.**

242. In Latin, the word **fōns** can mean either a _____ or a _____.

A: fountain   spring.

243. Pronounce and check. **Ā fonte pūrō pūrā dēfluit aqua.** √ ★ ○ • [Did you remember to pronounce *first* and check with the tape *second*?]

244. This means that a _____ s_____ _____.

A: from a pure spring flows pure water.

245. Copy Basic Sentence 35 and its English meaning in your Reference Notebook.

246. While it is true that an unpolluted water reservoir furnishes safe drinking water, the poetical meaning of this Basic Sentence is that from good parents come _____ _____ _____.

A: good children.

13-41

5-23

161. CapiT manuS mū----. ✓ ★ ○ •

Visual Check: CapiT manuS mūreM.

162. Now write the description of these same three pictures, writing the signals in large letters.

M‗‗Ø v‗‗‗‗‗ l‗‗‗‗.

A: MūsØ vesteM lavaT.

163. Write. E‗‗‗‗‗‗‗‗‗ l‗‗‗‗ v‗‗Ø.

A: ElephantuM lavaT virØ.

164. C‗‗‗‗ ma‗‗‗ mū‗‗‗.

A: CapiT manuS mūreM.

13-40

235. "Quālis vir blandā ōrātiōne nōn capitur?" "‗‗‗‗‗."

Respōnsum: Sapiēns.

236. "Quālī ōrātiōne vir stultus capitur?" "‗‗‗‗‗."

Respōnsum: Blandā ōrātiōne.

237. "Quō vir sapiēns nōn capitur?" "‗‗‗‗‗."

Respōnsum: Blandā ōrātiōne.

238. ★ ○ • ○ • Ā f‗‗‗‗ p‗‗‗ dēfl‗‗‗ aq‗‗‗.

Cōnfirmātiō: Ā fonte pūrō pūrā dēfluit aqua. (35)

239. Echo your teacher's description of this picture. ★ ○ • ○ • Ā f‗‗‗‗ dē‗‗‗‗ aq‗‗‗.

Cōnfirmātiō: Ā fonte dēfluit aqua.

240. Ā fonte dēfluit aqua means that ‗‗‗‗‗ is ‗‗‗‗ing from a f‗‗‗‗‗‗.

A: water is flowing from a fountain.

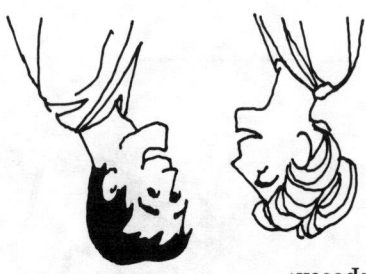

165. All our sentences so far have had subject, object, and verb. This is by far the most common type of sentence in Latin, and we call it the {-- -- --} type of sentence.

A: {-s -m -t}

166. In this abbreviation the {-s} stands for any _____, whether it has the old signal -- or the new signal ----.

A: subject -s
 zero.

167. The {-m} stands for any _____.

A: object.

168. The {-t} in an {-s -m -t} sentence stands for the part of speech called a ____.

A: verb.

169. Echo. ★ ○ • ○ • tránsitive (If you are not using a tape recorder, look at the Visual Check below to learn the pronunciation.)

Visual Check: "trán-zit-tive"

170. The type of verb that takes an object is called a "tránsitive" verb. The verbs in our {-s -m -t} sentences are all _____ verbs.

A: tránsitive

171. In English a tránsitive verb is the kind of verb that fills the slot between two nouns. In "The girl sees the snake," the verb "sees" comes between "girl" and "snake." Therefore in this sentence the verb "sees" is a _____ verb.

A: tránsitive

(Bottom half of page is printed upside-down:)

229. The word **blanda** refers not only to people who are pleasant but also to people who *pretend* to be pleasant. Therefore let's use the phrase "smooth speech."

Habet suum venenum blanda oratio = ----

A: Smooth speech has its own poison.

230. Copy Basic Sentence 34 and this English meaning in your Reference Notebook.

Question and Answer Drill: write.

231. "Qualis oratio habet suum venenum?" "_____."

Respōnsum: Blanda.

232. "Quid habet suum venenum?" "_____."

Respōnsum: Blanda oratio.

233. "Qualem virum blanda oratio capit, sapientem an stultum?" "_____."

Respōnsum: Stultum.

234. "Qualis vir blanda oratione capitur, stultus an sapiens?" "_____."

Respōnsum: Stultus.

172. Which of these verbs can normally fill the slot between the two nouns and are therefore *tránsitive* verbs?

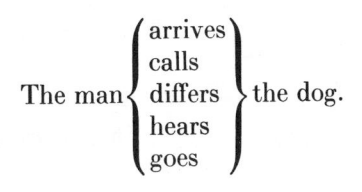

The man { arrives, calls, differs, hears, goes } the dog.

A: calls
   hears

173. Since the words "calls" and "hears" fill the slot between two nouns, they are both verbs.

A: tránsitive

174. In the English sentence "Fish swim," there is a subject and a verb but no .

A: object.

175. Echo a new technical term. ★ ○ • ○ • intransitive

Visual Check: "ín-tran-zit-tive"

176. To form a word that describes a verb like "swim" that does *not* take an object, we add the prefix "in" (which means "not") to the word "tránsitive." A verb like "swim" is an verb.

A: intransitive

177. For the present, verbs are either *tránsitive* or *íntransitive*. (There is a third type, which we will take up later, as in "The man is John.") Tell whether the verbs in the following sentences are transitive or intransitive. "The train hit the car." Since "hit" comes between two nouns ("train" and "car"), it is a verb.

A: transitive

223. The word **oratio** means not only a formal speech but also ordinary conv.

A: conversation.

224. The man is sorry now that he lost his temper. He is talking pleasantly. Find out what the woman is doing. ★ ○ ○

Confirmátio: Fémina oratiónem blandam laudat.

225. She is his plant speech.

A: praising his pleasant speech.

226. ★ ○ ○ H s v pl or. [There are four macrons]

Respónsum: Habet suum venénum blanda orátio.

227. This sentence means, "Pl has ."

A: Pleasant speech has its own poison. [Don't enter this meaning in your Notebook yet.]

228. This means that you cannot always trust a person who .

A: talks pleasantly.

5-26

178. "The fire glowed brightly." Since "glowed" does *not* come between two nouns it is an .... verb.

A: intransitive

179. "The moon shone clearly." The verb is a/an .... verb.

A: intransitive

180. "The cat purred happily." The verb is a/an .... verb.

A: intransitive

181. "The man insulted the policeman." The verb is a/an............ verb.

A: transitive

182. A transitive verb in English has a noun before it and a noun after it. An *intransitive* verb in English has a noun before it (like "Fish swim") but has ‒‒ noun after it.

A: no

183. Many verbs in English are commonly used as *either* transitive or intransitive verbs. Compare these two sentences.

    1) The girl *sees* the book.
    2) The blind girl now *sees*.

The verb "sees" in the first sentence is a/an .... verb, while the one in the second sentence is a/an .... verb.

A: transitive
       intransitive

13-37

218. **Ōrātiō** is .... case while **venēnō**, which also ends in long **ō**, is .... case.

A: nominative
    ablative

219. Write your teacher's description of this picture. ★ ○ ○ ————

220. This man was ————ing his ———— a sp————.

A: praising his friend with a speech.

221. Ask your teacher what the woman is irritated by. "Quō f———— irrītā————?" ∨ ★ ○ •

Cōnfīrmātiō: Quō fēmina irrītātur?

222. Write his answer. ★ ○ ○ "———— fēmina irrītātur."

Respōnsum: Intemperantī ōrātiōne fēmina irrītātur.

Cōnfīrmātiō: Vir amīcum suum ōrātiōne laudat.

184. The verb in "The girl sees the book" is a/an _____ verb because _____. [In your own words.]

A: transitive   it comes between two nouns.

185. The verb in "The blind girl now sees" is a/an _____ verb, because _____. [In your own words.]

A: intransitive   it does not come between two nouns.

186. In the example just given, the meaning of the verb "sees" does not change very much whether it is transitive or intransitive. But with many English verbs the meaning of the transitive verb is different from the meaning of the intransitive verb. Look at these two sentences. "The ship is sinking." (intransitive) This describes the picture labeled ____ (A/B). "The ship is sinking the rowboat." (transitive) This describes the picture labeled ____ (A/B).

Picture A

Picture B

A: Sentence 1) describes picture A.
   Sentence 2) describes picture B.

187. Identify the following verbs as transitive or intransitive. "The man ran the train." "Ran" is ____ (transitive/intransitive).

A: transitive.

---

213. We will now take up the meaning of the new words. Write your teacher's description of this pathetic scene. ★ ○ ○ ————. [If you have no tape recorder, study the answer.]

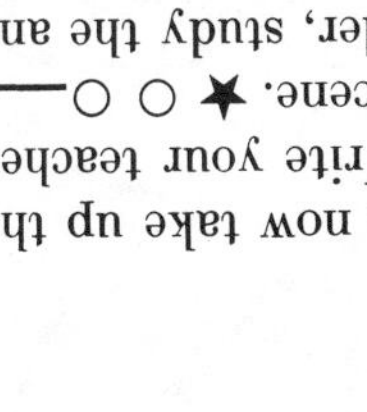

Cōnfirmātiō: Vipera aprum venēnō necat.

214. Find out why the doctor doesn't want the patient to drink the wine. ★ ○ ○

Cōnfirmātiō: Venēnum in vīnō est!

215. It turns out that the doctor believes that there is poi--- in the wine.

A: poison

216. ★ ○ • venēnum   venēnum
                   venēnum
                   venēnō

217. ★ ○ • ōrātiō   ōrātiō
                   ōrātiōnem
                   ōrātiōne

13-36

188. "The train ran quickly." "Ran" is ____ (transitive/intransitive).

A: intransitive.

189. "The girl dropped the cup." "Dropped" is ____.

A: transitive.

190. "The cup dropped." The verb is ____.

A: intransitive.

191. "The clock stopped when it was filled with dust." The verb is ____.

A: intransitive.

192. "The dust stopped the clock from running." The verb is ____.

A: transitive.

193. "This cloth will tear easily." The verb is ____.

A: intransitive.

194. "Will the dog bite?" The verb is ____.

A: intransitive.

195. "Will the dog bite the postman?" The verb is ____.

A: transitive.

---

207. "Quid amicus nōn quaerit?" "____ et ____."

Respōnsum: Spem et dictum.

208. "Dīligitne amīcus hilarem datōrem?"

Respōnsum: Dīligit.

209. "Quālem datōrem dīligit amīcus?"

Respōnsum: Hilarem.

210. "Dīligiturne hilaris dator ab amīcō?"

Respōnsum: Dīligitur.

211. "Quālis dator ab amīcō dīligitur?"

Respōnsum: Hilaris.

[If you had any trouble answering these questions, go back to the beginning of this sequence and try them again.]

212. ★ ○ • ○ • H____ s____m v____ēnum bl____ or____. (34)

Confirmātiō: *Habet suum venēnum blanda ōrātiō.* (34)

[If you can figure out the meaning, fine. Write it down in your Answer Pad and check later to see if you were right.]

5-29

196. "Bite" is transitive in "Will the dog bite the postman?" because it comes between _____.

A: two nouns.

197. "Bite" is intransitive in "Will the dog bite?" because _____. [In your own words.]

A: it does *not* come between two nouns.

198. Latin too has intransitive verbs. An intransitive verb in Latin has no {-m}, that is, it has no object. Echo. ★ ○ • ○ • **MūsØ curriT.**

199. **MūsØ curriT** means "The _____ is ru_____."

A: The mouse is running.

200. Describe this picture in two words.

M__Ø cur___.

A: **MūsØ curriT.**

13-34

199. "Quaeritne amīcus dictum an factum?" "___."
Respōnsum: **Factum.**

200. "Quis factum quaerit?" "___."
Respōnsum: **Amīcus.**

201. "Quaeritne ab amīcō rēs an spēs?" "___."
Respōnsum: **Rēs.**

202. "Quaeritne amīcus rem an spem?" "___."
Respōnsum: **Rem.**

203. "Quaeritne amīcus factum an dictum?" "___."
Respōnsum: **Factum.**

204. "Quid quaeritur ab amīcō, dictum an factum?" "___."
Respōnsum: **Factum.**

205. "Ā quō factum quaeritur?" "___."
Respōnsum: **Ab amīcō.**

206. "Quid amīcus quaerit?" "___ et ___."
Respōnsum: **Rem et factum.**

201. Because there is no {-m}, **curriT** is ____ (a transitive verb/an intransitive verb).

A: an intransitive verb.

202. The symbol for a sentence that contains subject, object and *transitive* verb is {-s -m -t}. The symbol for a sentence that contains a subject and an *intransitive* verb is the same as {-s -m -t} except that we omit the {-m}. The symbol for the type of sentence represented by **MūsØ currit** is therefore {__ __}.

A: {-s -t}.

203. An {-s -t} sentence contains a _____ and an _____ verb.

A: subject
         intransitive

204. The verb in an {-s -t} type of sentence is an _____ verb.

A: intransitive

205. But the verb in an {-s -m -t} type of sentence is a _____ verb.

A: transitive

206. Since there is no {-m}, we know that **MūsØ curriT** is an {__ __} type of sentence.

A: {-s -t}

207. The only intransitive Latin verb you know now is the verb c____T.

A: **curriT**.

5-31

208-211. Now for a new type of exercise. We will give you the Latin names of four kinds of people and animals who are running. Chorus as your teacher describes these four pictures.

208. snake **209.** bull **210.** dog **211.** old lady

★○○●● ★○○●● ★○○●● ★○○●●
Vípera∅ TaúruS CániS ÁnuS
curriT. curriT. curriT. curriT.

Referring to the list if you need, say aloud the correct title for each picture and check.

AnuS currit.
TauruS currit.
CaniS currit
Vīpera∅ currit.

212. √ ★ ○ •

Visual Check: **TauruS currit.**

213. √ ★ ○ •

Visual Check: **AnuS currit.**

214. √ ★ ○ •

Visual Check: **CaniS currit.**

13-32

185. ★ ○ • **dictum** ("talk.")
dictum
dictō

186. Write the paradigm of dictum.

Respōnsum: dictum
dictum
dictō

187. ★ ○ ○ R— n— sp—.

Respōnsum: Rem nōn spem.

188. **Rem and spem are both** ———— **case.**

A: accusative

189. **Rem and spem must be the {--} of an** {------} **sentence.**

A. {-m-} {-s-m-t}

190. **Rem and spem are antonyms: something blanks rem but it does not blank** ————.

Respōnsum: spem.

191. ★ ○ • **spēs** ("hope") 5th
spem   Declension
spē

192. However, **rēs** has a wide range of meanings. In the first place, it covers much of the territory that the English word "thing" includes. Then too, you know that the expression **in omni rē** means "in every s————."

A: situation.

5-32

215. √ ★ ○ •

Visual Check: **VīperaØ currit.**

This time, without using the list unless you find you have to, describe these same pictures.

216. C___s currit. √ ★ ○ •

Visual Check: **Canis currit.**

217. Vīp___Ø currit. √ ★ ○ •

Visual Check: **VīperaØ currit.**

218. An__ currit. √ ★ ○ •

Visual Check: **Anus currit.**

219. Tau___ currit. √ ★ ○ •

Visual Check: **Taurus currit.**

13-31

179. Which of these forms are the ambiguous nominative or accusative form?

 aure facile flūmine crūdēle

A: facile crūdēle

180. Which of these forms are the same case as facile?

 crūdēle hilare veste vulpe laude

A: crūdēle hilare

181. Which of these forms are nominative-accusative neuter?

 orbe jūdice quāle omne hilare facile

A: quāle omne hilare facile

182. ★ ○ • ○ • Rem nōn ___, f___ nōn d___, qu___ am___. (33)

183. ★ ○ • factum factum ("action") factō

Cōnfīrmātiō: Rem nōn spem, factum nōn dictum, quaerit amīcus. (33)

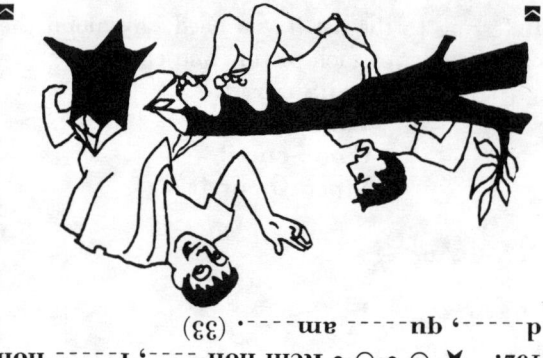

184. This new word is a ___ (1st/2d/3d/4th/5th) Declension ___ noun.

A: 2d neuter

5-33

220. Echo the Latin for "It is a dog." ★ ○ • ○ •
CaniS esT.

221-224. Here are the Latin names of four new animals. Chorus the titles of these pictures, using the intransitive verb **esT**.

221.	222.	223.	224.
fly	eagle	boar	fox

★○○○◉ ★○○○◉ ★○○○◉ ★○○○◉
MuscaØ esT. **AquilaØ esT.** **AperØ esT.** **VulpēS esT.**

[If you are not using a tape recorder ask your teacher to pronounce these new Latin words.]

Referring to the list if you need, say aloud the correct title for each picture and check.

> **MuscaØ est.**
> **AperØ est.**
> **AquilaØ est.**
> **VulpēS est.**

225. ✓ ★ ○ •

Visual Check: **VulpēS est.** Notice how the -s of **VulpēS** is pronounced with the **est**.

226. ✓ ★ ○ •

Visual Check: **MuscaØ est.**

---

174. Write Basic Sentence 31 ★ ○ ○ **Et g___ et f___ R___ P___ d___.**

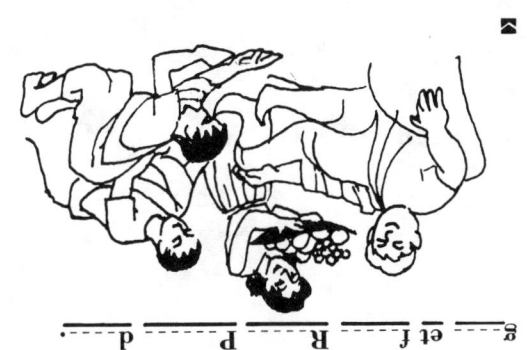

Respōnsum: **Et genus et formam Rēgīna Pecūnia dōnat.**

175. "Quāle genus pecūnia obumbrātur?" "**B___ g___.**"

Respōnsum: **Bonum genus.**

176. Write Basic Sentence 32 ★ ○ ○ **Īns___ m___ fl___ qu___ aqu___.**

Respōnsum: **Īnsānus mediō flūmine quaerit aquam.**

177. "Quālī ā virō aqua mediō flūmine quaeritur?" "**Ā v___.**"

Respōnsum: **Ā virō īnsānō.**

178. From now on you must learn to distinguish between "look-alikes," which end in the sound /e/. For example, **cane** is _____ case while **crūdēle** is _____ or _____ case.

A: nominative
accusative
ablative

13-30

227. √ ★ ○ •

Visual Check: Aquila∅ est.

228. √ ★ ○ •

Visual Check: Aper est.

229-232.   Give the title for each picture and check with the tape.

229.   Vul___ esT.   √ ★ ○ •

Visual Check: Vulpēs est.

230.   Aqu___∅ esT.   √ ★ ○ •

Visual Check: Aquila∅ est.

231.   Mu___∅ esT.   √ ★ ○ •

Visual Check: Musca∅ est.

---

168. "Quālis mēns possidet corpus sānum?" "_____ _____."

Respōnsum: Sāna mēns.

169. "Quid possidet mēns sāna?" "C_____ s_____."

Respōnsum: Corpus sānum.

We will now assume that an unhealthy body necessarily has an unhealthy mind, that is, **Mēns īnsāna in corpore īnsānō.** Answer these questions accordingly.

170. "Quālis mēns in corpore īnsānō est?" "_____ m_____."

Respōnsum: Īnsāna mēns.

171. "Quāle corpus mentem īnsānam habet?" "_____ c_____."

Respōnsum: Īnsānum corpus.

172. "Quālī in corpore est mēns īnsāna?" "_____ c_____."

Respōnsum: Īnsānō in corpore.

173. "Quāle corpus possidet mēns īnsāna?" "_____ c_____."

Respōnsum: Īnsānum corpus.

[If you do not understand any of these questions or answers, be sure to ask your teacher.]

5-35

232. Ap__Ø esT. √ ★ ○ •

▼

Visual Check: **AperØ est.**

233. Echo a new verb which means "sees."
★ ○ • ○ • videT

▼

234. In the eight pictures that follow a man sees one of these eight new people and animals. Complete the sentence by choosing the appropriate object form from the list at the right of each picture. Check your answers with the tape.

AnuM
ApruM
AquilaM
CaneM
MuscaM
TauruM
VīperaM
VulpeM

(If you have no tape recorder, use the Visual Check below.) V_____ virØ videT. √ ★ ○ •

▼

Visual Check: **Vulpem vir videt.** (Did you speak aloud?)

235. VulpeM virØ videT = ___ ___ ____ ___ ___.

▼

A: The man sees the fox.

236. Describe these pictures aloud.

Anum
Aprum
Aquilam
Canem
Muscam
Taurum
Vīperam
Vulpem

___m vir videt. √ ★ ○ •

▼

Visual Check: **Anum vir videt.**

13-28

162. Crūdēle is _____ or _____ case of the _____ gender.

▼

A: nominative or accusative neuter

163. The ablative form of crūdēle is _____.

▼

Respōnsum: crūdēlī.

164. Write Basic Sentence 30. M____ ○ ○ ★ • ○ ○ s__ __ c_____ s____.

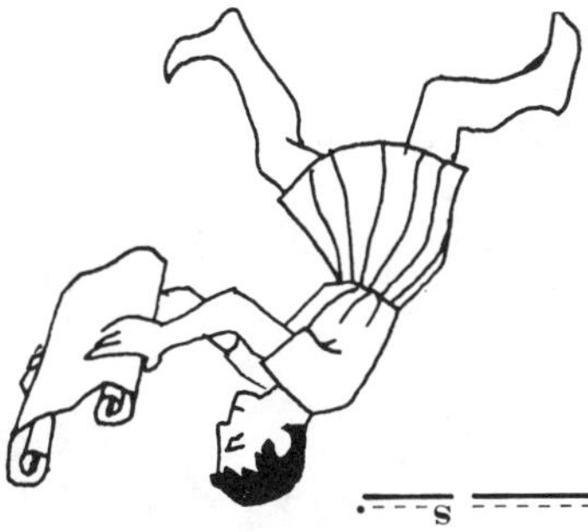

▼

Respōnsum: Mēns sāna in corpore sānō. (Macrons right?)

Question and Answer Drill

165. "Quālis mēns in corpore sānō est?" "____ m____."

▼

Respōnsum: Sāna mēns.

166. "Quālī in corpore est mēns sāna?" "_____."

▼

Respōnsum: Sānō in corpore.

167. "Quāle corpus possidet mēns sāna, sānum an īnsānum?" "_____." (Auxilium sub hāc līneā est.)

▲

Auxilium: Remember that an asks for one of the two words which it connects.

▼

Respōnsum: Sānum corpus.

5-36

237.

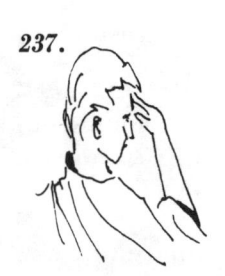

Anum
Aprum
Aquilam
Canem
Muscam
Taurum
Vīperam
Vulpem

------m v-- videt. √ ★ ○ •

Visual Check: **Vīperam vir videt.**

238.

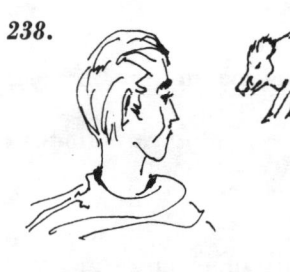

Anum
Aprum
Aquilam
Canem
Muscam
Taurum
Vīperam
Vulpem

----m v-- vid--. √ ★ ○ •

Visual Check: **Aprum vir videt.**

239.

Anum
Aprum
Aquilam
Canem
Muscam
Taurum
Vīperam
Vulpem

------ v-- v-----. √ ★ ○ •

Visual Check: **Taurum vir videt.**

240.

Anum
Aprum
Aquilam
Canem
Muscam
Taurum
Vīperam
Vulpem

------ --- ------. √ ★ ○ •

Visual Check: **Aquilam vir videt.**

13-27

154. • ○ ★ • masculine & feminine   neuter

nom	Quālis?	Quāle?
acc	Quālem?	Quāle?
abl	Quālī?	Quālī?

155. Enter the neuter forms of **Quāle?** in your Reference Notebook under "Forms."

156. • ○ ★ • **omne vitium** ("every fault")
omne vitium
omnī vitiō

157. The form **omne** is the same case as ---- (mūre/opus/īnfante/vīnum).

Respōnsum: **opus   vīnum.**

158. Write the paradigm of the Latin for "every fault." ------

Respōnsum: **omne vitium
omne vitium
omnī vitiō**

159. • ○ ★ • **crūdēle respōnsum** ("cruel answer")
crūdēle respōnsum
crūdēlī respōnsō

160. Write the paradigm of the Latin for "cruel answer." ------

Respōnsum: **crūdēle respōnsum
crūdēle respōnsum
crūdēlī respōnsō**

161. The form **crūdēle** could modify ---- (mente/auctōre/rēgnum/aciē).

Respōnsum: **rēgnum.**

5-37

241.

Anum
Aprum
Aquilam
Canem
Muscam
Taurum
Vīperam
Vulpem

•○★✓ ----------------

Visual Check: **Muscam vir videt.**

242.

Anum
Aprum
Aquilam
Canem
Muscam
Taurum
Vīperam
Vulpem

•○★✓ ----------------

Visual Check: **Canem vir videt.**

243-246. Here are the names of four new people and animals. Echo the titles of these pictures.

243.	244.	245.	246.
donkey	fish	monkey	baby

★○•○•★○•○•★○•○•★○•○•
ÁsinuSesT. PisciSesT. SīmiaØesT. ĪnfānSesT.

[If you have no tape recorder, ask your teacher to pronounce.]

13-26

148. On the model of **Lēx videt īrātum**, **īrātus lēgem nōn videt**, and using the word **flūmen**, describe this picture. **Ī____ fl____.**

A: -----

Respōnsum: Īrātus flūmen videt.

149-151. Adjectives like **malus, mala, malum** therefore have a three-way contrast. Adjectives of the Third Declension, however, have a *two-way* contrast. Study the paradigms.

       m   f   n

149. ★○• **150.** ★○• **151.** ★○•
masculine   feminine   neuter

omnis agnus   omnis rēs   omneØ opusØ
omnem agnum   omnem rem   omneØ opusØ
omnī agnō   omnī rē   omnī opere

152. In **omnis, omne** there is no contrast between the -------- and the -------- genders.

     m & f   n

A: masculine   feminine

153. An adjective like **omnis, omne** belongs to the Third Declension. The question word **Quālis? Quāle?** which asks for an adjective as an answer, belongs to the ---- (1st/2d/3d) Declension.

A: 3d

5-38

247-250. Choose from the list the correct title for each picture and check with the tape.

> PisciS est.
> SīmiaØ est.
> ĪnfānS est.
> AsinuS est.

247. √ ★ ○ •

▼

Visual Check: **PisciS est.**

248. √ ★ ○ •

▼

Visual Check: **AsinuS est.**

249. √ ★ ○ •

▼

Visual Check: **ĪnfānS est.**

250. √ ★ ○ •

▼

Visual Check: **SīmiaØ est.**

13-25

144. **Īnsānus aquam in flūmine nōn invenit** = The ----- doesn't f----- in the -----.

▲

A. The crazy person doesn't find water in the river.

[If you had any trouble answering these questions, go back to the beginning of this sequence and try them again.]

145. Write the paradigm of **flūmen**, remembering about the change of -men- to -min-.

▲

Respōnsum: flūmen
flūmen
flūmine

146. On the model of **Amīcus certus in rē incertā cernitur**, describe the following picture. Use the new word **flūmen**. A----- c----- in fl----- c-----.

▲

Respōnsum: **Amīcus certus in flūmine cernitur.**

147. On the model of **Cautus metuit foveam lupus**, describe this picture, using **flūmen**. C----- m----- fl----- v---.

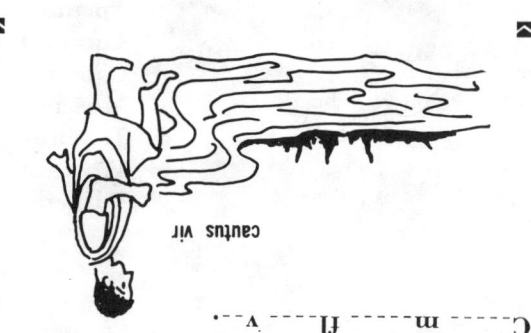

cautus vir

▲

Respōnsum: **Cautus metuit flūmen vir.**

5-39

251-254. Give the title for each picture and check with the tape.

251. Ī̄n___S esT. ✓ ★ ○ •

▼

Visual Check: **Ī̄nfānS est.**

252. S___aØ esT. ✓ ★ ○ •

▼

Visual Check: **SīmiaØ est.**

253. As___S esT. ✓ ★ ○ •

▼

Visual Check: **Asinus est.**

254. Pis___ esT. ✓ ★ ○ •

▼

Visual Check: **PisciS est.**

13-24

Question and Answer Drill

136. "Quaeritne aquam in flūmine sānus an īnsānus?" "_____."

Respōnsum: **Īnsānus.**

▲

137. "Quis aquam mediō flūmine quaerit?" "_____."

Respōnsum: **Īnsānus.**

▲

138. "Quaeritne aquam mediō flūmine sānus?" "_____."

Respōnsum: **Nōn quaerit.**

▲

139. "Estne aqua in flūmine?" "_____."

Respōnsum: Est.

▲

140. "Quid ab īnsānō mediō flūmine quaeritur?" "_____."

Respōnsum: **Aqua.**

▲

141. "Ā quō aqua mediō flūmine quaeritur?" "_____."

Respōnsum: **Ab īnsānō.**

▲

142. Your teacher, using a new verb which means "find," will ask you, "What doesn't the crazy person find in the river?" ★ ○ ○ Write your answer. "_____."

Cōnfirmātiō: "Quid īnsānus in flūmine nōn invenit?"

▲

Respōnsum: **Aquam.**

▲

143. "Quis aquam in flūmine nōn invenit?" "_____."

▲

Respōnsum: **Īnsānus.**

5-40

255-258. Here are the Latin names of four more animals. Echo the titles of these pictures.

255.	256.	257.	258.
frog	horse	lion	wolf

RānaØesT. EquuSesT. LeōØesT. LupuSesT.
★ ○ • • ★ ○ • • ★ ○ • • ★ ○ • •

Referring to the list if you like, say aloud the correct title for each picture and check.

        LupuS est.
        EquuS est.
        Leō∅ est.
        Rāna∅ est.

259. √ ★ ○ •

Visual Check: **LupuS est.**

260. √ ★ ○ •

Visual Check: **EquuS est.**

261. √ ★ ○ •

Visual Check: **Leō∅ est.**

13-23

130. **Insānus medio flūmine quaerit aquam** = The ----- l-----s for ----- in the ----- of the -----.

A: The crazy person looks for water in the middle of the river.

131. Copy Basic Sentence 32 and its English meaning in your Reference Notebook.

132. This saying is used to describe someone who is so stupid that he couldn't find ----- even if he were in the ----- of the -----.

A: water   middle   river.

133. There are four macrons in this sentence. Copy the sentence *without* the macrons. **Insanus medio flumine quaerit aquam.**

134. Listening to your teacher read the sentence, mark the vowels which are long. ★ ○ ○

Respōnsum: Insānus mediō flūmine quaerit aquam.

135. If the word **insānus** means "crazy person," then **sānus** must mean "s-----."

A: sane person.

262. ✓ ★ ○ •

Visual Check: **RānaØ est.**

263. Say and write the title for each picture.
R___Ø esT.

A: **RānaØ esT.**

264. **Eq___ ___.**

A: **EquuS esT.**

265. **Lu___ ___.**

A: **LupuS esT.**

266. **L__Ø esT.**

A: **LeōØ esT.**

---

125. Write his answer. ○ ○ ★ "v---- v---- b----."

Respōnsum: Vir vīnum bibit.

126. One problem with adjectives is that sometimes they do *not* modify any noun at all and are then used as nouns themselves. In the sentence **Īrātus lēgem nōn videt,** does the adjective **īrātus** modify any noun or is it used as a noun itself? ----

A: It is used as a noun itself (and means "angry person").

127. Write Basic Sentence 32. ○ ○ ★ **In---- m---- fl---- qu---- a----** (Listen for the long vowels.)

Respōnsum: Īnsānus mediō flūmine quaerit aquam. (Did you have four macrons?)

128. If the adjective **īnsānus** modifies a noun, draw an arrow in your answer pad from **īnsānus** to the noun with which it agrees in number and case. If there is no such noun, say so.

A: There is no such noun.

129. Therefore in this sentence **īnsānus** means "cr---- p----."

A: crazy person.

5-42

267. Here are eight more pictures where a man catches one of these new people and animals. Describe the pictures by choosing the appropriate object form from the list at the right of each picture. Check your answers with the tape.

Notice that we have put the subject **virØ** in the last place. Remember that the order of the words in Latin does not show whether the words are subject or object.

AsinuM
EquuM
ĪnfanteM
LeōneM
LupuM
PisceM
RānaM
SīmiaM

_____ capit virØ. √ ★ ○ •

Visual check: **Equum capit virØ.**

268. **EquuM capiT virØ** = The ___ _____ the _____ .

Visual Check: The man catches the horse.

269.

Asinum
Equum
Īnfantem
Leōnem
Lupum
Piscem
Rānam
Sīmiam

_____ capit vir. √ ★ ○ •

Visual Check: **Leōnem capit vir.**

13-21

120. Ask your teacher what the horse is doing.

"Q___ a___ eq___?" √ ★ ○ •

121. Echo his answer. ★ ○ • ○ •

Cōnfirmātiō: **Equus aquam bibit.**

122. **Equus aquam bibit** = The _____ is ____ing w____ .

A: The horse is drinking water.

123. You know that "aquatic sports" are sports that are played in or on the _____ .

A: water.

124. Ask your teacher what the man is doing.

"Q___ a___ v___?" √ ★ ○ •

Cōnfirmātiō: **Quid agit vir?**

5-43

270.

Asinum
Equum
Īnfantem
Leōnem
Lupum
Piscem
Rānam
Sīmiam

_____ cap__ vir. √ ★ ○ •

Visual Check: **Rānam capit vir.**

271.

Asinum
Equum
Īnfantem
Leōnem
Lupum
Piscem
Rānam
Sīmiam

_____ cap__ v___ √ ★ ○ •

Visual Check: **Lupum capit vir.**

272.

Asinum
Equum
Īnfantem
Leōnem
Lupum
Piscem
Rānam
Sīmiam

_____ c____ ___ √ ★ ○ •

Visual Check: **Piscem capit vir.**

273.

Asinum
Equum
Īnfantem
Leōnem
Lupum
Piscem
Rānam
Sīmiam

_____ √ ★ ○ •

Visual Check: **Asinum capit vir.**

13-20

114. In other words, the Romans expressed the idea of "in a place" *either with or without* the Latin preposition ___.

Respōnsum: in.

115. Ask your teacher where the mouse is standing. "___ l___ m___ st___?" √ ★ ○ •

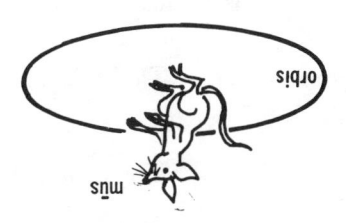

Cōnfirmātiō: **Quō locō mūs stat?**

116. Write the important part of his answer. "Mūs m___ o___ stat." ★ ○ ○ •

Respōnsum: mediō orbe

117. Ask your teacher where the statue is standing. "_____ ?" √ ★ ○ •

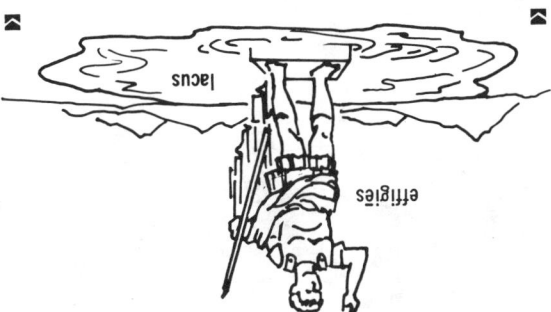

Cōnfirmātiō: **Quō locō effigiēs stat?**

118. Write the important part of his answer. "Effigiēs m___ l___ stat." ★ ○ ○ •

Respōnsum: mediō lacū

119. Echo the Latin for "What is he doing?" ★ ○ • ○ •

Cōnfirmātiō: **Quid agit?**

5-44

274.   Asinum
                              Equum
                              Īnfantem
                              Leōnem
                              Lupum
                              Piscem
                              Rānam
                              Sīmiam

----------------------- ✓ ★ ○ •

Visual Check: **Īnfantem capit vir.**

275.   Asinum
                              Equum
                              Īnfantem
                              Leōnem
                              Lupum
                              Piscem
                              Rānam
                              Sīmiam

----------------------- ✓ ★ ○ •

Visual Check: **Sīmiam capit vir.**

276. Now for English equivalent of these new words.
Vīperaǿ esT = It's a sn____.

A: It's a snake.

277. **AnuS curriT** = The old l____ is running.

A: The old lady is running.

278. **TauruS esT** = It's a b____.

A: It's a bull.

279. **Rānaǿ esT** = ___ a fr___.

A: It's a frog.

13-19

108. Write the three important words of his answer. ★ ○ ○ "**Equus m_____ f_____ stat.**"

Respōnsum: **mediō in flūmine**

109. **Equus mediō in flūmine stat** = The ____ is ____ing in the ____ of the r____.

A: The horse is standing in the middle of the river.

110. The English word "middle" in the expression "in the middle of the river" is a ____ (noun/adjective).

A: noun.

111. However, in the phrase **mediō flūmine** the Latin word **mediō** is an ____ and modifies the word ____.

A: adjective
flūmine.

112. There is no English adjective matching the Latin word **mediō**. Therefore we have to translate it by the expression, "In the ____."

A: middle of.

113. You may remember that for the expression "Where?" or "In what place?" we first used the three-word expression **Quō in locō?** We soon explained that the question was more commonly expressed by two words, "____?"

Respōnsum: **Quō locō?**
[We will use only the two-word form from now on to focus your attention on the ablative signal.]

5-45

280. AquilaØ esT = ___ an ea___.

A: It's an eagle.

281. LupuS curriT = The w___ is r_____.

A: The wolf is running.

282. VulpēS curriT = The ___ __ r_____.

A: The fox is running.

283. SīmiaØ esT = ___ a m_____.

A: It's a monkey.

284. PisciS esT = ___ a f____.

A: It's a fish.

285. MuscaØ esT = ___ a f___.

A: It's a fly.

286. EquuS curriT = The h____ is _____.

A: The horse is running.

287. ĪnfānS esT = ___ a b____.

A: It's a baby.

288. AperØ esT = ___ a b____.

A: It's a boar.

289. LeōØ esT = ___ a l____.

A: It's a lion.

13-18

Here is the vocabulary for this new Basic Sentence. Your teacher will describe this picture in three ways: write. [If you don't have a tape recorder, study the answer.]

103. ★ ○ • ○ • "Fl___ ___."

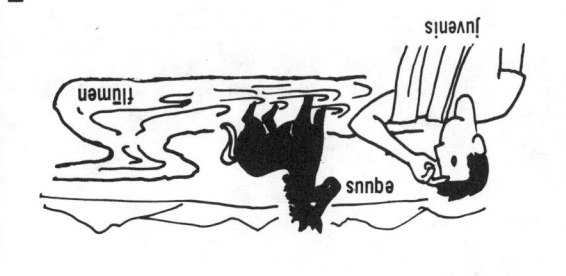

Respōnsum: Flūmen est.

104. ★ ○ • ○ • "J___ et ___ et ___ v___."

Respōnsum: Juvenis et equum et flūmen videt.

105. ★ ○ • ○ • "Eq___ ___ fl___ st___."

Respōnsum: Equus in flūmine stat.

106. ★ ○ • ○ • flūmenØ flūmenØ flūmine

107. Ask your teacher where the horse is stand-ing. "Q___ l___ e___ st___?" ∨ ★ ○ •

Confirmātiō: Quō locō equus stat?

290. **AsinuS curriT** = The d_____ is
_____.

A: The donkey is running.

291. **CaniS curriT** = The d__ __ _____.

A: The dog is running.

292. From now on we will drop the symbol [Ø] from the words that have the variant signal ____.

A: zero.

293. But to make sure that you understand which words have the old signal -s and which have the new signal zero, we will ask you to tell whether the signal for the subject form of the following words is -s or zero.

AnuS has the signal __ to signal subject form.

A: -s

294. **TauruS** has the signal __ and **rāna** has the signal ____.

A: -s
   zero.

295. **Aquila** has the signal ____ and **lupuS** has the signal ___.

A: zero
   -s.

296. **Musca** has the signal ____ and **aper** has the signal ____.

A: zero
   zero.

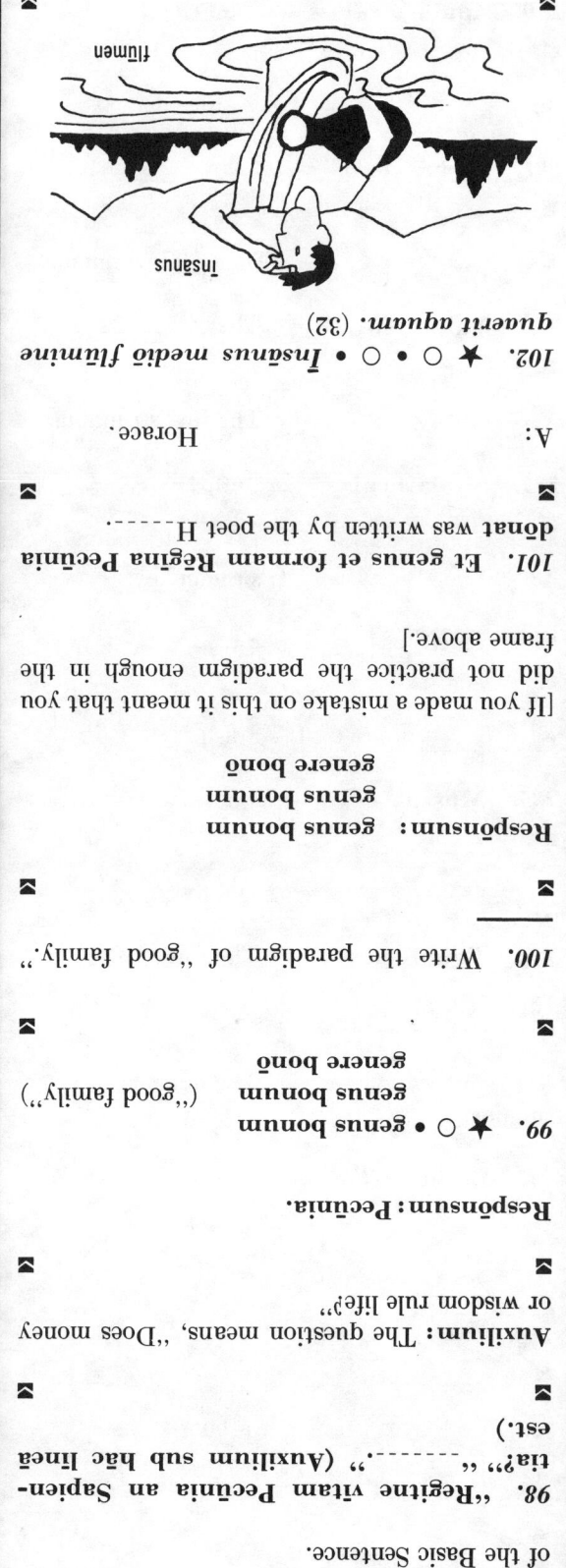

These questions are based on the general sense of the Basic Sentence.

98. "Régitne vitam Pecūnia an Sapien- tia?" "_____." (Auxilium sub hāc líneā est.)

Auxilium: The question means, "Does money or wisdom rule life?"

Respōnsum: Pecūnia.

99. ★ ○ • **genus bonum**
   genus bonum
   genere bonō   ("good family.")

100. Write the paradigm of "good family."

Respōnsum: **genus bonum**
   genus bonum
   genere bonō

[If you made a mistake on this it meant that you did not practice the paradigm enough in the frame above.]

101. Et genus et formam Rēgīna Pecūnia dōnat was written by the poet H_____.

A: Horace.

102. ★ ○ • ○ • *Īnsānus mediō flūmine quaerit aquam.* (32)

5-47

297-311. Describe the following pictures. Use the list below if you need to.

anuS	elephantuS	rāna
aper	lupuS	sīmia
aquila	mūs	tauruS
asinuS	musca	vīpera
caniS	pisciS	vulpēs

297. ---------- esT. √ ★ ○ •

Visual Check: **ElephantuS esT.**

298. ---- esT. √ ★ ○ •

Visual Check: **AnuS est.**

299. ------ esT. √ ★ ○ •

Visual Check: **Vīpera est.**

300. ------ esT. √ ★ ○ •

Visual Check: **TauruS est.**

301. ---- ---- √ ★ ○ •

Visual Check: **Aper est.**

---

92. Copy Basic Sentence 31 and its English meaning in your Reference Notebook.

93. The poet (Horace again) is saying that money has become so important that no matter how ugly you are or from what a poor background you come, if you have money there will be plenty of people who will say, because of your money, that you ---------- [In your own words.] ----------

A: ---------- are handsome and come from a distinguished family.

Question and Answer Drill

94. "Quis dōnat et genus et formam?"
"R---- P----."

Respōnsum: Rēgīna Pecūnia.

95. "Quid dōnat Rēgīna Pecūnia?"
"---- g---- ---- f----."

Respōnsum: Et genus et formam.

96. "Ā quō dōnātur et genus et forma?"
"---- R---- P----."

These questions are based on the transformation Et forma et genus ā Rēgīnā Pecūniā dōnātur.

Respōnsum: Ā Rēgīnā Pecūniā.

97. "Quid dōnātur ā Pecūniā?"
"---- g---- ---- f----."

Respōnsum: Et genus et forma.

13-16

5-48

anuS	elephantuS	rāna
aper	lupuS	sīmia
aquila	mūs	tauruS
asinuS	musca	vīpera
caniS	pisciS	vulpēS

302. ----- ---- . √ ★ ○ •

Visual Check: **LupuS** est.

303. ----- ---- . √ ★ ○ •

Visual Check: **VulpēS** est.

304. ----- ---- . √ ★ ○ •

Visual Check: **Sīmia** est.

305. ---- ---- . √ ★ ○ •

Visual Check: **Mūs** est.

306. ----- ---- . √ ★ ○ •

Visual Check: **Aquila** est.

13-15

85. • ○ • • ○ ★ ○ • English "genus," Latin **genus**.

86. The English word "genus," is used for a major subdivision or f___ly of plants or animals.

A: family

87. Queen Victoria of England was known as "Victoria Rēgīna." The Latin word **rēgīna** means "____."

A: queen

88. When you make a donation, you give something. **Dōnat** = ___s.

A: gives.

89. Since in this Basic Sentence, **pecūnia** is spelled with a capital you know that it is being used as a ____ (personal/non-personal) noun.

A: personal

90. ★ ○ ○ g___ f___ d___ R___ [Listen to the four long vowels.]

Cōnfirmātiō: Et genus et formam Rēgīna Pecūnia dōnat.

91. [Guess at the meaning of the new word **fōrma**.] This means that "Qu___ M___s b___ f___ and b___ty."

A: Queen Money gives both family and beauty.

5-49

anuS   elephantuS   rāna
aper   lupuS   sīmia
aquila   mūs   tauruS
asinuS   musca   vīpera
caniS   pisciS   vulpēs

307. ----- ---- √ ★ ○ •

Visual Check: **Rāna est.**

308. ----- ---- √ ★ ○ •

Visual Check: **AsinuS est.**

309. ----- ---- √ ★ ○ •

Visual Check: **PisciS est.**

310. ----- ---- √ ★ ○ •

Visual Check: **Musca est.**

311. ----- ---- √ ★ ○ •

Visual Check: **Canis est.**

13-14

77. You learned earlier that et was a connector which connected ----- things.

A: equal

78. The connector et is often used in pairs to mean "both . . . and." For example, Et lupus et fūr currit means, "----- the ----- --- the ----- are -----."

A: Both the wolf and the thief are running.

79. Anus et juvenem et infantem cognōscit = -----------------------------------.

A: The old lady recognizes both the young man and the baby.

80. In Et genus et formam, the word formam is a First Declension noun in the ---------- case.

A: accusative

81. Since the pair of connectors et . . . et connects equal things, then the unknown word genus must also be in the ---------- case.

A: accusative

82. Since genus is accusative case, it is declined like ----- (taurus/opus/asinus/corpus).

Respōnsum: opus ondo corpus.

83. In other words, genus is ----- gender.

A: neuter

84. ★ ○ • ○ ○ • genusØ
              genusØ
              genere

312-317. The {-s} form is used in Latin to show not only the subject of a sentence but also in giving the word in lists or in labeling pictures. Label these following pictures by using the {-s} form. In this sequence look back at the list if you need to.

    equuS   **leō**   **sīmia**
    īnfānS   **manuS**   **vir**

312. _____

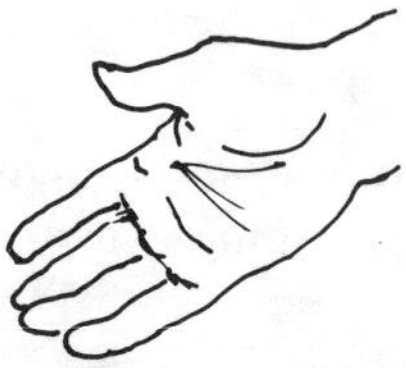

A: ManuS.

313. ___

A: Vir.

314. _____.

A: ĪnfānS.

315. _____.

A: EquuS.

---

71. This means, "A s____ m____ in a s_____."

A: A sound mind in a sound body.

72. Copy Basic Sentence 30 and its English meaning in your Reference Notebook.

73. Echo the author's name in English.

★ ● ○ ● ○ Juvenal

Visual Check: "jew-vuh-null"

74. The author, Juvenal, in the poem where this phrase occurs, says that we should pray to be healthy in _____.

A: both mind and body.

75. This was written by the poet J_____.

A: Juvenal.

76. All the new words in the next Basic Sentence have English derivatives. ★ ● ○ ● ○ • *Et genus et formam Rēgīna Pecūnia dōnat.*(31)

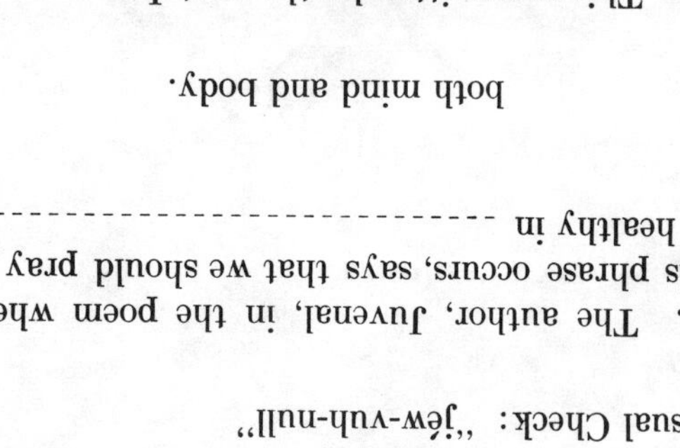

5-51

equuS   leō   sīmia
īnfānS   manuS   vir

316. ----.

A: Leō.

317. -----.

A: Sīmia.

318. Echo a new Basic Sentence. ★ ○ • ○ • *LupuS nōn mordeT lupuM.* [Don't look at this frame when doing the next.]

319. Write from dictation. ★ ○ ○ [This sentence has one macron.] L____ n__ m_____ l____. [If you have no tape recorder, write this from memory; look back if you can't remember the sentence.]

A: LupuS nōn mordeT lupuM.

320. The verb in this sentence is the unknown word _____.

A: mordeT.

321. If you use the colorless word "blanks," *LupuS nōn mordeT lupuM* means "One ____ doesn't blank another ____."

A: wolf ... wolf.

13-12

64. The final sound -s in **corpus** is not the signal {-s} (as in **vestis**) but rather, like the word **opus** and **mūs**, this -s is part of the st-- of the word.

A: stem

65. Instead of the form *corpose we have the form ——.

Respōnsum: corpore.

66. In Latin s between vowels changes to the sound ----.

Respōnsum: r.

67-69. The English words "sane" and "insane" come from a Latin adjective which means "sound." Echo the paradigms which illustrate the three different genders of this adjective.

67. ★ ○ •   **68.** ★ ○ •
sānus vir   sāna mēns
sānum virum   sānam mentem
sānō virō   sānā mente

69. ★ ○ •
sānum corpus
sānum corpus
sānō corpore

70. ★ ○ ○ M___ s_____ in c___ s_____. (30) [Careful; there are four macrons.]

Cōnfirmātiō: Mēns sāna in corpore sānō.

5-52

322. Echo your teacher as he describes this picture. ★ ○ • ○ • **Mūs mūreM mordeT**.

▼ ▼

323. Mūs mūreM mordeT = One _____ bi___ another _____ .

▼ ▼

A: One mouse bites another mouse.

324. LupuS nōn mordeT lupuM = ___ _____ .

▼ ▼

A: One wolf doesn't bite another wolf.
[The picture is crossed out to remind you that the statement is *negative*].

325. The "poetical meaning" of **LupuS nōn mordeT lupuM** is that members of the same group ought to _____ . [In your own words]

▼ ▼

A: get along together.

---

58. Now write the three nominative forms of **magnus**, putting in the abbreviations which indicate the gender.

_____, _____, _____ .

▼

    m   f   n

Respōnsum: **magnus, magna, magnum**

▼

59. An adjective like **magnus** has ____ (1/2/3/4/5) different forms for the nominative.

▼

A: 3

▼

60. The number (30) tells you that this is a Basic Sentence which you are to echo. ★ ○ • ○ •
(30) *Mēn s_a in c___re s_ō.*

▼

Cōnfirmātiō: **Mēns sāna in corpore sānō.** (30)

▼ ▼

61. ★ ○ • ○ • **corpusØ**
          corpusØ
          corpore

▼ ▼

62. "Corporal" punishment is punishment that is inflicted on the body, like whipping. The Latin word **corpus** means "_____".

▼

A: body.

▼

63. The ablative form of **corpus** is _____ .

▼

Respōnsum: **corpore**.

13-11

5-53

326. Copy Basic Sentence Six into your Reference Notebook.

327. We could express somewhat the same thought by using the verb **dīligiT** and saying **LupuS lupuM dīligiT**, which would mean, "‾‾‾‾‾‾‾‾‾‾‾‾‾‾‾‾‾‾‾‾‾‾‾‾‾‾‾‾‾‾‾‾‾‾‾‾."

A: One wolf loves another wolf.

In the following series of pictures, various animals are working in happy cooperation with each other. Describe the pictures on the pattern of **LupuS nōn mordeT lupuM**. We have labelled the animals. Remember to speak aloud: say the answer aloud, *then* check with the tape or the Visual Check.

328. Sīmia nōn mordeT ___iaM. √ ★ ○ •

Visual Check: **Sīmia nōn mordeT sīmiaM.**

329. ___ nōn m_____ mūreM. √ ★ ○ •

Visual Check: **Mūs nōn mordeT mūreM.**

13-10

52. Adjectives are listed in the nominative case with the gender contrast shown. For a while we will remind you of what this contrast means by writing the adjective like this:

    m   f   n
bonus, bona, bonum

The small letters m, f, and n stand for _____, _____ and _____ genders.

A: masculine, feminine, neuter

53. An adjective like **cautus, cauta, cautum**
                          m   f   n
is called a "First-and-Second Declension" adjective because _____ belongs to the First Declension and _____ and _____ belong to the Second Declension.

Respōnsum: **cauta cautus cautum**

54. Say these First-and-Second Declension adjectives in the nominative forms and check.

    m   f   n
nūllus, nūlla, nūllum √ ★ ○ •

    m   f   n
55. ūnus, ūn—, ūn— √ ★ ○ •

Cōnfirmātiō: **ūnus, ūna, ūnum**

    m   f   n
56. parv—, parv—, parv— √ ★ ○ •

Cōnfirmātiō: **parvus, parva, parvum**

    m   f   n
57. cert—, cert—, cert— √ ★ ○ •

Cōnfirmātiō: **certus, certa, certum**

48. The male animals **vulpēs** and **rāna** are modified by adjectives of the ―――― gender.

A: feminine

---

49. Nouns like **vīnum** and **opus**, which never have a contrast between nominative and accusative, are called "neuter" nouns. They are modified by the forms **bonum/bonum/bonō**. Four sentences may be made by choosing the neuter nouns in the parenthesis to say, "This is a bad something." Say the four sentences and then check your answer below. Est malum ―――― (lacus/opus/fūr/vīnum/musca/respōnsum/diēs/vitium).

Respōnsum: Est malum opus.
Est malum vīnum.
Est malum respōnsum.
Est malum vitium.

---

50. Things, objects, instruments, concepts, etc. which do not have any biological sex may belong to any one of the three genders. Which nouns in this list of nominatives are feminine gender? [Look at the adjectives!]

malum opus, nūlla poena, ūna nox, spatiōsum corpus

Respōnsum: poena   nox

---

51. In the accusative case, **bonum** can be both masculine and neuter. Therefore to do *this* frame, you must *remember* which nouns are neuter. Which of the {-m}'s in these sentences are neuter nouns?

Leō parvum asinum capit.
Vir suum capillum habet.
Juvenis sānum corpus habet.
Amīcus auxilium nūllum quaerit.
Fūr perīc'lum certum cernit.
Sīmia parvum saccum tenet.

Respōnsum: corpus   auxilium   perīc'lum

---

330. R―――――――――――――――――. ✓ ★ ○ •

Visual Check: **Rāna nōn mordeT rānaM.**

331. ――――――――――――――――――. ✓ ★ ○ •

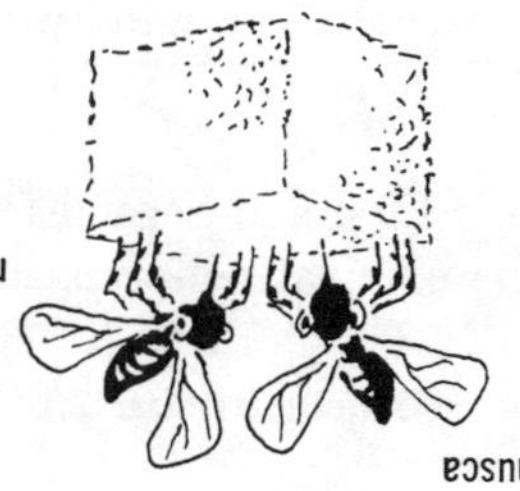

Visual Check: **Musca nōn mordeT muscaM.**

332. ――――――――――――――――――. ✓ ★ ○ •

Visual Check: **CaniS nōn mordeT caneM.**

333. ---------------------------- ✓ ★ ○ •

elephantus   elephantus

Visual Check: **ElephantuS nōn mordeT elephantuM.**

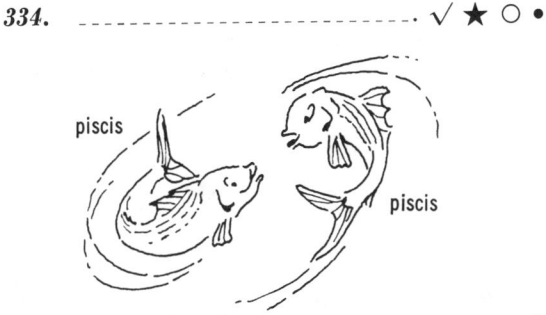

334. ---------------------------- ✓ ★ ○ •

piscis   piscis

Visual Check: **PisciS nōn mordeT pisceM.**

335. ---------------------------- ✓ ★ ○ •

aper   aper

Visual Check: **Aper nōn mordeT apruM.**

336. For the next series you will have to learn a new part of speech. The word "and" in English is called a "connector." Connectors connect *equal* things. In the sentence "The dog and the cat were fighting in the back yard," the word "and" ------s the two nouns "dog" and "cat."

A: connects

---

43. **We call locus a "masculine" noun because** -------------- [In your own words]

▲

A: it is modified by an adjective which is masculine gender, here **spatiōsus.**

▲

44. Which nouns in the following list of nominatives are masculine nouns and are therefore modified by masculine adjectives? [All you have to do is to look at the adjectives.]

magnus gradus, magna fovea, magnum opus, magnum vitium, magnus arcus

▲

Respōnsum: gradus   arcus

▲

45. Why the name "masculine"? The answer is that many (but not all) Latin names for *male* persons and *male* animals are masculine ------.

▲

A: gender.

▲

46. Here, however, is a list of male animals and people. Which ones are masculine *gender*? [Remember, they are all males in this list, but they are not all modified by the class of adjectives called "masculine." Just look at the adjectives.]

cauta vulpēs, magnus taurus, īrātus fūr, parva rāna, malus aper

▲

Respōnsum: taurus   fūr   aper

▲

47. Nominative forms like **cauta** and **parva** belong to the "feminine" gender. The *male* animals above, **cauta vulpēs** and **parva rāna** are ---- (masculine/feminine) gender.

▲

A: feminine

337. Now a dog and a cat are certainly not "equal" things in the usual sense of the word. In fact, in this particular fight the dog is getting the worst of it. But the *words* "dog" and "cat" are equal things because they are both the same ____ of _____.

A: part   speech.

338. "Connectors" in English connect words that are _____.
[In your own words.]

A: the same part of speech (equal things, etc.)

339. Echo your teacher as he describes this picture. ★ ○ • ○ • **AsinuS lupuM et leōneM videT.**

340. **LupuM** and **leōneM** are both nouns. They are connected by the Latin connector ___.

A: et.

---

38. Which nouns in this list are modified by adjectives of the same gender? [Again, just look at the adjectives.]

mala rēs, malum opus, malum vitium, malus auctor

Respōnsum: opus   vitium

39. Adjectives differ from nouns in having gender as well as case. You now know three cases for nouns. An adjective like **bonus**, however, not only has cases, but it has three separate _____s as well.

A: genders

40. The technical names for these genders you will find confusing at first because they are common words which have an entirely different meaning in ordinary speech. A person who is "masculine" is someone who _____.
[In your own words.]

A: _____ is a real he-man.

41. It will surprise you to discover that **sānus** is called the "masculine" gender. Which nouns in this list are modified by the "masculine" form like **sānus**? [Just look at the adjectives.]

malus oculus, cauta mēns, ūnus capillus, magnum opus, spatiōsus locus

Respōnsum: oculus   capillus   locus

42. Since **oculus, capillus,** and **locus** are modified by the masculine gender adjectives (**malus, ūnus,** and **spatiōsus**), we say that these three nouns are "m_____ nouns."

A: masculine

5-57

341. In Latin, as in English, a connector may connect only *equal* things (like two nouns). **LupuM** and **leōneM** are not only both nouns but they are both _____ forms of the nouns.

A: object

342. In Latin the connector **et** connects nouns that are ____ (the same form/different forms).

A: the same form.

343. [Just a reminder: always read all the Latin aloud whether the directions tell you to or not.] **AsinuS lupuM et leōneM videT** = ___ _____ sees ___ ____ and ___ ____.

A: The donkey sees the wolf and the lion.

344. Like the word **nōn** this new word **et** does not _____ form.

A: change

345. Because it connects, the word **et** is called a "_____."

A: connector.

346. Since **et** is a part of speech that does not change form and since it is a connector, is the sound **t** on the end of the word the same signal as the **-t** on the verb **dīligiT**? ____(Yes/No)

A: No

347. In the next sequence we will show situations where someone sees *two* different people and animals. Say aloud the description of each picture. Remember: there will be *one* subject and *two* objects (each ending in **-m**) in each of the next seven frames.

13-6

32. When we use the English adjective "good" to modify "judge," "mind," or "work," does the English word "good" change form? ____ (Yes/No)

A: No

33. In Latin, however, while we say **Bonus jūdex est**, we must change the adjective **bonus** when we wish to say, "It's a good work," and say, **B____ op__ est**.

Respōnsum: **Bonum opus est**.

34. "It's a good law" = **B____ lēx est**.

Respōnsum: **Bona lēx est**.

35. Echo a new technical term. ● ○ ● ○ ★ gender.

Visual Check: "jĕnn-der"

36. This contrast between the forms **bonus**, **bona**, and **bonum** is called "gender." The word **bonus** in **Bonus jūdex est** and the word **bona** in **Bona lēx est** belong to different _____s.

A: genders.

37. Which two nouns in this list are modified by adjectives of the same gender? [Look at the adjectives; which ones are the same?]

ūnus capillus, ūna vulpēs, ūnum rēgnum, ūnus fūr

A:

Respōnsum: **capillus : fūr**

348. M__aM et as___M anuS videT.

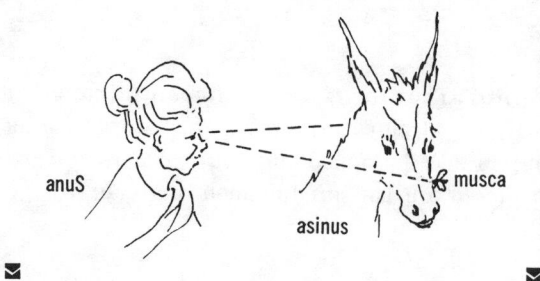

A: MuscaM et asinuM anuS videT.

349. The forms **musca** and **asinuS** are used in the picture because they are merely used as _____s.

A: labels.

350. However, when we wish to say that the old lady sees the fly and the donkey, we must use the {__} form.

A: {-m}

351. Vi__M et mū__M c____ videT.

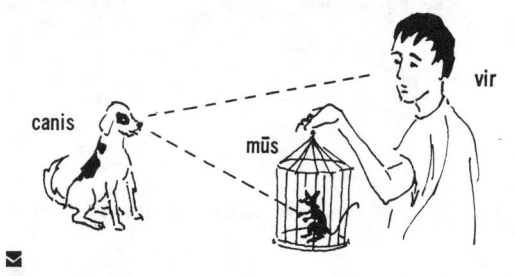

A: ViruM et mūreM caniS videT.

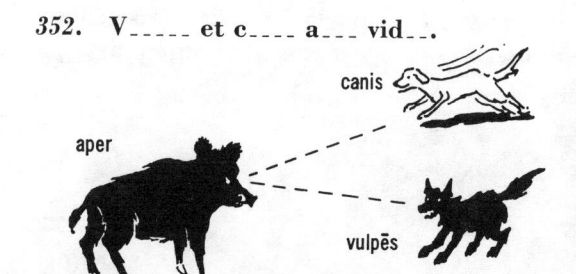

352. V_____ et c____ a___ vid___.

A: VulpeM et caneM aper videT.

---

24. Respōnsum est → B_____ r_____.
∨ ★ ○ •

Cōnfirmātiō: Bonum respōnsum est.

25. Rēgnum est → B_____ r_____.
∨ ★ ○ •

Cōnfirmātiō: Bonum rēgnum est.

26. In this sequence you will have some of the same sentences to expand to say that these are good ones. However, this time you must choose between **bonus, bona,** and **bonum. Vīnum** est → v_____ B_____.
∨ ★ ○ •

Cōnfirmātiō: Bonum vīnum est.

27. Vulpēs est → v_____ B_____.
∨ ★ ○ •

Cōnfirmātiō: Bona vulpēs est.

28. Leō est → B_____ l_____.
∨ ★ ○ •

Cōnfirmātiō: Bonus leō est.

29. Taurus est → B_____ t_____.
∨ ★ ○ •

Cōnfirmātiō: Bonus taurus est.

30. Vestis est → B_____ v_____.
∨ ★ ○ •

Cōnfirmātiō: Bona vestis est.

31. Rēgnum est → B_____ r_____.
∨ ★ ○ •

Cōnfirmātiō: Bonum rēgnum est.

5-59

353. V_____ et s_____ v_____ vid___.

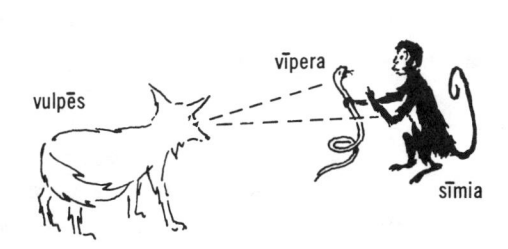

A: VīperaM et sīmiaM vulpēS videT.

354. Equ__ et el_____ īn____ v____.

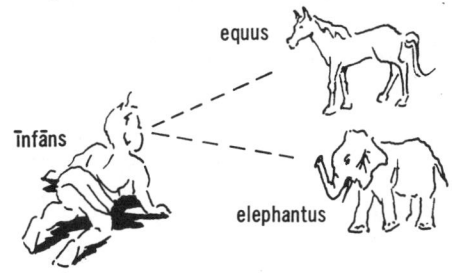

A: EquuM et elephantuM īnfānS videT.

355. Aq____ et t____ s____ v____.

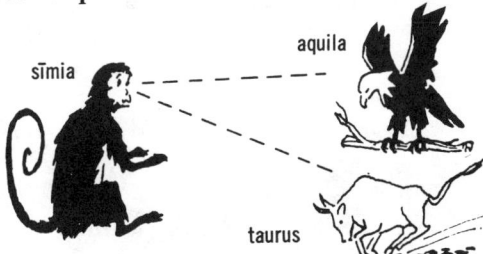

A: AquilaM et tauruM sīmia videT.

356. P____ et r____ e____ ____.

A: PisceM et rānaM equuS videT.

---

17. Lēx est → B___ ‧‧‧‧‧‧ ∧ ★ ○ •

Cōnfirmātiō: Bona lēx est.

18. Vīta est → B___ ‧‧‧‧‧‧ ∧ ★ ○ •

Cōnfirmātiō: Bona vīta est.

19. Ōrātiō est → B___ ‧‧‧‧‧‧ ∧ ★ ○ •

Cōnfirmātiō: Bona ōrātiō est.

The next three nouns, however, are all like **jūdex**: they are modified in the nominative by the form **bonus**. Expand to say that these are good ones.

20. Vir est → Bon___ vir est. ∧ ★ ○ •

Cōnfirmātiō: Bonus vir est.

21. Taurus est → B___ t___. ∧ ★ ○ •

Cōnfirmātiō: Bonus taurus est.

22. Leō est → B___ ‧‧‧‧‧‧ ∧ ★ ○ •

Cōnfirmātiō: Bonus leō est.

23. Finally, the next three nouns are like **opus**: expand with **bonum** to say that these are good ones. Vīnum est → Bon___ vīnum est. ∧ ★ ○ •

Cōnfirmātiō: Bonum vīnum est.

357. You remember the Basic Sentence **ElephantuS nōn capiT mūreM**, which means that elephants ignore mice. Echo your teacher as he uses this same pattern to describe this picture. ★ ○ • ○ •

Visual Check: **Aquila nōn capit rānam.**

358. Now write down the sentence you just echoed, which meant that an eagle doesn't catch a frog.
Aq____ n__ c____ r_____. (There are two macrons.)

A: **Aquila nōn capiT rānaM.** [Were you careful not to look back when you wrote?]

359–366. Now describe the following pictures in the same way to say that one animal ignores another. Use the same {-s -m -t} pattern as in **Elephantus nōn capit mūrem**, and check your answers with your tape.

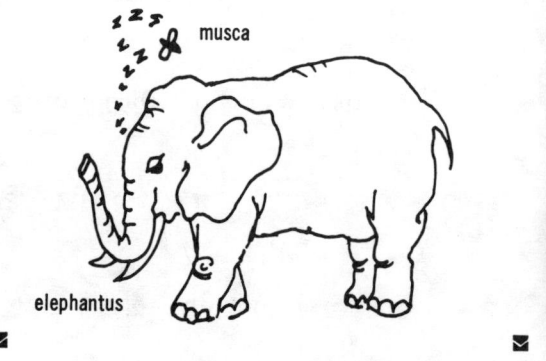

359. El_____s nōn capit m___am. √ ★ ○ •

Visual Check: **Elephantus nōn capit muscam.**

5-61

360. Eq___ nōn capit s____m. ✓ ★ ○ •

equus / sīmia

Visual Check: **Equus nōn capit sīmiam.**

361. V__ ___ ca___ īn_____. ✓ ★ ○ •

vir / īnfāns

Visual Check: **Vir nōn capit īnfantem.**

362. T_____ ___ c____ v_____. ✓ ★ ○ •

vulpēs / taurus

Visual Check: **Taurus nōn capit vulpem.**

363. L__ ____ ____ an___. ✓ ★ ○ •

anus / leō

Visual Check: **Leō nōn capit anum.**

13-2

6. If the noun is in the same class as **jūdex**, however, then the adjective which modifies it will be, in the nominative, ____ (bonus/bona/bonum).

Respōnsum: **bonus.**

7. If the noun is in the same class as **opus**, the adjective which modifies it will be ____ (bonus/bona/bonum).

Respōnsum: **bonum.**

8. Notice how different this is from English. Put the adjective "good" in the slots indicated to make them modify these three different nouns: "the g___ mind," "the g___ judge," "the g___ work."

A: good / good / good

9. It will naturally puzzle you at first to discover that Latin adjectives change form depending on the class of noun which they m_____.

A: modify.

10. ★ ○ • ○ • **bonus jūdex, bona mēns, bonum opus** [Remember that this sign means that you are to echo at least twice.]

11. Try to understand that there is no real "explanation" for the fact that **bonus** changes form in this way. Just remember that it is one of the facts of the Latin language that while we say **Bona mēns est,** we say **B__us jūdex est,** and **B__um opus est.**

Respōnsum: **Bonus / Bonum**

UNIT THIRTEEN

13-1

1. We will now introduce you to a point of structure which is found in many languages but which English does not have. Echo the paradigm of "a good (noble) mind."

★ ○ •   bona mēns
("good mind")   bonam mentem
                 bonā mente

2. But here is a surprise. Notice what happens to the adjective which means "good" when it modifies **jūdex**.

★ ○ •   bonus jūdex
("good judge")   bonum jūdicem
                  bonō jūdice

3. When the adjective modifies **jūdex** it has ____ (the same forms as/different forms from) when it modifies **mēns**.

Answer: different forms from

4. And finally, echo the paradigm of "good work."

★ ○ •   bonum opus
("good work")   bonum opus
                 bonō opere

5. All nouns in Latin fall into one of three classes. If they are in the same class as **mēns**, the adjective which modifies them will be, in the nominative, ____ (bonus/bona/bonum).
[Look back if you wish.]

Respōnsum: bona.

5-62

364. C____ ___ p____. ✓ ★ ○ •

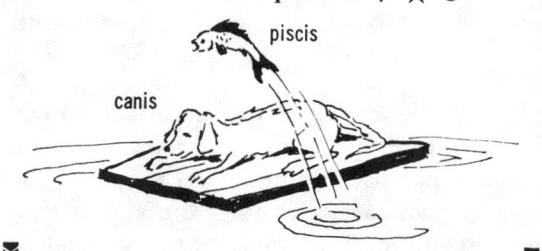

canis   piscis

Visual Check: **Canis nōn capit piscem.**

365. L____ ___ m____. ✓ ★ ○ •

lupus   mūs

Visual Check: **Lupus nōn capit mūrem.**

366. Ap__ ___ v____. ✓ ★ ○ •

aper   vīpera

Visual Check: **Aper nōn capit vīperam.**

367. So far we have had only two Latin words that *do not* change form. These have been the word for "not," which was ___ and the connector "and," which was ___.

A: nōn
         et.

368. The next word you will learn, like **nōn** and **et**, does not _____ form.

A: change

369. Echo the Latin word for "never."
★ ○ • ○ • **numquam**

370. VestiS viruM numquam reddiT. = Clothes _____ make the man.

A: never

371. ElephantuS numquam capiT mūreM = An _____ _____ catches a _____.

A: An elephant never catches a mouse.

372. Time never discloses the truth = Vēr_____ d___ n_____ ap____. [There are three macrons.]

A: VēritāteM diēS numquam aperiT.

373. Because **numquam** is a word that never changes form, the last sound of the word ____ (is/is not) the signal **-m** that shows object form.

A: is not

374. **Numquam** is not a noun because it never _____s ____.

A: changes form

375. Echo the first two words of a new Basic Sentence. ★ ○ • ○ • **VēritāS numquam** [You will be asked to write this in the next frame.]

376. Write these same two words. ★ ○ ○ [Write from memory if you are not using a tape recorder.] V_____ n_____ [Did you remember the two macrons?]

A: VēritāS numquam

377. VēritāS numquam = _____ _____ blanks.

A: Truth never blanks.

5-63

TEST INFORMATION

From now on we will not be quite so definite about the test. For one thing, we will not refer you to specific frame numbers. But we will make sure that you know what you are supposed to have learned.

On this test you will be asked only questions which were asked in this Unit. When asked to produce paradigms, you will be given only paradigms which you have practiced. The Latin questions will be the same questions which are in this Unit. Be sure to be able to do the seven ambiguous nouns (**vitium**, **opus**, etc.).

VOCABULARY INVENTORY

In this Unit you learned seven nouns whose nominative and accusative cases are *always* alike:

perīc'lum (118), vitium (173), auxilium (208), vīnum (227), rēgnum (290), respōnsum (312), opus (388), and the question word Quid? (13).

You learned four other nouns: nēmō (195), mēns (293), cōnfirmātiō (262), auctor (389).

You learned new adjectives: bona (304), mala (311), quālis (317), stultus (271), sapiēns (271).

Three new verbs: obumbrat (239), possidet (306), laudat (392).

A new meaning for **est** (199).

There were two new expressions: **Quid agit** (412) and **Auxilium sub hāc līneā est** (209).

468. Copy in your Reference Notebook the paradigm of the word which asks for an adjective.

quālis
quālem
quālī

12-69

5-64

378. Echo the entire sentence. ★ ○ • ○ •
VēritāS numquam periT.

379. Write. ★ ○ ○
VēritāS numquam p____.

A: **VēritāS numquam periT.**

380. Although the word **numquam** ends in the sound **-m** it is *not* the object case, because **numquam** is the kind of word that _____ _____[In your own words.]

A: _____ never changes form.

381. If we tell you that **periT** means "dies," then you know that **VēritāS numquam periT** means "____ ____ ____."

A: Truth never dies.

382. Copy this in your Reference Notebook as Basic Sentence Seven.

383. Truth never dies = **Vēr____ num____ per___.**

A: **VēritāS numquam periT.**

384. A Latin verb which patterns with an {-m} is called a transitive verb. A verb like **periT** that does not pattern with an {-m} is called an _____ verb.

A: intransitive

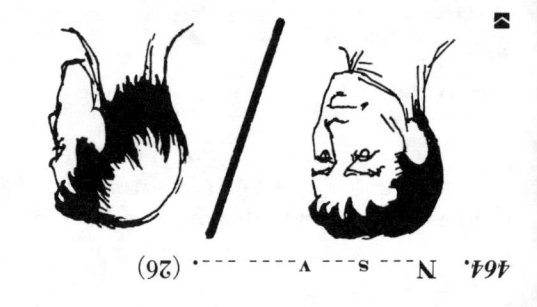

463. M____ r____ b____ p_____ (28)

Respōnsum: **Mēns rēgnum bona possidet.** (28)

464. N____ s____ v____ ____ (26)

Respōnsum: **Nēmō sine vitiō est.** (26)

465. Copy in your Reference Notebook the paradigm of the question word.

Personal	Non-personal
Quis?	Quid?
Quem?	Quid?
Quō?	Quō?

466. Copy in your Reference Notebook the paradigm of this typical Second Declension noun which has the nominative and accusative forms alike.

vitium
vitium
vitiō

467. Copy in your Reference Notebook the paradigm of this typical Third Declension noun which has the nominative and accusative forms alike.

opus
opus
opere

12-68

5-65

385. You now know three intransitive verbs, the kind that form {-s -t} sentences: runs = c_____, is = e___, dies = p____.

▼

A: **currit   est   perit.**

386. Say aloud the Basic Sentences which describe the following pictures.
V_____ d___ ap____. ✓ ★ ○ •

▼

Visual Check: **Vēritātem diēs aperit.**

If you made any error, you should study the first seven Basic Sentences before going further in the program.

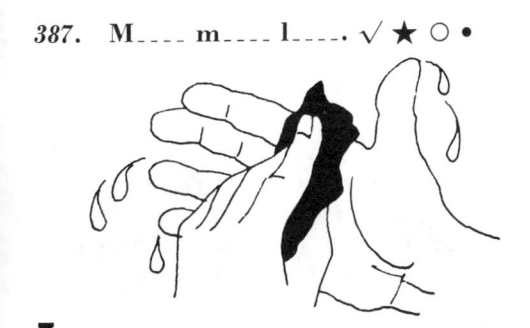

387. M____ m____ l____. ✓ ★ ○ •

▼

Visual Check: **Manus manum lavat.**

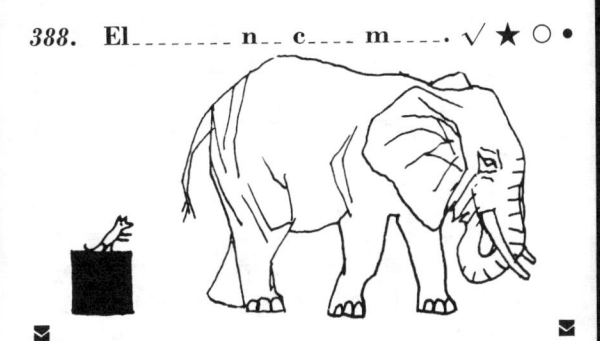

388. El_____ n__ c____ m____. ✓ ★ ○ •

▼

Visual Check: **Elephantus nōn capit mūrem.**

12-67

457. If we change the sentence to **Semper hilarem datōrem dīligit Deus** we have _____ed by adding **semper.**

▼

A: expanded

458. All our question and answer drills are based upon these three manipulations of s_____, tr_____, and ex_____.

▼

A: substitution, transformation, and expansion.

459. In the word **opus** you had another example of the consonant **s** changing to --- between vowels.

▼

Respōnsum: -r- (as in **mūre**)

You learned five Basic Sentences, 25-29.
Give the Basic Sentences.

460. S_____ v_____ o_____. (27)

▼

Respōnsum: Sapientia vīnō obumbrātur.

461. N_____ p_____ s_____ p_____ v_____. (25)

▼

Respōnsum: Numquam perīc'lum sine perīc'lō vincitur. (25)

462. A_____ o_____ l_____. (29)

▼

Respōnsum: Auctor opus laudat. (29)

5-66

389. H‿‿‿ d‿‿‿ d‿‿‿ D‿‿. ✓ ★ ○ •

Visual Check: **Hilarem datōrem dīligit Deus.**

390. V‿‿‿ v‿‿‿ r‿‿‿. ✓ ★ ○ •

Visual Check: **Vestis virum reddit.**

391. Lupu‿ ‿‿ morde‿ lupu‿. ✓ ★ ○ •

Visual Check: **Lupus nōn mordet lupum.**

SUMMARY

450. In this Unit you learned about nouns like **Quid?, rēgnum,** and **opus.** These nouns are different from **vestis** and **quercus** because the ‿‿‿‿‿ and ‿‿‿‿‿‿‿‿‿‿‿s are always alike.

A: nominative   accusative cases

▲

451. While **Quis?** asks for a personal noun, the question word **Quid?** asks for a ‿‿‿‿‿‿ noun.

A: non-personal

▲

452. Since **Quid?** is an ambiguous form, you must look at the rest of the context to decide whether it asks for the subject or the object. In the sentence **Quid fēmina quaerit?** the word **Quid?** asks for the {‿‿}.

A: {-m}.

▲

453. In the sentence **Quid metuit iūdex?** the word **Quid?** asks for the {‿‿}.

A: {-m}. [If you missed this frame, it means that you were not really working, that you just assumed that the answer to this frame would be different. Don't try to outguess the program: work with it.]

▲

454. In the sentence **Quid anum vincit?** the word **Quid?** asks for the {‿‿}.

A: {-s}.

▲

455. When we ask the question **Quis dīligit hilarem datōrem?** we have ‿‿‿‿‿‿‿ed **Quis?** for the original word **Deus.**

A: substituted

▲

456. If we change the sentence to **Hilaris dator dīligitur ā Deō** we have ‿‿‿‿‿‿‿ed from the active to the passive voice.

A: transformed

▲

12-66

5-67

392. Vēritā_ numqua_ peri_. √ ★ ○ •

Visual Check: **Vēritās numquam perit.**

393-396. An English derivative is almost always *pronounced differently* from the Latin word. Here is a list of English words with the Latin words from which they are derived. Echo your teacher as he pronounces first the English word and then the Latin word. If you do not have a tape recorder, your teacher will probably do these four frames in class.

	ENGLISH	LATIN
393. ★ ○ • ○ •	simian ("sim-mee-yun")	**sīmia**
394. ★ ○ • ○ •	infant ("inn-funt")	**īnfāns**
395. ★ ○ • ○ •	viper ("vye-purr")	**vīpera**
396. ★ ○ • ○ •	canine ("kay-nine")	**canis**

SUMMARY

397. In this Unit you concentrated mostly on learning to handle the subject and object forms of different nouns. You learned that the signal for subject can be either _ _ or _ _ _ _ _.

A: **-s** zero.

398. Write the seven forms which have the signal **Ø**.

anuS	aquila	sīmia	equuS	vīpera
musca	leō	asinuS	īnfānS	tauruS
aper	pisciS	lupuS	rāna	caniS

A: **musca aper aquila leō sīmia rāna vīpera**

12-65

441. There is an English word which sounds like "eyerate." Listen to your teacher as he uses this English word in a sentence. ★ ○ ○
When we broke his window the man became so "eyerate" that we were afraid he would call the police.

442. Because you know the Latin word **īrātus**, you know that this English word is spelled _____.

A: irate.

443. Pronounce English "irate," Latin **īrātus**. √ ★ ○ •

444. ★ ○ • ○ • English "irritate," Latin **irritat**.

445. You can remember that the English word "irritate" is spelled with two r's because it is derived from the Latin word _____.

Respōnsum: irritat.

446. Echo an English word which means "full of life" or "necessary to life." ★ ○ ○

447. Because this word is derived from Latin **vīta**, you know that it is spelled ____ (vytal/vighbal/vītal/vaytal). _____

A: vital.

448. Pronounce English "vital," Latin **vīta**. √ ★ ○ •

449. You know that "vital" is spelled with an "i" in English because you know the Latin word for "life," which is _____.

Respōnsum: vīta.

399. You also learned that there are two kinds of verbs, those that take objects and those that do not. Those that take objects are called _____ verbs.

A: transitive

400. Those that do not take objects are called _____ verbs.

A: intransitive

401. Because you were busy learning to form subjects and objects of new words, in this Unit you learned only two new Basic Sentences. Say and write this Basic Sentence. Lup__ n__ mor___ l_____.

A: LupuS nōn mordeT lupuM.

402. Say and write the Basic Sentence. Vērit__ n_____ pe__T.

A: VēritāS numquam periT.

Now follows a Vocabulary Inventory which will help you review any words you are not sure of.

---

434. Some of you have not yet learned the system of spelling Latin perfectly and therefore are still having some trouble in spelling Latin words. When you have learned the system, however, you will be able to _____.
[In your own words]

A: spell Latin without any difficulty.

435. We have other good news for you, too. Everyone knows that English is a difficult language to spell, but not everyone realizes that a knowledge of Latin will help tremendously in spelling English correctly. Echo your teacher as he says a word which is probably new to you. ★ ○ ● ○ ●

436. If you did not know Latin you might very well misspell this word in some such way as "averiss" (which is certainly the way it sounds), but here is how a knowledge of Latin will help you. This English word means "greed"; it is a derivative of the Latin word for "greed" which you know, av___tia.

Respōnsum: avāritia

437. Latin -tia frequently shows up in English as "-ce." So you can figure out that this new English word which means "greed" is spelled _____.

A: avarice.

438. Pronounce English "avarice," Latin avāritia. ✓ ★ ○ ●

439. We have seen that Latin -tia often becomes English "____."

A: -ce.

440. There is a Latin word scientia whose English derivative is "scien__."

A: science.

5-69
VOCABULARY INVENTORY

In this Unit you learned the names of fourteen different animals. Read them aloud from the list given below. The number in parentheses is the number of the frame in which the word was given. If you cannot remember the meaning, go back and review the frames that drilled a word.

aper		musca	
aprum	(223)	muscam	(221)
aquila		piscis	
aquilam	(222)	piscem	(244)
asinus		rāna	
asinum	(243)	rānam	(255)
canis		sīmia	
canem	(210)	sīmiam	(245)
equus		taurus	
equum	(256)	taurum	(209)
leō		vīpera	
leōnem	(257)	vīperam	(208)
lupus		vulpēs	
lupum	(258)	vulpem	(224)

You also learned the names of two kinds of people:

| anus | | īnfāns | |
| anum | (211) | īnfantem | (246) |

In addition, you learned five new verbs:

est	(220)
currit	(198)
mordet	(322)
perit	(378)
videt	(233)

And finally two other words which do not change form:

| et | (342) |
| numquam | (369) |

5-70

TEST INFORMATION

You will be asked to perform the following tasks:

1) To identify subjects that have the new signal zero, as in frame 67.
2) To describe the pictures which occurred in frames 267–275, 328–335, 347–358, and elsewhere.
3) To describe *new* pictures, similar to those in frames 267–275 and elsewhere. You will use the words which you have practiced in this program.
4) To write some of the seven Basic Sentences when shown the picture and with prompting by first letters.

Here is a suggestion which will be useful for some of you. Get some 3 by 5 filing cards and on one side write the two forms of each word you know, one under the other, like this:

vir
virum

On the reverse side of the card write the Basic Sentence in which this word occurred (**Vestis virum reddit**) and finally the English meaning of this word in this sentence ("man"). When you are directed to write forms in your Reference Notebook, you may write them on these cards instead.

You can use these cards to review. The most convenient feature of this system is that you can weed out the words which you are sure of, leaving only the ones which you feel you need more practice on.

Not everyone will need to use this system; the program gives a lot of review. But *if* you find that you have any trouble remembering either the words or the Basic Sentences, give this a try.

12-62

415. **Vītam regit Fortūna, nōn Sapientia.** (18)

416. **Parva necat morsū spatiōsum vīpera taurum.** (21)

417. **Lēx videt īrātum, īrātus lēgem nōn videt.** (13)

418. **Fūrem fūr cognōscit et lupum lupus.** (14)

419. **Lupus nōn mordet lupum.** (6)

420. **Pecūnia nōn satiat avāritiam, sed irrītat.** (17)

421. **Auctor opus laudat.** (29)

[Read these through again if you feel it necessary.]

422. **"Quid agit Deus?" "H______ d______ d______."** ✓ ★ ○ •

Cōnfirmātiō: **Hilarem datōrem dīligit.**

423. **"Quid agit vēritās?" "Im_________ vin___."** ✓ ★ ○ •

Cōnfirmātiō: **Imitātiōnem vincit.**

424. **"Quid agit Fortūna?" "Vīt__ reg__."** ✓ ★ ○ •

Cōnfirmātiō: **Vītam regit.**

425. **"Quid agit parva vīpera?" "Nec__ t_____."** ✓ ★ ○ •

Cōnfirmātiō: **Necat taurum.**

426. **"Quid agit auctor?" "Op__ l_____."** ✓ ★ ○ •

Cōnfirmātiō: **Opus laudat.**

UNIT SIX

1. We will now introduce a new part of speech. We said earlier that **hilareM datōreM** was the object form of "cheerful giver." Later we identified **datōreM** as a noun meaning "giver." Therefore the word that means "cheerful" must be the word ⎯⎯⎯⎯.

A: **hilareM**.

2. The subject form of the word **hilareM** is **hílariS**. Echo your teacher as he describes this picture. ★ ○ • ○ • **HílariS dátor esT** = It's a ⎯⎯⎯⎯ ⎯⎯⎯⎯.

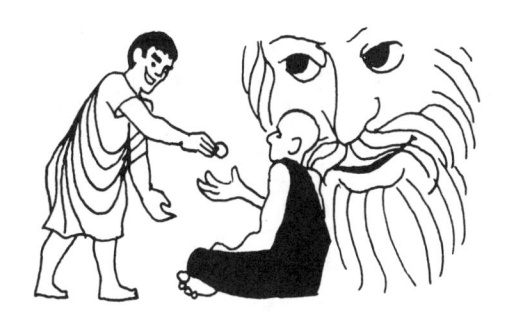

A: cheerful giver.

3. Echo a new technical term. ★ ○ • ○ • **ádjective**

Visual Check: "ádd-jeck-tive"

4. The word **hilariS** is not a noun, it is an "adjectōre." But what is an adjective? Let us first look at English. We use the term "adjective" in English to describe a word that fills the slot between noun marker and noun. For example, the word "happy" in the expression "The happy man" is an adjective because it fills the slot between the words "⎯⎯⎯" and "⎯⎯⎯."

A: the   man

---

405. **Opus** is either ⎯⎯⎯⎯ or ⎯⎯⎯⎯ case.

A: nominative or accusative

406. Write the passive transformation of **Auctor opus laudat.** ★ ○ ○
O⎯⎯ ab a ⎯⎯ l⎯⎯⎯⎯.

Respōnsum: **Opus ab auctōre laudātur.**

407. "Ā quō opus laudātur?" "⎯⎯⎯."

Respōnsum: **Ab auctōre.**

408. "Quid auctor laudat?" "⎯⎯⎯."

Respōnsum: **Opus.**

409. "Irrītāturne auctor opere suō?" "⎯⎯⎯."

Respōnsum: **Nōn irrītātur.**

410. "Satiātūrne auctor opere suō?" "⎯⎯⎯."

Respōnsum: **Satiātur.**

411. "Quō auctor satiātur?" "⎯⎯⎯."

Respōnsum: **Opere suō.**

412. The question **Quid agit?** ("What's he doing?") is answered by a verb. If the verb is a transitive verb, you add to your answer the ⎯⎯⎯ of that verb.

A: object

In the next sequence, we will ask **Quid agit?** questions on these Basic Sentences. Review them here. ★ ●

413. **Hilarem datōrem dīligit Deus.** (3)

414. **In omnī rē vincit imitātiōnem vēritās.** (22)

6-2

5. Say the words that can normally fill the adjective slot in the sentence.

The {walked, happy, was, this, quickly, John, cold} man came into the room.

▼

A: happy
cold

6. "Happy" and "cold," because they can fill this slot, are the part of speech we call ---------s.

▼

A: adjectives.

7. But words other than adjectives can fill this particular slot between noun marker and noun: we can also put a *noun* in the slot between "The" and "man." For example, in the sentence "The radio man came into the room," the word "radio" is *not* an adjective, and here is why. English adjectives must *also* be able to fill a *second* slot, one that comes after such verbs as "is," "seems," "appears," and the like. Say the words that can normally fill the adjective slot in this sentence.

The man seems {fat. goes. gently. thing. bright. stupid. radio.}

▼

A: fat.
bright.
stupid.

8. Therefore, the words "fat," "bright," and "stupid," are ----------

▼

A: adjectives.

---

396. ★ ○ • auctor   397. ★ ○ • opus

Confirmátio: aúctor   opus
                auctórem opus
                auctóre ópere

398. Say both the question and the answer aloud; then write down the answer. "Quis opus laudat?" "----------."

Respónsum: Auctor.

399. "Quid auctor laudat?" "----------."

Respónsum: Opus.

400. In this answer the word opus is in the ---------- case.

A: accusative

401. "Quid ab auctóre laudátur?" "----------."

Respónsum: Opus.

402. In this answer opus is in the ---------- case.

A: nominative

403. To answer this last Latin question you had to transform the original accusative opus in Auctor opus laudat to the nominative opus in Opus ab auctóre laudátur. In other words, you transformed the accusative form opus to the nominative form ----------.

Respónsum: opus.

404. The reason that there is no change in form is that opus is an ---------- form.

A: ambiguous

9. In addition to filling these *two* slots, English adjectives may be compared, as in "This box is small, the second one is smaller yet, but the third one is the _____ of all."

A: smallest

10. There does not happen to be any such word as *"beautifuller," but we can say "She is m___ beautiful than her sister."

A: more

11. Therefore "small" and "beautiful," because they can both show comparison, are both the part of speech called an _____.

A: adjective

12. Let us see if the word "large" is an adjective. It must fit *both* of these slots.
    The _____ man came into the room.
    The man seems _____.
Does "large" fit into both these slots? ____ (Yes/No)

A: large
    large.
    Yes

13. Does it meet the additional test: can we show comparison and say "large," "larger," and "largest"? ____ (Yes/No)

A: Yes

14. Then the word "large" is an _____ because it fills the ___ slots and has the endings "___" and "___" to show comparison.

A: adjective
    two
    -er   -est

15. Do we have in English the forms "hot," "hotter," "hottest"? ____ (Yes/No)

A: Yes

---

390. ✶ ○ • ○ ✶ • *Auctor opus laudat.* (29)

391. ✶ ○ ○ A___ o___ l_____.

Respōnsum: **Auctor opus laudat.**

392. Since you already know the noun **laus/laudem/laude**, you should be able to guess the meaning of the new verb **laudat**.
Auctor opus laudat = An _____ _____ _____.

A: An author praises his work. [Don't copy this meaning into your Reference Notebook.]

393. You knew that the ambiguous nominative-accusative form **opus** in this sentence was the {-m} because _____ is the {-̄}.

Respōnsum: **auctor** {-s}.

394. "An author praises work," makes sense, that is, an author comes out in favor of working hard. But it is not what **Auctor opus laudat** means, and we know this only from the context in which this sentence is used. People use it when they see someone pleased with what he has done himself. We therefore know that **Auctor opus laudat** means.
"An _____ h_____ w_____."

395. Copy this Basic Sentence and its meaning in your Reference Notebook.

A: An author praises his own work.

396-397. To remind you of the forms that you will use in the next sequence, echo once again the paradigm of the two nouns that you will be using.

16. Therefore "hot" is an _____.

A: adjective.

17. Do we have in English the forms "dog," "dogger," "doggest"? ____ (Yes/No)

A: No

18. Therefore "dog" ____ (is/is not) an adjective.

A: is not

19. In English, the position of the adjective is important. In the sentence "The small boy sees the dog," we know it is the ____ (boy/dog) which is small.

A: boy

20. In the sentence "The boy sees the small dog," it is the ___ which is small.

A: dog

21. Is "The boy small sees the dog" a normal English sentence? ____ (Yes/No)

A: No

22. If "small" comes before "dog" (as in "The small dog sees the boy"), it means that "small" describes the word ___.

A: dog.

---

383. To make a general statement, where we would expect a single -s- between vowels we find the sound ___ instead.

Respōnsum: r

384. Instead of *ŏpese the actual ablative form of **opus** is _____.

Respōnsum: opere.

385. Note also that the **u** of **opus** becomes ___ in **opere**.

Respōnsum: e

386. English "opus," Latin **opus**. ★ ○ • ○

387. Musical works are often labeled "Opus Such and Such," "Opus Twenty-Three" would mean that this was the author's twenty-third ____.

A: work.

388. Write the paradigm of the Latin word for "work." _____

Respōnsum: opus
opus
opere

389. Echo the paradigm of the Third Declension noun "author." ★ ○ • **auctor**
auctōrem
auctōre

23. If "small" comes before "boy" it means that "small" describes the word "___."

A: boy.

24. Does it make any difference in the meaning where "small" occurs in the English sentence? ____ (Yes/No)

A: Yes (it sure does!)

25. Echo a new technical term. ★ ○ • ○ • modify

Visual Check: "máw-dee-fy"

26. When an adjective comes between a noun marker and a noun, as in "The old man," we say that the adjective "modifies" the noun. In the phrase "The happy cat," the adjective "happy" _____s the noun "cat" and describes it.

A: modifies

27. Adjectives describe the noun which they _____.

A: modify.

28. In the sentence "The dog is small," the word "small" modifies "___."

A: dog (or "the dog").

29. Pick out the words that will fill *both* of these slots. The ____ cat is purring by the fire. The cat is ____.
(ran/never/big/is/small/sick/kind.)

A: big   small sick kind.

---

378. Now you know that the word **rēgnum** can be either the _____ or the _____ of the verb.

A: subject   object

379. Nouns with this ambiguous nominative-accusative form are also found in the Third Declension, where the signal is zero. Here is the paradigm of an ambiguous Third Declension noun with one form missing. Say the paradigm, supplying the missing form. [Remember that neuters *always* have the nominative and accusative alike.]

nom   opusØ   ("work")
acc   ____
abl   opere   ∧ ★ ○ •

Cōnfirmātiō: opusØ
               opusØ
               opere

380. You will remember that the form **mūs** did not have the signal -s but rather the variant -----

A: zero.

381. The nominative was therefore **mūsØ**. You then learned that the imaginary accusative form ***musem** is actually ------

Respōnsum: mūrem.

382. In other words, it is a fact of the Latin language that a single -s- between two vowels does not occur in native Latin words (although it shows up in a few words borrowed from other Latin languages, and under special conditions in a few Latin words). The imaginary ablative of **opus** would be *opese, but it turns out instead to be the form ------

Respōnsum: opere.

30. Because they can fill these two slots, the words "big," "small," "sick," and "kind" are _____.

A: adjectives.

31. We say "this cat is big, the second one is still _____, and that one is the _____ of all."

A: bigger   biggest

32. "Big," "small," "sick," and "kind" can also be identified as adjectives by the fact that they have forms in "-er" and "-est" to show c_____son.

A: comparison.

33. What part of speech is the word "cowardly" in the sentence, "The cowardly man ran away"? First, let us consider the slots it fills. Does it fill an adjective slot in this sentence? ____ (Yes/No)

A: Yes

34. It fills the slot between the noun marker "___" and the noun "___."

A: the   man.

35. Secondly, can it fill a slot after the verb "is"? Can we say, "The man is cowardly"? ____ (Yes/No)

A: Yes

36. So we have met two of the requirements. Can we compare two people and say, "He is more cowardly"? ____ (Yes/No)

A: Yes

37. "Cowardly" therefore fulfills *all three* of the requirements and is an _____.

A: adjective.

---

369. We also associate words with their opposites, or antonyms. Say the antonym of each word. intemperāns ≠ c___us ∨ ★ ○ •

Cōnfirmātiō: cautus

370. magnus ≠ p___us ∨ ★ ○ •

Cōnfirmātiō: parvus

371. numquam ≠ s___er ∨ ★ ○ •

Cōnfirmātiō: semper

372. nūllus ≠ om___s ∨ ★ ○ •

Cōnfirmātiō: omnis

373. nox ≠ d___ ∨ ★ ○ •

Cōnfirmātiō: diēs

374. So far we have had six nouns whose nominative and accusative cases were alike. They were perīc'l__, vīn__, auxili__, viti__, respōns__, and rēgn__.

Respōnsum: perīc'lum, vīnum, auxilium, vitium, respōnsum, rēgnum.

375. These nouns all belong to the ____ (1st/2nd/3d/4th) Declension.

A: 2d

376. There was also the irregular question word which asks for nonpersonal nouns, whose ambiguous nominative-accusative form is ____.

Respōnsum: Quid?

377. Until you met nouns like vitium, every noun which ended in -m was _____ case and _____ of the verb.

A: accusative   object

38. Is "new," in "The new horse ran swiftly" an adjective? Does it fulfill *all three* requirements? ____ (Yes/No)

A: Yes

39. New fills ____ slots, and has the forms "_____" and "_____."

A: both (two) newer newest.

40. Let's look at a sentence very much like the last one in some ways, "The race horse ran swiftly." Remember: an adjective must fulfill *all three* requirements. "Race" fulfills the requirement about filling the slot between noun marker and noun. Is "The horse is race" a normal sentence? ____ (Yes/No)

A: No

41. Therefore "race" in this sentence ____ (is/is not) an adjective.

A: is not

42. "Race" doesn't show comparison either, because there are no forms for "race" meaning "____ race" and "____ race."

A: more most

43. What part of speech *is* "race" then? We can say, "The race is won" and we can say, "The races are won." Therefore "race" in these sentences is a ____.

A: noun.

44. From the expression "The race horse" we see that a noun ("race" in this example) can fill the slot between a n___ m_____ and a ___.

A: noun marker noun.

---

363. In the changed sentence, we left the same words in the same order, but we changed the structural signals that show {--} and {--}.

A: {-s} and {-m}.

364. It is not enough, of course, to know *just* the structural meaning; you must also know the dictionary meaning of the sentence. This is why we will have drills where you will practice vocabulary.

To learn the meaning of a word, however, you must "associate" it with something. Perhaps the easiest way is to learn a meaningful sentence containing that word. When you see or hear the word **diligit,** you now _____ it with the Basic Sentence Hilarem datōrem diligit Deus.

A: associate

365. You associate the word **reddit** with the sentence V____ v____ r____.

Respōnsum: Vestis virum reddit.

366. There are also other kinds of association. A word that means *about* the same thing as another word is called a "synonym." We say that "house" and "home" are _____s.

A: synonyms.

367. "House" and "home" do not mean *exactly* the same thing. A ____ (house/home) can be empty, but a ____ (house/home) has people living in it.

A: house home

368. Later in this course, new Latin words will usually be explained by familiar Latin _____

A: synonyms.

6-9

45. In other words, in the expression "The race horse," the word "race" is a noun which _____s the word "horse."

◼

A: modifies

46. In the expression "The junk man," the word "junk" is a ____ and _____s the word "____."

◼

A: noun   modifies   man.

47. An English noun can _____ another noun.

◼

A: modify

48. A "junk man" is a man who _____. [In your own words]

◼

A: collects junk.

49. A "station bus" is a ___ that goes to and from the _____.

◼

A: bus   station.

50. On the other hand, a "bus station" is a _____ where people take _____.

◼

A: station (place, etc.)   busses.

51. In the expression "The station bus," the word "_____" _____ the word "___."

◼

A: station   modifies   bus.

52. The word "bus" in "the bus station" is not an adjective because _____. [Two reasons, in your own words.]

◼

A: We cannot say *"busser" (or *"more bus" and *"most bus") and we cannot say *"The station is bus."

---

357. In D, **manus** describes a small group of men, or, as we would say, only a _____ of men.

◼

A: handful

358. *Webster's Collegiate Dictionary* lists thirteen meanings for the English noun "shadow." A Latin dictionary of about the same size (*Cassell's*) has eight meanings for **umbra**, among them "idleness," "uninvited guest," and "a kind of fish."

This diagram means that *some* meanings of Latin **umbra** are about the same as ____ meanings of English "shadow."

A: some

◼

359. Here is a sentence which may or may not be a familiar Basic Sentence. Pronounce and check. **Parvam neat morsu spatiosus viperam taurus.** √ ★ ○ •

360. The sentence above describes picture ____.

A.

◼

361. This ____ (is/is not) the original Basic Sentence.

A: is not

◼

362. This sentence is different from the original Basic Sentence not in the dictionary meaning but in the _____ meaning.

A: structural

6-9

53. The asterisk [*] shows a form or sentence which does not actually ___ in the language.

A: occur (exist, etc.)

54. In English it is *position* in the sentence which tells us which noun an adjective ___.

A: modifies.

55. Remembering that Latin and English have different structures, can we assume that in Latin it is position in the sentence which tells us which noun an adjective modifies? ___ (Yes/No)

A: NO! NO! NO! NO! NO! NO! NO!

56. Let's see then how Latin adjectives *do* work. Pronounce and check. **HilareM datōreM dīligiT DeuS.** √ ★ ○ •

57. You were told earlier that **datōreM** was a ___ and **hilareM** was an ___.

A: noun   adjective.

58. DatōreM is the ___ form of the noun.

A: object

59. HilareM is the ___ form of the adjective.

A: object

60. In Latin, if the noun is object form, then the adjective that modifies it is also the ___ form.

A: object

12-53

350. Write his answer. ★ ○ ○ " ___ ."

Respōnsum: **Manū.**

351. Because of the picture we know that the teacher has said that the sack is being held by the elephant's ___.

A: trunk.

352. In other words, although **manus** has so far meant a part of the human body, you now discover that it can also mean a part of an ___'s body.

A: elephant's

353. When talking about people, **manū** means "by someone's ___," but when talking about elephants, **manū** means "by the elephant's ___."

A: hand   trunk.

354. To the Romans, an elephant's trunk was like a human h___.

A: hand.

manus   *manus*   *manus*   *manus*
  A   B   C   D

355. The instrument illustrated by B was a grappling iron which seized an enemy ship just the way a human ___ might.

A: hand

356. In C, the amount of sand which the man holds is a ___ful.

A: handful.

61. If you read the label you see that, if the noun is subject form, then the adjective that modifies it is also _____ form.

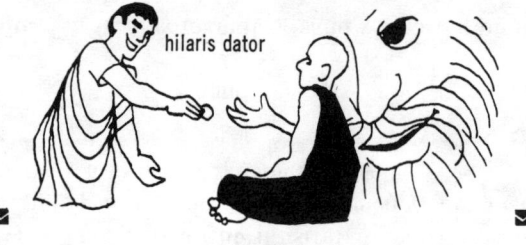

A: subject

62. In other words, in Latin you can tell which noun in the sentence an adjective modifies because the adjective will be the ____ form as the noun it modifies.

A: same

63. HilareM modifies nouns that are *object* form; hilariS modifies nouns that are _____ form.

A: subject

64. The position of a Latin adjective does *not* tell you which noun it modifies. We will now take our Basic Sentence and change hilareM to hilariS but we will keep the same position, which in Latin is not a structural signal. HilariS datōreM dīligiT DeuS. Since the new form hilariS is *subject* form, it now modifies the *subject*, which is ____.

A: DeuS.

65. Copy the sentence **Hilaris datōrem dīligit Deus** in your answer pad and draw a line from the adjective **hilaris** to the subject form which it now modifies.

A: Hilaris datōrem dīligit Deus.

66. Hilaris datōrem dīligit Deus = A _____ ___ ____s a _____.

A: A cheerful God loves a giver.

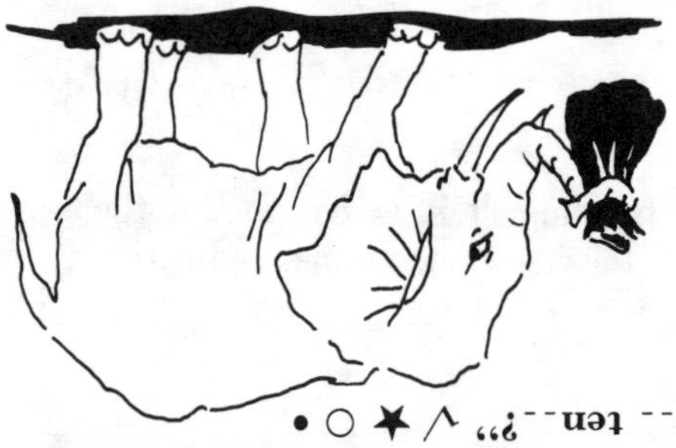

Cōnfirmātiō: Quō elephantus saccum tenet?

345. We are able here to peek into this man's ____ of cards.

A: hand

346. This actor is getting a "good ____" from the audience.

A: hand

347. Someone who works on a farm or boat is often called a "____."

A: hand.

348. In **Manus lavat**, the word **manus** meant ____ of the human ____.

A: part body.

349. Ask your teacher in Latin, "By what is the elephant holding the sack?" "Quā el_____ sacc__ ten___?"

6-11

67. In English, to make "cheerful" modify "God," we would have to move it from one ____ to another ____.

A: slot (position) slot (position).

68. In English it is always the ____ that shows which noun an adjective modifies.

A: slot (position)

69. In Latin it is not the position of an adjective that shows which noun the adjective modifies, but the signal {-_-} or {-_-}.

A: {-s} {-m}.

If you have no tape recorder, get help from your teacher on frames 70-78.

70. Now back briefly to pronunciation. In Unit Three you listened to the contrast between English "dough" and Latin dō. Listen to this contrast again. ★ ○ ○ Which word ends in a "w" sound, the English word or the Latin word? _____

A: The English word.

71. Listen to English "Dee" and Latin dī. ★ ○ ○ Which word ends in a "y" sound, the English word or the Latin word? _____.

A: The English word.

72. Echo a new technical term. ★ ○ • ○ • diphthong

Visual Check: "díp-thong" or "díf-thong"

The vowel sounds in the English words "dough" and "Dee" are not simple vowels but diphthongs. A diphthong is a combination sound where one vowel glides into another. You used a diphthong in the last unit, although you didn't know it. Describe this picture and check.

12-31

340. You must recognize the structural meaning of a word along with its d_____ m_____.

A: dictionary meaning.

341. So far the only dictionary meaning you know for canis is "____."

A: dog.

342. We have tried to show you that words almost always have ____ (several meanings/just one meaning).

A: several meanings.

The English word "dog" has twelve meanings according to *Webster's Collegiate Dictionary*. The Latin word canis happens to have eleven meanings given in a comparable dictionary. The English word "dog" fits only *some* of these meanings. Among other things, Latin canis is "a person who sponges off his friends," "the worst throw at dice," and "someone who is wild with rage."

343. When we say, "Canis means 'dog,'" this is only a short way of saying, "The most common meaning of Latin canis is about the same as the most _____ meaning of the English word 'dog.'"

A: common

344. As the course progresses you will learn that in Latin, as in all languages, words have *wide areas of meaning*. In other words, a word means not just one thing but several. We think of "hand" perhaps as part of the human body. But the markers on this clock are called "____s."

A: hands.

6-12

73. √ ★ ○ • T_ _rus _ _t.

Visual Check: **Taurus est.**

74. Notice how the letters **au** represent a gliding from one vowel to another. This kind of sound we call a _____ . [Check your pronunciation.] √ ★ ○ •

Visual Check: diphthong.("díp-thong" or "díf-thong")

75. We will now learn a new Basic Sentence, this one by Horace. In the first word occurs this Latin diphthong. Echo this first word. ★ ○ • ○ • **CautuS**

76. [If you don't have a tape recorder, write the last word from memory.] ★ ○ ○ C_____ [Write the signal in a big letter.]

A: **CautuS**

77. Echo the first two words. ★ ○ • ○ • **CautuS metuiT**

78. ★ ○ ○ CautuS m_____

A: **metuiT**

79. In **CautuS metuiT** we see the {_-} and {-t} parts of the sentence.

A: {-s}

12-30

336. It was necessary to emphasize *structural meaning* in this way because people who have not studied a foreign language almost always believe that the only problem is the *dictionary meaning*. We hope that you are now aware of the importance, for example, of telling subject from object, which is not dictionary meaning but _____ al _____ ing.

A: structural meaning.

337. If a foreigner were to read an English textbook on chemistry, he could find out with the aid of a dictionary what the words "water," "sulphuric acid," "pour," and "into" meant. But in order to know whether he should pour the water into the acid or the acid into the water, he would have to understand the English _____ signal of word order.

A: structural

338. This person has studied his English structural signals properly. Let's see how he makes out. "Pour the sulphuric acid into the water."

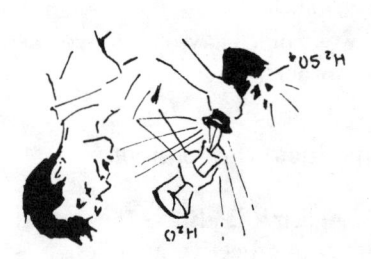

339. His friend, however, could not be bothered with the structural signals. "Be sure not to pour the water into the acid."

6-13

80. Remembering that Latin v sounds like English "w," echo the first three words.
★ ○ • ○ • **CautuS metuiT foveaM**

81. ★ ○ ○ **CautuS metuiT f____M**

A: **foveaM**

82. FoveaM is the {--} part of this sentence.

A: {-m}

83. Chorus the complete Basic Sentence.
★ ○ ○ ◉ ◉ *CautuS metuiT foveaM lupuS.*

84. ★ ○ ○ C_____ m_____ f_____ l_____.

A: **CautuS metuiT foveaM lupuS.**
[If you made a mistake in spelling, copy the sentence again.]

85. In **Cautus metuiT foveaM lupuS** there are two different words that have the signal {--}.

A: {-s}.

86. One word, therefore, must be the part of speech we call a ____, and the other must be an _____ modifying it.

A: noun
   adjective

87. You already know that **lupuS** is a ____ and means "____."

A: noun
   wolf.

12-49

328. Quālem aurem nōn semper habet Fēlīcitās?" "_____."

Respōnsum: **Facilem.**

329. "Quālem datōrem dīligit Deus?"

Respōnsum: **Hilarem.**

330. "Quālis mēns rēgnum possidet?"

Respōnsum: **Bona.**

331. "Quālis lupus metuit foveam?"

Respōnsum: **Cautus.**

332. "Quālem medicum facit aeger intemperāns?" "_____."

Respōnsum: **Crūdēlem.**

333. "Quālis amicus in rē incertā cernitur?" "_____."

Respōnsum: **Certus.**

334. "Quālis aeger medicum crūdēlem facit?" "_____."

Respōnsum: **Intemperāns.**

335. So far we have emphasized heavily the *structural* meanings of the Latin sentences. We have tried to get you to see the kernel and modifiers in a sentence instantly, even before you knew the _____ meanings of the individual words.

A: dictionary

6-14

88. Therefore **cautuS** must be an _____ which _____ **lupuS**.

A: adjective
    modifies

89. ★ ○ • ○ • English "cautious" and Latin **cautuS**. [Of course, without a tape recorder or a teacher you can't be sure that you are right, but you should still be able to make a sound in Latin that is different from English.]

90. The adjective **cautus** means "c_____s."

A: cautious.

91. Show that you know which noun **cautuS** modifies in this sentence by connecting adjective and noun with an arrow in your answer pad. **CautuS metuiT foveaM lupuS.**

A: CautuS metuiT foveaM lupuS.
       ⌒_____⌒

92. In English an adjective occurs just _____ the noun it modifies.

A: before

93. You certainly realize that in presenting new material teachers cannot tell you everything at once. We make general statements and then add to these later. For example, we have just said that adjectives in English come *before* the noun they modify. However, in such phrases as "The house beautiful," "God Almighty," and so forth, it is apparent that these particular adjectives come _____ the noun they modify.

A: after

94. If you think of some examples, you will realize that *most* adjectives in English come ____ (before/after) the noun they modify.

A: before

12-48

317. Echo the paradigm of the adjective that means "What kind of?" ★ ○ • ○ • **quālis**

quālem
quālī
[Note the ablative form.]

318. Write the paradigm of quālis. _____

Respōnsum: quālis
quālem
quālī

We will now do a question and answer drill with the word quālis using the following Basic Sentences.

319. Cautus metuit foveam lupus. (8) ★ ◉

320. Nōn quaerit aeger medicum ēloquentem. (9)

321. Nōn semper aurem facilem habet Fēlicitās. (10)

322. Crūdēlem medicum intemperāns aeger facit. (12)

323. Mēns rēgnum bona possidet. (28)

324. Hilarem datōrem dīligit Deus. (2)

325. Amīcus certus in rē incertā cernitur. (24)

326. Remember that quālis asks for an adjective. Give the adjective which was in the original Basic Sentence. These will be simple substitution questions, that is, you ____ (do/do not) have to change the form of the original word.

Respōnsum: do not

327. "In quālī rē amīcus certus cernitur?" "_____ ___ __.."

Respōnsum: Incertā in rē.

6-15

95. There are *very few* English adjectives that come after their noun, but in any case in English it is always the p_____ of the adjective which tells us which noun it modifies.

A: position

96. Which statement completes the sentence correctly? In Latin an adjective
1) comes just before the noun it modifies.
2) comes just after the noun it modifies.
3) can come anywhere in the sentence.

A: 3) can come anywhere in the sentence.

97. For example, in **CautuS metuiT foveaM lupuS** the adjective **cautuS** is the _____ word in the sentence and **lupuS**, the noun it modifies, is the ____ word in the sentence.

A: first
    last

98. Word order in English serves as a structural signal. In Latin, word order
1) is the same as in English and is a structural signal.
2) is a different order from English but is still a structural signal.
3) is almost entirely free.

A: 3) is almost entirely free.

99. Enter this information under "Facts About Latin."

100. Let us now go through this last Basic Sentence word by word and try to understand how a Roman would react to it. **CautuS** means "cautious." But who is cautious? The signal {-s} tells us that it is the person who is the _____ of the sentence.

A: subject

---

310. Here is the same Basic Sentence in unemphatic word order: **Mēns bona rēgnum possidet.** Put it in the original order that emphasizes the words **mēns** and **bona** by separating them. ____ **rēgnum** ____ **possidet.**

A: **Mēns rēgnum bona possidet.**

311. The antonym of **bona** is **mala**. An evil mind does not possess a kingdom = M___ _____ m__a p_____ t.

A: **Mēns rēgnum mala nōn possidet.**

312. The Latin word for "answer" is the noun **respōnsum**. From now on, when the answer is in Latin we will use the Latin word "_____" instead of "answer."

A: **respōnsum**

313. Question and answer drill on the Basic Sentence **Mēns rēgnum bona possidet.** Say both question and answer aloud, then write your answer. "**Quid rēgnum possidet?**" "_____."

Respōnsum: **Mēns bona.**

314. Echo your teacher as he asks, "What kind of mind possesses a kingdom?" ★ ○ • ○ •

Confirmātiō: "**Quālis mēns rēgnum possidet?**"

315. Now ask him the same question and check. "**Quāl__ m__ rēg___ possi___?**" ∨ ★ ○ •

Confirmātiō: **Quālis mēns rēgnum possidet?**

316. Write down his answer. "_____ ★ ○ ○ ."

Respōnsum: **Bona.**

6-16

101. CautuS means, "A _____ person blanks."

A: cautious

102. We use the colorless verb "blanks" to show that the person who is cautious is _____ of the English sentence.

A: subject

103. We know that the phrase "A cautious person" is subject of our English sentence because it _____.

A: comes before the word blanks, (etc.)

[From now on we will not emphasize the verb ending **T** by printing it in heavy letters.]

104. ★ ○ • ○ • CautuS metuit

105. This second word is the part of speech called a ____.

A: verb.

106. We know it is a verb because of the signal {-_}.

A: {-t}.

107. The meaning of **metuit** is "fears." Drop "fears" into the slot previously occupied by "blanks." **CautuS metuit** = A _____ ____ ____ (something or somebody).

A: A cautious person fears (something or somebody).

108. ★ ○ • ○ • CautuS metuit foveaM

---

304. The adjective **bona** ("good", "noble",) is _____ case.

A: nominative

305. Draw an arrow in your answer pad connecting the adjective **bona** with the noun it modifies.

A: Mens rēgnum bona possidet.
              ⟵

306. The verb **possidet** is a synonym of the verb **habet**. Mens rēgnum bona possidet = A _____ _____ _____ a _____.

A: A noble mind possesses a kingdom.

307. Copy this Basic Sentence and its meaning in your Reference Notebook.

308. Echo a new technical term. ★ ○ • ○ • Stoic

Cōnfirmātiō: "stow'-wick"

309. The author of this saying was Seneca, a Stoic philosopher. You will learn a great deal about the point of view of the Stoics. One of their principles was that the true philosopher could rise above any misfortune; he was master of himself. The philosopher was therefore the equal of any ____ on earth.

A: king

12-46

6-17

109. **FoveaM** has the signal {--}. It is therefore the ------ of the verb.

A:
    object   {-m}

110. Echo these contrasting forms.
★ ○ • ○ • **fovea**
            foveaM

111. **Fovea** means "pitfall" (a hole for catching animals). **CautuS metuit foveaM** =
A -------- ------ ----s the -------.

A: A cautious person fears the pitfall.

112. Echo the entire sentence. ★ ○ • ○ •
CautuS metuit foveaM lupuS = A --------
---- ----s the -------. (In case you are unacquainted with a pitfall, it is a hole in the ground, concealed by branches, to catch animals.)

A: A cautious wolf fears the pitfall.

113. Copy this eighth Basic Sentence and its meaning in your notebook.

12-45

295. **mēns** = "------."

A: mind

296. **Mēns** belongs to the ---- (1st/2d/3d/4th/5th) Declension.

A: 3d

297. From the paradigm you can see that **mēns** ---- (is/is not) one of the ambiguous nouns we have been studying.

A: is not

298. Echo the first two words of a new Basic Sentence. ★ ○ • ○ • **Mēns rēgnum**

A: **Mēns rēgnum**

299. Write. ★ ○ • ○ • M--- r--- ----

A: **Mēns rēgnum**

300. Although **rēgnum** is an ambiguous form, you know that in this sentence it must be ---------- case because **mēns** is ---------- case.

A: accusative   nominative

301. Using the colorless verb "blanks," "**Mēns rēgnum** means, "----------------."

A: A mind blanks a kingdom.

302. ★ ○ • ○ • **Mēns rēgnum bona possidet.** (28) [Observe which vowels are long.]

303. ○ ○ ★ **Mēns rēgnum b--- p--------.**

A: **Mēns rēgnum bona possidet.**
[Did you include the two macrons?]

6-18

114. Pronounce the Latin saying by Horace that describes the picture and check. C_____ m_____ f_____ l_____. ✓ ★ ○ •

▼

Visual Check: **Cautus metuit foveam lupus.**

115. This sentence, like the others we have studied, has been widely quoted because it describes in vivid fashion a common experience. It means that a person will not get into trouble if he is sensible enough to be afraid of d_____ous things.

▼

A: dangerous

116. The sentence was written by the Latin poet H_____.

▼

A: Horace.

117. "A cautious wolf fears the pitfall." = C_____ m_____ f_____ l_____.

▼

A: CautuS metuit foveaM lupus.

118. You know now *two* adjectives, h_____, and c_____.

▼

A: hilariS
    cautuS

119. The combination of sounds *au* is called a _____. ✓ ★ ○ •

▼

Visual Check: ("dip-thong" or "diff-thong") diphthong

12-44

286. This means, "_____."

▼

A: A cautious young man fears wine.

287. Write the paradigm of perīc'lum. _____

▼

A: perīc'lum
   perīc'lum
   perīc'lō

288. Write the paradigm of vitium. _____

▼

A: vitium
   vitium
   vitiō

289. Write the paradigm of vīnum. _____

▼

A: vīnum
   vīnum
   vīnō

290. regnum ★ ○ • ○ • regnum
   regnum ("kingdom")
   regnō

▼

291. The word **regnum** belongs to the ____ (1st/2d/3d/4th/5th) Declension.

▼

A: 2d

292. From the paradigm you can tell that **regnum** ____ (is/is not) one of the ambiguous nouns we have been studying.

▼

A: is

293. mēns ★ ○ • ○ • mēns
   mentem
   mente

▼

294. An English derivative of **mēns** is "mental," which is an adjective that means "pertaining to the m____."

▼

A: mind.

120. Say aloud the Basic Sentence that describes each picture. H_____ d_____ d_____ D____.

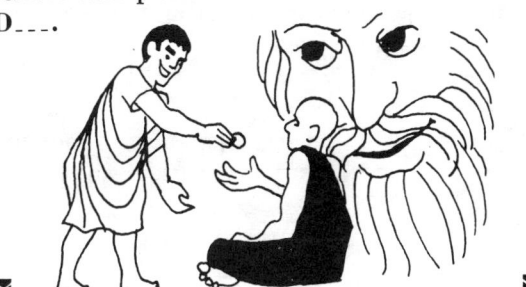

A: HilareM datōreM dīligit Deus.

121. V_____ n_____ p_____.

A: VēritāS numquam perit.

122. Cau___ met___ fov___ lu____.

A: CautuS metuit foveaM lupuS.

123. El_____ n__ c____ m_____.

A: ElephantuS nōn capit mūreM.

---

279. Amīcus certus in rē incertā cernitur. Amīcus certus in _____ cernitur.

A: Amīcus certus in vīnō cernitur.

280. This means, "_____." [In your own words]

A: A sure friend is discovered in wine.

281. Here is a well-known saying, popular in German drinking songs. Pronounce and check with the tape. **In vīnō vēritās.** ✓ ○ ★ •

282. This expresses the same idea as the sentence which you have just constructed, namely, that when people have been drinking wine they are likely to _____.

A: tell the truth (sometimes unfortunately!)

283. Numquam perīc'lum sine perīc'lō vincitur. Numquam perīc'lum sine _____ vincitur.

A: Numquam perīc'lum sine vīnō vincitur.

284. This means, "_____." [In your own words]

A: Danger is never overcome without wine. (There are certain people who can never bring themselves to do something dangerous or difficult without first taking a drink. For some reason, this kind of encouragement is known as "Dutch courage.")

285. Notice that in this frame we have substituted *juvenis* for the original word *lupus*. Cautus metuit *foveam juvenis*. Cautus metuit _____ juvenis.

A: Cautus metuit vīnum juvenis.

6-20

124. L___ n__ m____ l____.

A: **LupuS nōn mordet lupuM.**

125. Echo a new technical term. ★ ○ • ○ • nominative

Visual Check: "nóm-min-nay-tive"

126. "Nominative" is the technical term for the Latin subject form. We also use the technical term "case," and say that **vestiS** is the _____ case.

A: nominative

127. **Vir,** because it has the new signal zero, is also _____ case. ✓ ★ ○ •

Visual Check: nominative

128. Echo another technical term. ★ ○ • ○ • accusative

Visual Check: "ack-kúze-zuh-tive"

129. "Accusative" is the technical term for the Latin object form. From now on we will not say that **vēritāteM** is the object form; we will say instead that it is the _____ case.

A: accusative

130. **FoveaM** is the _____ case; **fovea** is the _____ case.

A: accusative
   nominative

---

272. "Facitne vīnum virum stultum an sapientem?" "Vīnum facit virum _____." (Sub hāc līneā auxilium est.)

Auxilium: The question asks, "Does wine make a man stupid or wise?"

A: **Vīnum facit virum stultum.**

In the next sequence we will substitute the forms of **vīnum** in the Basic Sentences listed below.

If you have any question, stop the tape player and look in your Reference Notebook. If there is still any question, ask your classroom teacher to explain the sentence to you. ★ ●

273. **Amīcus certus in rē incertā cernitur.** (24)

274. **Cautus metuit foveam lupus.** (8)

275. **Vestis virum reddit.** (1)

276. **Numquam perīc'lum sine perīc'lō vincitur.** (25)

Substitute the right form of **vīnum** for the italicized word in each sentence; pronounce your sentence and check with the tape. Then write down the correct form of **vīnum.** Give an English translation for the new sentence.

277. *Vestis* virum reddit.
   Vīn_____ virum reddit.

A: **Vīnum virum reddit.**

278. This means, "_____."
   [In your own words]

A: Wine makes the man.
   (Meaning that he is a coward unless he is drunk. This is not an attractive picture but is sometimes true.)

12-42

131. The signal that shows that **fovea** is nominative case is the signal ‒‒‒‒.

A: zero.

132. **FoveaM** is the ‒‒‒‒‒‒‒‒‒‒ case. √ ★ ○ •

Visual Check: accusative ("ack-kúze-zuh-tive")

133. **Dator** is the ‒‒‒‒‒‒‒‒‒‒ case. √ ★ ○ •

Visual Check: nominative ("nóm-min-nay-tive")

134. **ManuM** is the ‒‒‒‒‒‒‒‒‒‒ ‒‒‒‒.

A: accusative case.

The next nine frames will ask you to identify the case of different nouns.

135. **Mūs** is the ‒‒‒‒‒‒‒‒‒‒ ‒‒‒‒.

A: nominative case.

136. **VesteM** is the ‒‒‒‒‒‒‒‒‒‒ ‒‒‒‒.

A: accusative case.

137. **VēritāS** is the ‒‒‒‒‒‒‒‒‒‒ ‒‒‒‒.

A: nominative case.

138. **Deum** is the ‒‒‒‒‒‒‒‒‒‒ ‒‒‒‒.

A: accusative case.

139. **Sīmiam** is the ‒‒‒‒‒‒‒‒‒‒ ‒‒‒‒.

A: accusative case.

---

265. The ablative of **leō** is ‒‒‒‒‒‒.

A: leōne.

266. The nominative of **virō** is ‒‒‒‒.

A: vir.

267. **Tauro** and **virō** rhyme. They ‒‒‒‒ (are/ are not) the same case.

A: are

268. **Leō** and **aprō** rhyme. They ‒‒‒‒ (are/ are not) the same case.

A: are not

269. Here are two new adjectives. Echo your teacher's description of this picture. ★ ○ ○ •

J‒‒‒‒‒s st‒‒‒‒e‒‒‒‒t.

Cōnfirmātiō: **Juvenis stultus est.**

270. ★ ○ ○ • V‒‒‒‒s s‒‒‒‒t.

Cōnfirmātiō: **Vir sapiēns est.**

271. **Stultus** and **sapiēns** are antonyms; we will use them in the next question. **Stultus** means "st‒‒‒d," and **sapiēns** means "w‒‒‒."

A: stupid wise.

6-22

140. **Vulpēs** is the _____ ____.

A: nominative case.

141. **Aquila** is the _____ ____.

A: nominative case.

142. **Leōnem** is the _____ ____.

A: accusative case.

143. During the last sequence we vanished the heavy letters which called attention to the signals for _____ and _____.

A: subject   object.

144. The nominative case has two variant signals, __ and ____.

A: -s   zero.

145. The sound **au** in the Latin word **cautus** is not a simple vowel but a _____.

A: diphthong.

146. Echo your teacher as he says a new Latin diphthong. ★ ○ • ○ • **ae**

147. Pronounce **ae** and check. √ ★ ○ •

148. ★ ○ • ○ • **au, ae**

149. Your teacher will say one of these two diphthongs. ★ ○ • ○ • **au? ae?**

A: ae

---

259. N __ s __ v _____ (26) √ ★ ○ •

Cōnfirmātiō: Nēmō sine vitiō est. (26)

260. Sap ____ v ___ ob _____ (27) √ ★ ○ •

Cōnfirmātiō: Sapientia vīnō obumbrātur.

261. From the three frames above it is obvious that the Latin word **cōnfirmātiō** is used for the English expression, "V____ Ch____."

A: Visual Check.

262. The English derivative of **cōnfirmātiō** is "____tion."

A: confirmation.

263. The form **cōnfirmātiō** is ____ (ablative like **taurō**/nominative like **imitātiō**).

A: nominative like **imitātiō**.

264. Pick out the nouns in this list which are *nominative case*: **capillō, imitātiō, nēmō, aegrō, cōnfirmātiō, virō, leō, magnō.**

A: **imitātiō, nēmō, cōnfirmātiō, leō**

150. Your teacher will now say a word that contains this new diphthong. ★ ○ • ○ • **quaerit**

151. Pronounce this word and check. **quaerit** √ ★ ○ •

152. Echo a new technical term. ★ ○ • ○ • **negator**

Visual Check: "nee-gáy-tor"

153. The word **nōn** is a "negator." You learned it in the sentence **Elephantus ---- capit mūrem.**

A: **nōn**

154. **Nōn** is a _____.

A: negator.

155. We call **nōn** a "negator" because it makes the idea *negative*; that is, the **nōn** in **Elephantus nōn capit mūrem** shows that elephants ____ catch mice.

A: don't

156. We will now build up a Basic Sentence one word at a time. Echo the first word. ★ ○ • ○ • **Nōn**

157. This word **nōn** is a negator; we know that the sentence will say that something does ___ happen.

A: not

158. Since **nōn** makes the sentence negative, it is the part of speech called a _____.

A: negator.

---

254. **Sapientiam vīnum obumbrat.** In this transformed sentence you can tell whether **vīnum** is subject or object because the word **sapientiam** is the _____ of the sentence. (Sub hāc līneā auxilium est.)

Auxilium: Look at the signal on **sapientiam.**

A: object

255. Therefore you know that **vīnum** is here the _____.

A: subject.

256. "Aperītne an obumbrat vīnum sapientiam?" "_____."

A: **Obumbrat.**

257. We will try to have the program contain less and less English and more and more _____.

A: Latin.

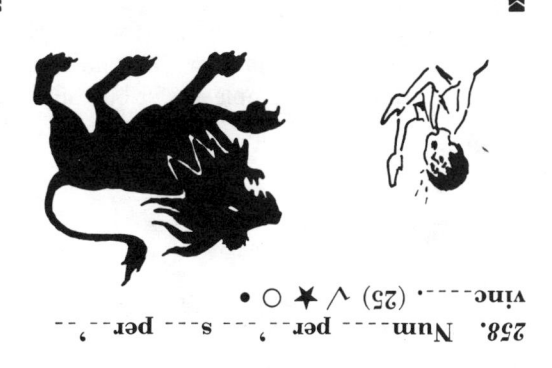

Give the Basic Sentence which these pictures illustrate and check with the tape.

258. Num ---- per ´-- s ---- per ´-- vinc ---- (25) √ ★ ○ •

Cōnfirmātiō: Numquam perīc'lum sine perīc'lō vincitur. (25)

159. Echo the first two words. ★ ○ • ○ •
Nōn quaerit

160. In saying Latin **ae** the tongue glides from one position to another. The new sound **ae** therefore is not a simple vowel but, like **au**, it is a ———.

A: diphthong.

161. Write. ★ ○ ○ **N__ qu_____** [If you do not have a tape recorder, write from memory: if necessary, look back.]

A: **Nōn quaerit**

162. **Nōn** is a ———.

A: negator.

163. We know from the signal {-t} that **quaerit** is a ____ (noun/verb/adjective/negator).

A: verb.

164. **Quaerit** is a "transitive" verb. Pronounce this technical term. transitive √ ★ ○ •

Visual Check: "trán-zit-tive"

165. You will remember that transitive verbs pattern with an object. You therefore expect to find in this sentence not only a noun in the nominative case (the subject), but also another noun in the ———— case.

A: accusative

166. In other words, **quaerit** is the {-t} part of an {__ __ -t} sentence.

A: {-s -m -t}

167. Still to come in the sentence are both the {--} and {--}.

A: {-s} {-m}.

168. The dictionary meaning of **quaerit** is "seeks." **Nōn quaerit** = Somebody doesn't ____ s_____.

A: Somebody doesn't seek something (or somebody).

169. The person who doesn't seek will have the signal {--}, and what he doesn't seek will have the signal {--}.

A: {-s}
     {-m}.

170. **Nōn** is the part of speech we call a _____.

A: negator.

171. Echo the first three words of this new Basic Sentence. ★ ○ • ○ • **Nōn quaerit aeger**

172. Write. ★ ○ ○ **Nōn quaerit ae___**

A: **aeger**

173. There is the same _____ in the first syllable of **aeger** as there is in the first syllable of **quaerit**.

A: diphthong

174. Echo the contrasting forms of the Latin words for "sick person." ★ ○ • ○ • **aeger aegrum**

175. **Aeger** must be the _____ case.

A: nominative

---

242. This means that when a person drinks too much wine, the wine takes away his _____.

A: wisdom.

243. Many of the prefixes on Latin verbs serve to strengthen the verb. Whereas **umbrat** would mean "to shadow," **obumbrat** means "to ----shadow."

A: overshadow.

244. "Overshadow" means to put something compl---ly in the shade.

A: completely

245. The prefix **ob-** in the verb **obumbrātur** serves to _____ the simple verb **umbrat**.

A: strengthen (intensify, etc.)

246. The sentence **Sapientia vīnō obumbrā- tur** was written by a famous Roman scientist who is called "Pliny the Elder," to distinguish him from his nephew who is called "_____ the Younger."

A: Pliny

247. Contrary to the impression we get from movies about ancient Rome, most Romans were temperate in the use of wine. Although they drank it regularly with meals, they mixed it with water, adding more water than wine. Pliny the Elder tells us that people sometimes drank a mixture as weak as eight parts of _____ to one part of _____.

A: water
   wine.

176. The signal that shows that **aeger** is nominative case is ----.

A: ∅ (or zero).

177. The form **aeger** ("sick person") is the expected {--} of the sentence.

A: {-s}

178. Because it has the signal zero the structural meaning of **aeger** is "------ of the sentence."

A: subject

179. The dictionary meaning of **aeger** is "---------."

A: sick person.

180. To show both dictionary meaning and structural meaning we say that **Nōn quaerit aeger** means, "A ---- ------ does --- ---- s--------."

A: A sick person does not seek somebody (or something).

181. Echo the first four words. ★ ○ • ○ •
Nōn quaerit aeger medicum

182. Write. ★ ○ ○ **Nōn quaerit aeger m-------.**

A: **medicum.**

183. **Medicum** is the expected {--} of the sentence.

A: {-m}

---

234. The noun **umbra** means "-------."

A: shadow.

235. Write your teacher's description of this picture. ★ ○ ○ **Qu----- t----- ob--------**

A: **Quercus taurum obumbrat.**

236. This means that the s----- ---- ---- the -----.

A: oak tree shades the bull.

237. The first two letters of **obumbrat** are the ------ of the word.

A: prefix

238. The prefix in **obumbrat** is -------.

A: **ob-.**

239. In our new Basic Sentence the verb **obumbrat** has the meaning "overshadow"; the passive form **obumbrātur** means "--------------."

A: is overshadowed.

240. **Sapientia vīnō obumbrātur** (27) = "-------------- is -----------------."

A: Wisdom is overshadowed by wine.

241. Copy this Basic Sentence and its meaning in your Reference Notebook.

184. When we wish to talk about contrasting forms of words we will often indicate this by means of a slash [/]. For example, **medicus/medicum** means that the form **medicus** contrasts with the form ———.

A: medicum.

185. In the same way, **mūs/mūrem** means that **mūs** ———s with **mūrem**.

A: contrasts

186. The dictionary meaning of **medicus/medicum** is "doctor." **Nōn quaerit aeger medicum** = A ———— ——— doesn't ——— a ———.

A: A sick person doesn't seek a doctor.

187. As it stands, this statement is absurd, because sick people are the very ones who *do* seek doctors. What we expect is a modifier of some part of the {-s} {-m} {-t}. A modifier would ——— additional information.

A: give (add, provide, etc.)

188. Perhaps a sick person doesn't seek an *untrained* doctor, or perhaps a *foolish* sick person doesn't seek a doctor. In this example, "foolish" would be a ———— of "sick person."

A: modifier

189. And "untrained" would be a ———— of "doctor."

A: modifier

190. Now let us see what the modifier actually is in this sentence. Echo the complete Basic Sentence. ★ ○ ● ● *Nōn quaerit aeger medicum ēloquentem.* [Just a reminder: give a loud, clear answer for all the Latin frames.]

---

227. ★ ● ○ ● **vīnum**
vīnum ("wine")
vīnō

228. Say the paradigm of the word for "wine."

———
———
———
———— ∨ ★ ○ ●

VCh: **vīnum**
vīnum
vīnō

229. Pronounce and check. *Sapientia vīnō obumbrātur.* ∨ ★ ○ ●

230. The last three letters of **obumbrātur** are ———— ———— ————

A: passive voice.

231. In a previous Basic Sentence, the first two letters of **incertus** were called a "p———x."

A: prefix.

232. Like the **in-** of **incertus**, the **ob-** of **obumbrātur** is a ————.

A: prefix.

233. If we remove both the prefix **ob-** and the verb signal **-tur** from **obumbrātur**, we have five letters left. This is the word's stem, which is: -————-.

A: -umbrā-.

191. Write. ★ ○ ○ <u>Nōn</u> <u>quaerit</u> <u>aeger</u> <u>medi-cum</u> <u>ēl</u>________. [There should be two macrons in the complete sentence.]

A: **Nōn quaerit aeger medicum ēloquentem.**

192. The modifier is the word **ēloquentem,** which has the signal --.

A: **-m.**

193. Echo these contrasting forms.
★ ○ • ○ • **ēloquēns**
ēloquentem

194. Pronounce and check. **Nōn quaerit aeger medicum ēloquentem.** √ ★ ○ •

195. The adjective **ēloquentem,** because it ends in **-m,** modifies -------.

A: **medicum.**

196. The structural meaning of **ēloquentem** is "------- of **medicum.**"

A: modifier

197. The dictionary meaning of **ēloquentem** is "talkative." **Nōn quaerit aeger medicum ēloquentem** = -------------------------.

A: A sick person doesn't seek a talkative doctor.

198. Enter this ninth Basic Sentence in your Reference Notebook.

219. **"Quid in omnī virō est?"** "------."

A: **Vitium.**

220. ★ ○ • ○ • ***Sapientia vīnō obumbrātur.*** (27)

221. We are trying to make the directions as short and clear as possible. The number 27 in parenthesis following this sentence tells you that this is a new ----- --------.

A: Basic Sentence.

222. ★ ○ ○ <u>S-------</u> <u>v---</u> <u>ob--------</u>. [Include the three macrons!]

A: **Sapientia vīnō obumbrātur.**

223. This sentence is an ---- {**-s -t**}
{**-s -m -t**}
{**-s -tur**} type of sentence.

A: {**-s -tur**}

224. If you saw the word **vīnō** all by itself, you could not tell whether it was, like **leō** in the --------- case or, **lupō,** in the -------- case.

A: nominative ablative

225. But in the sentence **Sapientia vīnō obumbrātur,** you know that **vīnō** is -------- case. (**Auxilium sub hāc līneā est.**)

Auxilium: The subject of the sentence is **sapientia.** Therefore **vīnō** cannot be nominative.

A: ablative

226. Because the characteristic vowel in the ablative form **vīnō** is **o,** you know that this noun belongs to the ---- (1st/2d/3d/4th) Declension.

A: 2d

6-29

199. That is, he wants the doctor to ____ him, not ____ to him.

A: cure (etc.)
   talk

200. Again, we will give you practice in learning to *ignore* what seem to you like the "natural" signals of the position of the words. Position of the words is a "natural" signal to a speaker of English, but it is a *false* and *misleading* "signal" if you are trying to learn the ____ language.

A: Latin

201. We are going to make *some kind of change* in the last Basic Sentence. If the change is one of position, then the meaning of the Latin sentence ____ (does/does not) change.

A: does not

202. If the change is, for example, from **aeger** to **aegrum,** then the meaning of the sentence ____ (does/does not) change.

A: does

203. Here is the original sentence: **Nōn quaerit aeger medicum ēloquentem.** Here is the changed sentence: **Nōn quaerit aegrum medicus ēloquentem.**
The original **aeger** has been changed to _____, and the original **medicum** has been changed to _____.

A: aegrum
   medicus.

12-33

213. "**Habetne omnis vir vitium?**" "_____." (Auxilium sub hāc lineā est.)

Auxilium: This means, "Does every man possess a fault?"

A: Habet.

214. "**Quid habet omnis vir?**" "_____." (Auxilium sub hāc lineā est.)

Aux: You can find the answer for this question in one of the questions above. Look back if you need to.

A: Vitium.

215. "**Quis nūllum vitium habet?**" "_____."

A: Nēmō.

216. "**Estne vitium in nūllō virō an in omnī virō?**" "_____." (Auxilium sub hāc lineā est.)

Auxilium: This means, "Is there a fault in no man or in every man?"

A: In omnī virō.

217. "**Estne vitium in omnī virō?**" "_____."

A: Est.

218. "**In quō est vitium**," "_____." (Auxilium sub hāc lineā est.)

Auxilium: Look back at the previous frames.

A: In omnī virō.

204. So we have interchanged the _____ and the _____ of the sentence.

A: subject
    object

205. Nōn quaerit aegrum medicus ēloquentem. = _____.

A: A doctor doesn't seek a talkative sick person. (But they certainly seem to get a lot of them, just the same.)

206. Here is the original again. **Nōn quaerit aeger medicum ēloquentem.** √ ★ ○ •

207. Look carefully at this changed sentence to see whether the change is one of signals or merely of position. **Medicum ēloquentem nōn quaerit aeger.**
The change in this sentence is a change of
_____.

A: position.

208. This changed sentence means, "_____."

A: A sick person doesn't seek a talkative doctor.

209. Give the meaning of another changed sentence. **Medicum nōn quaerit aeger ēloquēns** = _____

A: A talkative sick person doesn't seek a doctor. He goes around and tells everybody what is wrong with him instead of _____.

A: seeking medical advice.

---

207. To ask the question, **Quid vult fēmina?** on the Basic Sentence **Vulpēs vult fraudem, lupus agnum, fēmina laudem** (15), it was necessary to _____ **fēmina laudem.**

A: expand

208. In this next sequence, we will make use of all three techniques at once, thus giving us many more possibilities. Since these questions are harder, we will give you extra help if you need it. Here is how we will give you that extra help. First echo the paradigm of the Latin word for "help."

★ ○ • ○ • auxilium
              auxilium
              auxiliō   ("help,")
              auxilio

209. The sentence "**Sub hāc līneā auxilium est.**" means, "There is ____ h____ b____ w this l____."

A: help below this line.

210. The word **hāc** is ablative case and means "_____."

A: this.

[If you *know* the answer, say it, and pull the mask down to the answer section, ignoring the section marked Auxilium. But if you feel that you would like more help in finding the right answer, pull down the mask to reveal the Auxilium section. Then answer and lower the mask again to check your answer.]

211. "**Quis sine vitiō est?**" "_____."

A: Nēmō.

212. "**Sine quō est nēmō?**" "_____."

A: Sine vitiō.

6-31

210. Now to refresh your mind on the original that means, "A sick person doesn't seek a talkative doctor," chorus the original Basic Sentence. ★ ○ ○ ● ● N__ qu_____ ae___ _____ ē_.

Visual Check: **Nōn quaerit aeger medicum ēloquentem.**

211. Describe the following pictures, using the familiar Basic Sentences. V_____ v____ r_____.

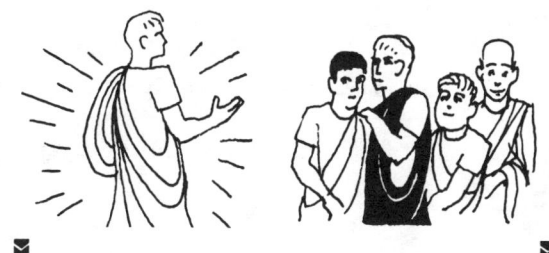

A: **Vestis virum reddit.**

212. L____ __ m_____ l____.

A: **Lupus nōn mordet lupum.**

213. V_____ n_____ p____.

A: **Vēritās numquam perit.**

12-31

200. Although **nēmō** and **vitiō** end in the same sound, **nēmō** is _____ case and **vitiō** is _____ case.

A: nominative
ablative

201. Which words in this list are nominative case? **perīc'lō, leō, taurō, agnō, imitātiō, deō, nēmō.**

A: leō nēmō
imitātiō

202. The ablative form of **leō** is _____.

A: **leōne.**

203. The ablative form of **imitātiō** is _____.

A: **imitātiōne.**

204. The ablative form of **nēmō** is _____.

A: **nēmine.**

205. You have now had three kinds of questions. The easiest question is represented by **Quem vestis reddit?**, where you merely have to the accusative **virum** for the accusative **Quem?**.

A: substitute

206. In other words, you don't have to make any change in the form of the noun. Then the questions got a little more complicated. To answer the question, "**Quis ā Deō dīligitur?**" you had to transform the accusative **Hilarem** to **Hilāris dator**, which is in the _____ case.

A: nominative

6-32

214. Ca____ me____ fo____ l____.

A: **Cautus metuit foveam lupus.**

215. N__ quaer__ aeg__ medic__ ēloquent__.

A: **Nōn quaerit aeger medicum ēloquentem.**

216. Word order in Latin ____ (does/does not) show which noun an adjective modifies.

A: does not

217. Word order in Latin ____ (does/does not) show which word is subject and which word is object.

A: does not

218. What word order *does* do in Latin is to show *emphasis*. The *most common* word order is subject, object, verb. It is for this reason that we placed the {-s} and the other elements in the order {__}, {__}, {__} in talking about the most common Latin sentence type.

A: {-s}, {-m}, {-t}

219. The order subject, object, verb in Latin is the most _____ order.

A: common

---

192. Echo your teacher as he says that no one catches a mouse. ✱ ○ • ○ •

VCh: **Nēmō capit mūrem.**

193. **Nēmō capit mūrem** is built upon Elephantus nōn capit mūrem by omitting the word ___ and substituting ____ for _____.

A: **nōn** **nēmō** **elephantus**

194. Since **nēmō** has been substituted for **elephantus** it is obvious that the new word **nēmō** must be _____ case.

A: nominative

195. ✱ ○ • **nēmō**
nēminem
nēmine

196. Nobody bites a wolf = ____ l____.

A: **Nēmō mordet lupum.**

197. Nobody seeks a talkative doctor = ____ qu____ _____ _____.

A: **Nēmō quaerit medicum ēloquentem.**

198. Nobody has a sympathetic ear. ____ f____ h____.

A: **Nēmō aurem faciłem habet.**

199. Here is Basic Sentence 26. In it the intransitive verb **est** means "exists."
✱ ○ • ○ • **Nēmō sine vitiō est.**

220. The last word in the sentence is the one that receives the heaviest emphasis, because we are waiting for it to complete the sentence. Thus in **Vestis virum reddit,** we first hear **vestis,** then **virum.** But what is it that clothes do to a man? We do not know until we come to the Latin word _____.

A: reddit.

221. The most important word in the average sentence is often the verb. It is for this reason that the verb is often the l___ word in the sentence.

A: last

222. Look at the nine Basic Sentences in your Reference Notebook. The last word is the **-m** in ____ (1/2/3/4/5/6/7/8/9) of them.

A: 3

223. The last word was the **-s** in ____ (1/2/3/4/5/6/7).

A: 2.

224. The last word was the **-t** in ____ (1/2/3/4/5/6).

A: 4.

225. Perhaps we can describe the importance of Latin word order by comparing it with a play. When we have the word **mūs,** we know that whatever action takes place, a _____ will do it.

A: mouse

---

184. Substitute the correct form of **vitium** for the italicized word and check your sentence with the tape. Then write down the form of **vitium.**

Vēritātem diēs aperit.
√ ○ ★ ● Vit_____ diēs aperit.

A: **Vitium** diēs aperit.

185. This means, "_____." [In your own words; do not expect your translation to be exactly like the one given in the answer.]

A: Time discloses a flaw (crime, fault, vice).

186. **Sub jūdice līs est.**
Sub jūdice vit___ est.

A: Sub jūdice vitium est.

187. This means, "_____."

A: The crime is before the judge.

188. Notice that we have substituted **vir** for **lupus.**
Cautus metuit *lupum* vir.
Cautus metuit vit___ vir.

A: Cautus metuit vitium vir.

189. This means, "_____."

A: A cautious man fears crime (vice, etc.)

190. *Hilarem datōrem* nōn dīligit Deus.
Vit___ nōn dīligit Deus.

A: Vitium nōn dīligit Deus.

191. This means, "_____."

A: God does not love crime (vice).

226. Now the word **leōnem** appears. The tension mounts! The mouse is going to do something to the lion, but the big question is: _____ _____? [In your own words.]

A: _____ What is he going to do to the lion?

227. Now we find out. Listen to your teacher's description of this picture. ★ ○ ○ M _ _ l _ _ _ _ _
m _ _ _ _ _ _.

Visual Check: **Mūs leōnem metuit.**

228. This means that _____.

A: _____ the mouse fears the lion.

229. Now suppose we were to change the order. Here is an elephant, and we know what he does: he's afraid. What we want to know is, "_____ _____?" [In your own words.]

A: _____ What is he afraid of?

230. Listen to what he does. ★ ○ ○
El_____ m_____ c____.

Visual Check: **Elephantus metuit canem.**

231. In the last sentence, the word that we were waiting for was the word _____.

A: **canem.**

232. Because of its position in the sentence, the most important word in **Vestis virum reddit** is _____.

A: **reddit.**

233. In the sentence **Elephantus nōn capit mūrem,** we are not told what it is that an elephant doesn't catch until we come to the ____ word in the sentence.

A: last

234. Therefore the word that receives the heaviest emphasis in **Elephantus nōn capit mūrem** is the Latin word _____.

A: **mūrem.**

235. Here is a new sequence. In the next frames you will find pictures describing four situations. Your teacher will say sentences describing some, but not all of them. He may describe some more than once. You will be tempted to rely on English word order. *Resist!* Listen to the *Latin* signals of {-s} and {-m}.

---

168. Substitute a form of peric'lum.
Vestis virum reddit.
_____ virum reddit.

A: Peric'lum virum reddit.

169. This means, "_____."

A: Danger makes the man. (That is, it is danger that makes a man out of a boy.)

170. Substitute a form of peric'lum.
Vēritās numquam perit.
_____ numquam perit.

A: Peric'lum numquam perit.

171. This means, "_____."

A: Danger never dies. (That is, there is always danger.)

172. ★ ○ • ○ • vitium
vitium
vitiō

[Cover this frame before you go to the next frame.]

173. Write the paradigm. ★ ○ ○ _____.

A: vitium
vitium
vitiō

174. In the ablative case can be seen the characteristic vowel ___, so you can tell that **vitium** belongs to the ___ Declension.

A: o
2d

175. You can tell from the paradigm that two of the forms of **vitium** are alike, the _____ case and the _____ case.

A: nominative
accusative

6-36

A   B

C   D

236. Here is the first sentence. ★ ○ ○ **Vulpēs** ____m ____t.

Visual Check: **Vulpēs rānam metuit.**

237. This describes picture ____.

A: B.

238. ★ ○ ○ **Rānam** ____t ____s.

Visual Check: **Rānam metuit vulpēs.**

239. This describes picture ____.

A: B.

240. ★ ○ ○ ___m ____s ____t.

Visual Check: **Anum īnfāns quaerit.**

241. This describes picture ____.

A: C.

242. ★ ○ ○ ____m ___s ____t.

Visual Check: **Īnfantem anus quaerit.**

243. This describes picture ____.

A: D.

---

162. Create new sentences, using Basic Sentences as models.

1) Substitute the corresponding case of perīc'lum for the italicized word in the Basic Sentence by writing and then reading aloud what you have written.

2) Give an English translation of what you have written. Do not expect that your translation will always be like the one in the answer. If in doubt, ask your teacher.

Here is the first sentence: **Cautus metuit *foveam* lupus.** Which form of perīc'lum do you choose? You know that *foveam* is the _____ case.

A: accusative

163. Therefore you should substitute the _____ case of perīc'lum.

A: accusative

164. **Cautus metuit p_____ lupus.**

A: **Cautus metuit perīc'lum lupus.**

165. This means, "_____."

A: A cautious wolf fears danger.

166. Proceed in the same way, substituting a form of perīc'lum for the italicized word.

Nūlla avāritia sine *poenā* est.
Nūlla avāritia sine _____ est.

A: **Nūlla avāritia sine perīc'lō est.**

167. This means, "_____."

A: There is no greed without danger.

6-37

In this sequence your teacher will describe some of these pictures. Write from dictation. If you do not have a tape recorder, copy the sentence.

A   B

C   D

244. Write. ★ ○ ○ _____ .

A: **Sīmiam lavat vir.**

245. This describes picture _____ .

A: A.

246. Write. ★ ○ ○ _____ .

A: **Rānam mordet piscis.**

247. This describes picture _____ .

A: D.

248. ★ ○ ○ _____ .

A: **Vir sīmiam lavat.**

249. This describes picture _____ .

A: A.

250. ★ ○ ○ _____ .

A: **Piscem rāna mordet.**

251. This describes picture _____ .

A: C.

A: perīc'lum
  perīc'lum
  perīc'lō

161. Write the paradigm of perīc'lum.

A: nominative
    accusative

160. We know that in this sentence perīc'lum is _____ case, because vēritātem is _____ case.

A: Vēritātem perīc'lum aperit.

[This sentence has three macrons] p_____ ap_____
Vēritātem diēs aperit. ★ ○ ○ V_____
Write as your teacher says in Latin, "Danger discloses the truth," based on the model of

159. We will now substitute the new word perīc'lum in those familiar Basic Sentences.

158. Vēritās numquam perit. (7)

157. Vestis virum reddit. (1)

156. Nūlla avāritia sine poenā est. (19)

155. Vēritātem diēs aperit. (2)

154. Cautus metuit foveam lupus. (8)

★ ●

A: adding or subtracting.

whether by _____ or _____ .

153. This may seem like a strange use of the word "expand," but we need to use the term to describe the process of changing the sentence,

12-25

252. Back to pronunciation. We have told you before that while in English one letter may stand for several *different* sounds, in Latin a letter always stands for the ____ sound.

A: same

253. Pronounce this familiar Latin word and then check. **capit** √ ★ ○ •

254. The **c** in **capit** is pronounced like English "k." From what we said you know that Latin **c** is *always* pronounced like English "____."

A: k.

255. Echo your teacher as he pronounces a Latin syllable. ★ ○ • ○ • **ce**

256. Pronounce, remembering to make a sound like English "k." **ce** √ ★ ○ •

257. Echo your teacher as he pronounces another Latin syllable. ★ ○ • ○ •

258. Pronounce, remembering to make a sound like English "k." **ci** √ ★ ○ •

259. Pronounce. **ce, ci.** √ ★ ○ •

260. Echo a new Latin word containing this Latin sound that sounds like English "k." ★ ○ • ○ • **facilis**

261. Pronounce **facilis.** √ ★ ○ •

262. Echo another Latin word that contains Latin **c.** ★ ○ • ○ • **Fēlīcitās**

263. Pronounce **Fēlīcitās.** √ ★ ○ •

---

147. In changing **Elephantus nōn capit mūrem** to **Ab elephantō nōn capitur mūs,** we transformed the verb from _____ to _____ voice.

A: active to passive

148. A third form of manipulation is called "expansion." One way of expanding is to *add* something. For example, the words **fēmina laudem** make no sense by themselves. They become sensible only when they are found in a context like **Vulpēs vult fraudem, lupus agnum, fēmina laudem,** where they can be expanded with the verb ____.

A: **vult.**

149. When we change **fēmina laudem** to **fēmina laudem vult,** we say that we have _____ the words **fēmina laudem.**

A: expanded

150. If we say, **In omnī rē vestis virum reddit,** we have _____ the sentence **Vestis virum reddit.**

A: expanded

151. We expanded by the addition of the phrase _____.

A: **In omnī rē.**

152. In ordinary speech we use the word "accelerate" to mean "make an object go faster." In physics, however, we use "accelerate" in a special sense to mean "make an object go either faster or slower." In the same way, in this program we use the word "expand," to mean "change by either adding or subtracting something." Therefore, when we change **Vēritās numquam perit** to **Vēritās perit** by subtracting the modifier **numquam,** we say that we have _____ the sentence.

A: expanded

6-39

264. In English, the letter "c" stands for several different sounds. In "central" the letter "c" has the same sound as the letter ___.

A: s.

265. In "cat" the letter "c" has the sound of the letter ___.

A: k.

266. In the word "delicious" the letter "c" has the sound of ___.

A: sh.

267. However, in Latin the letter "c" always has the sound like the English ___.

A: k.

268. We will give you some practice in remembering to pronounce Latin **c** like "k" by giving you English derivatives and the Latin word from which they come. You have not had these words, and don't worry about the meaning of them. We are merely using these for practice in getting you to pronounce Latin **c** like English "___."

A: k.

(If you do not have a tape recorder, your teacher will probably practice these in class.) Echo the Latin word.

269. ★ ○ • ○ • English "certain," Latin **certus**

270. ★ ○ • ○ • English "cent," Latin **centum**

271. ★ ○ • ○ • English "celerity," Latin **celeritās**

272. ★ ○ • ○ • English "discern," Latin **cernit**

12-23

141. The words **metuit** and **sine** cannot replace **virum** in the sentence **Vestis virum reddit**, because they are not the same p___ of sp___ as **virum**.

A: part of speech

142. The words **manū, fēmina,** and **jūdice** cannot replace **virum** in the sentence **Vestis virum reddit** either, but for a different reason: although they are nouns, as **virum** is, they are not the same ___ as **virum**.

A: case

143. For an accusative you can substitute only an ___.

A: accusative.

Later you will discover that in Latin, as in English, you can have a whole group of words as an object (as in "The man sees *that the dogs are running*"), but we will worry about that later.

144. The second kind of manipulation is "transformation." For example, we changed the sentence, **Ā cane nōn magnō saepe tenētur aper** to **Canis nōn magnus saepe tenet aprum** by ___ing the verb from passive to active.

A: transforming

145. We also transformed the ablative **Ā cane nōn magnō** to ___.

A: **Canis nōn magnus.**

146. Finally we transformed the subject **Aper** to the object form, ___.

A: **Aprum.**

6-40

273. Echo these contrasting forms. ★ ○ • ○ •
auris
aurem

We have now had two Latin diphthongs.

274. Pronounce **quaerit**. √ ★ ○ •

275. Now pronounce **auris**. √ ★ ○ • [Remember to say it *first*, then listen to the tape.]

276. The first syllable of **auris** contains the
_____ au.

A: diphthong

277. Write down your teacher's description of this picture. ★ ○ ○ V__ a____ habet.

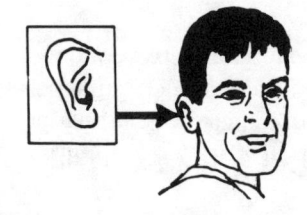

A: **Vir aurem habet.** [If you have no tape recorder, copy.]

278. Vir aurem habet = ___ ___ has an ____.

A: The man has an ear.

279. Vir vestem habet = _____.

A: The man has clothes.

280. Describe this picture. V__ m____ h_____

A: **Vir mūrem habet.**

12-22

137. You can substitute only things that are similar. To answer a nominative **Quis?** you must substitute a word that is in the _____ case.

A: nominative

138. In the English sentence "The man sees the bear," we can substitute a great many words for the word "bear," but they must all be similar to the word "bear." Which of these similar words can be substituted?

The man sees the { dog. tree. was. of. rapidly. almost. argument. }

A: { dog. tree. argument. }

139. "Dog," "tree," and "argument" are all similar because they are all three the part of speech which we call a _____.

A: noun.

140. Which of the following words can be substituted for **virum** in **Vestis virum reddit** to make an {-s – m –t} sentence?

Vestis { manū fēmina fūrem medicum metuit sine datōrem jūdice anum } reddit.

A: Vestis { fūrem medicum datōrem anum } reddit.

6-41

281. Echo these contrasting forms.
★ ○ • ○ • facilis
              facilem

282. **Auris/aurem** means that the form **auris** ....s with **aurem**.

A: contrasts

283. Write down the two forms of **auris** using the symbol that means that these two forms contrast with one another. _____

A: **auris/aurem**

284. In the Basic Sentence you will soon meet, the adjective **facilis/facilem** means "sympathetic." **Vir aurem facilem habet** = The ___ ___ a _____ ___.

A: The man has a sympathetic ear. (That is, he listens sympathetically.)

285. Here is the new Basic Sentence. We will take it up word by word: the first word is **nōn**. **Nōn** is a _____.

A: negator.

286. Because of the negator, we know that this is a negative statement; that is, something ____ ___ happen.

A: does not

287. Echo the first two words. ★ ○ • ○ •
Nōn semper

288. Write. ★ ○ ○ _____

A: **Nōn semper** [Did you write without looking at the last frame?]

12-21

132. You now know 25 Basic Sentences. These sayings come from many different authors, most of them from the "Classical" period, which was 2,000 years ago. These sentences and others like them form the "Basic Text" of Latin Level One. You are learning Latin by doing two things:
1) by studying the Basic Text,
2) by "manipulating" the Basic Text.
By "manipulating," we mean making changes. You have already learned two ways of m_____ the Basic Text.

A: manipulating

133. The first kind of manipulation is "substitution." Substitution is used in both asking and answering questions. When we ask, **Quis hilarem datōrem dīligit?**, we have s-------ed the word **Quis?** for **Deus** in the Basic Sentence.

A: substituted

134. You answer the question **Quis hilarem datōrem dīligit?** by substituting for **Quis?** the original subject ____.

A: **Deus.**

135. **Quis?** asks for a personal noun as the ------- of a sentence.

A: subject

136. If you wish to ask for the *object* of the sentence **Hilarem datōrem dīligit Deus**, you substitute the question word **Quem?** for -------.

A: **Hilarem**
    datōrem (the object).

289. **Semper** is a word that, like **nōn** and **numquam**, does not change form. It is a modifier of the verb and means "always." **Nōn semper** = Something does ___ _____ happen.

A: not always

290. "Not always" = ___ _____

A: Nōn semper

291. ★ ○ • ○ • Nōn semper aurem

292. ★ ○ ○ Nōn semper a____

A: aurem

293. **Aurem** is the {__} of the sentence.

A: {-m}

294. Since the {-m} has appeared before either the {-s} or the {-t} the sentence is in the ____ (emphatic/common) order.

A: emphatic

295. The first three words of this Basic Sentence were **Nōn semper aurem**. This means, "Somebody _____."

A: Somebody doesn't always blank an ear.

296. Since **aurem** has the signal **-m**, we know that we will have an {_____} type of sentence.

A: {-s -m -t}

297. ★ ○ • ○ • Nōn semper aurem facilem

298. ★ ○ ○ Nōn semper aurem f_____

A: facilem

---

127. **Numquam sine perīc'lō vincitur.** [Remember to say the Latin first and *then* listen to the tape] √ ★ ○ •

128. _____ = _____ is _____ od _____ (further)

A: Danger is never conquered without (further) danger.

129. Copy this Basic Sentence and English translation in your Reference Notebook.

130. This means that when the situation is completely desperate, since you have nothing to lose, you should _____ [In your own words]

131. If you are ahead 7-6 in a football game with thirty seconds to play, don't try a risky play just to get an extra touchdown. But suppose that you are *behind* 7-6; it's a fourth down on your own twenty with thirty seconds to play and seven yards to go. The quarterback wants to kick. In such a situation we would strongly urge you to say to him.

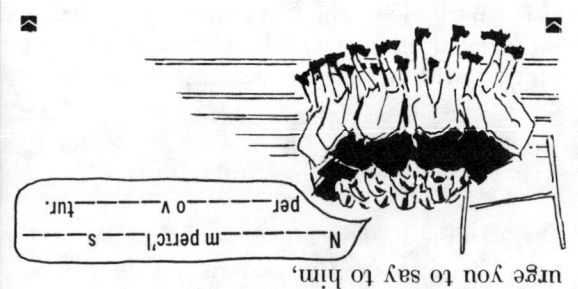

A: take a chance.

A: **Numquam perīc'lō sine vincitur.**

(There was a high school football team in Illinois who were all members of the same Latin class. By calling signals in Latin on the field they were able to change assignments without the opposition knowing what they were doing. In Latin Level Two we will have an optional section which will give you a chance to learn how to do this in several sports.)

6-43

299. **Aurem** and **facilem** both have the signal {--}.

▼

A: {**-m**}.

300. **Aurem** is a ____ and **facilem** is an _____.

▼

A: noun adjective.

301. "Facilis/facilem" means that the word **facilis** _____s with the word _____.

▼

A: contrasts **facilem**.

302. However, when we talk about the meaning of a word we usually mention just the nominative case. We have told you that words have many meanings. The word **facilis** means "easy to do, convenient, favorable, clever, easygoing, good-natured, generous, sympathetic." In this Basic Sentence it has the last meaning. **Nōn semper aurem facilem** = Somebody _____ _____.

▼

A: Somebody doesn't always blank a sympathetic ear.

303. Echo the complete Basic Sentence. ★ ○ • ○ • *Nōn semper aurem facilem habet Fēlīcitās.*

▼

304. Write. ★ ○ ○ **Nōn semper aurem facilem habet F_____**.

▼

A: **Nōn semper aurem facilem habet Fēlīcitās.**

305. Look at the sentence: there are *four* macrons in it. Listen to the tape again and notice which vowels take about twice as long to say as the other ones. ★ ○ ○ [Without a tape recorder you can't practice this.]

▼

---

122. Therefore, as you write this first part of the sentence, put down **peric'lum** twice to remind you that it is ambiguous. ★ ○ ○

$$\text{N} \underline{\quad\quad} \begin{cases}(\text{nom.?}) \\ (\text{acc.?})\end{cases} \underline{\text{p}\underline{\quad},} \\ \underline{\text{p}\underline{\quad},}$$

▼

A: **Numquam** $\begin{cases}(\text{nom.?}) \\ (\text{acc.?})\end{cases}$ **peric'lum**

▼

123. Echo the entire Basic Sentence. ★ ○ • ○ • *Numquam peric'lum sine peric'lo vincitur.* (25)

▼

124. Write the last part of the sentence. ★ ○ ○

Numquam $\begin{cases}(\text{nom.?}) \\ (\text{acc.?})\end{cases}$ **peric'lum** s_____ p_____ v_____.

▼

A: **Numquam peric'lum sine peric'lo vincitur.**

▼

125. Now we can tell what case **peric'lum** is, because **vincitur** is a _____ verb and therefore doesn't take an object.

▼

A: passive

▼

126. In your answer pad, cross out the form of **peric'lum** that does not fit into the sentence pattern.

Numquam $\begin{cases}(\text{nom.?}) \\ (\text{acc.?})\end{cases}$ **peric'lum** **sine peric'lo vincitur.**

▼

A: **Numquam** $\begin{cases}(\text{nom.?}) \\ \cancel{(\text{acc.?})}\end{cases} \begin{cases}\text{peric'lum} \\ \cancel{\text{peric'lum}}\end{cases}$ **sine peric'lo vincitur.**

12-19

306. Long vowels take about twice as long to say as short vowels. Diphthongs take about ――――― ―― ――― to say as short vowels.

A: twice as long

307. Diphthongs take about twice as long to say as ordinary short vowels because a diphthong is a combination of ――― vowel sounds.

A: two

308. Habet is the {――} of the sentence.

A: {-t}

309. Echo these contrasting forms. ★ ○ • ○ •
Fēlīcitās
Fēlīcitātem

310. The word **fēlīcitās** often means "prosperity." In this Basic Sentence, however, it means "the Goddess of Prosperity," and we therefore print it with a capital letter because it refers to a g――dess.

A: goddess.

311. Nōn semper aurem facilem habet Fēlīcitās = ――――――――――――――
―――――――――――.

A: The Goddess of Prosperity doesn't always have a sympathetic ear.

312. Enter Basic Sentence Ten in your Notebook.

---

116. "**Quid pecūnia irrītātur?**" "―――――."

117. "**Quō avāritia irrītātur?**" "―――――."

A: Avāritia.

A: Pecūnia.

[Just a reminder. Going through the program will be only a waste of time unless you *learn* while you are doing it. If your error rate was more than 10% on the last few sequences, you are *not* working properly. If this is true in your case, go back *now* to a place where you feel confident and go through the program again. This is a responsibility which *you* must take upon *yourself*.]

118. Chorus the paradigm of an ambiguous noun of the Second Declension which means "danger." ★ ○ ○ • •

peric'lum
peric'lum
peric'lō

(The apostrophe means that there is a longer form, **perīculum**, for this word. In this program we will use only this short form, peric'lum.)

119. Echo the first part of the new Basic Sentence. ★ ○ • ○ • **Numquam peric'lum**

120. The form **peric'lum** is an ambiguous form and can be either ――――― or ―――――. case.

A: nominative accusative

121. At this point we ―― (can/cannot) tell which case it is.

A: cannot

313. This means that although we may pray to this goddess to aid us,' _. [In your own words.]

A: she doesn't always grant our prayers.

314. In the sentence above, the subject **Fēlīcitās** is in the _ _ _ _ place in the sentence.

A: last

315. Therefore the emphatic word in the sentence is _ _ _ _ _ _ _ _ _.

A: **Fēlīcitās**.

316. Putting **Fēlīcitās** last in the sentence gives it unusual _ _ _ _ _ _ _ _.

A: emphasis.

317. In the following Basic Sentences the *subjects* have all been omitted. Read these sentences aloud, supplying the missing subject. [Give the whole Latin Sentence, not just the missing parts.]

318. **Nōn semper aurem facilem habet F _ _ _ _ _ _ _ _.**

A: **Nōn semper aurem facilem habet Fēlīcitās.**

---

108. "Quid nōn semper habet Fēlīcitās?" "_ _ _ _ _ _ _ _ _."

A: Aurem facilem.

109. "Quid habet etiam capillus ūnus?" "_ _ _ _ _ _ _ _."

A: Umbram suam.

110. "Quid habet umbram suam?" "Etiam _ _ _ _ _ _ _ _ _."

A: Etiam capillus ūnus.

111. "Quid vult vulpēs?" "_ _ _ _ _ _ _ _ _."

A: Fraudem.

112. "Quid fēmina vult?" "_ _ _ _ _ _ _ _."

A: Laudem.

113. "Quid avāritiam nōn satiat?" "_ _ _ _ _ _ _ _."

A: Pecūnia.

114. "Quid pecūnia nōn satiatur?" "_ _ _ _ _ _ _ _."

A: Avāritia.

115. "Quid pecūnia irrītat?" "_ _ _ _ _ _ _ _."

A: Avāritiam.

6-46

319. Nōn quaerit _____ medicum ēloquentem.

▼ ▼

A: Nōn quaerit aeger medicum ēloquentem.

320. In this Basic Sentence the *object* has been omitted. Read this sentence aloud, supplying the missing object. **Nōn quaerit aeger m_____ ēl_____.**

▼ ▼

A: Nōn quaerit aeger medicum ēloquentem.

SUMMARY

321. In this unit you learned a new part of speech, one which modifies the noun. This part of speech is called an _____.

▼ ▼

A: adjective.

322. In *English* we know which noun an adjective modifies from _____ [In your own words].

▼ ▼

A: its position in the sentence.

323. In *Latin* we know which noun an adjective modifies because the adjective has the same s_____ as the noun it modifies.

▼ ▼

A: signal

12-16

From now on, you will not usually be told in words to chorus; you will be given the direction by the sign. ★ ●

98. Manus manum lavat. (4)

99. Nōn semper aurem facilem ∙ habet Fēlīcitās. (10)

100. Etiam capillus ūnus habet umbram suam. (11)

101. Vulpēs vult fraudem, lupus agnum, fēmina laudem. (15)

102. Pecūnia nōn satiat avāritiam sed irrītat. (17)

▲ ▲

103. "Quid manum lavat?" "_____."

▲ ▲

A: Manus.

104. "Quid manus lavat?" "_____."

▲ ▲

A: Manum.

105. "Quō manus lavātur?" "_____."

▲ ▲

A: Manū.

106. In the first question, Quid manum lavat?, you knew that Quid? asked for the subject because the object was _____.

▲ ▲

A: manum.

107. In the second question, Quid manus lavat?, you knew that Quid? asked for the _____ because _____.

▲ ▲

A: object because manus was the subject.

6-47

324. You also learned that while position is not used to show structure in Latin, it *is* used to show ‗‗‗‗‗‗‗‗.

A: emphasis.

325. The word which receives most emphasis because of word order is the word which comes ‗‗‗‗ in the sentence.

A: last

326. You also learned that **nōn** is the part of speech called a ‗‗‗‗‗‗‗.

A: negator.

327-329. You learned three new Basic Sentences. Write the Basic Sentence which describes each situation.

327. N‗‗ sem‗‗‗ au‗‗‗ facil‗‗ hab‗‗ Fēlīci‗‗‗‗.

A: **Nōn semper aurem facilem habet Fēlīcitās.** (10)

328. C‗‗‗‗‗ m‗‗‗‗‗ f‗‗‗‗‗ l‗‗‗‗‗.

A: **Cautus metuit foveam lupus.** (8)

12-15

Anus sacco mūrem tenet.

90. "Ā quō mūs tenētur?" "Ab ‗‗‗‗."

A: Ab anū.

91. "Quid mūrem tenet?" "‗‗‗‗‗."

A: Saccus.

92. "Quis saccō tenētur?" "‗‗‗‗‗."

A: Mūs.

93. "Quō mūs tenētur?" "‗‗‗‗‗."

A: Saccō.

Anus jūdicem lite irrītat.

94. "Quis irrītat?" "‗‗‗‗‗."

A: Anus.

95. "Quis irrītātur?" "‗‗‗‗‗."

A: Jūdex.

96. "Quō jūdex irrītātur?" "‗‗‗‗‗."

A: Līte.

97. "Quid jūdicem irrītat?" "‗‗‗‗‗."

A: Līs.

6-48

329. N__ quae___ ae___ medi___ ēloque____.

A: Nōn quaerit aeger medicum
ēloquentem. (9)

The number in parentheses shows which number this sentence is in the Basic Text in case you wish to refer to it. This number will regularly occur with the Basic Sentences from now on.

VOCABULARY INVENTORY

In this Unit you learned the Latin names of three kinds of people; read the words aloud.

medicus (186)   **aeger** (174)   **Fēlīcitās** (309)
medicum   aegrum   Fēlīcitātem

You also learned two other nouns:

    auris (277)   **fovea** (110)
    aurem   foveam

In addition, you learned three new adjectives:

ēloquēns (191)   **cautus** (88)   **facilis** (284)
ēloquentem   cautum   facilem

Three new verbs were added to your inventory of Latin words:

metuit (104)   **quaerit** (163)   **habet** (278)

And finally a modifier:
        semper (287)

If you wish to review the meaning of these words, study the frame on which they were introduced. The frame number appears in parentheses beside each word.

12-14

83. "Quō lupus capitur?" "_____." ∧ ✱ ○ •
VCh: Foveā.

84. "Quis foveā capitur?" "_____." ∧ ✱ ○ •
VCh: Lupus.

85. "Ā quō lupus capitur?" "_____." ∧ ✱ ○ •
VCh: Ā virō.

Juvenis arcū leōnem necat.

86. "Quid leōnem necat?" "_____." ∧ ✱ ○ •
VCh: Arcus.

87. "Quō juvenis leōnem necat?" "_____." ∧ ✱ ○ •
VCh: Arcū.

88. "Quem arcus necat?" "_____." ∧ ✱ ○ •
VCh: Leōnem.

89. "Ā quō leō necātur?" "_____." ∧ ✱ ○ •
VCh: Ā juvene.

6-49

TEST INFORMATION

You will be asked to perform the following tasks:

1) To identify English adjectives, as in frames 5-54.

2) To pronounce one of the three Basic Sentences you learned in this Unit, paying particular attention to the diphthongs and the sound represented in Latin by **c**.

3) To identify the adjectives in one of these new Basic Sentences.

4) To produce any one of the first seven Basic Sentences when shown the picture and given just the first letter of each word. This type of question will be on every Unit test.

5) To pick out the word in a sentence which receives the most emphasis from the word order, as in frames 218-234.

6) To match a Latin sentence with the correct picture, as in frames 235-243. The pictures, however, will be different.

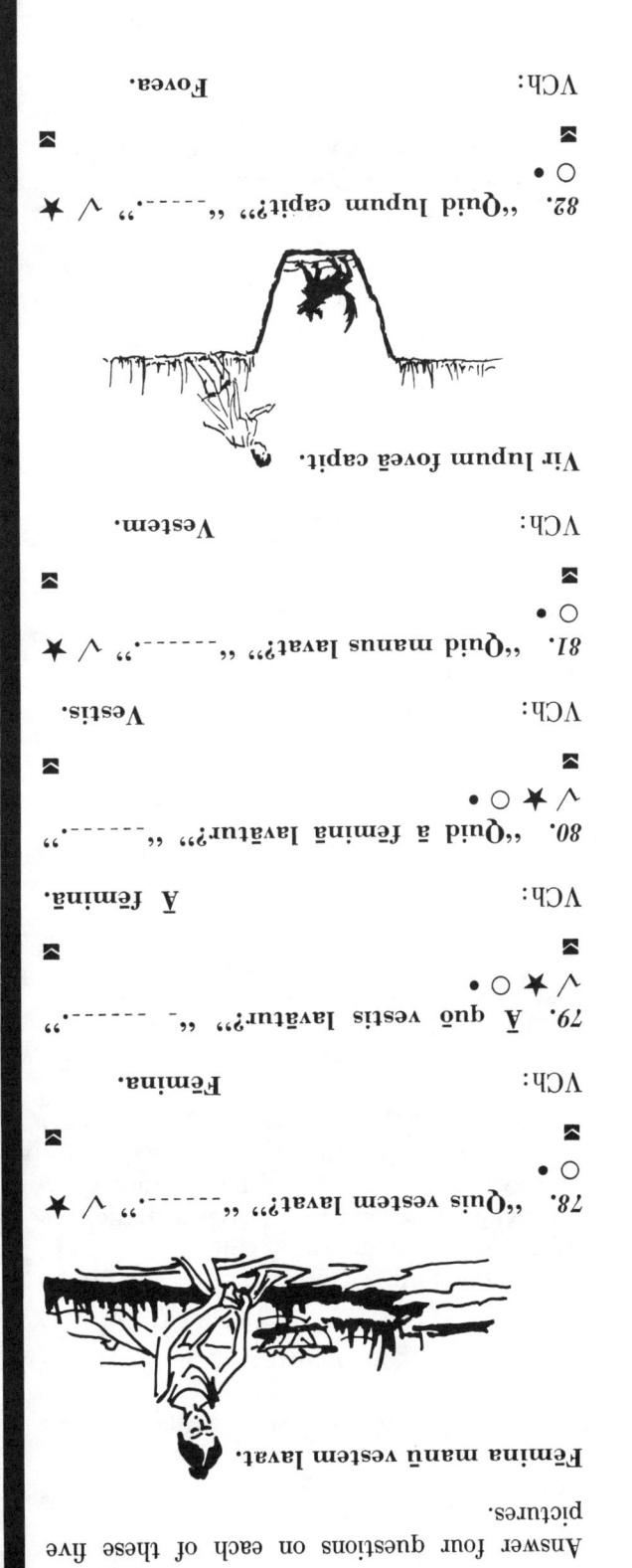

12-13

Answer four questions on each of these five pictures.

Fēmina manū vestem lavat.

78. "Quis vestem lavat?" "⎯⎯⎯." ∧ ★
   ○ •
   ⋈
   VCh: Fēmina.
   ⋈

79. "Ā quō vestis lavātur?" "⎯⎯⎯."
   ∧ ★ ○ •
   ⋈
   VCh: Ā fēminā.
   ⋈

80. "Quid ā fēminā lavātur?" "⎯⎯⎯."
   ∧ ★ ○ •
   ⋈
   VCh: Vestis.
   ⋈

81. "Quid manus lavat?" "⎯⎯⎯." ∧ ★
   ○ •
   ⋈
   VCh: Vestem.
   ⋈

Vir lupum foveā capit.

82. "Quid lupum capit?" "⎯⎯⎯." ∧ ★
   ○ •
   ⋈
   VCh: Foveā.

UNIT SEVEN

1. As you progress in this course, you will do more and more work in Latin and less and less in English. In the last unit you had a drill where we asked you in English for the subjects of certain Basic Sentences. We will now show you how to ask *in Latin* for the subject of a sentence. Echo a new word. ★ ○ • ○ • quiS?

2. Chorus as your teacher asks for the *subject* of the Basic Sentence **ElephantuS nōn capit mūrem.** ★ ○ ○ ◉ ◉

Visual Check: **QuiS nōn capit mūrem?**

3. Ask your teacher the same question: **QuiS nōn capit mūrem?** √ ★ ○ •

4. Write down his answer to your question. ★ ○ ○ [If you have no tape recorder, see if you can answer your own question.] "E_____."

A: **ElephantuS.**

5. The question word **quiS?** has the familiar signal **-s** that indicates the {-s} of the sentence, in the _____ case.

A: nominative [Notice that we have temporarily gone back to using the heavy letter to show the signal for subject.]

6. To answer the question **quiS?** all you have to do is to answer with the {-s} of the sentence. For example, you are asked the question **QuiS nōn capit mūrem?** In the original Basic Sentence **ElephantuS nōn capit mūrem,** the {-s} is the word _____.

A: **elephantuS.**

7. Therefore, the answer to **quiS?** in this question is _____.

A: **ElephantuS.**

---

77. But when something is done by a thing that is *not* a person or animal (for example, **manus**), then Latin uses the _____ case without any _____.

A: ablative preposition.

76. From these examples it is apparent that when something is done by a *person or animal,* Latin uses the preposition - (or its variant --) plus the _____ case.

A: **ā** **ab** ablative

75. **Ā fēmina** tells "by _____," but **manū** tells "by _____."

A: whom what.

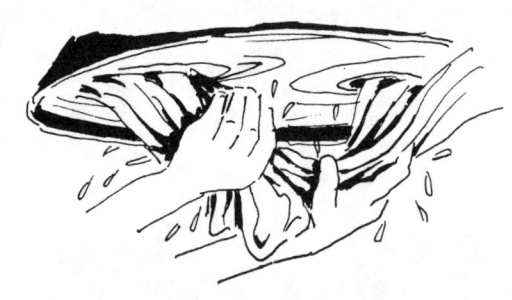

A: by a hand (or we might say, "by hand").

74. The sentence **Manū vestis lavātur** says that the clothes are washed -- a _____.

A: by a woman.

73. The sentence **Ā fēmina vestis lavātur** says that the clothes are washed -- a _____.

8. When you are asked a **quiS?** question about a Basic Sentence, you substitute for **quiS?** the word that was _____ case in the original Basic Sentence.

A: nominative

9. The English equivalent of **quiS?** is "who?". "**QuiS nōn capit mūrem?**" = ___ doesn't catch a mouse?

A: Who

10. And the answer to "Who doesn't catch a mouse?" is in English "__ _____."

A: An elephant.

11. Of course there are other possible answers to "Who doesn't catch a mouse?" (like "A lazy cat"), but in this program you are supposed to give the answer that makes sense according to the _____ _____ to which the question refers.

A: Basic Sentence

12. You will find that this type of question is much easier to answer if you do not try to translate it into English, but instead you *think directly in Latin*. Here is how you do this. The word **quis?** ends in the sound ___.

A: -s.

13. You must remember that the signal {-s} also has a variant signal, zero. Therefore, the question **QuiS?** may be answered *either* by a word that ends in the variant **-s** *or* by one that ends in the variant zero. The answer to **QuiS nōn quaerit medicum ēloquentem?** is the nominative word ae____.

A: aeger.

---

68. In the following questions, remember that the question words **Quis?**, **Quem?**, and **Ā quō?** are answered by ____ (personal/non-personal) nouns.

A: personal

69. The question words **Quid?** and **Quō?** are answered by _____ nouns.

A: non-personal

70. But you will have to remember also that the ambiguous form **Quid?** asks for either the _____ or the _____ of the sentence.

A: subject or the object of the sentence.

71. Echo and write your teacher's description of this picture. ★ ○ ○ • = ____ f____ v____ l____. [If you have no tape recorder, then copy the sentence.]

72. Echo and write another description of the same picture. ★ ○ • M____ v____ l____.

A: Manū vestis lavātur.

A: Ā fēminā vestis lavātur.

7-3

14. Latin makes a distinction between "personal" and "non-personal" nouns. Because **medicus** refers to a *person*, it is a _____ noun.

A: personal

15. **Manus** is not the name of a person (although it refers to a part of the body); therefore **manus** is a _____ noun.

A: non-personal

16. Although animals are not people, in this program we will read stories where animals talk; therefore we will consider the names for animals as _____ nouns.

A: personal

17. Pick out the *personal* nouns from this list (people or animals): **canis fovea leō diēs vestis aper anus**

A: canis leō aper anus

18. In Latin, **quiS?** asks for *personal* nouns. Answer these **quiS?** questions, all of which ask for the person or animal that was the _____ of the original Basic Sentence.

A: subject

19. "QuiS hilarem datōrem dīligit?" "D___."

A: DeuS.

---

62. Answer the question, "Quid sub quercū stat?" "_____."

A: Effigiēs sub quercū stat.

63. Here is a question on another Basic Sentence, "Quid numquam perit?" "V____s."

A: Vēritās.

64. Echo this transformation of a familiar Basic Sentence. ★ ○ ● ○ ● Vēritās diē aperitur.

65. Passive verbs *do not* take objects. Therefore if you were asked, Quid aperitur?, you would know that Quid? asked for the {---} of the passive verb.

A: {-s}

66. "Quid diē aperītur?" "_____."

A: Vēritās.

67. You know that Quid? could not ask for the object because _____.

A: aperītur is a passive verb and passive verbs do not take objects.

12-10

7-4

20. "QuiS nōn capit mūrem?" "El_____."

A: ElephantuS.

21. "QuiS aurem facilem nōn semper habet?" "F_____."

A: FēlīcitāS.

22. Here the answer consists of *two* words, a noun and an adjective. "Quis metuit foveam?" "C_____ l_____."

A: CautuS lupuS.

23. The question "QuiS nōn capit mūrem?" means: "Who _____?"

A: Who doesn't catch a mouse?

24. QuiS metuit foveam? = _____?

A: Who fears the pitfall?

12-9

55. The question **Quid vult vulpēs?** may be represented by **Quid** {-t} {-s}? Since **vulpēs** is the {-s}, **Quid?** therefore asks for the {--} of the original Basic Sentence.

A: {-m}

56. Now answer this question, "**Quid vult vulpēs?**" "_____."

A: Fraudem.

57. Quid dies aperit? Since **dies** is the {--} of the sentence, **Quid?** must ask for the {--}.

A: {-s}
      {-m}

58. "**Quid dies aperit?**" "_____."

A: Vēritātem.

59. The verbs **stat, est, perit,** and **currit** are not transitive verbs but _____ ones.

A: intransitive

60. Intransitive verbs ____ (do/do not) take objects.

A: do not

61. Therefore if you were to hear the question **Quid stat?**, you would know that **Quid?** asks for the {--} of the sentence.

A: {-s}

25. **QuiS nōn semper aurem facilem habet?** = _____?

A: Who doesn't always have a sympathetic ear?

26. We are trying to get you to think directly in Latin. Once you learn to think in Latin, the kind of questions which you have been asked seems almost ridiculously easy. When you hear **quis?** you answer with the word that was the {--} of the Basic Sentence.

A: {-s}

27. This kind of **quis?** question is exactly like the questions they sometimes ask on quiz shows to cheer up a contestant who hasn't been doing very well. "When was the war of 1812 fought?" This question is so easy that you might even miss it, thinking that there must be a trick. But if we assure you that there is no trick, then you answer that the War of 1812 was fought in the year of _____.

A: 1812.

28. Try to answer this Latin question which is of the same type: **"Cujus colōris est equus albus quem possidet Caesar?"** You can't do it because you do not yet know the necessary Latin signals. But if we were to translate it for you, you should not have too much trouble. "What is the color of Caesar's white horse?" "It's a _____ horse."

A: white

29. **QuiS?** has another form, ★ ○ • ○ • **QueM?**

30. From the signal {-m} you can see that **queM?** is the _____ case.

A: accusative

49. Therefore **Quid?** is an _____ form.

A: ambiguous

50. Since **Quid?** is an ambiguous form, how do we know whether it asks for the subject or the object? Let us look at an example. Can you tell which it is? **"Quid virum reddit?"** You know that **reddit** is a transitive verb and takes both subject and object. Since **virum** is the object, then **Quid?** must ask for the _____.

A: subject.

51. Answer the question by saying the subject of **Vestis virum reddit.** **"Quid virum reddit?"** "V___s."

A: **Vestis.**

52. Let us illustrate this by means of the symbols which we have used for our various types of sentences. **Vestis virum reddit** is an {--------} type of sentence.

A: {-s- m -t}

53. The question **Quid virum reddit?** may therefore be represented in symbols by **Quid?** {-m} {-t}?, which makes it clear that **Quid?** asks for the {--} of the original Basic Sentence.

A: {-s}

54. **"Quid virum reddit?"** "_____."

A: **Vestis.**

7-6

31. While **quiS?** ask for the {-s} of the sentence, **queM?** asks for the {__} of the sentence.

A: {-m}

32. Write this last frame in your Reference Notebook under "Facts About Latin."

33. Chorus with your teacher as he asks for the *object* of the Basic Sentence **Vestis viruM reddit.** ★ ○ ○ ◉ ◉ "Qu__ v____ r____?"

34. Ask your teacher the same question. _____? √ ★ ○ •

VCh: **Quem vestis reddit?**

35. Now write his answer to your question. ★ ○ ○ [Or give the answer yourself, if you can.] _____.

A: **ViruM.**

36. Answer these **queM?** questions on familiar Basic Sentences. Remember: all you have to do is to repeat the object. **"QueM vestis reddit?"** "V____."

A: **ViruM.**

37. "Quem dīligit Deus?" "H_____ d_____."

A: **Hilarem datōrem.**

38. "Quem elephantus nōn capit?" "M____."

A: **Mūrem.**

39. "Quem lupus nōn mordet?" "L____."

A: **Lupum.**

12-7

43. "Quid nōn semper habet Fēlicitās?" "_____." ∨ ★ ○ •

VCh: **Aurem facilem.**

44. "Quid habet etiam capillus ūnus?" "_____." ∨ ★ ○ •

VCh: **Umbram suam.**

45. "Quid pecūnia nōn satiat sed irrītat?" "_____." ∨ ★ ○ •

VCh: **Avāritiam.**

46. Echo the paradigm of the question word that asks for a *personal* noun. • ○ • ○ ★

Quis?
Quem?
Quō?
[Repeat until learned.]

47. Echo the paradigm of the question word that asks for a *non-personal* noun. • ○ • ○ ★

Quid?
Quid?
Quō?
[Repeat until learned.]

48. You are familiar by now with the fact that, although we always tell you the truth about Latin, we almost never tell you the *whole truth* at once. For example, we have stressed over and over the importance of the *contrast* between the nominative and accusative cases. And yet Quid? there is *no* contrast between the word you see from the paradigm that in this word _____ and _____ cases.

A: nominative accusative

40. "Quem vestis reddit?" = Who do _____ _____?

▼ ▼

A: Who do clothes make? (Some people might say, "Whom do clothes make?")

41. "Quem dīligit Deus?" = ___ does ___ _____?

▼ ▼

A: Who does God love?

42. "Quem elephantus nōn capit?" = ___ ____ an _____ not _____?

▼ ▼

A: Who does an elephant not catch?

43. Some of you may be puzzled by the fact that we used the form "who" in saying "Who do clothes make?" In speaking, almost no one (and this includes educated people) uses the word "whom" at the beginning of a sentence. "Whom" in this position sounds strange to most of us. For this reason there are jokes about it.

"Whom" is used in formal writing. But since this program is written as a conversation between you and your tape teacher, we have used the form "____."

▼ ▼

A: who.

44. From now on, instead of being asked, "What is the subject?", you will be asked in Latin "Qu__?".

▼ ▼

A: Quis?

---

33. If you could not see what slot in the sentence the word "watches" fills, then "watches" would be an _____ form.

▼ ▼

A: ambiguous

34. Quid? is an ambiguous form since it can also ask for a non-personal noun as *object* of the sentence. Echo your teacher as he asks what it is that a fox likes. ★ ○ ○ Qu___ v___ v___?

▼ ▼

VCh: Quid vulpēs vult?

35. Answer in terms of Basic Sentence 15. "Fr___ v___ v___."

▼ ▼

A: Fraudem vulpēs vult.

Chorus the Basic Sentences which you will use in the next sequence. ★ ●

36. Vulpēs vult fraudem, lupus agnum, fēmina laudem. (15)
37. Vēritātem diēs aperit. (2)
38. Nōn semper autem facilem habet Fēlīcitās. (10)
39. Etiam capillus ūnus habet umbram suam. (11)
40. Pecūnia nōn satiat avāritiam sed irrītat. (17)

▼ ▼

Answer your teacher by giving the non-personal noun which is the answer to his question.

41. "Quid fēmina vult?" "_____."
∨ ★ ○ ●

▼ ▼

VCh: Laudem.

42. "Quid diēs aperit?" "_____."
∨ ★ ○ ●

▼ ▼

VCh: Vēritātem.

7-8

45. And instead of "What is the object, you will be asked "____?".

◪

A: **Quem?**.

Here are the same **Quis?** and **Quem?** questions as before. [Be sure to give the answer first; then check. Occasionally students forget and do not give the answer first. They are therefore merely echoing. You will learn *faster* if you follow directions.]

46. "Quem elephantus nōn capit?" "____." ✓ ★ ○ •

◪

VCh: **Mūrem.**

47. "Quis metuit foveam?" "_____." ✓ ★ ○ •

◪

VCh: **Cautus lupus.**

48. "Quis nōn semper aurem facilem habet?" ✓ ★ ○ • "_____."

◪

VCh: **Fēlīcitās.**

49. "Quem dīligit Deus?" "_____." ✓ ★ ○ •

◪

VCh: **Hilarem datōrem.**

50. "Quem lupus nōn mordet?" "____." ✓ ★ ○ •

◪

VCh: **Lupum.**

51. "Quis hilarem datōrem dīligit?" "____." ✓ ★ ○ •

◪

VCh: **Deus.**

12-5

28. From these examples you can see that **Quid?** asks for a ____ (personal/non-personal) noun which is the { -- } of the sentence.

◪

A: non-personal { -s }

29. Echo a new technical term. ★ ○ • ○ •

◪

VCh: "am-bíg-you-us"

30. An "ambiguous" statement is a statement that can mean two different things. "I live in Washington" could mean either that you lived in the *city* of Washington, D.C., or in the *state* of Washington. Therefore the statement is _____.

◪

31. In English, the word "watches" would be ambiguous if it occurred alone. But of course words never occur alone. In the expression "He watches the show every night" the word "watches" is the part of speech called a ____.

◪

A: verb.

32. In the expression "The watches are all keeping accurate time" the word "watches" is the part of speech called a ____.

◪

A: noun.

52. "Quem vestis reddit?" "_____."
√ ★ ○ •

VCh: **Virum.**

53. "Quis nōn capit mūrem?"
"_____." √ ★ ○ •

VCh: **Elephantus.**

54. "Quem aeger nōn quaerit?" √ ★ ○ •
"M_____ ēl_____."

VCh: **Medicum ēloquentem.**

55. "Quis medicum ēloquentem nōn quaerit?" "_____." √ ★ ○ •

VCh: **Aeger.**

56. If we wish to give an English equivalent, we can say that **"Quis medicum ēloquentem nōn quaerit?"** means, "___ doesn't seek a talkative doctor?"

A: Who

57. **Quem aeger nōn quaerit?** means, "___ doesn't a ____ _____ ____?"

A: Who doesn't a sick person seek? (or "whom," if you really insist).

58. Here follows a series of pictures. If asked **quis?**, you are to answer with the name of a person or animal in the _____ case, and if asked **quem?** you are to answer with a person or animal in the _____ case.

A: nominative
                accusative

---

19. **Pecūnia nōn satiat avāritiam sed irrītat.** (17)

20. Now answer your teacher as he asks you: "**Quid vēritātem aperit?**" "What discloses the truth?" ★ ○ ○

VCh: **Vēritās.**

21. "D____." √ ★ ○ •

VCh: **Diēs.**

22. "**Quid numquam perit?**" "What never dies?" ★ ○ ○

23. "V_____." √ ★ ○ •

24. "**Quid habet umbram suam?**" "What casts its own shadow?" ★ ○ ○

VCh: **Capillus ūnus.**

25. "C____ū____." √ ★ ○ •

26. "**Quid nōn satiat avāritiam?**" "What does not satisfy greed?" ★ ○ ○

27. "P____." √ ★ ○ •

VCh: **Pecūnia.**

7-10

59. "Quem piscis capit?" "_____."
 √ ★ ○ •

VCh: Muscam.

60. "Quis rānam mordet?" "_____."
 √ ★ ○ •

VCh: Piscis.

61. "Quis mūrem quaerit?" "_____."
 √ ★ ○ •

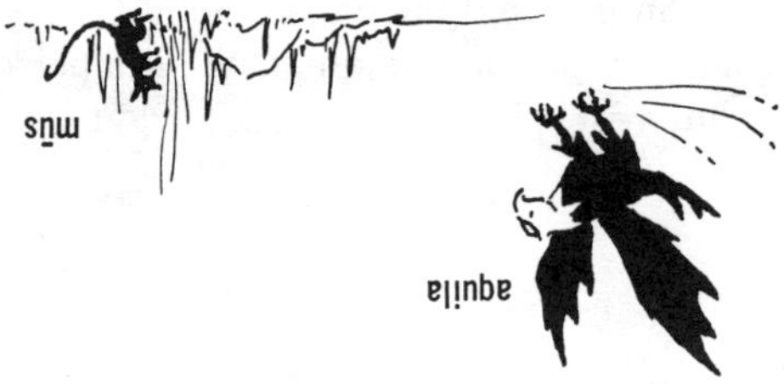

VCh: Aquila.

62. "Quem dīligit īnfāns?" "_____."
 √ ★ ○ •

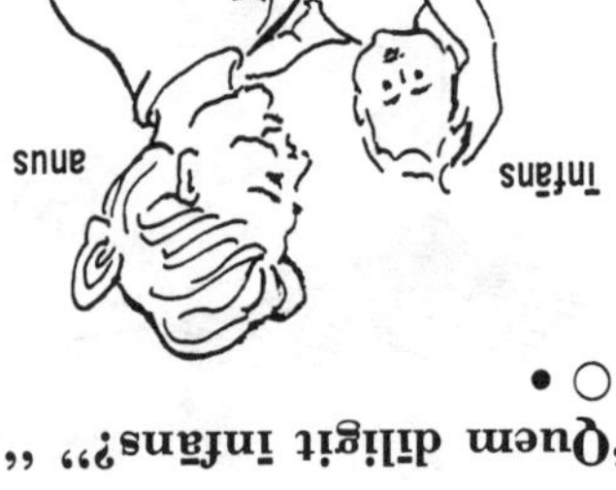

VCh: Anum.

12-3

12. But when **Fēlīcitās** is capitalized and means "Goddess of Prosperity," then it is a _____ noun.

A: personal

13. In order to ask for a non-personal subject of a sentence, Latin uses the word **Quid?**. Listen to your teacher ask, "What makes a man?" ★ ○ ○ Then answer him.

VCh: "Quid virum reddit?"

14. "V_____ virum reddit."

A: Vestis virum reddit.

Chorus the Basic Sentences which you will use in the next sequence. ★ ●

15. Vēritātem diēs aperit. (2)
16. Vēritās numquam perit. (7)
17. Vulpēs vult fraudem, lupus agnum, fēmina laudem. (15)
18. Etiam capillus ūnus habet umbram suam. (11)

7-11

63. "Quem musca mordet?" "_____."
√ ★ ○ •

musca
leō

VCh: **Leōnem.**

64. "Quis metuit lupum?" "_____."
√ ★ ○ •

asinus
lupus

VCh: **Asinus.**

65. "Quis rānam capit?" "_____."
√ ★ ○ •

vīpera
rāna

VCh: **Vīpera.**

66. "Quem lavat vir?" "_____." √ ★ ○ •

vir
sīmia

VCh: **Sīmiam.**

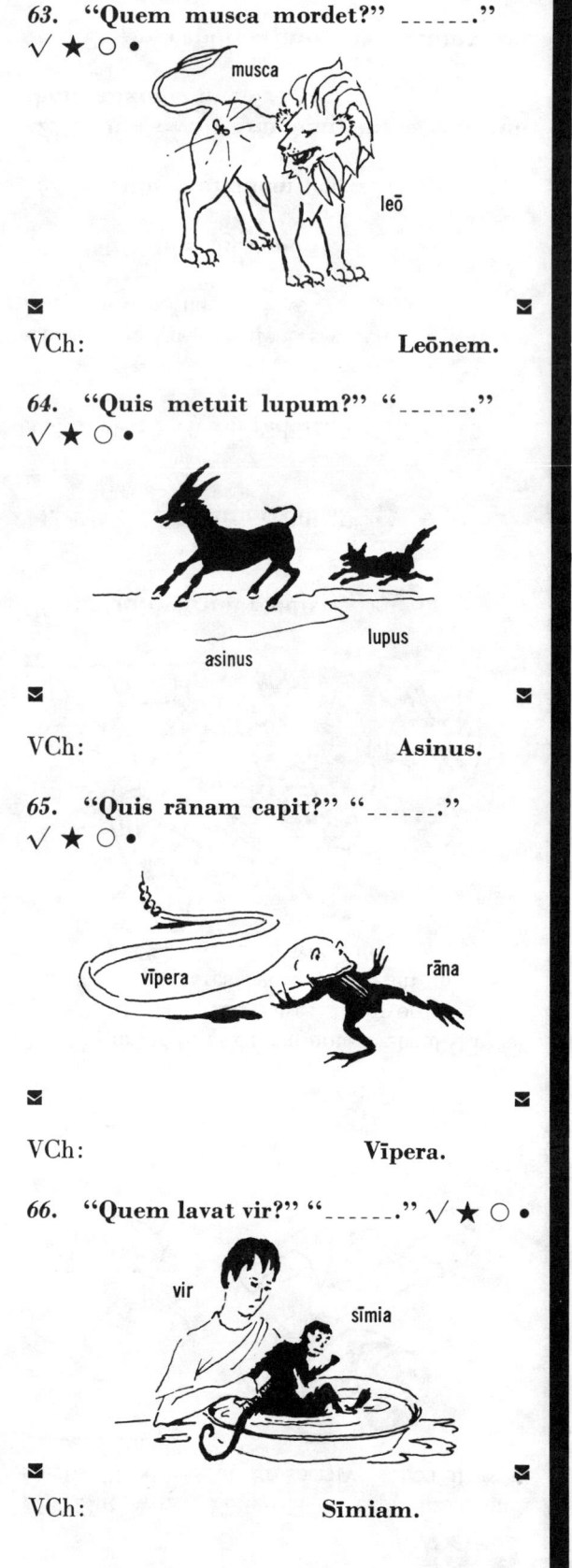

12-2

5. For things which are not people we would say, not "Who is that?" but, "____ is that over in the corner?"

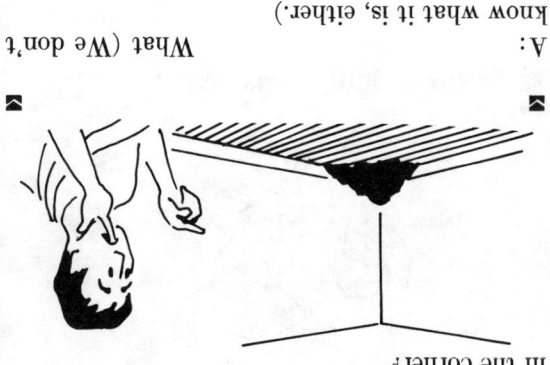

A: What (We don't know what it is, either.)

6. A "non-personal" noun is a noun that is *not* the name of a person or animal. **Vir** is a personal noun, but **vestis** is a _____ noun.

A: non-personal

7. **Vēritās** is a ____ (personal/non-personal) noun.

A: non-personal

8. **Manus** is a _____ noun.

A: non-personal

9. **Juvenis** is a _____ noun.

A: personal

10. **Mūs** is a _____ noun.

A: personal

11. Some words are used as personal nouns part of the time and as non-personal nouns the rest of the time. For example, when **fēlicitās** means "prosperity," it is used as a _____ noun.

A: non-personal

7-12

67. "Quem vir quaerit?" "_____."
√ ★ ○ •

vir — *equus*

VCh: Equum.

68. "Quem capit elephantus?" "_____."
√ ★ ○ •

elephantus — *aper*

VCh: Aprum.

69. "Quem metuit canis?" "_____."
√ ★ ○ •

canis — *rāna*

VCh: Rānam.

70. "Quem metuit mūs?" "_____."
√ ★ ○ •

mūs — *vulpēs*

VCh: Vulpem.

UNIT TWELVE

1. You remember that **Quis?** asks for the nominative of a "personal" noun, that is, a noun that is the name of a _____ or an _____.

A: person   animal.

2. **Anus, medicus, fēmina,** and **canis** are all _____ nouns.

anus   medicus   fēmina   canis

A: personal

3. On the other hand, nouns like **manus, angulus, saccus,** and **gradus** are _____ nouns.

manus   angulus   saccus   gradus

A: non-personal

4. The same distinction exists in English; for persons we say, "____ (Who/What) is over in the corner?"

A: Who

7-13

71. The most common type of Latin sentence is the {-s -m -t} sentence. But it almost never occurs in literature as a simple three word sentence. Sentences such as **Vestis virum reddit** are rare, because one or more of the three parts (subject, object, verb) are usually m_____ed by other words.

A: modified

72. **Nōn quaerit aeger medicum ēloquentem** contains not three words but ____ words.

A: five

73. The two extra words are the modifiers ___ and _____.

A: **nōn**, **ēloquentem**.

74. The word **nōn** modifies _____ and the word **ēloquentem** modifies _____.

A: **quaerit**, **medicum**.

75. **Ēloquentem** is the part of speech called an _____, and **nōn** is a _____.

A: adjective   negator.

76. The {-s-m-t} part of a sentence we call the "kernel" of the sentence. **Quaerit aeger medicum** is the _____ of the sentence **Nōn quaerit aeger medicum ēloquentem**.

A: kernel

77. The kernel of **Nōn quaerit aeger medicum ēloquentem** is _____ _____ _____. [Put the kernel in the same order as in the Basic Sentence.]

A: **quaerit aeger medicum**.

VOCABULARY INVENTORY 11-54

The number shows the frame where the words were first introduced. Review them there if you have forgotten any of them. There was one noun, **amīcus** (229), one verb, **cernit** (248), two adjectives, **certus** (229) and **incerta** (242), a preposition, **ā, ab** (78), and a new verbal modifier, **saepe** (176).

TEST INFORMATION

In the test for Unit Eleven you will be asked to perform the following tasks:

1) To answer questions on pictures, as in frames 108-111, where some of the questions will require the use of the passive voice. The pictures will be different but similar.

2) To transform sentences from active to passive, as in frames 164-173. They will be the same sentences.

3) To say one of the two new Basic Sentences from looking at the picture, prompted by letters, as in frames 341 and 343.

4) To answer questions on Basic Sentence 23 as in frames 195-207.

5) To answer questions on familiar Basic Sentences which will require the use of transformation, as in frames 211-214.

6) To identify the word which receives emphasis in a sentence, as in frames 293 and 304.

7) To give the paradigm of one of the adjective-noun combinations in frames 335 and 338.

7-14

78. Add the modifier of **quaerit**: ___ quaerit

A: **nōn quaerit**

79. Add the modifier of **medicum**: medicum _____.

A: medicum **ēloquentem**

80. The combination of subject, object and verb is called the k_____.

A: kernel.

81. Nōn semper aurem facilem habet Fēlīcitās. The kernel of this sentence, that is, the {-s -m -t} part, is _____ _____ _____. [Put the kernel in the same order as in the Basic Sentence.]

A: **aurem habet Fēlīcitās.**

82. To find the kernel of this sentence we strip off all the modifiers until we are left with just the {__ __ __} part.

A: {-s -m -t}

83. In the four word sentence **Cautus metuit foveam lupus,** the word that is added to the kernel is the modifier _____.

A: **Cautus.**

84. Therefore the kernel of this sentence is the rest of the sentence, namely the three words _____ _____ _____.

A: **metuit foveam lupus.**

85. In this sentence by Horace the parts of the kernel occur in the order {-_} {-_} {-_}.

A: {-t} {-m} -{s}.

---

341. You also learned the Basic Sentence that describes this picture. Say it aloud. A c___ n___ m___ ō s___ e ten___ a___. (23)

342. This means, "_____."

A: A boar is often held by a small dog.

A: **Ā cane nōn magnō saepe tenētur aper.**

343. Say the Basic Sentence that describes this picture. A___ s___ in___ ā cer___. (24)

A: **Amīcus certus in rē incertā cernitur.**

344. The meaning of this Basic Sentence is, "_____."

A: A sure friend is recognized in an unsure situation.

86. In **Hilarem datōrem dīligit Deus** the word that is added to the kernel is the modifier _____.

A: **Hilarem**.

87. Therefore the kernel of this sentence is the three words _____ _____ _____.

A: **datōrem dīligit Deus**.

88. In this sentence the parts of the kernel occur in the order {--} {--} {--}.

A: {-m} {-t} {-s}.

89. The {-s} in **Elephantus nōn capit mūrem** is the word _____.

A: **Elephantus**.

90. The {-m} in this sentence is _____.

A: **mūrem**.

91. And the {-t} in this sentence is _____.

A: **capit**.

92. The kernel of this sentence is _____ _____ _____.

A: **Elephantus capit mūrem**.

93. In this sentence the parts of the kernel occur in the order {--} {--} {--}.

A: {-s} {-t} {-m}.

94. **Vēritātem diēs aperit.** In this sentence the parts of the kernel occur in the order {--} {--} {--}.

A: {-m} {-s} {-t}.

---

335. Write the paradigm of **canis magnus**.

A: canis magnus
canem magnum
cane magnō

336. Write the paradigm of **rēs incerta**.

A: rēs incerta
rem incertam
rē incertā

337. Write the paradigm of **crūdēlis medicus**.

A: crūdēlis medicus
crūdēlem medicum
crūdēlī medicō

338. Write the paradigm of **hilaris dator**.

A: hilaris dator
hilarem datōrem
hilarī datōre

SUMMARY

339. In this Unit you learned chiefly one thing: you learned how to transform active sentences containing active verbs into sentences containing _____ _____-s.

A: passive verbs.

340. From now on, verbs will end in either **--** or **--**.

A: **-t** -**tur**.

95. The {-s} of this sentence is _____.

A: diēs.

96. The {-m} of this sentence is _____.

A: vēritātem.

97. And the {-t} of this sentence is _____.

A: aperit.

98. The sentence **Vēritātem diēs aperit**, like the sentence **Vestis virum reddit**, has no m_____s.

A: modifiers.

99. In a Latin {-s -m -t} sentence the elements {-s} and {-m} and {-t} ____ (can occur only in this order/may occur in any order).

A: may occur in any order.

100. In an {-s -t} sentence, the kernel consists of just a subject and a _____.

A: verb.

101. Vēritās numquam perit is an {__ __} type of sentence.

A: {-s -t}

102. In this {-s -t} sentence, the {-s} is the Latin word _____ and the {-t} is the Latin word _____.

A: vēritās
   perit.

331-334. Here are paradigms of adjective-noun phrases. You will be asked to write them in the next sequence.

331. ✱ ○ •
canis magnus
canem magnum
cane magnō

332. ✱ ○ •
rēs incerta
rem incertam
rē incertā

333. ✱ ○ •
crūdēlis medicus
crūdēlem medicum
crūdēlī medicō

334. ✱ ○ •
hilaris dator
hilarem datōrem
hilarī datōre

---

327. ✱ ○ ○
VCh: "Ā quō taurus spatiōsus morsū necātur?" "_____."

VCh: Ā parva vipera.

328. ✱ ○ ○
VCh: "Quis taurum spatiōsum morsū necat?" "_____."

VCh: Parva vipera.

329. ✱ ○ ○
VCh: "Quis ā parvā viperā morsū necātur?" "_____."

VCh: Spatiōsus taurus.

330. ✱ ○ ○
VCh: "Quem morsū parva vipera necat?" "_____."

VCh: Spatiōsum taurum.

7-17

103. The kernel of **Vēritās numquam perit** is the subject _____ and the verb _____.

A: vēritās perit.

104. The kernel of **Lupus nōn mordet lupum** is _____.

A: lupus mordet lupum.

105. Write down your teacher's description of this picture. ★ ○ ○ [Without a tape recorder you cannot, of course, do this kind of frame. Instead copy the answer and say it aloud several times.] C_____ l__ __t.

A: Cautus leō est.

106. The kernel of the sentence you wrote is ___ ___.

A: Leō est.

107. Echo your teacher's description of this picture. ★ ○ • ○ • H_____ r___ e___.

108. Write down the sentence you just echoed. H_____ r____ ____.

A: Hilaris rāna est.

---

321. **Parva necat morsū spatiōsum vīpera.** Now we are told that it is a small _____ which kills a large something by biting.

A: snake

322. **Parva necat morsū spatiōsum vīpera taurum.** We don't discover until the last word in the sentence that the large something which the small snake kills is a _____.

A: bull.

323. Write from dictation the passive transformation of Basic Sentence 21. Parva necat morsū spatiōsum vīpera taurum. ← Ā p___ā v___ā t____ss___ m s m____ū tur. ★ ○ ○

VCh: Ā parva vīpera taurus spatiōsus morsū necātur.

324. A reminder: **Quō?** means "By what?" and is answered by a noun in the _____ case.

A: ablative

325. **Ā quō** means "By whom?" and is answered by a p____al noun in the ablative case.

A: personal

326–330. Listen to the question, then say your answer. Look back to the original and the transformation if you need help.

326. ★ ○ ○

VCh: "Quō parva vīpera taurum necat?" "_____."

VCh: Morsū.

II-50

7-18

109. The sentence which you wrote is an {-- --} type of sentence.

A: {-s -t}

[If you have no tape recorder, skip to frame 130.]

110. We will return to a point of pronunciation which we drilled on briefly before, that is the double consonant such as we had in the word **reddit**. Listen to your teacher say a pair of contrasting Latin words and echo. ★ ○ • ○ •
vīlis, vīllis

111. Pronounce: vīlis, vīllis √ ★ ○ •

112. Your teacher will now say another Latin pair. ★ ○ • ○ • **ager, agger**

113. ager, agger √ ★ ○ •

114. Your teacher will say another pair. ★ ○ • ○ • **erās, errās**

115. erās, errās √ ★ ○ •

116. Your teacher will say one of two words. ★ ○ • ○ • **colis? collis?**

117. Write the word you just echoed. ——

A: collis

118. colis, collis √ ★ ○ •

119. Your teacher will say one of two words. ★ ○ • ○ • **sumus? summus?**

120. Write the word you just echoed. ——

A: sumus

11-49

314. Let us rewrite the sentence in an unemphatic order. **Parva vipera spatiōsum taurum morsū necat.** First we have a small snake as the subject, then a ---- ---- as the object.

A: large bull

315. Next we find out how the small snake does what he does to the bull: he does it -- a ----

A: by a bite.

316. Finally we find out that what the snake does to the bull is to ---- him.

A: kill

In the original Basic Sentence, through the device of word order, the author Ovid has emphasized the contrast between the tiny snake and the mighty bull. Let us look at it word by word.

317. **Parva.** First we are told that the subject is ---- (large/small).

A: small.

318. **Parva necat.** Then we are told that this small person ---- somebody.

A: kills

319. **Parva necat morsū.** Then we are told how this small person kills: he kills by ----ing.

A: biting.

320. **Parva necat morsū spatiōsum.** Next we are told that the person whom the small person is killing is ----.

A: large.

121. **sumus, summus.** √ ★ ○ •

122. Your teacher will say either one of two words. ★ ○ • ○ • **erās? errās?**

123. Write the word you just echoed. _____

A: **erās**

124. **erās, errās.** √ ★ ○ •

125. Your teacher will say one of two words. ★ ○ • ○ • **ager? agger?**

126. Write the word you just echoed. _____

A: **agger**

127. **ager, agger.** √ ★ ○ •

128. Your teacher will say one of two words. ★ ○ • ○ • **redit? reddit?**

129. Write the word you just echoed. _____

A: **reddit**

130. Pronounce **Vestis virum reddit**, being careful with the double **d**. √ ★ ○ •

131. Now for a new Basic Sentence. Latin nouns, adjectives, and verbs change their form according to their use in the sentence. Words like **nōn, numquam, et** and **semper** _____ _____ [In your own words]

A: **do not change form.**

132. ★ ○ • ○ • **etiam**

309. Let us look in detail at one of our recent sentences. Write from dictation. ★ ○ • ○ _____

A: **Parva necat morsū spatiōsum vipera taurum.**

310. In your answer pad, draw arrows connecting the two adjectives in the sentence above with the nouns they modify.

A: **Parva necat morsū spatiōsum vipera taurum.**

311. The first impression on the learner of Latin is that the poet must have been clumsy indeed to write in such a mixed-up fashion. The arrows show that the word order is indeed involved: not only are the adjectives separated from each other but the arrows cr--- each other.

A: **cross**

312. **Parva necat morsū spatiōsum vipera taurum.** Before we come to the noun that **parva** modifies, that is, **vipera**, we come across a second adjective, one which modifies _____

A: **taurum.**

313. We will show you that this apparently haphazard order is actually one of the devices which the author is using to _____ certain words.

A: **emphasize**

133. This new word **etiam** is like **et, nōn** and **numquam** because it also does ___ ___ ___ ___.

A: not change form.

134. Therefore, even though the word **etiam** happens to end in the sound **-m**, it is not the {-m} in an {-s -m -t} sentence because **etiam** is a word which ___ ___ ___ form.

A: does not change

135. Echo a new technical term. ★ ○ • ○ • intensifier.

VCh: "in-tense-sif-fier"

136. The word **etiam** "intensifies" the meaning of the word next to it; that is, it calls special attention to this word. The word "even" in the English sentence "Even a cat may look at a queen" calls special attention to the word "___."

A: cat.

137. The English word "even" is an intensifier. The Latin word **etiam** means "even" and is an ___ ___ ___.

A: intensifier.

138. For example, **Etiam lupus** would mean: "___ a wolf blanks."

A: Even

139. **Etiam vestis virum reddit** = ___ ___ ___ ___.

A: Even clothes make the man.

140. In the expressions **Etiam lupus** and **Etiam vestis**, the word **etiam** comes right ___ to the word it emphasizes.

A: next

303. In **Hilarem datōrem dīligit Deus,** the adjective **hilarem** is placed ___ (just before/just after/separated from) the noun it modifies.

A: just before

304. Therefore the position of the adjective **hilarem** is ___ (emphatic/unemphatic).

A: unemphatic.

305. **Cautus metuit foveam lupus.** The adjective **cautus** ___ (comes just before or after/is separated from) the noun it modifies.

A: is separated from

306. The effect of separating **cautus** and **lupus** is to ___ ___ ___ ___. [In your own words.]

A: emphasize them both.

307. In the sentence **Cautus metuit foveam lupus,** the word **lupus** is emphasized by two devices:
1) ___ ___ ___ ___ ___ ___.
2) ___ ___ ___ ___ ___ ___.

A: 1) It is the last word in the sentence.
2) It is separated from its adjective.

308. Because of the fact that the word order in Latin is almost entirely free, word-order is perhaps the *most important* single ___ which the Romans used to obtain their effects.

A: device

141. The word **etiam** means "____."

A: even.

142. The purpose of **etiam** is to _____ the word next to it, so it is the part of speech called an _____.

A: intensify intensifier.

143. We have constantly called your attention to the fact that in Latin position is not a signal for showing subject or object. We have even shortened this to say that in Latin position is of no importance at all. We must now change this statement slightly. The position of the word **etiam** is important, because it calls attention to the word ____ to it.

A: next

144-147. There are now four Latin words you know which do not change form:

nōn, semper, numquam, etiam, meaning:
"___," "_____," "_____," "____."

A: not   always   never   even.

148. The word **etiam,** because it intensifies the meaning of the word next to it, is the part of speech called an _____

A: intensifier.

Echo these contrasting forms of two nouns.

149. ★ ○ • ○ • capillus
                    capillum

150. ★ ○ • ○ • umbra
                    umbram

---

296. The word that receives special emphasis in *Parva necat morsū spatiōsum vīpera taurum* is the word _____.

A: taurum.

297. The Romans used word order also to emphasize adjectives. The unemphatic position for an adjective is either just before or just after the noun it modifies. In the sentence *Etiam capillus ūnus habet umbram suam,* the adjective **ūnus** is in the _____ case.

A: nominative

298. So we know that **ūnus** modifies the nominative noun _____.

A: capillus.

299. **Suam** is _____ case; it modifies the noun _____.

A: accusative umbram.

300. We know that **suam** modifies **umbram** because **suam** and **umbram** are the s___ c____.

A: same case.

301. We have said that the unemphatic position for an adjective is either just *before* or just *after* the noun it modifies. When an adjective is *separated* from its noun, both the adjective and the noun receive special _____

A: emphasis.

302. In the sentence *Etiam capillus ūnus habet umbram suam,* the adjectives **ūnus** and **suam** are in an ____ (emphatic/unemphatic) position with regard to the nouns they modify.

A: unemphatic

7-22

151. Echo the first word of the new Basic Sentence. ★ ○ • ○ • **Etiam**

152. Write. ★ ○ ○ <u>E____</u>

A: Etiam

153. ★ ○ • ○ • **Etiam capillus**

154. Write. ★ ○ ○ Etiam <u>c_____</u>

A: capillus

155. **Capillus** is a noun whose dictionary meaning you do not know. However, you do know that it is the {_ _} of the sentence.

A: {-s}

156. You know that **capillus** is an important word in this sentence because your attention has been called to it by the intensifier _____.

A: etiam.

157. ★ ○ • ○ • **Etiam capillus ūnus**

158. Write ★ ○ ○ Etiam capillus <u>ū___</u>

A: ūnus

159. **Ūnus** also has the signal **-s**. If **capillus** is a noun, then **ūnus** is an _____ modifying it.

A: adjective

160. ★ ○ • ○ • **Etiam capillus ūnus habet**

161. Write. ★ ○ ○ Etiam capillus ūnus <u>h____</u>

A: habet

---

289. An especially important part of a Latin sentence is the verb, so in about half of our sentences the last word is the _____.

A: verb.

290. In an {-s – -m – -t} sentence, the word order {-s} {-m} {-t} is the most common of the six possible arrangements of the parts. We therefore say that a sentence with the order {-s} {-m} {-t} is written in the un_____ order.

A: unemphatic

291. However, a sentence like **Lupus nōn mordet lupum**, which has the order {-s} {-t} {-m}, is said to be written in the *emphatic* order, because the word that comes last and receives emphasis is not the verb but the word _____.

A: lupum.

292. A sentence written with the order {-s} {-m} {-t} has the ____ (emphatic/unemphatic) order.

A: unemphatic

293. In **Hilarem datōrem dīligit Deus**, the word that receives the most emphasis from its position is _____.

A: **Deus**.

294. Because the last word is not the verb but the noun **Deus**, we say that this sentence is written in the _____ _____.

A: emphatic order.

295. **Vestis virum reddit** is written in the _____ _____.

A: unemphatic order.

11-45

162. **Habet** is the {--} of the sentence.

A: {-t}

163. ★ ○ • ○ • **Etiam capillus ūnus habet umbram**

164. Write. ★ ○ ○ **Etiam capillus ūnus habet u**_____

A: umbram

165. Although you do not know the meaning of the noun **umbram**, you do know that it is the {--} of the sentence.

A: {-m}

166. Now echo the entire Basic Sentence.
★ ○ • ○ • **Etiam capillus ūnus habet umbram suam.**

167. Write. ★ ○ ○ **Etiam capillus ūnus habet umbram s**____.

A: **Etiam capillus ūnus habet umbram suam.**

168. **Umbram** is a noun; **suam**, which is the same form, is an _____.

A: adjective.

169. **Etiam capillus ūnus habet umbram suam.** The subject and object both have modifiers. The subject (with its modifier) is _____.

A: **capillus ūnus.**

170. The object (with its modifier) is _____.

A: **umbram suam.**

7-23

280. ★ ○ • **amīcus
amīcum
amīcō**

281. **Amīcus** belongs to the _____ Declension.

A: Second

282. ★ ○ • **lacus
lacum
lacū**

283. **Lacus** belongs to the _____ Declension.

A: Fourth

284. ★ ○ • **poena
poenam
poenā**

285. **Poena** belongs to the _____ Declension.

A: First

286. Earlier in the Unit we said that our Basic Sentences are important not only for the message which they convey, but also for the striking way in which the message is conveyed. We said that the writers obtained these effects through different _____.

A: devices.

287. We have already pointed out that the Romans used word order not to show such structures as subject and object (as English does) but to show _____.

A: emphasis.

288. The word that receives the most emphasis in a Latin sentence is the ____ word in the sentence.

A: last

II-44

7-24

171-173. Echo your teacher as he describes these pictures.

171. ★ ○ • ○ • **Capillus est.**

172. ★ ○ • ○ • **Umbra est.**

173. ★ ○ • ○ • **Capillus habet umbram.**

174. Give the nominative and accusative cases of the Latin word for "shadow." [Look back if you need to.]

    nominative: _____
    accusative: _____

A: **umbra**
                      umbram

175. Give the nominative and accusative cases of the Latin word for "hair." [Look back if you need to.]

                _____
                _____

A: **capillus**
                      capillum

11-43

271. In the same way, we list *two* samples of the Third Declension because --- ---------- ---
---------.

A: the nominatives are different.

272. **Fūr** has the signal --- and **līs** has the signal ---.

A: zero (∅)
   -s.

273. The Fourth and Fifth Declensions have *only* the signal -- for the nominative.

A: -s

274. The First Declension has *only* the signal --- for the nominative.

A: zero (∅)

275. But the Second and Third Declensions have as signal for the nominative case ---------.

A: *both* -s *and zero* (∅).

276. √ ○ • **aciēs**
        aciem
        aciē

277. Aciēs belongs to the ----- Declension.

A: Fifth

278. ★ ○ • **jūdex**
        jūdicem
        jūdice

279. Jūdex belongs to the ----- Declension.

A: Third

176. The kernel of the sentence **Etiam capillus ūnus habet umbram suam** is _____ _____ _____.

A: **capillus habet umbram**.

177. The parts of the kernel occur in the order {--} {--} {--}.

A: {-s} {-t} {-m}.

178. **Capillus habet umbram** is the _____ of the sentence.

A: kernel

179. Pronounce and check. **Etiam capillus ūnus habet umbram suam.** √ ★ ○ •

180. Write *just* the kernel. ★ ○ ○ _____ _____

A: **capillus habet umbram**

181. The first time we met **habet** it was in the Basic Sentence **Nōn semper aurem facilem habet Fēlīcitās**, where it meant "____."

A: has.

182. However, we do not usually say that an object *has* a shadow; we say rather that an object c___s a shadow.

A: casts

183. **Capillus habet umbram** = A ____ _____ a _____.

A: A hair casts a shadow.

---

259. Echo the complete sentence again, paying special attention to these repeated sounds of c and r. • ○ • √ ★ **Amīcus certus in rē incertā cernitur.**

260. It is by such "devices," as repetition that these sayings are made effective. It will be one of the goals of this course to point out the different d_____s by which the Latin authors made their writing effective.

A: devices

261. Once you have had your attention called to these Latin sayings, you may improve your own writing in English by employing some of these same _____s.

A: devices.

262. Now write Basic Sentence 24. ★ ○ ○ Am___ c____ r. in____ c_____.

A: **Amīcus certus in rē incertā cernitur.**

263-269. Pronounce and check these sample paradigms of each Declension.

263.	264.	265.
First	Second	
vīta	angulus	vir
vītam	angulum	virum
vītā	angulō	virō
√ ★ ○ •	√ ★ ○ •	√ ★ ○ •

266.	267.	268.	269.
Third	Fourth	Fifth	
līs	arcus	rēs	
lītem	arcum	rem	
līte	arcū	rē	
√ ★ ○ •	√ ★ ○ •	√ ★ ○ •	√ ★ ○ •

270. We list *two* samples of the Second Declension because the nominatives are different. **Vir** has the signal ___ and **angulus** has the signal ___-s.

A: zero (∅)

7-26

184. A hair casts a shadow = Ca_____ ha___ umb____.

A: **Capillus habet umbram.**

185. The dictionary meaning of **ūnus** is "one." One hair casts a shadow = Ca_____ ūn__ ha___ umb____.

A: **Capillus ūnus habet umbram.**

186. ★ ○ • ○ • sua suam

187. The adjective **sua/suam** modifies something that belongs to the subject of the sentence. We can translate it as "his own," "her own," or "its own." **Capillus ūnus habet umbram suam** = ___ h___ c___s ___ ___ _____.

A: One hair casts its own shadow.

188. The Basic Sentence **Etiam capillus ūnus habet umbram suam** therefore means: "_____ _____."

A: Even one hair casts its own shadow.

189. It might sound better to say that even a s___le hair casts its own shadow.

A: single

II-41

252. The "-cern" part is a derivative of the new verb _____.

A: **cernitur.**

253. We have told you that many of these sayings are famous. The reason for their fame is not quite so much *what* they say as the *way* they say it. Look at the new Basic Sentence. **Amīcus certus in rē incertā cernitur.** (24) There is one syllable of three letters that is repeated three times: this is the syllable ____.

A: **cer.**

254. The adjectives **certus** and **incerta** are connected in meaning with the verb **cernitur**: something that is discovered is something that is now s____ or c____.

A: sure certain.

255. Echo as your teacher pronounces these three words. ★ • ○ • ○ • **certus, incerta, cernitur.**

256. The **cer-** stem that occurs in these words begins with the sound __.

A: c.

257. The sound **c** occurs in another word in the sentence. Pronounce this word and check. _____ ∨ ★ ○ •

VCh: **Amīcus**

258. In the same way, the sound **r** of the cer- stem also occurs in the noun __ and in the verb _____.

A: rē cernitur.

7-27

190. Even a single hair casts its own shadow =
Et___ cap_____ ū___ h____ um____ s____.

A: Etiam capillus ūnus habet umbram suam.

191. Enter Basic Sentence 11 in your Notebook.

192. The expression **capillus ūnus** is emphasized because it is preceded by the intensifier _____.

A: etiam.

193. The words **umbram suam** receive emphasis from the fact that they come ____ in the sentence.

A: last

194-198. Pronounce and check. [Look up the meaning in your Reference Notebook if you have forgotten it.]

194. Nōn quaerit aeger medicum ēloquentem. √ ★ ○ •

195. Vēritātem diēs aperit. √ ★ ○ •

196. Etiam capillus ūnus habet umbram suam. √ ★ ○ •

197. Nōn semper aurem facilem habet Fēlīcitās. √ ★ ○ •

198. Cautus metuit foveam lupus. √ ★ ○ •

---

245. The verb ends in ____ (-t/-tur).

A: -tur.

246. Therefore, this sentence says that in an unsure situation a sure friend ____ (does something/has something done to him).

A: has something done to him.

247. Write the entire Basic Sentence. ★ ○ ○
Am____ c____ r_ in____ c____.

A: Amīcus certus in rē incertā cernitur.

248. Here is a situation which this saying might describe. **Amīcus certus in rē incertā cernitur** = A ____ is disc____ in ____.

A: A sure friend is discovered in an unsure situation.

249. Copy this Basic Sentence and its meaning in your Reference Notebook.

250. This means that you discover your real friends when _____.
[In your own words.]

A: things are difficult.

251. The English word "discern" means "to recognize something clearly." It is made up of two parts. The "dis-" part we call the pr___x.

A: prefix.

11-40

7-28

199. Say the Basic Sentence which describes each picture. N__ s_____ au___ f_____ h____ Fēl_____.

A: **Nōn semper aurem facilem habet Fēlīcitās.**

200. Et___ cap_____ ū___ h____ um____ s____.

A: **Etiam capillus ūnus habet umbram suam.**

201. V_____ d___ a_____.

A: **Vēritātem diēs aperit.**

202. N__ qu_____ ae___ m_____ ēl_____.

A: **Nōn quaerit aeger medicum ēloquentem.**

II-39

237. But **Amīcus certus cognōscitur** would mean that a _____ is _____ed.

A: a sure friend is being recognized.

238. Because **Amīcus certus** is the subject, we know that the verb will describe a sure friend, whether he does the action or whether he has the action d___ to ____.

A: done to him.

239. Echo the first two phrases. ★ ○ • ○ •
Amīcus certus in rē incertā.

A: _____

240. Write. ★ ○ ○ **Amīcus certus __ r_ in____.**

VCh: **Amīcus certus in rē incertā.**

241. In Basic Sentence 22 **in omnī rē** meant "__ _____."

[If you don't know the answer, stop right here. Look up Basic Sentence 22 in your Basic Text and *learn* it. Then learn *all the other 23* Basic Sentences you have had.]

A: in every situation.

242. The prefix **in-** means "not." Since **certus** means "sure," the phrase **rē incertā** means "a ___ s___ _____."

A: a not sure situation.

243. However, instead of "a not sure situation," we would probably say "an uns___ _____."

A: unsure situation.

244. Echo the entire Basic Sentence. ★ ○ • ○ •
Amīcus certus in rē incertā. (24)

7-29

203. C_____ m_____ f_____ l_____.

A: Cautus metuit foveam lupus.

204. Here is a new Basic Sentence. Echo the first two words. ★ ○ • ○ • **Crūdēlem medicum**

205. These two words form the {--} of the sentence.

A: {-m}

206. Write. ★ ○ ○ Cr_____ m_____

A: **Crūdēlem medicum**

207. When the words in a sentence are in the order {-s} {-m} {-t}, the order is the ____ (common/emphatic) order.

A: common

208. Since **Crūdēlem medicum** occurs first in this new Basic Sentence we know that we have the ____ (common/emphatic) order.

A: emphatic

209. ★ ○ • ○ • **Crūdēlem medicum intemperāns aeger**

210. Write. ★ ○ ○ **Crūdēlem medicum in_____ ae___**

A: **intemperāns aeger**

---

229. We will take up Basic Sentence 24 a phrase at a time to see how the Latin thought develops. Echo the first phrase. ★ ○ • ○ • **Amīcus certus**

230. Here we have the {--} of the sentence.

A: {-s}

231. The phrase **Amīcus certus** means, "A sure friend (blanks)." Echo. ★ ○ • ○ • English "certain" Latin **certus**.

232. "Certain" is a synonym for "sure." In **Amīcus certus** the word that means "sure" is _____.

A: **certus**.

233. And the word that means "friend" must be _____.

A: **Amīcus**.

234. Until you knew about the passive voice, you would have interpreted **Amīcus certus** as "A _____ _____ blanks."

A: A sure friend blanks.

235. But now that you know that there is a passive voice, the verb may end not in -t but in ____.

A: -tur.

236. **Amīcus certus cognōscit** would mean that a ____ _____ re_____ (s_____) or s_____).

A: sure friend recognizes (somebody or something).

11-38

7-30

211. The {-s} of this sentence is the noun-and-adjective combination _____ _____.

A: intemperāns aeger.

212. ★ ○ • ○ • *Crūdēlem medicum intemperāns aeger facit.*

213. Write. ★ ○ ○ <u>Crūdēlem medicum intemperāns aeger</u> f_____.

A: Crūdēlem medicum intemperāns aeger facit.

214-216. Now for the dictionary meaning of the words. (We give the nominative form of nouns and adjectives.) Echo the words after your teacher.

214. ★ ○ • ○ • **facit** = makes somebody be something

215. ★ ○ • ○ • **intemperāns** = intemperate (that is, uncontrolled)

216. ★ ○ • ○ • **crūdēlis** = cruel

217-220. Pronounce, then check with the tape, and give the English.

217. **Fovea lupum cautum facit.** √ ★ ○ •

218. = A p_____ makes a w___ _____.

A: A pitfall makes a wolf cautious.

219. **Vestis virum hilarem facit.** √ ★ ○ •

220. = C_____ m___ a ___ _____.

A: Clothes make a man cheerful.

221. A pitfall makes a wolf cautious = F____ l____ m c____m facit. √ ★ ○ •

VCh: **Fovea lupum cautum facit.**

---

221. "Ā quō vīta regitur?" "_____."

A: Ā Fortūnā.

222. "Quis vītam nōn regit?" "_____."

A: Sapientia.

223. "Ā quō vīta nōn regitur?" "_____."

A: Ā Sapientiā.

224. "Quis vītam regit?" "_____."

A: Fortūna.

225. Until this unit you knew only *two* sentence types. The type that contains an active transitive verb with an object (like **Manus manum lavat**) is the {-- -- --} type.

A: {-s- -m- -t}

226. The type that contains an intransitive verb (like **Medicus est**) is the {-- --} type.

A: {-s- -t}

227. Since we represented the sentence **Manus manum lavat** by the symbol {-s- -m- -t} and the sentence **Medicus est** by {-s -t}, you may be able to figure out that we will represent this third type of sentence like **Piscis mordētur** by the symbols {-- --}.

A: {-s -tur}

228. **Mūs capitur** is an {-- --} sentence.

A: {-s -tur}

7-30

7-31

222. Clothes make a man cheerful = Ve____
v____ hil____ f____.

VCh: **Vestis virum hilarem facit.** ✓ ★ ○ •

223. A person who is "intemperate" is a person who has no self control. An intemperate sick person would be one who would not ____ the doctor's orders.

A: obey (follow)

224. *Crūdēlem medicum intemperāns aeger facit* = An int_____ s___ p_____ makes a d_____ _____.

A: An intemperate sick person makes a doctor cruel. In other words, if the patient doesn't obey doctor's orders the doctor will be forced to be strict.

225. Copy this sentence (12) in your Reference Notebook.

226. An intemperate sick person makes a doctor cruel = Cr_____ med____ int_____ ae___ f____.

A: **Crūdēlem medicum intemperāns aeger facit.**

---

215. Write down the passive transformation of this sentence. ★ ○ ○
N____ qu____ ab____
m____ el____.

VCh: **Nōn quaeritur ab aegrō medicus ēloquēns.**

216. "Quis ab aegrō nōn quaeritur?" "____."

A: **Medicus ēloquēns.**

217. "Ā quō medicus ēloquēns nōn quaeritur?" "____."

A: **Ab aegrō.**

218. "Quis nōn quaerit?" "____."

A: **Aeger.**

219. "Quem aeger nōn quaerit?" "____."

A: **Medicum ēloquentem.**

220. Write the passive transformation. ★ ○ ○
V____ r____, n____ ā F____, n____ S____.

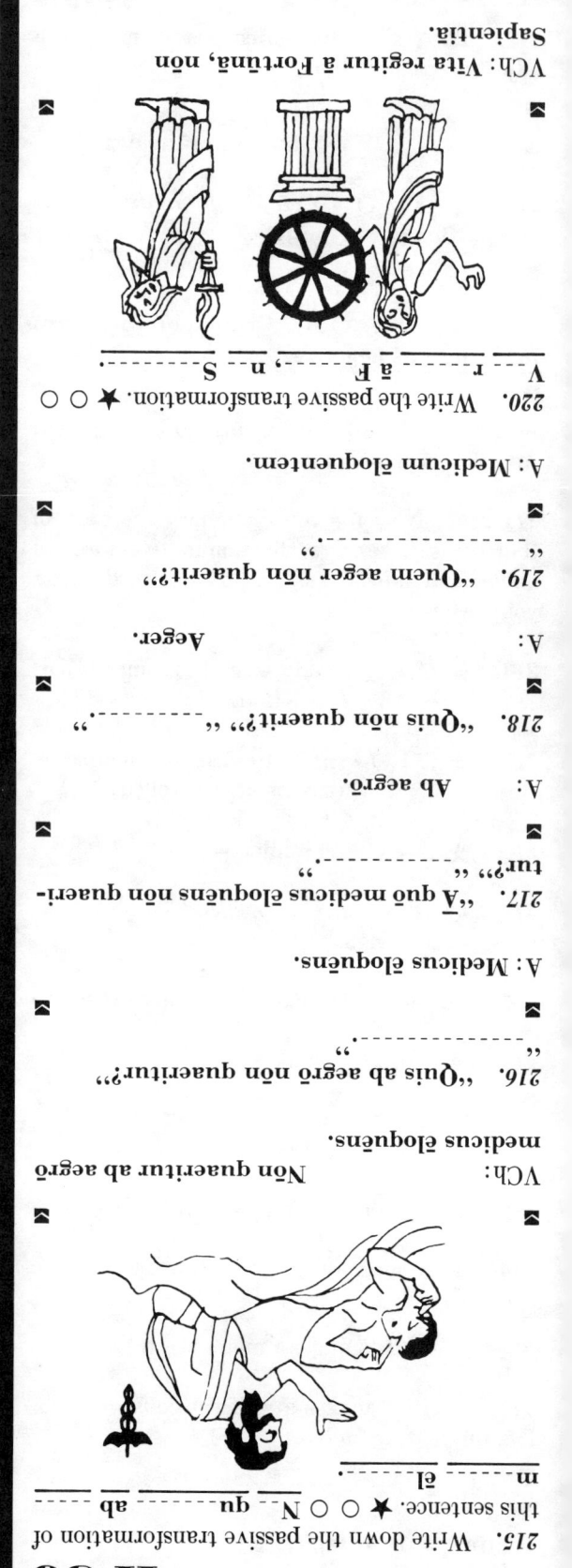

VCh: **Vīta regitur ā Fortūnā, nōn Sapientiā.**

227. Once again we will present you with situations where you must *ignore* your lifelong habit as a speaker of English, of reacting to position as a structural signal. We will change the last Basic Sentence in some way. If we change just the *position* of the Latin words, then we ____ (have/have not) changed the structural signals of the sentence.

A: have not

228. If we change the position of English words we usually have changed the _____ _____ of the sentence.

A: structural signals

229. If we change the position of Latin words, then we have changed the em_____ of these words but not the _____ _____ of the sentence.

A: emphasis
structural signals

230. There will be a sentence using these same dictionary words, perhaps in the same order as the original, perhaps not, perhaps switching the signals for the {-s} and the {-m} and perhaps not. Force yourself to ignore _____ _____. [In your own words.]

A: the position of the words.

231. Not only should you ignore the position, but you must observe the Latin signals for the {__} and the {__}.

A: {-s}   {-m}.

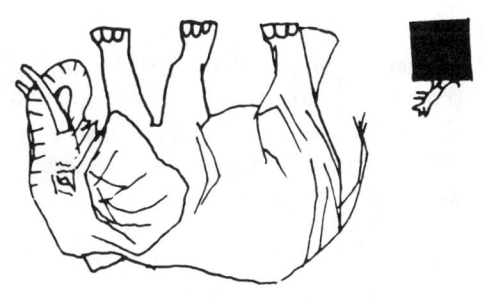

210-224. In this sequence your teacher will dictate the passive transformation of a Basic Sentence. Write it down, then answer four questions, two of which will be asked on the original Basic Sentence and two on the passive transformation. Elephantus nōn capit mūrem. ⟵

210. Passive Transformation: ★ ○ ○ Ab el_____ n_____ c_____ m_____. [If you have no tape, *study* the answer.]

ACh: Ab elephantō nōn capītur mūs.

Now the questions. Notice that the dashes do not indicate the length of the answer. Look back, of course, if you need to.

211. "Ā quō mūs nōn capitur?" "_____."

A: Ab elephantō.

212. "Quem elephantus nōn capit?" "_____."

A: Mūrem.

213. "Quis nōn capitur?" "_____."

A: Mūs.

214. "Quis mūrem nōn capit?" "_____."

A: Elephantus.

7-33

232. Here is the original Basic Sentence: **Crūdēlem medicum intemperāns aeger facit.** Here is the changed version: **Crūdēlem medicum facit aeger intemperāns.** In this new sentence we have changed ____ (the position of the words/the structural signals).

A: _____ the position of the words.

233. Since we have changed the position of the words, this sentence now means, "_____."

A: _____ An intemperate sick person makes a doctor cruel.

234. The structure is the same as in the original Basic Sentence, but the emphasis has been changed. The word emphasized most because of its position in this changed version is the adjective _____.

A: **intemperāns.**

235. Here is another way of saying "An intemperate sick person makes a doctor cruel": **Facit aeger intemperāns crūdēlem medicum.** Here the word emphasized most is the noun _____.

A: **medicum.**

236. Look at a changed version. To understand the structure, ignore the position and respond to the real signals {-s} and {-m}. **Crūdēlis medicus intemperantem aegrum facit.** Are the Latin structural signals for {-s} and {-m} on the same words as before or on different words? _____

A: On different words.

237. Therefore the structural meaning ____ (has been changed/has not been changed).

A: _____ has been changed.

---

202. **Quem canis nōn magnus saepe tenet?**

A: **Aprum.**

203. **Ā quō aper saepe tenētur?** _____

A: **Ā cane nōn magnō.**

204. Ask your teacher the question which will get as an answer the italicized words and check. **A cane nōn magnō** *saepe tenētur aper.* "_____,"

VCh: **Ā quō saepe tenētur aper?**

205. Write down your teacher's answer. If you don't have a tape recorder, see if you can give the answer yourself. "_____,"

A: **Ā cane nōn magnō.**

206. Ask the question that will get the italicized word as answer. **Canis nōn magnus** *aprum saepe tenet.* "_____,"

VCh: **Quem canis nōn magnus saepe tenet?**

207. Write down your teacher's answer. "_____."

A: **Aprum.**

208. Again, ask the question that will get the italicized words as answer. **Canis nōn magnus** *aprum saepe tenet.* "_____,"

VCh: **Quis aprum saepe tenet?**

209. Write down your teacher's answer. "_____."

A: **Canis nōn magnus.**

7-34

238. Crūdēlis medicus intemperantem aegrum facit = _____.

A: _____ A cruel doctor makes a sick person intemperate.

239. In the next frame we will give you another version of this same Basic Sentence. We will use the same dictionary words as the original, but we may change the position of the words and the structural signals for {-s} and {-m}. You must remember to _____ the position (as far as structure goes) and respond to the s_____ for {-s} and {-m}.

A: ignore

signals

240. Intemperantem aegrum facit crūdēlis medicus = _____.

A: _____ A cruel doctor makes a sick person intemperate.

241. Since we have been making all these changes, let's make sure that you can remember the Basic Sentence in its original form.
★ ○ ○ ◉ ◉ Cr____ m____ in_____ a____ f____.

VCh: Crūdēlem medicum intemperāns aeger facit.

242. When a Roman writer wished to give special emphasis to either the {-s} or the {-m} of a sentence, he would place it ____ in the sentence.

A: last

---

195. Ā cane nōn magnō saepe tenētur aper may be transformed to Canis nōn magnus saepe tenet aprum. From now on if you hear the word "Quis?" you must notice whether the verb is active (tenet) or passive (tenētur).

"Quis aprum saepe tenet?" _____

A: Canis nōn magnus.

196. The question "Quis aprum saepe tenet?" asks for the subject of ____. (Ā cane nōn magnō saepe tenētur/Canis nōn magnus saepe tenet aprum.)

A: Canis nōn magnus saepe tenet aprum.

197. "Quis ā cane nōn magnō saepe tenētur?" "_____."

A: Aper.

198. "Quem canis nōn magnus saepe tenet?" "_____."

A: Aprum.

199. "Ā quō aper saepe tenētur?" "_____."

A: Ā cane nōn magnō.

200. Write the answers to these same questions. [If you have to look back, you had better do the last few frames again.] "Quis saepe tenētur?" "_____."

A: Aper.

201. "Quis saepe tenet?" "_____."

A: Canis nōn magnus.

II-33

243. The *second* most important position in the sentence is that of the first word in the sentence. In the common order the first word in the sentence is the {--}.

A: {-s}.

244. If the {-t} or the {-m} should come first in the sentence, then it would receive special _____ because of this unusual position.

A: emphasis

245. In the original Basic Sentence **Crūdēlem medicum intemperāns aeger facit,** the {-m} comes _____ in the sentence.

A: first

246. The expression **crūdēlem medicum** therefore _____.

A: receives special emphasis.

247. In **Vēritātem diēs aperit,** where there is a variation of the {-s} {-m} {-t} order, the word given special emphasis is the word that has been *shifted* from its expected position to appear first in the sentence, the word _____.

A: **vēritātem.**

248. Echo the Basic Sentence you hear on the tape. ★ ○ • Et___ c_____ ū___ h____ um____ s____.

VCh: **Etiam capillus ūnus habet umbram suam.**

249. ★ ○ • El_____ n__ c____ m_____.

VCh: **Elephantus nōn capit mūrem.**

250. ★ ○ • N__ qu_____ a____ m_____ ēl_____.

VCh: **Nōn quaerit aeger medicum ēloquentem.**

---

190. For example, until this unit, when you saw or heard the Basic Sentence **Hilarem datōrem dīligit Deus** and were then asked "**Quis?**" you did not even need to listen to the rest of the question to give the answer "____."

A: **Deus.**

191. But now that we have the active-passive transformation you now have two possibilities when you hear the question "**Quis?**" about the sentence **Hilarem datōrem dīligit Deus.** If the question is "**Quis hilarem datōrem dīligit?**" then you answer "____," just as before.

A: **Deus**

192. But if the question is "**Quis ā Deō dīligitur?**" you know that the question is based on the transformation of the original Basic Sentence into **Hilaris dator dīligitur ā Deō.** The answer to "**Quis ā Deō dīligitur?**" is "_____."

A: **Hilaris dator.**

193. If this were a program designed to teach someone English, we might have had "God loves a cheerful giver." as a Basic Sentence. The answer to "Who is loved by God?" would be "_____."

A: A cheerful giver.

194. "A cheerful giver is loved by God" is a _____ of the original sentence "God loves a cheerful giver."

A: transformation

7-36

251. ★ ○ • N__ s_____ au___ f_____
h____ F_____.

VCh: Nōn semper aurem facilem habet Fēlīcitās.

252. ★ ○ • Cr_____ m_____ in_____
a____ f____.

VCh: Crūdēlem medicum intemperāns aeger facit.

253. We will now ask **Quis?** and **Quem?** questions on Basic Sentences. "**Quem elephantus nōn capit?**" "_____." √ ★ ○ •

VCh: Mūrem.

254. "**Quis medicum ēloquentem nōn quaerit?**" "_____." √ ★ ○ •

VCh: Aeger.

255. "**Quem aeger nōn quaerit?**"
"_____." √ ★ ○ •

VCh: Medicum ēloquentem.

256. "**Quis aurem facilem nōn semper habet?**" "_____." √ ★ ○ •

VCh: Fēlīcitās.

257. "**Quis mūrem nōn capit?**"
"_____." √ ★ ○ •

VCh: Elephantus.

258. "**Quis medicum crūdēlem facit?**"
"In_____ ae____." √ ★ ○ •

VCh: Intemperāns aeger.

---

186. We had another Basic Sentence that expressed about the same thought, although its point was rather that small people can often be dangerous to larger people because of some particular power (in this case it was poison) that they possess. See if you can remember what it was. Say and write.

P_ a_ n_ t_ m__ sp___ū_ m__ v_____ t_____.

A: **Parva necat morsū spatiōsum vipera taurum.**

187. Now for questions on the Basic Sentence "**Ā cane nōn magnō saepe tenētur aper.**" "**Quis saepe tenētur?**" "_____."

A: Aper.

188. "**Ā quō aper saepe tenētur?**" "_____."

A: Ā cane nōn magnō.

189. Up until this point, this kind of "simple substitution" has been the only kind of question which you have had on the Basic Sentences. It was simple, very simple, and this is why we began with it. Until this Unit, whenever you heard the question word **Quis?** you needed only to repeat the _____ of the Basic Sentence.

A: subject

SUMMARY

259. In this Unit you learned how to answer Latin questions. You now know two question words, ____ and ____.

A: **quis?**   **quem?.**

260. You learned that the {-s -m -t} or {-s -t} part of a sentence is called the _____.

A: kernel.

261. You also learned the intensifier _____.

A: **etiam.**

262. You learned that while position is *not* a *structural* signal in Latin to show such relations as subject and object, the Roman authors used it to show _____.

A: emphasis.

263. You learned two new Basic Sentences. Give the Latin. E____ c_____ ū___ h____ u_____ s____.

A: **Etiam capillus ūnus habet umbram suam.**

264. Cr_____ m_____ i_____ ae___ f_____.

A: **Crūdēlem medicum intemperāns aeger facit.**

---

180. This sentence means:"A ____ is often ____ by a not l____ ____."

A: A boar is often held by a not large dog.

181. "Large" and "small" are a_____s of each other.

A: antonyms

182. It would sound better in English to change "by a not large dog" to "by a _____ dog."

A: small

183. **Ā cane nōn magnō saepe tenētur aper** = A ____ is ____ ____ by a ____ ____.

A: A boar is often held by a small dog.

184. Copy Basic Sentence 23 and its meaning in your Notebook.

185. This means that little or unimportant people are often victorious, through sheer persistence, over big or _____ people.

A: important

7-38
VOCABULARY INVENTORY

In this Unit you learned two forms of a word that is used to ask questions about people or animals:

   quis?
   quem? (6)

You learned four new adjectives:

crūdēlis	**sua**
crūdēlem (212)	**suam** (187)
intemperāns	**ūnus**
intemperantem (213)	**ūnum** (185)

In this Unit there was a new verb, and a new meaning for an old verb:

   facit (217) **habet** (181)

There was also a new kind of word, called an intensifier:

   etiam (138)

And finally two new nouns:

capillus	**umbra**
capillum (169)	**umbram** (172)

If you cannot recall the meaning of these new words, you can refer to the Frames where they first occurred. The number is indicated in parenthesis beside each word.

TEST INFORMATION

You will be asked to perform the following tasks:

1) when shown a picture of the two new Basic sentences, with prompting with the first letter of each word, to write the sentence.

2) to answer **Quis?** and **Quem?** questions on some of the Basic Sentences, as in frames 46–55.

3) to identify the kernel of Basic Sentences, as in frame 77.

4) to produce any of the review Basic Sentences (1–9) when clued by the picture and the first letter of each word.

---

172. Simia infantem lavat. ⟶ ─────

A: Ā simia īnfāns lavātur.

173. Canis aprum premit. ⟶ ─────

A: Ā cane aper premitur.

174. Here is Basic Sentence 23. Echo the first four words. ★ ○ • ○ • Ā cane nōn magnō

175. Write. ★ ○ ○ = c──── n──── m────

A: Ā cane nōn magnō

176. Echo the complete Basic Sentence. (23) ★ ○ • ○ • Ā cane nōn magnō saepe tenētur aper.

177. Echo. ★ ○ • ○ • saepe. The word *saepe* is a word that does not change form and means "often."

178. A boar is often held = S───e t───── a────

A: Saepe tenētur aper.

179. Write. ★ ○ ○ • Ā cane nōn magnō s──── t──── r.

A: Ā cane nōn magnō saepe tenētur aper. (23)

UNIT EIGHT

1. The English word "vest" is derived from Latin **vestis**. We therefore say that English "vest" is a .... of Latin **vestis**.

A: derivative

2. In the Basic Sentence which we will take up next, *every* Latin word has an English derivative. Echo a new Latin word. ★ ○ • ○ • **lēx**

3. The letter **x** in Latin stands for the combination sound **cs**. If we were to rewrite **lēx** as *****lēcs**, it would be clear that the signal for nominative case is the sound ....

A: -s.

4. Echo the nominative and accusative of this word. ★ ○ • ○ • **lēx**
                    lēgem

5. The English word "legal" is derived from the Latin word **lēx/lēgem**. "Legal advice" is advice concerning the law. The Latin word **lēx/lēgem** means "...."

A: law.

6. The English word "irate" means "angry." "Irate" is a .... of the Latin word **īrātus**, which also means "an...."

A: derivative
             angry.

7. ★ ○ • ○ • **videt**

---

162. **Īnfāns** sīmiam lavat. → ★ ○ •

VCh: Ab **īnfante** sīmia lavātur.

163. **Canis** aprum premit. → ★ ○ •

VCh: Ā **cane** aper premitur.

164. Now write the transformation of these same sentences from active to passive. **Vīpera** piscem mordet. →

A: Ā **vīperā** piscis mordētur.

165. **Anus** juvenem tenet. →

A: Ab **anū** juvenis tenētur.

166. **Aper** canem premit. →

A: Ab **aprō** canis premitur.

167. **Vir** fēminam quaerit. →

A: Ā **virō** fēmina quaeritur.

168. **Juvenis** anum tenet. →

A: Ā **juvene** anus tenētur.

169. **Īnfāns** sīmiam lavat. →

A: Ab **īnfante** sīmia lavātur.

170. **Fēmina** virum quaerit. →

A: Ā **fēminā** vir quaeritur.

171. **Piscis** vīperam mordet. →

A: Ā **pisce** vīpera mordētur.

8-2

8. When television was first invented it was often called "video," which is a derivative of the Latin verb **videt**. On the radio, you can only hear the performance, but on "video" (or television) you can both hear and ___ the performance.

A: see

9. The verb **videt** means "___s."

A: sees.

10. As a matter of fact, the "-vision" part of "television" is also a derivative of another form of this same verb **videt** which means "___s."

A: sees.

11. You now know the dictionary meaning of all the words in our new sentence. However, we must first explain a new point about sentence structure. An {-s -m -t} sentence of only three words is rare in Latin because _____ _____. [In your own words]

A: the subject, the object, and the verb may all be modified by other words.

12. The use of modifying words "expands" a sentence. For example, the adjective **cautus** _____s the kernel **metuit foveam lupus.**

A: expands

13. Besides having modifiers, a sentence may be expanded by having two (or more) kernels. Echo the first kernel of a new Basic Sentence. ★ ○ • ○ • **Lēx videt īrātum,** [Do not look at this frame when you do the next.]

14. Write. L__ v____ ī_____, ★ ○ ○

A: **Lēx videt īrātum,**

11-27

152. Ā virō fēmina quaeritur. ⟶ _____

A: **Vir fēminam quaerit.**

153. Ab aprō canis premitur. ⟶ _____

A: **Aper canem premit.**

154. Now we will do the reverse. Echo as your teacher transforms these same sentences from active to passive. Vir fēminam quaerit. ⟶ ★ ○ •

VCh: Ā virō fēmina quaeritur.

155. Fēmina virum quaerit. ⟶ ★ ○ •

VCh: Ā fēminā vir quaeritur.

156. Piscis vīperam mordet. ⟶ ★ ○ •

VCh: Ā pisce vīpera mordētur.

157. Juvenis anum tenet. ⟶ ★ ○ •

VCh: Ā juvene anus tenētur.

158. Simia īnfantem lavat. ⟶ ★ ○ •

VCh: Ā simiā īnfāns lavātur.

159. Aper canem premit. ⟶ ★ ○ •

VCh: Ab aprō canis premitur.

160. Vīpera piscem mordet. ⟶ ★ ○ •

VCh: Ā vīperā piscis mordētur.

161. Anus juvenem tenet. ⟶ ★ ○ •

VCh: Ab anū juvenis tenētur.

15. Chorus the whole Basic Sentence. *Lēx videt īrātum, īrātus lēgem nōn videt.* (13)
★ ○ ○ ● ●

16. L__ v____ ī_____, ī_____ l____ n__ v____.
★ ○ ○ [Seven macrons in this sentence.]

A: Lēx videt īrātum, īrātus lēgem nōn videt.

17. How many kernels are there in this sentence?

A: Two.

18. We can expand a sentence not only by having modifiers but by having _____ .
[In your own words]

A: two or more kernels.

19. Lēx videt īrātum, īrātus lēgem nōn videt. The word lēx/lēgem is subject of the first kernel and _____ of the second kernel.

A: object

20. And the word īrātus/īrātum is _____ of the first kernel and _____ of the second.

A: object
subject

---

143. "Ā quō īnfāns lavātur?" "_____."

A: Ā simiā.

144. Transform these ten passive sentences to active. Ā cane aper premitur. → C___ s a___ m p___t.

A: Canis aprum premit.

145. Ab anū juvenis tenētur. → A____ j_____ m t___t.

A: Anus juvenem tenet.

146. Ā simiā īnfāns lavātur. → S____ i_____ l_____.

A: Simia īnfantem lavat.

147. Ā viperā piscis mordētur. → _____ _____.

A: Vipera piscem mordet.

148. Ab īnfante simia lavātur. → _____.

A: Īnfāns simiam lavat.

149. Ā juvene anus tenētur. → _____.

A: Juvenis anum tenet.

150. Ā fēminā vir quaeritur. → _____.

A: Fēmina virum quaerit.

151. Ā pisce vipera mordētur. → _____.

A: Piscis viperam mordet.

8-4

21. Lēx videt īrātum, īrātus lēgem nōn videt = The ___ ___s an ____ p_____, the _____ p_____ does not ___ the ____.

A: The law sees an angry person, the angry person does not see the law.

22. Copy this Basic Sentence in your Reference Notebook.

23. Say the Basic Sentence which this picture describes. L__ v____ ī_____, ī_____ l____ n__ v____.

A: **Lēx videt īrātum, īrātus lēgem nōn videt.**

24. This means that although when we are angry *we* may forget about the law and overlook it, the law will certainly not _____ our actions.

A: _____ overlook (forget, etc.)

25. In answering these questions, remember that all you have to do is to repeat the {-s} part of the kernel for **Quis?** and the {-m} part for **Quem?** However, remember to say your answer first, and *then* check with either the tape or the Visual Check. "Quis lēgem nōn videt?" "_____." ✓ ★ ○ •

VCh: **Īrātus.**

---

136. "Quem vir quaerit?" "_____."

A: **Fēminam.**

137. "Ā quō fēmina quaeritur?" "_____."

A: **Ā virō.**

138. "Quis quaerit?" "_____."

A: **Vir.**

139. "Quis quaeritur?" "_____."

A: **Fēmina.**

140. "Quis lavat?" "_____."

141. "Quem simia lavat?" "_____."

A: **Simia.**

142. "Quis īnfantem lavat?" "_____."

A: **Īnfantem.**

A: **Simia.**

8-5

26. "Quem lēx videt?" "_____." ✓ ★ ○ •

VCh: Īrātum.

27. "Quis īrātum videt?" "_____." ✓ ★ ○ •

VCh: Lēx.

28. "Quem īrātus nōn videt?" "_____."
✓ ★ ○ •

VCh: Lēgem.

29. Now using the same pattern, describe this picture to say that the monkey sees the bull, but the bull does not see the monkey. Say the entire sentence aloud. **Sīmia videt taurum, t___us s___am nōn videt.**

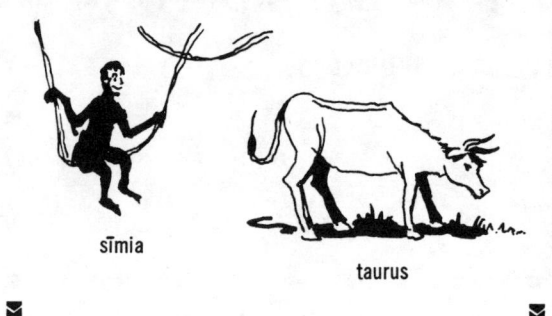

sīmia   taurus

A: Sīmia videt taurum, taurus sīmiam nōn videt.

30. Piscis capit _____, _____ piscem nōn capit.

musca   piscis

A: Piscis capit muscam, musca piscem nōn capit.

---

129. "Quis ab aprō premitur?" "_____."

A: Canis.

130. "Quem aper premit?" "_____."

A: Canem.

131. "Ā quō canis premitur?" "_____."

A: Ab aprō.

132. "Quis anum tenet?" "_____."

133. "Quis tenētur?" "_____."

A: Juvenis.

134. "Quem juvenis tenet?" "_____."

A: Anus.

135. "Ā quō anus tenētur?" "_____."

A: Anum.

A: Ā juvene.

11-24

31. Anus dīligit ____tem, īn___ s a__m nōn dīligit.

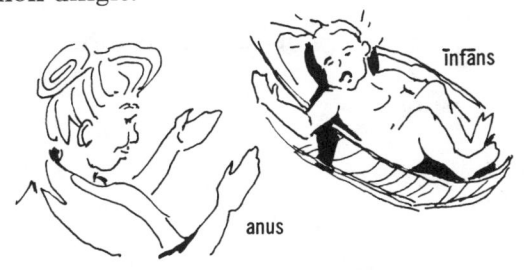

A: Anus dīligit īnfantem, īnfāns anum nōn dīligit.

32. Agnus metuit lupum, ____ ____ __ ____.

A: Agnus metuit lupum, lupus agnum nōn metuit.

33. We will now show you a new type of question. Although you probably never thought about it, asking and answering a "Yes" or "No" type of question is complicated in English. Observe: "Do you have any money?" "Yes, I have s___ money."

A: some

34. In the answer above, we changed the three-word verb form "do you have" to the two words "_ _____."

A: I have.

35. And we also changed the "any" of the question to "_____."

A: some.

---

122. "Ā quō aper premitur?" "_____."

A: Ā cane.

123. "Quis premitur?" "_____."

A: Aper.

124. "Quis ā fēminā quaeritur?" "_____."

A: Vir.

125. "Quis virum quaerit?" "_____."

A: Fēmina.

126. "Ā quō vir quaeritur?" "_____."

A: Ā fēminā.

127. "Quem fēmina quaerit?" "_____."

A: Virum.

128. "Quis premit?" "_____."

A: Aper.

8-7

36. In addition, we also added the word "____."

A: Yes.

37. Although it may surprise you to learn that there are no single words for "yes" and "no" in Latin, this type of Yes-or-No question and answer is easy in Latin. Write down your teacher's description of this picture. ★ ○ ○
L____ v__ v_____.

A: **Lavat vir vestem.**

38. Echo your teacher as he asks whether the man in the picture is washing the clothes. ★ ○ • ○ • **Lavatne vir vestem?**

39. To ask the question he added the question element **-ne** to the ____ (first/second/third) word in the sentence.

A: first

40. Ask your teacher in Latin the same question. ("Is the man washing the clothes?") "**Lavatne vir vestem?**" √ ★ ○ •

41. Write down his answer that means, "Yes, he is." ★ ○ ○ L____ v__ ve____.

A: **Lavat vir vestem.**

11-22

115. "Ā quō piscis mordētur?" "_____."

A: Ā vīperā.

116. "Quis ab īnfante lavātur?" "_____."

A: Simia.

117. "Quem īnfāns lavat?" "_____."

A: Simiam.

118. "Ā quō simia lavātur?" "_____."

A: Ab īnfante.

119. "Quis simiam lavat?" "_____."

A: Īnfāns.

120. "Quis aprum premit?" "_____."

A: Canis.

121. "Quem canis premit?" "_____."

A: Aprum.

42. Because the man is actually washing the clothes, your teacher gave an "affirmative" answer (one that says "yes"). He did this by repeating the sentence but leaving off the ___

A: -ne.

43. Your teacher will now ask you in Latin the same question ("Is the man washing the clothes?") ★ ○ • ○ •

VCh: **Lavatne vir vestem?**

44. Tell him that he is. "_____ ___ _____."

A: **Lavat vir vestem.**

45. Here is a question about this picture. ★ ○ ○ "**Lavatne anus vestem?**" Write your affirmative answer. "_____ _____ _____."

A: **Lavat anus vestem.**

46. Now ask your teacher if the *man* is washing clothes. "L____ne v__ ve____?" ✓ ★ ○ •

VCh: "**Lavatne vir vestem?**"

47. Echo his answer. ★ ○ • ○ •

VCh: "**Nōn lavat vir vestem.**"

8-8

In this picture and in the ones that follow you will be asked these four questions: two **Quis?** questions, one **Ā quō?** question, and one **Quem?** question.

108. "**Quis juvenem tenet?**" "_____."

A: **Anus.**

109. "**Quis ab anū tenētur?**" "_____."

A: **Juvenis.**

110. "**Quem anus tenet?**" "_____."

A: **Juvenem.**

111. "**Ā quō juvenis tenētur?**" "**Ab** _____."

A: **Ab anū.**

112. "**Quem vipera mordet?**" "_____."

A: **Piscem.**

113. "**Quis piscem mordet?**" "_____."

A: **Vipera.**

114. "**Quis ā viperā mordētur?**" "_____."

A: **Piscis.**

8-9

48. To give a "negative" answer ("No") your teacher repeated the sentence as before, but he added the word "____."

A: nōn.

49. Answer the question. "Lavatne anus vestem?" "___ _____ ____ _____."

A: Nōn lavat anus vestem.

50. Write down your teacher's question about this picture. ★ ○ ○ "M____ne p_____ r____?"

VCh: Mordetne piscis rānam? [If you have no tape recorder, copy this.]

51. He asked you whether _____ _____. [In your own words]

A: the fish is biting the frog.

52. Since the fish *is* biting the frog, give a "Yes" answer. "_____ _____ _____."

A: Mordet piscis rānam.

53. Listen to another question about the same situation. ★ ○ ○

VCh: "Mordetne piscem rāna?"

11-20

103. "_____," ∨ ★ ○ •

VCh: Ā fēminā vir quaeritur.

104. While these sentences both describe the same picture, tenet is _____ voice, while tenētur is _____ voice.

Anus juvenem tenet.
Ab ānū juvenis tenētur.

A: active
   passive

105. Each of the two sentences contains two nouns, and we can therefore ask four different questions on the situation. Quem? would ask for the {--} of the verb tenet.

A: {-m}

106. Quis? would ask for the {--} of either tenet or tenētur.

A: {-s}

107. Ā quō? would ask for ā (or ab) plus a noun in the _____ case.

A: ablative

8-10

54. Write your answer. "_____."

A: Nōn mordet piscem rāna.

55. Here is a new picture. Ask your teacher whether the fish is biting the frog.

    A   B

"M_____ne pisc___ rān___?" √ ★ ○ •

VCh: "Mordetne piscis rānam?"

56. Listen to his answer. ★ ○ ○

VCh: "Piscis rānam nōn mordet."

57. His answer describes Picture ____ (A/B).

A: B.

58. Here are a series of **-ne** questions on more pictures. Give an affirmative ("Yes") or negative ("No"). Answer as necessary to describe each picture. Remember to *ignore* the word order; observe the Latin signals. "**Lavatne sīmia elephantum?**" "_____."
[A line of dashes like this does not indicate either the length of words or the number of words expected in the answer.]

A: "Lavat sīmia elephantum."

11-19

97. "_____," ∨ ★ ○ •

VCh: Ab aprō canis premitur.

98. ★ ○ ○ "___ l___ in ___?"

99. "_____," ∨ ★ ○ •

VCh: "Ā quō īnfāns lavātur?"

VCh: Ā sīmiā īnfāns lavātur.

100. ★ ○ ○ ",, ___ j___ t___?"

101. "_____," ∨ ★ ○ •

VCh: "Ā quō juvenis tenētur?"

VCh: Ab anū juvenis tenētur.

102. ★ ○ ○ "___ qu___ v___ qu___?"

VCh: "Ā quō vir quaeritur?"

59. "Lavatne elephantus virum?"
"_____."

A: Nōn lavat elephantus virum.

60. "Peritne lupus?" "_____."

A: _____ Perit.

61. "Vīdetne aquilam vīpera?" "_____."

A: _____ Nōn videt.

62. If you were asked in English, "Is the elephant washing the man?", you might answer "No, the elephant isn't washing the man," but it would be much more common to say, "No, he ___'t."

A: isn't.

---

91. "_____."
VCh: Ab īnfante sīmia lavātur.

92. ★ ○ ○ "Ā ___ a___ t_____?"

VCh: "Ā quō anus tenētur?"

93. "_____." ∧ ★ ○ •

VCh: Ā iuvene anus tenētur.

94. ★ ○ ○ "_____ v___ m_____?"

VCh: "Ā quō vīpera mordētur?"

95. "_____." ∧ ★ ○ •

VCh: Ā pisce vīpera mordētur.

96. ★ ○ ○ "_____ c___ pr_____?"

VCh: "Ā quō canis premitur?"

8-12

63. In the same way, it is more common in Latin to answer a **-ne** question by merely repeating the *one word* (usually the verb) to which the **-ne** was attached. Ask your teacher whether the mouse is washing clothes and check your question. "La_ _ _ _ _?" ✓ ★ ○ •

VCh: "Lavatne vestem mūs?"

64. Echo his one word answer. ★ ○ • ○ •

VCh: **Lavat.**

65. Now answer these questions on these new pictures by repeating just the verb, either with or without **nōn**, depending on the situation. "Mordetne anum canis?" "_ _ _ _ _."

A: **Nōn mordet.**

66. "Quaeritne piscem rāna?" "_ _ _ _ _."

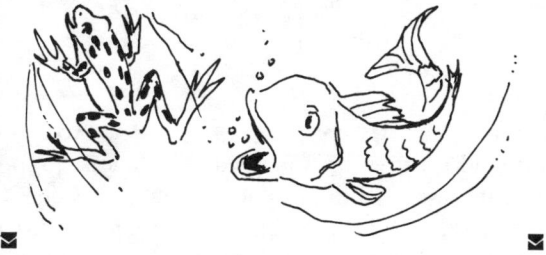

A: **Nōn quaerit.**

11-17

86. Your teacher will now ask you "by whom?" (**ā quō?**) the action in each picture is being done. Answer with a complete sentence. "A p_ _ _ m_ _ _ _ ?" ★ ○ ○

VCh: "Ā quō piscis mordētur?"

87. "_ _ _ _ _ _ _ _ _ _ _ _ _ ," ∧ ★ ○ •

VCh: Ā vipera piscis mordētur.

88. ★ ○ ○ "Ā _ _ _ a _ _ _ pr _ _ _ _ ?"

VCh: "Ā quō aper premitur?"

89. "_ _ _ _ _ _ _ _ _ _ _ _ _ _ ," ∧ ★ ○ •

VCh: Ā cane aper premitur.

90. ★ ○ ○ "Ā _ _ _ _ s _ _ _ l _ _ _ _ ?"

VCh: "Ā quō simia lavātur?"

8-13

67. We will now ask you this same kind of **-ne** question about some of our Basic Sentences. For example, we had a Basic Sentence **Vestis virum reddit**. The question would be **Redditne vestis virum?** ("Do clothes make the man?") Now since the Basic Sentence says that they *do*, you give the one-word affirmative answer. "**Redditne vestis virum?**" "_____."

A: Reddit.

68. In other words, all you have to do is to remember whether the Basic Sentence says that something is so or isn't. "**Metuitne foveam cautus lupus?**" "_____."

A: Metuit.

69. "**Quaeritne aeger medicum ēloquentem?**" "_____."

A: Nōn quaerit.

70. "**Capitne elephantus mūrem?**" "_____."

A: Nōn capit.

71. "**Habetne semper aurem facilem Fēlīcitās?**" "_____."

A: Nōn habet.

72. "**Lavatne manus manum?**" "_____."

A: Lavat.

73. "**Facitne crūdēlem medicum intemperāns aeger?**" "_____."

A: Facit.

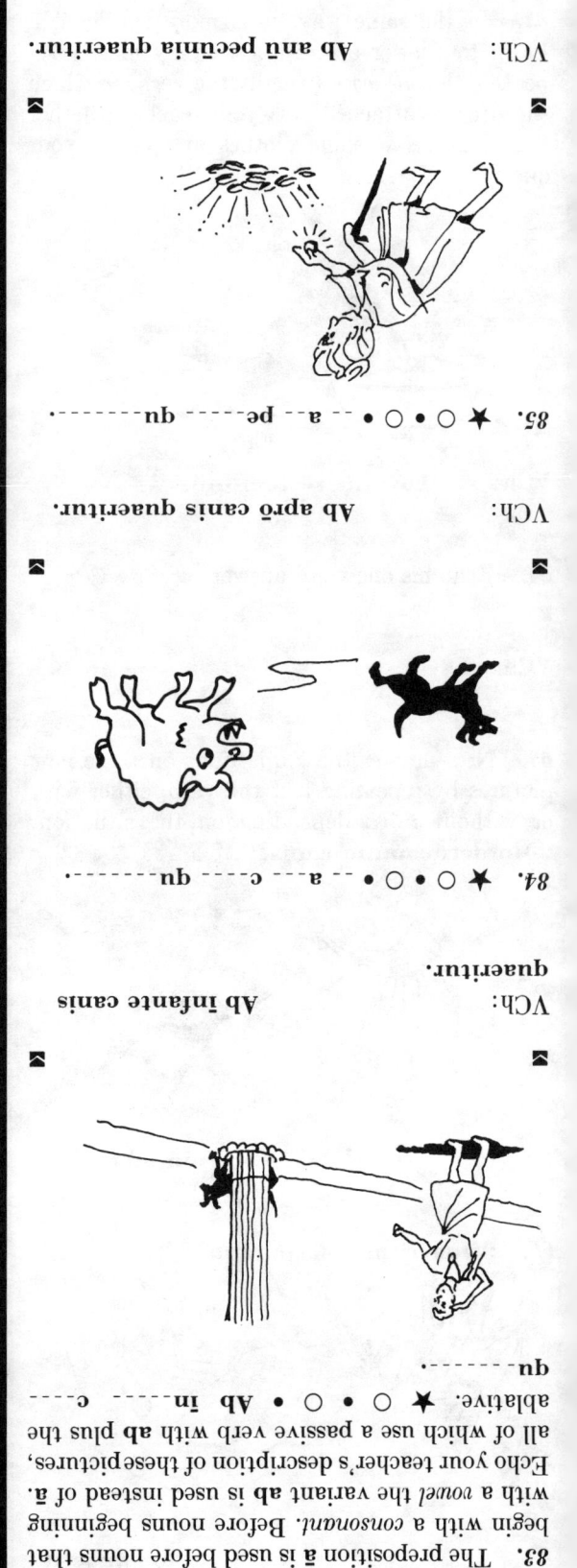

11-16

83. The preposition **ā** is used before nouns that begin with a *consonant*. Before nouns beginning with a *vowel* the variant **ab** is used instead of **ā**. Echo your teacher's description of these pictures, all of which use a passive verb with **ab** plus the ablative. ★ ○ • ○ • **Ab in**____ c_____nb_____

VCh: **Ab īnfante canis quaeritur.**

84. ★ ○ • ○ • **a**___ c____ qu_____nb_____

VCh: **Ab aprō canis quaeritur.**

85. ★ ○ • ○ • **a**__ **pe**____ qu_____nb_____

VCh: **Ab anū pecūnia quaeritur.**

8-14

74. These questions are on the two-kernel sentence **Lēx videt īrātum, īrātus lēgem nōn videt.** Because the two kernels are so much alike, you will have to observe closely to see which kernel we are asking about. "Vidētne īrātus lēgem?" "_____."

A: Nōn videt.

75. "Vidētne lēx īrātum?" "_____."

A: Videt.

76. We sometimes want to give a person a choice: "Is it *this* or is it *that*?" The person in these pictures is asking some very foolish questions. Echo as he asks whether it is an elephant or a monkey, using the new connector **an**.

★ ○ ● ○ ●

Estne elephantus an sīmia?

77. As you can see, we use the familiar question element **-ne** on the first word, but the new word **an** connects the words from which you will choose the answer. Well, which is it, an elephant or a monkey? Answer the question in Latin. "_____ est."

A: "Sīmia est."

11-15

80. On the same pattern as **Ā sīmia rāna capitur**, describe the following pictures. **Ā j_____ p_____ c_____.**

A: juvene pisce capitur.

81. **Ā v_____ f_____ c_____.**

A: Ā virō fūr capitur.

82. **Ā f_____ as_____.**

A: Ā fēminā asinus capitur.

8-15

78. These are certainly stupid questions that this person is asking, but he is an older person, so answer them patiently. Remember, you merely *choose* between the words on either side of the connector **an**. "‗ ‗ ‗ ‗ ‗ ‗ ‗ ‗ ."

> Estne equus an lupus?

A: Lupus est.

79. Write down the question that means, "Is it a horse or a wolf?" ‗ ‗ ‗ **ne** ‗ ‗ ‗ ‗ **an** ‗ ‗ ‗ ‗ ?

A: Estne equus an lupus?

80. Please have patience with this man. His Latin seems to be all right; perhaps he just doesn't see very well. "‗ ‗ ‗ ‗ ‗ ‗ ‗ ‗ ."

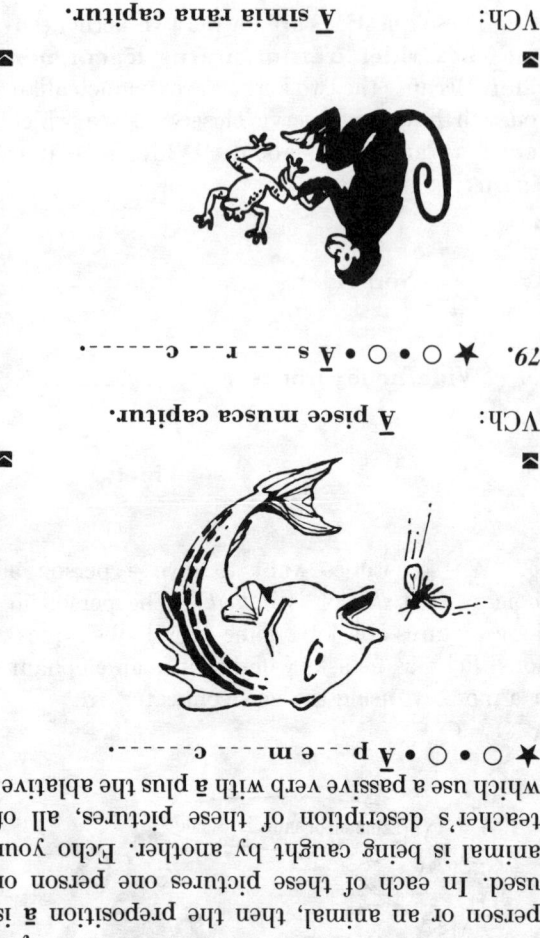

> Estne rāna an vir?

A: Rāna est.

---

76. "Quis virum quaerit?" "‗ ‗ ‗ ‗ ‗ ‗ ." ∧ ★ ○ •

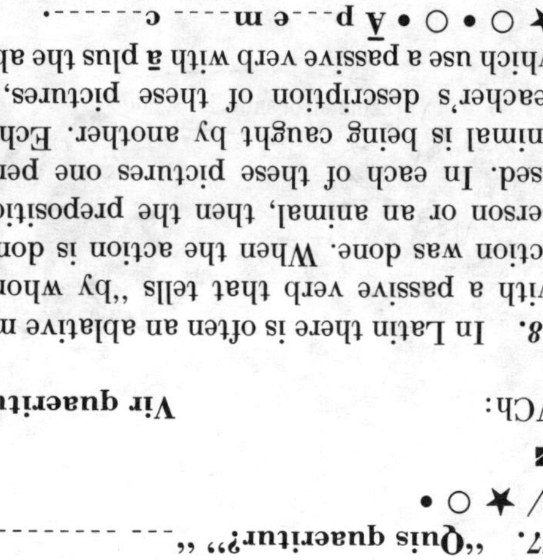

VCh: Canis.

77. "Quis quaeritur?" "‗ ‗ ‗ ‗ ‗ ‗ ‗ ." ∧ • ○ ★ •

VCh: Vir quaeritur.

78. In Latin there is often an ablative modifier with a passive verb that tells "by whom," the action was done. When the action is done by a person or an animal, then the preposition **ā** is used. In each of these pictures one person or animal is being caught by another. Echo your teacher's description of these pictures, all of which use a passive verb with **ā** plus the ablative.

★ • ○ • ∧ **Ā** p‗ ‗ ‗ **e m** ‗ ‗ ‗ **c** ‗ ‗ ‗ ‗ ‗ .

VCh: **Ā** pisce musca capitur.

79. ★ ○ ○ • ∧ **Ā** s‗ ‗ ‗ ‗ **r** ‗ ‗ ‗ ‗ **c** ‗ ‗ ‗ ‗ ‗ .

VCh: **Ā** simiā rāna capitur.

11-14

8-16

81. Now just listen to his questions and then answer him. Remember that it's not really his fault that he can't tell the difference between an elephant and a monkey. "‑ ‑ ‑ ‑ ‑ ‑ ‑ ‑ ‑ ‑."
√ ★ ○ •

VCh: "Estne elephantus an sīmia?"

A: Elephantus est.

82. "‑ ‑ ‑ ‑ ‑ ‑ ‑." √ ★ ○ •

VCh: "Estne canis an īnfāns?"

A: Īnfāns est.

83. "‑ ‑ ‑ ‑ ‑ ‑ ‑." √ ★ ○ •

VCh: "Estne mūs an taurus?"

A: Taurus est.

11-13

71. "Quis leōnem premit?" "‑ ‑ ‑ ‑ ‑ ‑."
√ ★ ○ •

VCh: Taurus.

72. "Quis lavātur?" "‑ ‑ ‑ ‑ ‑ ‑." √ ★ ○ •

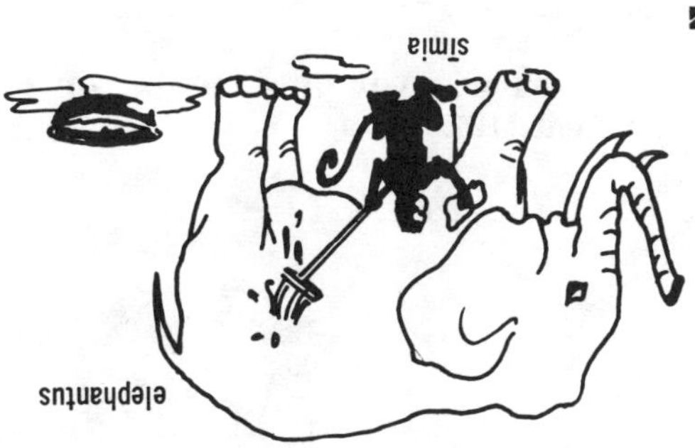

VCh: Elephantus.

73. "Quis elephantum lavat?" "‑ ‑ ‑ ‑ ‑."
√ ★ ○ •

VCh: Sīmia.

74. "Quis irrītātur?" "‑ ‑ ‑ ‑ ‑ ‑ ‑ ‑."
√ ★ ○ •

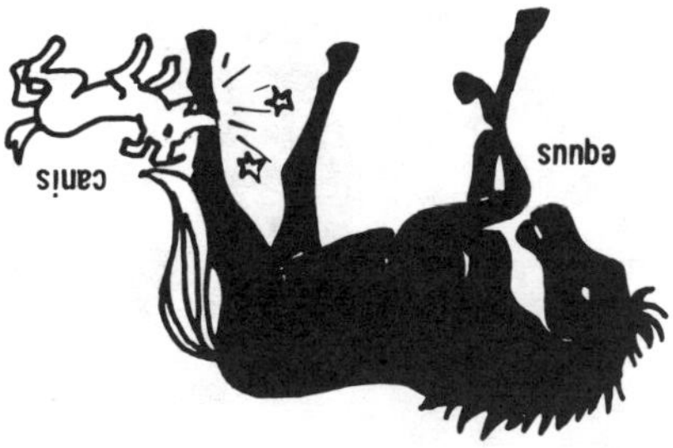

VCh: Equus irrītātur.

75. "Quis irrītat?" "‑ ‑ ‑ ‑ ‑ ‑ ‑."
√ ★ ○ •

VCh: Canis irrītat.

8-17

84. To a question like **Peritne piscis an taurus?** you answer with *one* of the two words which ------------------- [In your own words]

A: were connected by **an**.

85. Say the Basic Sentences for the following pictures. E____ c_____ ū___ h____ um____ s___. (11)

A: Etiam capillus ūnus habet umbram suam. (11)

86. Cr_____ med____ intemp_____ ae___ f_____. (12)

A: Crūdēlem medicum intemperāns aeger facit. (12)

87. N__ s_____ au___ f_____ h____ Fēl_____. (10)

A: Nōn semper aurem facilem habet Fēlīcitās. (10)

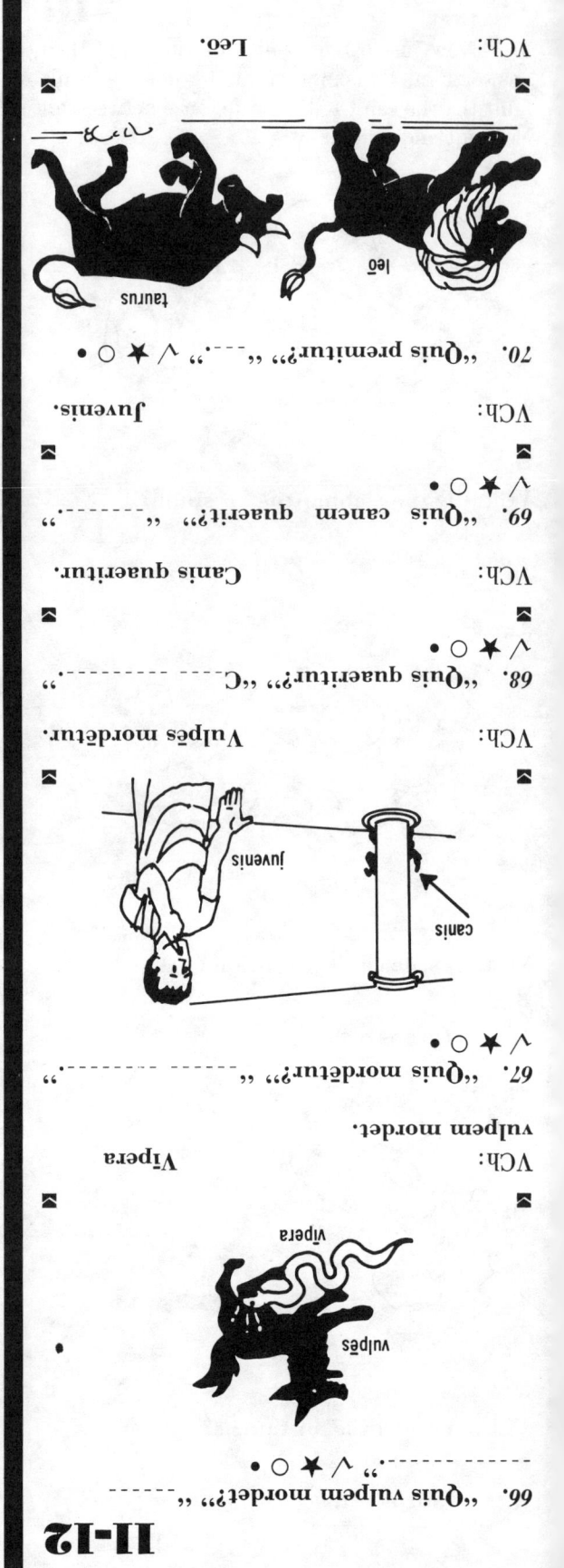

11-12

66. "Quis vulpem mordet?" "--------." ∧ ★ ○ •

VCh: **Vīpera** vulpem mordet.

67. "Quis mordētur?" "--------." ∧ ★ ○ •

VCh: **Vulpēs** mordētur.

68. "Quis quaeritur?" "C----." ∧ ★ ○ •

VCh: **Canis** quaeritur.

69. "Quis canem quaerit?" "------." ∧ ★ ○ •

VCh: **Juvenis**.

70. "Quis premitur?" "-----." ∧ ★ ○ •

VCh: **Leō**.

8-18

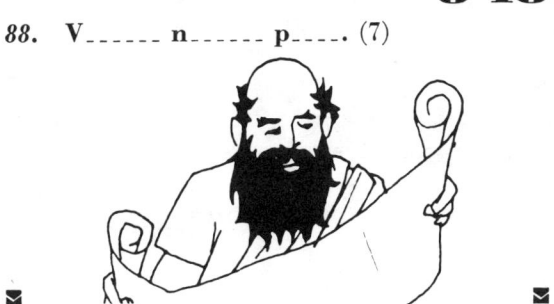

88. V_____ n_____ p_____. (7)

A: Vēritās numquam perit. (7)

89. L__ vid__ īrāt__, īrāt__ lēg__ n__ vid___. (13)

A: Lēx videt īrātum, īrātus lēgem nōn videt. (13)

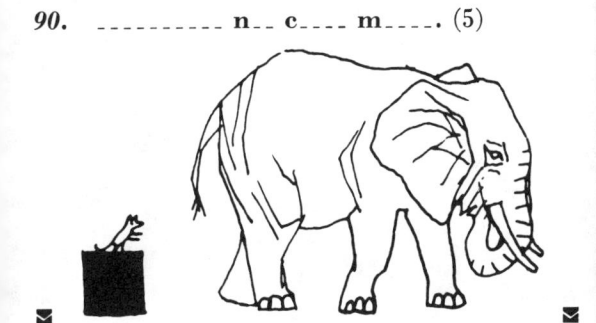

90. _____ n__ c____ m____. (5)

A: Elephantus nōn capit mūrem. (5)

91. Here is Basic Sentence 14. Echo the first kernel. ★ ○ • ○ • Fūrem fūr cognōscit

92. There are ____ (1/2/3/4) macrons in this kernel.

A: 3

93. Write. ★ ○ ○ F____ f__ c_____

A: Fūrem fūr cognōscit

II-11

60. **Taurus premit** = The ____ is ____ing (somebody).

A: bull pursuing

61. **Juvenis premitur** = _____

A: The young man is being pursued (by somebody).

62. "Quis simiam lavat?" [Be sure to answer before you listen to the tape.] "____ s____ l____." ∨ ★ ○ •

63. "Quis lavatur?" "_____." ∨ ★ ○ •

VCh: Simia lavātur.

64. "Quis irritātur?" "_____." ∨ ★ ○ •

VCh: Canis irritātur.

65. "Quis canem irritat?" "____ ____ ____." ∨ ★ ○ •

VCh: Musca canem irritat.

8-19

94. Chorus the entire sentence. ★ ○ ○ ● ●
Fūrem fūr cognōscit et lupum lupus. (14)

95. ★ ○ ○ Fūrem fūr cognōscit __ l____ l____.

A: et lupum lupus.

96. Because the word **et** connects equal things, it is called a _____.

A: connector.

97. The connector **et** can connect kernels. In the sentence **Fūrem fūr cognōscit et lupum lupus** it connects the three-word kernel **Fūrem fūr cognōscit** with the two-word kernel l___ m l___s.

A: lupum lupus.

98. But in what way can we say that **Fūrem fūr cognōscit** is equal to **lupum lupus**? This sentence illustrates one of the most characteristic things about the Latin language, which is this: *important parts* of the sentence must often be *supplied* by the reader. This is not so hard as it sounds, and we will give you plenty of practice in doing it. Here is how it works. In **Fūrem fūr cognōscit et lupum lupus, lupum** is the {-m} of the second kernel, and **lupus** is the {-s}. The only thing missing to make this second kernel a complete {-s -m -t} phrase is a {__}.

A: {-t}.

99. When the {-t} is missing, *you must supply it from the other kernel.* Expand the sentence then, by supplying the {-t} that you find in the other kernel.
Fūrem fūr cognōscit et lupum lupus
        _____t.

A: **cognōscit.**

11-10

54. We also use the technical term "voice," and say that **mordet** is "active voice,"; the form **mordētur** is therefore "passive _____."

A: _____ voice.

55. Premit is _____ voice and **premitur** is _____ passive _____

A: active _____ voice.

56. Quaeritur is _____ voice and **quaerit** is _____ voice.

A: passive _____ active

57. Lavātur is _____ and **lavat** is _____ _____.

A: passive voice active voice.

58. Here is a new set of pictures. About each one you will be asked two **quis?** questions, with either a passive or an active verb. For example, if you are asked about this picture **Quis premit?** you answer, "_____ _____."

A: **Taurus premit.**

59. If you are asked **Quis premitur?** you answer, "_____ _____."

A: **Juvenis premitur.**

taurus

juvenis

8-20

100. When we added **cognōscit** we ex_____ed the second kernel.

A: expanded

101. The dictionary meaning of **fūr** is "thief." The kernel **Fūrem fūr cognōscit** therefore means, "A thief blanks another _____."

A: thief.

102. And the kernel **lupum lupus cognōscit** means, "A ____ _____ another ____."

A: A wolf blanks another wolf.

103. The word **cognōscit** means "recognizes." **Fūrem fūr cognōscit et lupum lupus** = A _____ r_____ another _____ and a ____ _____ another ____.

A: A thief recognizes (another) thief and a wolf recognizes (another) wolf. (Basic Sentence 14).

104. Copy Basic Sentence 14 and its meaning in your Notebook.

105. While **Vēritātem diēs aperit** was a one-kernel sentence, **Fūrem fūr cognōscit et lupum lupus** is a ___ kernel sentence.

A: two-kernel

---

48. ★ • ○ • ○ • **Fēmina quaeritur.**

49. ★ • ○ • ○ • **Simia lavātur.**

A: **Fēmina quaeritur.**

A: **Simia lavātur.**

50. The form of the verb that ends in -**t** is called the "active" form; the form that ends in -**tur** is called the "passive" form. **Capit** is the _____ form of the verb.

A: active

51. **Mordet** is the _____ form of the verb.

A: active

52. **Capitur** is the _____ form of the verb.

A: passive

53. **Mordētur** is the _____ form of the verb.

A: passive

8-21

106. Write the Basic Sentence that describes this picture. F____ fūr cogn_____ et _____ lupus.

A: **Fūrem fūr cognōscit et lupum lupus.**

107. An English equivalent might be to say that it takes a th___ to catch a _____.

A: thief   thief.

Now for some questions on Basic Sentence 14.

108. "Quem fūr cognōscit?" "_____."
√ ★ ○ •

VCh: **Fūrem.**

109. "Quem lupus cognōscit?" "_____."
√ ★ ○ •

VCh: **Lupum.**

110. "Quis lupum cognōscit?" "_____."
√ ★ ○ •

VCh: **Lupus.**

111. "Quis fūrem cognōscit?" "____."
√ ★ ○ •

VCh: **Fūr.**
[Did you remember to answer first and *then* check?]

A: **Vīpera mordētur.**

47. ★ ○ • ○ • **Vīpera mordētur.**

A: **Juvenis tenētur.**

46. ★ ○ • ○ • **Juvenis tenētur.**

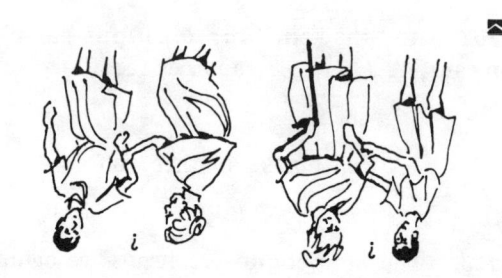

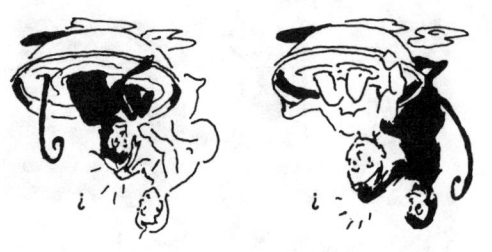

A: **Īnfāns lavātur.**

45. ★ ○ • ○ • **Īnfāns lavātur.**

A: **Piscis mordētur.**

44. ★ ○ • ○ • **Piscis mordētur.**

8-22

112. We will now ask you some **-ne** questions, the kind that call for an affirmative or negative answer. If we ask you (in Latin), "Does a thief recognize another thief?" you will of course give an affirmative answer. What answer would you give *in terms of the Basic Sentence*, if your teacher were to ask (in Latin), "Does a thief recognize a wolf?" ____ (An affirmative answer/A negative answer.)

A: A negative answer.

113. Here are four **-ne** questions about this Basic Sentence. Give the short answer, one word for an affirmative answer, two words for a negative one. "Cognōscitne lupus lupum?" "_____."

A: Cognōscit.

114. "Cognōscitne lupus fūrem?" "_____."

A: **Nōn cognōscit.**

115. "Cognōscitne fūr lupum?" "_____."

A: **Nōn cognōscit.**

116. "Cognōscitne fūr fūrem?" "_____."

A: **Cognōscit.**

117. Use the same pattern of **Fūrem fūr cognōscit et lupum lupus** to say that the mouse recognizes the mouse and the lion recognizes the lion. **Mūrem ___ cognōscit et ____em ___.**

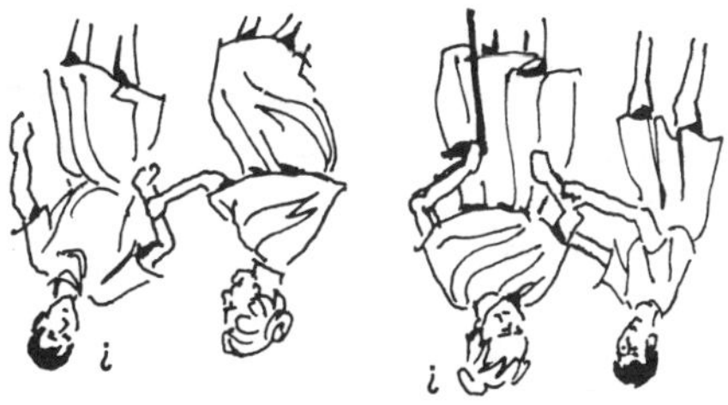

A: **Mūrem mūs cognōscit et leōnem leō.**

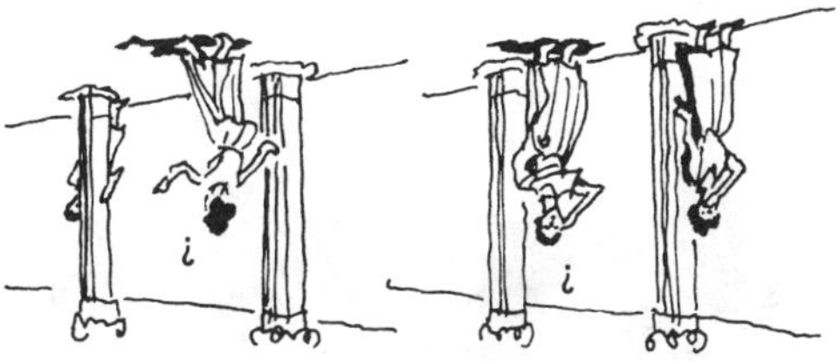

8-23

118. Use this same pattern to describe the following pictures. **Vulpem _____ cognōscit et ____m ____.**

▼

A: **Vulpem vulpēs cognōscit et rānam rāna.**

119. M_____ _____ _____ et _____ _____.

▼

A: **Muscam musca cognōscit et piscem piscis.**

120. S_____ _____ _____ et _____ _____.

▼

A: **Sīmiam sīmia cognōscit et equum equus.**

(reversed text from facing page:)

35. While **Vir quaerit** means, "The man is seeking (something not yet mentioned)," **Vir quaeritur** means, "The ___ is being _____ (by somebody not yet mentioned)."

▲

A: man   sought

▲

36. If the verb ends in **-t**, it means that the subject of the sentence is *doing* the action; if the verb ends in **-tur**, it means that the subject is having the action d____ to ____.

▲

A: done to him (her, it).

▲

37. **Canis capit** = The ___ is _____ (something not yet mentioned).

▲

A: The dog is catching

▲

38. **Canis capitur** = The ___ is _____.

▲

A: The dog is being caught.

39-49. This sequence will give you practice in the new {-tur} form. Your teacher will describe one of two pictures; you are to decide which picture he has described. The description will be repeated under the *correct* picture. Let us first try it in English.

39. The dog is being pursued.

▲

(Which picture is it, the right or the left?)

▲

A: The dog is being pursued.

8-24

121. El------------------------------.

elephantus elephantus asinus asinus

A: Elephantum elephantus cognōscit et asinum asinus.

122. C------------------------------.

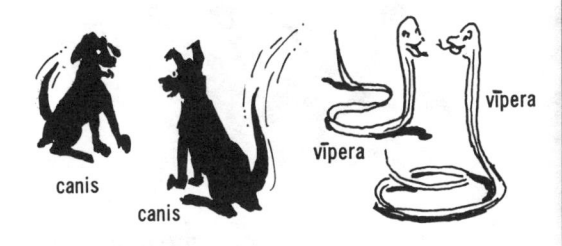

canis canis vīpera vīpera

A: Canem canis cognōscit et vīperam vīpera.

123. Describe the pictures aloud and check.
L____ n__ m_____ l____. (6) √ ★ ○ •

VCh: Lupus nōn mordet lupum. (6)

124. E____ c_____ ū___ h____ um____ s____. (11) √ ★ ○ •

VCh: Etiam capillus ūnus habet umbram suam. (11)

11-5

Echo the descriptions of these two pictures which have the same subject but different forms of the verb.

28.   29.

★ • ○ •   ★ • ○ •
Vulpēs agnum mordet.   Vulpēs mordētur.

30. In both sentences the subject is the Latin ------ word.

A: **vulpēs.**

31. In the left hand picture [look back if necessary] the verb is ------ but as you will notice, the verb in the right hand picture is ---------.

A: **mordet   mordētur.**

32. In the first picture, **Vulpēs agnum mordet**, the fox is ----ing the ----, while in the second, **Vulpēs mordētur**, the fox is being ------.

A: biting   lamb   bitten.

33. You know now that verbs end not only in -t but they may also end in ----.

A: **-tur**.

34. ★ • ○ • ○ • **quaerit, quaeritur**.

8-25

125. L__ vi__ īrā___, īrā___ lē__ n__ vi__.
(13) ✓ ★ ○ •

VCh: **Lēx videt īrātum, īrātus lēgem nōn videt.** (13)

126. Cr_____ med____ int_____ ae___ f_____. (12) ✓ ★ ○ •

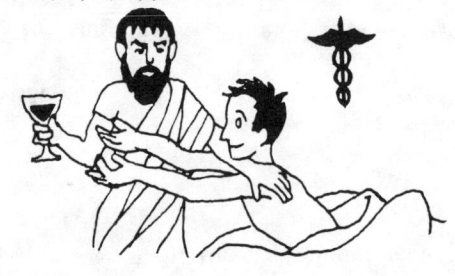

VCh: **Crūdēlem medicum intemperāns aeger facit.** (12)

127. Fūr__ fū_ cognōsc__ et ____ m ____ s.
(14) ✓ ★ ○ •

VCh: **Fūrem fūr cognōscit et lupum lupus.** (14)

128. Here is new vocabulary. Echo your teacher as he describes this picture. ★ ○ • ○ • **Fēmina vestem lavat.**

---

22. Any sentence that contains a transitive verb can be "transformed" into a different construction: we can say, "The mouse is _____ by the dog."

A: caught

23. "The old lady is washing the baby" can be transformed to "The ____ is being washed by the ___ ____."

A: baby
    old lady.

24. When we change "The old lady is washing the baby" to "The baby is being washed by the old lady," we say we have tr____ ed the verb.

A: transformed

25-26. Transitive verbs in Latin have this same kind of transformation. Echo your teacher as he describes this picture in two different ways.

25. ★ ○ • ○ • **Canis mūrem capit.**

26. ★ ○ • ○ • **Mūs capitur.**

27. **Capitur** is a new form of the verb **capit**. **Mūs capitur** therefore means, "The ____ is being ____."

A: The mouse is being caught.

8-26

129. He said that the w___n is ___ing _____.

A: the woman is washing clothes.

130. Anus means "old woman." Fēmina describes a woman of any age. Now write the same sentence as your teacher says it again. ★ ○ ○

F_____ v_____ l____.

A: Fēmina vestem lavat.

131. "Quis vestem lavat?" "F_____ v_____ l____."

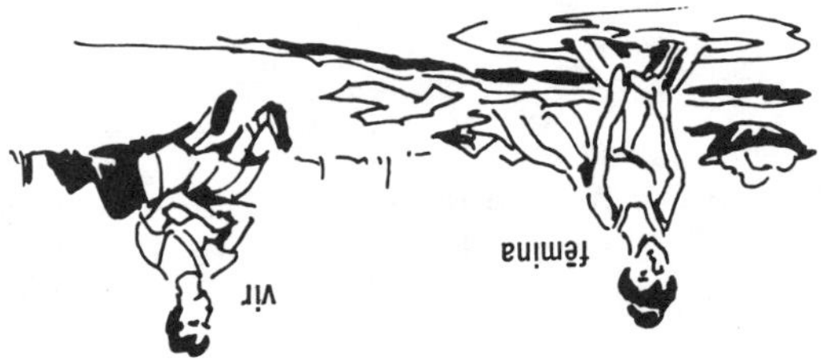

A: Fēmina vestem lavat.

132. "Quem lupus mordet?" "_____."

A: Agnum.

133. Quem vulpēs metuit? "_____."

A: Leōnem.

---

16. Et ____ (does/does not) change shape.

A: does not

17. Et is the part of speech called a _____.

A: connector.

18. At first all sentences had been of the {-s – m – t} type. You then learned to distinguish between the {-s – m – t} type and the {– – –} type.

A: {-s -t}

19. You then learned that while Vestis virum reddit is a one-kernel sentence, Lēx videt īrātum, īrātus lēgem nōn videt is a _____ sentence.

A: two kernel

20. The next distinction was learning to tell the _____ case from the nominative and accusative cases.

A: ablative

21. We will now move on to a new distinction. Look at this picture. We could describe it in English by saying "The dog is catching a mouse." "Catch" is ____ (a transitive/an intransitive) verb.

A: a transitive verb.

134. Echo the first kernel of Basic Sentence 15.
★ ○ • ○ • **Vulpēs vult fraudem.**

135. Write. ★ ○ ○ V_____ v___ fr_____,
[This kernel has one macron.]

A: **Vulpēs vult fraudem,**

136. Even without knowing the meaning of two of the three words, you can see that this is an {_ _ _} kernel.

A: {-s -m -t}

137. The {-s} is the word _____.

A: **vulpēs.**

138. The {-m} is the word _____.

A: **fraudem.**

139. And the {-t} is the word ____.

A: **vult.**

140. Echo the first two kernels of this sentence.
★ ○ • ○ • **Vulpēs vult fraudem, lupus agnum,**

141. ★ ○ ○ **Vulpēs vult fraudem,** l____ a____,

A: **lupus agnum,**

142. **Lupus agnum** is also an {-s -m -t} kernel. {-s} is the word _____.

A: **lupus.**

143. The {-m} is _____.

A: **agnum.**

---

8. Examples of subject forms with the signal zero are the words for "man" = v--, "boar" = ap--, and "frog" = r---.

A: vir   aper   rāna.

9. **Vir** and **aper** both belong to the ___ Declension.

A: 2d

10. **Rāna** belongs to the ___ _____.

A: 1st Declension.

11. **Numquam** is ____ (nominative case/accusative case/is not a noun at all and has no case).

A: is not a noun at all and has no case.

12. While most words in Latin change their shape, some Latin words do ____.

A: not.

13. You then learned that some words ending in **-s** and **-m** are not nouns; they are the part of speech we call an _____.

A: adjective.

14. You were told at first that verbs ended in **-t** and for a while all words that ended in **-t** were ___-s.

A: verbs.

15. The word **et** ____ (is/is not) a verb.

A: is not

8-28

144. But missing in the kernel is the {--}.

A: {-t}.

145. To complete the kernel **lupus agnum** we must repeat the {--} that occurred in the first kernel of the sentence, **Vulpēs vult fraudem**.

A: {-t}

146. Expand with the missing {-t}: **Lupus ---t agnum**.

A: vult

147. Chorus the entire Basic Sentence.
★ ○ ○ ◉ ◉ *Vulpēs vult fraudem, lupus agnum, fēmina laudem.*

148. ★ ○ ○ **Vulpēs vult fraudem, lupus agnum, f_____ l_____**.

A: **Vulpēs vult fraudem, lupus agnum, fēmina laudem**.

149. **Fēmina laudem** is also an {-s -m -t} kernel. The {-s} is the word ------.

A: **fēmina**.

150. The {-m} is ------.

A: **laudem**.

151. But missing in the kernel is the {--}.

A: {-t}.

152. To complete the third kernel **fēmina laudem** we must repeat the {--} that occurred in the first kernel of the sentence.

A: {-t}

UNIT ELEVEN

1. In this course you are constantly required to make distinctions. The first thing you did after you learned to operate the book (and the tape) was to distinguish between consonants and ------.

A: vowels.

2. This was easy for those of you who had heard the term ''consonant'' and ''vowel'' before. But then you had to learn to distinguish the ---- (1/2/3/4/5/6/7/8/9) Latin short vowels.

A: 5

3. After you learned the five short Latin vowels, you learned to distinguish them from the five corresponding ---- vowels.

A: long

4. You then learned to distinguish between Latin verbs and ------.

A: nouns.

5. At that point all Latin nouns ended in -- or **-m** and all verbs ended in --

A: **-s- -t**.

6. The next distinction was between Latin nouns in s- and in ---

A: **-m**.

7. Nouns in **-s** were ------, and those in **-m** were ------.

A: subjects
   objects.

11-1

8-29

153. Expand the third kernel with the missing {-t}. **Fēmina** ____ **laudem**

A: **vult**

154. Here is the sentence with the second and third kernels expanded. **Vulpēs vult fraudem, lupus vult agnum, fēmina vult laudem.** Write the *original* sentence. _____.

A: **Vulpēs vult fraudem, lupus agnum, fēmina laudem.**

155. Echo and write the Latin verb for "likes."
★ ○ • ○ • ____

A: **vult**

156. Echo and write the nominative and accusative of the Latin word for "trickery." [If you are working without a tape recorder, study the answer by saying and writing it.]
★ ○ • ○ • ____

A: **fraus**
   fraudem

157. Echo and write the nominative and accusative of the Latin word for "praise."
★ ○ • ○ • ____

A: **laus**
   laudem

158. In ancient times (as today) foxes had a reputation for trickery. **Vulpēs vult fraudem** =
A ___ l____ _____.

A: A fox likes trickery.

TEST INFORMATION

10-75

You will be asked to perform the following tasks:

1) To describe pictures, as in frames 13-20. They will be different, although similar, pictures.

2) To write the paradigm of nouns of all five declensions, as in frames 362-366. You will be asked only nouns whose paradigm you have practiced in this Unit.

3) To answer questions on the new Basic Sentences, as in frames 356-361. You will not have the Basic Sentence visible.

4) To write the paradigm of the adjectives which you practiced in this Unit.

8-30

159. When expanded with the missing {-t}, the **lupus agnum** kernel in this Basic Sentence means, "A ____ ____s a l___."

A: A wolf likes a lamb.

160. The **fēmina laudem** kernel means, "_____."

A: A woman likes praise.

161. Vulpēs vult fraudem, lupus agnum, fēmina laudem (15) = A ___ ____ _____, a ____ ____ a ____, a _____ ____ _____.

A: A fox likes trickery, a wolf likes a lamb, a woman likes praise.

162. Copy Basic Sentence 15 and its meaning in your Notebook.

163. Latin uses position to show _____.

A: emphasis.

10-74

435. In o... r. v.... im........ v....... (22)

A: In omnī rē vincit imitātiōnem vēritās.

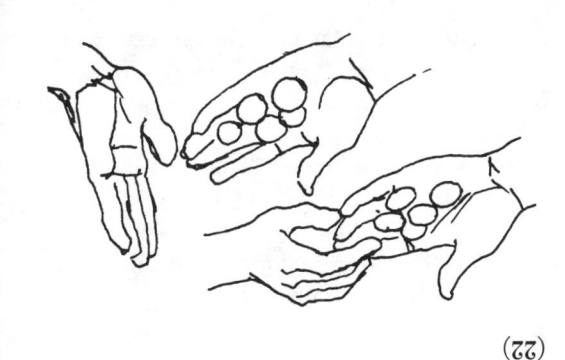

VOCABULARY INVENTORY

Here is the usual vocabulary review. From now on we will give only the nominative form of nouns and adjectives.

You have learned these seventeen nouns:

aciēs (141)   imitātiō (403)   orbis (79)
angulus (68)   jūdex (231)   plānitiēs (142)
arcus (273)   lacus (3)   porticus (2)
effigiēs (144)   līs (239)   quercus (1)
faciēs (143)   morsus (279)   rēs (399)
gradus (4)   saccus (67)

You also learned the following new adjectives: magnus (250), omnis (400), spatiōsus (347), parva (250).

And you learned three new verbs: necat (271), tenet (275), vincit (406).

You learned a new preposition: sub (221).

And three new question phrases: cum quō? (58), quō? (33), quō locō? (29).

If you wish to review any of these words you can refer to the frame in which its English meaning was given.

164. The word that gets the greatest emphasis is the one that comes ____ (first/in the middle/last) in the sentence.

A: last

165. And the *kernel* which receives the greatest emphasis in a sentence is the kernel that comes last. Therefore in this sentence the kernel that receives the greatest emphasis is _____ _____.

A: **fēmina laudem.**

166. The author could just have started off by saying that fish like frogs or dogs like rabbits, but the saying would have lost all its point if he had changed the part that says that women like _____.

A: praise.

167. Therefore the author put **fēmina laudem** in the ____ part of the sentence.

A: last

168. In other words, the point of this saying is to show that women _____. [In your own words]

A: are conceited.

169. In your own words, write why you think we put this sentence into the program. _____

A: Listen to the tape for the answer. ★ ○ [If you have no tape, you will have to ask your teacher.]

170. ★ ○ • ○ • English "laud," Latin **laudem**

171. In the hymn "Glory, Laud and Honor," the word "laud" means "pr____."

A: praise.

---

432. You learned a new preposition meaning "under" or (in the Basic Sentence) "before"; it was _____.

A: sub.

433-435. Say the Basic Sentences which describe these situations. The number shows the number of this Basic Sentence. If you forgot to write the sentence in your Reference Notebook, do so when you have completed this sequence.

433. P____ n____ m____ sp____ v____ t_____. (21)

A: Parva necat morsū spatiōsum vīpera taurum.

434. S__ j_____ l__ e__. (20)

A: Sub jūdice līs est.

8-32

172. There are several English derivatives of **laus/laudem**. A "laudatory" message is one that is full of _____ for the one who receives it.

A: praise

173. The English derivative of the word **fraus/fraudem** is "_____."

A: fraud.

174. Pronounce and check. **Vulpēs vult fraudem, lupus agnum, fēmina laudem.** √ ★ ○ •

175-186. Now for some questions on this Basic Sentence. Remember that you are to answer in terms of what the Basic Sentence says, not your own opinion. *You* may not think that women like praise (particularly if you are a woman yourself), but in this kind of practice you will just have to swallow your pride and answer "yes" if the question is "Does a woman like praise?"

175. "Vultne laudem lupus an fēmina?"
"_____."

A: Fēmina.

176. "Vultne vulpēs laudem an fraudem?"
"_____."

A: Fraudem.

177. "Vultne lupus an fēmina agnum?"
"_____."

A: Lupus.

10-72

427. While they all lived within a hundred years of each other, the earliest was C_____, who died in 43 B.C.

A: Cicero

428. The latest was Seneca, who died in 65 ____ (B.C./A.D.).

A: A.D.

SUMMARY

429. You have learned that there are ____ different declensions of nouns.

A: five

430. In your Reference Notebook in the section labelled "Forms," copy the paradigm of **morsus** under "Fourth Declension."

morsus
morsum
morsū
[Check your work.]

431. Now enter the forms of a Fifth Declension noun:

diēs
diem
diē

8-33

178. "Vultne lupus agnum an laudem?"
"‗‗‗‗‗."

A: **Agnum.**

179. "Vultne fēmina agnum an laudem?"
"‗‗‗‗‗."

A: **Laudem.**

180. "Vultne fraudem vulpēs an lupus?"
"‗‗‗‗‗."

A: **Vulpēs.**

181. "Quis agnum vult?" "‗‗‗‗‗‗‗‗."
[Give the short answer.]

A: **Lupus.**

182. "Quis laudem vult?" "‗‗‗‗‗‗."

A: **Fēmina.**

183. "Quis fraudem vult?" "‗‗‗‗‗‗."

A: **Vulpēs.**

184. "Vultne lupus agnum?" "‗‗‗‗‗."

A: **Vult.**

185. "Vultne fēmina agnum?" "‗‗‗‗‗."

A: **Nōn vult.**

186. "Vultne vulpēs agnum?" "‗‗‗‗‗."

A: **Nōn vult.**

10-71

421. In omnī rē vincit imitātiōnem vēritās was written by the statesman C‗‗‗‗‗.

A: Cicero.

422. Diem nox premit, diēs noctem was written by S‗‗‗‗‗.

A: Seneca.

423. Echo the name of a Latin poet.
★ • ○ • ○ • Ovid

VCh: "ăwe-vĭd"

424. Parva necat morsū spatiōsum vipera taurum was written by this poet ‗‗‗‗‗.

A: Ovid.

425. You know the names of four Latin authors now; they are C‗‗‗‗‗, S‗‗‗‗‗, O‗‗‗‗‗, and H‗‗‗‗‗.

A: Cicero, Seneca, Ovid, and Horace.

426. Ovid was a younger contemporary of H‗‗‗‗‗.

A: Horace.

8-34

187. The next frame is just for the women students. Men students must skip to frame 188. Give your answer to the following question based on *this* picture, not on the Basic Sentence. "Quis laudem vult?" "___ laudem vult."

▼

A: Vir

188. Using the pattern **Vulpēs vult fraudem, lupus agnum, fēmina laudem,** describe.
P____s vult m____m, ___ _____m, ____s _____m.

▼

A: Piscis vult muscam, leō taurum, īnfāns sīmiam.

189. _____ metuit _____, _____ _____, ___ _____.

▼

A: Sīmia metuit leōnem, īnfāns canem, fūr lēgem.

---

415. saccus ———

▲

A: saccus
    saccum
    saccō

416. umbra ———

▲

A: umbra
    umbram
    umbrā

If you did have any trouble, then by all means go back to Frame 362 and go through the sequence again.

417. Echo the name of a Roman author and philosopher. ★ • ○ • ○ Seneca

▲

VCh: "sěnn-neck-kuh"

418. Vēritātem diēs aperit was written by this philosopher named S-----.

▲

A: Seneca.

419. Vītam regit Fortūna, nōn Sapientia, however, was written by the author, philosopher, and statesman whose name was C-----.

▲

A: Cicero.

420. Nōn quaerit aeger medicum ēloquentem was written by S-----.

▲

VCh: Seneca.

10-70

8-35

190.
V_____ quaerit _____, aq____ _____, ae___ _____.

vīpera   aquila
rāna   agnus   medicus aeger

A: **Vīpera quaerit rānam, aquila agnum, aeger medicum.**

191. Your teacher will ask you questions on Basic Sentences. Write the answer. ★ ○ ○
_____ _____. √ ★ ○ •

VCh: **"Quis crūdēlem medicum facit?"**

VCh: **Intemperāns aeger.**

192. ★ ○ ○ ____. √ ★ ○ •

VCh: **"Quis fūrem cognōscit?"**

VCh: **Fūr.**

193. ★ ○ ○ _____. √ ★ ○ •

VCh: **"Quem īrātus nōn videt?"**

VCh: **Lēgem.**

194. ★ ○ ○ _____ _____. √ ★ ○ •

VCh: **"Quis metuit foveam?"**

VCh: **Cautus lupus.**

10-69

409. **"Vincitne imitātiō vēritātem?"**
"_____."

A: **Nōn vincit.**

410. ★ ○ • **omnis rēs**
                    omnem rem
                    omnī rē

411. Write the paradigm of **omnis rēs**:
_____.

A: **omnis rēs**
   omnem rem
   omnī rē

412-416. Here is a chance for you to check on your judgment. See if you can decline these nouns. They are from the frames which you were told you might skip *if* you felt that you could decline nouns perfectly. Write these and see if you actually do know them.

412. **plānitiēs** _____

A: **plānitiēs**
   plānitiem
   plānitiē

413. **gradus** _____

A: **gradus**
   gradum
   gradū

414. **laus** _____

A: **laus**
   laudem
   laude

8-36

195. ★ ○ ○ ----- ·√ ★ ○ •

VCh: "Quem lupus vult?"

VCh: Agnum.

196-207. Ask your teacher the question which will require the italicized word as an answer. Remember that if it is the subject that is italicized you substitute the word **quis?**, and if the object is italicized you substitute the word **quem?**. Check your question and echo his answer.

196. Fūrem *fūr* cognōscit et lupum lupus. (14) Ask the question that calls for the italicized word. "Q___ f____ c_____?" √ ★ ○ •

VCh: "Quis fūrem cognōscit?"

197. Echo the answer to your question.
★ ○ • "____."

VCh: Fūr

198. Crūdēlem medicum *intemperāns aeger* facit. (12) Ask the question that calls for the italicized word. "Q___ cr_____ m_____ f____?" √ ★ ○ •

VCh: "Quis crūdēlem medicum facit?"

199. Echo the answer. ★ ○ • "_____ _____."

VCh: Intemperāns aeger.

200. *Cautus* metuit foveam *lupus*. (8) Ask the question. "____ _____?" √ ★ ○ •

VCh: "Quis metuit foveam?"

201. Echo the answer. ★ ○ • "_____ _____."

VCh: Cautus lupus.

10-68

404. Are **imitātiō** and **capillō** the same case? (Yes/No)

A: No

405. Pronounce and check. **In omnī rē vincit imitātiōnem vēritās.** √ ★ ○ •

406. If we tell you that the verb **vincit** means "conquer," then **In omnī rē vincit imitātiōnem vēritās** means, "In _____ s_____ s_____ _____."

A: In every situation truth conquers imitation. (The student on the left has been a good boy; the character on the right tried to take some short cuts and got caught. Isn't this course wonderful for improving your way of life?)

407. Write. ★ ○ ○ **In om__ r__ v_____ im_____ v_____.**

A: **In omnī rē vincit imitātiōnem vēritās.**

408. Give short answers [one or two words]. "Vincitne imitātiōnem vēritās?" "_____."

A: Vincit.

8-37

202. Vulpēs vult fraudem, lupus *agnum*, fēmina laudem. (15) Ask the question. "____ ____ _____?" √ ★ ○ •

VCh: "Quem vult lupus?"

203. Echo the answer. ★ ○ • "_____."

VCh: Agnum.

204. Lēx videt īrātum, īrātus *lēgem* nōn videt. (13) Ask the question. "____ _____ ___ _____?" √ ★ ○ •

VCh: "Quem īrātus nōn videt?"

205. Echo the answer. ★ ○ • "_____."

VCh: Lēgem.

206. Vestis *virum* reddit. (1) Ask the question. "____ _____ _____?" √ ★ ○ •

VCh: "Quem vestis reddit?"

207. Echo the answer. ★ ○ • "_____."

VCh: Virum

208. You need more vocabulary to read a new Basic Sentence. ★ ○ • ○ • nox noctem

209. You will remember that the word lēx is _____ case.

A: nominative

210. Listen to the last *sound* in the word lēx. ★ ○ ○ The last *sound* of lēx is the sound ____.

A: s.

10-67

397. Because of the long e, you know that the new word rē belongs to the ___ Declension.

A: 5th

398. Omni is an adjective modifying rē; like crūdēlī and hilarī it belongs to the ___ Declension and is _____ case.

A: 3d ablative

399. Echo the paradigm of a Latin word that in this Basic Sentence means "situation." ★ ○ • rēs
rem
re

400. Echo the paradigm of the Third Declension adjective that means "every." ★ ○ • omnis
omnem
omnī

401. An *omnivorous* animal is one that eats _____thing.

A: everything

402. In omnī rē = __ _____ _____

A: In every situation

403. Echo the paradigm of this Latin word. ★ ○ • imitātiō
imitātiōnem
imitātiōne

211. In Latin the letter **x** stands for the two letters ___.

A: **cs.**

212. Listen to the last sound of **nox**. ★ ○ ○ Does **nox** end in the *sound* **s**? ____ (Yes/No)

A: Yes [It ends in the letter **x,** which stands for **cs.**]

213. Therefore, just like **lēx,** the word **nox** is _____ case.

A: nominative

214. Is the signal for nominative case on **nox** the variant **-s** or the variant zero? It is ___.

A: **-s.**
[Remember, the **x** stands for **cs.**]

215. Echo a new technical term. ★ ○ • ○ • antonym

VCh: "ánn-toe-nim"

216. An "antomym" is a word that means the opposite of another word. For example, an antonym of "always" is "n____".

A: never.

217. Pronounce "antonym" and check. √ ★ ○ •

VCh: "ánn-toe-nim"

218. "Good" is an _____ of "bad."

A: antonym

219. The Latin words **numquam** and **semper** are examples of _____s.

A: antonyms.

---

390. Now for a new Basic Sentence. Echo the first three words. ★ ○ • ○ • **In omnī rē**

391. Write. ★ ○ ○ **o__ __**

A: **In omnī rē**

392. Echo the entire Basic Sentence. ★ ○ • ○ • *In omnī rē vincit imitātiōnem vēritās.* (22)

A: **In omnī rē**

393. Write. ★ ○ ○ **In omnī rē v_____.**

A: **In omnī rē vincit imitātiōnem vēritās.**

394. This is an {__ __ __} type of sentence.

A: {-s -m -t}

395. **In omnī rē vincit imitātiōnem vēritās.** The {-s} is _____, the {-m} is _____, and the {-t} is _____.

A: **vēritās**   **imitātiōnem**   **vincit**

396. Although you have never seen the form before, you can guess that the word **rē** must be _____ case.

A: ablative

8-38

10-66

8-39

220. The familiar word **diēs** has a new meaning in the new Basic Sentence. It is an antonym of **nox**. The word **nox** means "n___t" and its antonym **diēs** means "____."

Diēs   Nox

A: night   day.

221. ★ ○ • ○ • Lupus agnum premit.

222. This sentence means that the ____ is pur___ng the ____.

A: the wolf is pursuing the lamb.

223. Answer your teacher's question about this picture. ★ ○ ○

VCh: "Premitne leō taurum an sīmiam?"

224. Answer his question. "_____ pr_____."

A: Leō taurum premit.

10-65

In this sequence, look back if necessary.

383. with a cheerful giver = c--- h----- d----
A: cum hilarī datōre

384. by a sympathetic ear = a--- f-----
A: aure facilī

385. with an intemperate sick person = c--- in--------- ae---
A: cum intemperantī aegrō

386. without a cautious wolf = s--- c--- l---
A: sine cautō lupō

387. with a cruel doctor = c--- cr----- m---
A: cum crūdēlī medicō

388. with a small snake = c--- p----- v-----
A: cum parvā viperā

389. The last vowel in the ablative case of Third Declension adjectives is ----.
A: ī.

225. Describe this picture, using the new verb.
Canis ap___ p_____.

▼

A: Canis aprum premit.

226. Echo the first kernel of Basic Sentence 16.
★ ○ • ○ • Diem nox premit,
▼

227. Write. ★ ○ ○ D___ n__ pr____.
▼
A: Diem nox premit.

228. This ____ (is/is not) a complete {-s -m -t} kernel.
▼
A: is

229. However, the order is not {-s} {-m} {-t} but {--} {--} {--}.
▼
A: {-m} {-s} {-t}.

230. Pay careful attention to the structural signals for {-s} and {-m} in the kernel and ignore the position of the words. Diem nox premit = _____ _____s ____.
▼
A: Night pursues day.

231. Echo the entire Basic Sentence. ★ ○ • ○ •
Diem nox premit, diēs noctem.
▼

232. Write. ★ ○ ○ Diem nox premit, d___ n_____.
▼
A: Diem nox premit, diēs noctem.

---

373. The characteristic vowel of the Third Declension is --- or ---.
△
A: e   i.

374. The characteristic vowel in the ablative of canis is ----.
△

375. Echo the paradigm of the Third Declension adjective that means "cheerful." ★ ○ •
hilaris
hilarem
hilari
△
A: e.

376. The characteristic vowel in the ablative of hilaris is ----.
△
A: i.

377-382. Echo until learned.

377.
★ ○ •
intemperāns aeger
intemperantem aegrum
intemperantī aegrō

378.
★ ○ •
auris facilis
aurem facilem
aure facilī

379.
★ ○ •
cautus lupus
cautum lupum
cautō lupō

380.
★ ○ •
parva vīpera
parvam vīperam
parvā vīperā

381.
★ ○ •
crūdēlis medicus
crūdēlem medicum
crūdēlī medicō

382.
★ ○ •
hilaris dator
hilarem datōrem
hilarī datōre

8-40

10-64

8-41

233. **Diēs noctem** ____ (is/is not) a complete {-s -m -t} kernel.

A: is not

234. Missing to make it a complete kernel is a {--}.

A: {-t}.

235. When the {-t} is missing, we must expand the kernel by supplying the {-t} from the other k_____.

A: kernel.

236. Expand in the way you were told above. **Diem nox premit, diēs noctem** _____.

A: premit.

237. Pronounce and check. **Diem nox premit, diēs noctem.** (16) ✓ ★ ○ •

238. The most noticeable thing in the Basic Sentence **Diem nox premit, diēs noctem** is that **nox** is the subject of the first kernel, but **noctem** is the _____ of the second.

A: object

239. Diem is _____ of the first kernel, and **diēs** is _____ of the second.

A: object
        subject

8-42

240. Diem nox premit, diēs noctem (16)
= _____ _____s ___, ___ _____s _____.

▼ ▼

A: Night pursues day, day pursues night.

241. Copy Basic Sentence 16 and its meaning in your Reference Notebook.

▼ ▼

242. This means that nothing can stop the _____. [In your own words]

▼ ▼

A: passage of time.

243. The antonym of **nox** is _____.

▼ ▼

A: **diēs.**

244. Numquam is the antonym of **semper** because they have _____ meanings.

▼ ▼

A: opposite

245. Diēs and **nox** are _____s.

▼ ▼

A: antonyms.

246. To express the rapid passage of time we say in Latin: **Die_ no_ premi_, di__ noct_m.** (16)

▼ ▼

A: **Diem nox premit, diēs noctem.**

361. "Necatne taurum vipera an leō?"
_____

▼

A: Necat taurum vipera.

362-366. This sequence will give you practice in paradigms. Many students find this kind of drill extremely helpful. We are going to give you an opportunity here to choose for yourself how much of this drill you wish to do. In column A are examples of each of the five declensions. Do these. If you made no errors, then you may skip columns B, C, D, and E. If you made an error or if you wish more practice, then do as many of the extra columns as you wish. Some of the paradigms on the examination will be taken from these 25 nouns.

A	B	C	D	E
362.	*363.*	*364.*	*365.*	*366.*
fraus	vestis	aciēs	asinus	gradus
fraus	vestis	aciēs	asinus	gradus
fraudem	vestem	aciem	asinum	gradum
fraude	veste	aciē	asinō	gradū
diēs	oculus	pecūnia	arcus	laus
diēs	oculus	pecūnia	arcus	laus
diem	oculum	pecūniam	arcum	laudem
diē	oculō	pecūniā	arcū	laude
equus	effigiēs	aeger	fovea	saccus
equus	effigiēs	aeger	fovea	saccus
equum	effigiem	aegrum	foveam	saccum
equō	effigiē	aegrō	foveā	saccō
vita	lacus	auris	faciēs	umbra
vita	lacus	auris	faciēs	umbra
vitam	lacum	aurem	faciem	umbram
vitā	lacū	aure	faciē	umbrā
manus	poena	quercus	nox	plānitiēs
manus	poena	quercus	nox	plānitiēs
manum	poenam	quercum	noctem	plānitiem
manū	poenā	quercū	nocte	plānitiē

If you wish more practice, try another column (B). If not, proceed with the frame below.

8-43

247. Now two questions. Give a one-word answer. "Premitne nox diem?" "_____."

A: Premit.

248. "Premitne diēs noctem?" "_____."

A: Premit.

249. Describe the picture. Aprum v__ premit, ___r ____m.

A: Aprum vir premit, aper virum.

250. In this sentence the word **vir** is subject of the first kernel and _____ of the second kernel.

A: object

251. And the word **aper** is _____ of the first kernel and _____ of the second.

A: object
   subject

252. Using the same pattern, write the descriptions of the next two pictures. **Leōnem _____s premit, ___ _____m.**

A: Leōnem elephantus premit, leō elephantum.

---

354. Pronounce and check. **Parva necat morsū spatiōsum vīpera taurum.** ✓ ★ ○ •

355. Answer these questions on the sentence. These are easy; all you have to do is repeat the part of the sentence which the question asks for, remembering that **Quis?** asks for the _____, **Quem?** asks for the _____, and **Quō?** asks for the m_____ of the verb.

A: subject
   object
   modifier

356. "Quis spatiōsum taurum necat?" "_____." [Look back only if you need to.]

A: Parva vīpera.

357. "Quō parva vīpera spatiōsum taurum necat?" "_____."

A: Morsū.

358. "Quem necat parva vīpera?" "_____."

A: Spatiōsum taurum.

359. "Necatne vīperam taurus?" "_____."

A: Nōn necat vīperam taurus.

360. "Necatne vīpera taurum morsū an arcū?" "_____."

A: Necat vīpera taurum morsū.

10-61

8-44

253. S____m ___ dīligit, ____ ____.

A: Sīmiam mūs dīligit, sīmia mūrem.

254. Write the Basic Sentences which fit these pictures. N__ qu_____ ae___ m_____ ēl_____. (9)

A: Nōn quaerit aeger medicum ēloquentem.

255. L__ v____ īr____, īr____ l____ n__ v____. (13)

A: Lēx videt īrātum, īrātus lēgem nōn videt.

---

350. Write. ○ ○ ★ ○ ○ Parva necat morsū spatiōsum v____ t_____. [There are three macrons in this sentence.]

A: Parva necat morsū spatiōsum vipera taurum.

351. A   B

A: Parva necat morsū spatiōsum vipera taurum.

The Basic Sentence describes Picture ____.

A.

352. Parva necat morsū spatiōsum vipera taurum then means, "A ____ _____ s a ____ ____ by a ____."

A: A small snake kills a large bull by a bite.

353. The "poetical meaning" of this Basic Sentence is that victory does not always go to the _____. [In your own words.]

A: big and powerful people.

8-45

256. Fū___ f__ cognō____ et lu___ lu___. (14)

A: Fūrem fūr cognōscit et lupum lupus. (14)

257. Di__ n__ pre___, di__ noc___. (16)

A: Diem nox premit, diēs noctem. (16)

258. Vul___ vu__ frau___, lu__ ag___, fēm____ lau___. (15)

A: Vulpēs vult fraudem, lupus agnum, fēmina laudem. (15) [If you had *any* trouble with these five sentences it means that you are hurrying too much. Time spent now in reviewing all 16 Basic Sentences will save you much time later. *If you need to,* turn now to your Reference Notebook and review the Basic Sentences.]

259. The Latin word **sed** means "but." Because **sed,** like **et,** connects equal things, we call it a c_____.

A: connector.

10-59

344. **Parva necat morsū.** We know now that: "A_____ (or _____) a___ _____ s____ a _____."

345. Echo the first four words. ★ ○ • ○ •

Parva necat morsū spatiōsum

346. Write. ★ ○ ○ Parva necat morsū sp_____

A: Parva necat morsū spatiōsum

347. **Spatiōsus** is a synonym of **magnus** and its English derivative is "spacious"; in the Basic Sentence it means "large." The sentence now means, "A _____ (or _____) s____ a l_____ somebody."

A: A small something (or somebody) kills a large somebody by (means of) a bite.

348. Well, it seems like David and Goliath all over again. There are just two words left in the Basic Sentence, and they will have to be the _____ and the _____ of the verb.

A: subject   object

349. ★ ○ • ○ • *Parva necat morsū spatiōsum vipera taurum.* (21)

8-46

260. Echo your teacher as he describes this picture. ★ ○ • ○ • **Nōn vir sed fēmina vestem lavat.**

261. Your teacher said that not the ___ but the _____ is ___ing _____s.

A: _____ not the man but the woman is washing clothes.

262. Echo your teacher as he describes this picture. ★ ○ • ○ •

VCh: **Nōn agnus sed vulpēs fraudem vult.**

263. Without looking back, see if you can write this last sentence from memory.
N__ a____ s__ v_____ fr_____ v___.

A: **Nōn agnus sed vulpēs fraudem vult.**

264. Write your teacher's description of this picture. ★ ○ ○ A____ l____ n__ d_____ s__ m_____.

VCh: **Agnus lupum nōn dīligit sed metuit.**

10-58

337. Echo the first two words. ★ ○ • ○ •

Parva necat

338. Write. ★ ○ ○ **Parva n____** (Don't look back at the previous frame.)

A: **Parva necat**

339. Which of these statements is true?
1) The word **necat** shows that we have an {-s - m - t} sentence.
2) The word **necat** shows that we have an {-s - m - t} sentence.
3) We can't tell which type we have until we see more of the sentence.

A: The word **necat** shows that we have an {-s - m - t} sentence (because **necat** is a transitive verb and will therefore take an object).

340. Missing to complete the {-s - m - t} sentence are the {- - -} and {- - -}.

A: {-s-} {-m-}

341. The words **Parva necat** tell us that: "A _____ somebody (or something) _____s somebody."

A: small kills

342. Echo the first three words. ★ ○ • ○ •

Parva necat morsū

343. Write. ★ ○ ○ **Parva necat m____**

A: **Parva necat morsū**

8-47

265. This sentence means that the lamb doesn't ____ the wolf but ____ (him).

A: doesn't love the wolf but fears him.

266. ★ ○ ○ N__ m____ s__ v____ m____ m__.

A: Nōn muscam sed vulpem metuit mūs.

267. This last sentence means that _____ _____. [In your own words]

A: _____ the mouse doesn't fear the fly but (he does fear) the fox.

268. Write one-word answers to questions on these same pictures. "**Metuitne mūs vulpem an muscam?**" "____."

A: Vulpem.

269. "Lavatne vestem fēmina an vir?" "____."

A: Fēmina.

10-57

330. Now we will take up a new Basic Sentence one word at a time so that you can see how the thought in a Latin sentence develops.

★ ○ ○ • **Parva**

331. Write ★ ○ ○ P____

A: Parva

332. **Parva** is the ____ case.

A: nominative

333. Both nouns and adjectives have nominative cases. **Parva** is ____ (a noun/an adjective).

A: an adjective.

334. Therefore **parva** is not the subject itself but is an adjective which ____s the subject.

A: modifies

335. The word **parva** therefore means, "A ____ somebody (or something) blanks."

A: small

336. Which of these statements is true?
1) The word **parva** shows that we have an {-m -t} sentence.
2) The word **parva** shows that we have an {-s -t} sentence.
3) The word **parva** could modify the subject of either an {-s -m -t} sentence or an {-s -t} sentence, and we can't tell which type we have until we see more of the sentence.

A: 3 [We can't tell yet.]

8-48

270. In the next question the connector **an** will connect two Latin verbs. You will answer with one of the two ____s.

A: verbs.

271. "Metuitne an dīligit agnus lupum?"
"_____."

A: Metuit.

272. "Vultne fraudem agnus an vulpēs?"
"_____."

A: Vulpēs.

273. Say the answer aloud. Give a double answer where indicated. "Quis vestem lavat?"
"Nōn ___ sed _____ v_____ l_____."

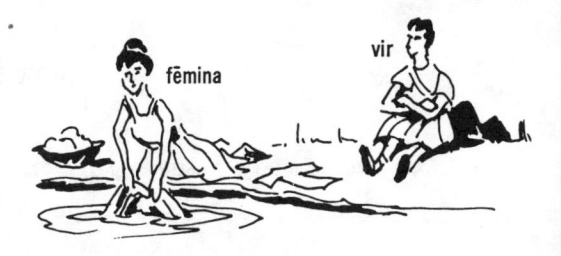

A: Nōn vir sed fēmina vestem lavat.

---

322. by means of a step = gr_____

A: gradū

323. by means of a face = fa_____

A: faciē

324. by means of money = pec_____

A: pecūniā

325. by means of a bow = ar_____

A: arcū

326. by means of life = v_____

A: vītā

327. by means of night = n_____

A: nocte

328. by means of praise = l_____

A: laude

329. by means of law = l_____

A: lēge

8-49

274. "Quis fraudem vult?" "Nōn _____ sed _____ fr_____ v____."

A: Nōn agnus sed vulpēs fraudem vult.

275. "Quem agnus nōn dīligit sed metuit?" "_____."

A: Lupum.

276. "Quem mūs metuit? Nōn _____ sed _____ _____ ___."

A: Nōn muscam sed vulpem metuit mūs.

277. Echo the first part of Basic Sentence 17. ★ ○ • ○ • Pecūnia nōn satiat avāritiam

278. There are ____ (1/2/3/4) macrons in this kernel.

A: 3

---

314. by means of life = v___ ★ ○ •

VCh: vīta

315. by means of a bow = ar___ ★ ○ •

VCh: arcū

316. by means of a battle line = ac___ ★ ○ •

VCh: aciē

317. by means of a face = fa___ ★ ○ •

VCh: faciē

Now write the Latin for these same 12 expressions.

318. by means of a battle line = ac_____

A: aciē

319. by means of wisdom = sap_____

A: sapientiā

320. by means of an eye = oc_____

A: oculō

321. by means of trickery = fr_____

A: fraude

10-55

8-50

279. Write. ★ ○ ○ P_____ n__ s_____ av_____.

A: **Pecūnia nōn satiat avāritiam**

280. Echo the entire Basic Sentence.
★ ○ • ○ • *Pecūnia nōn satiat avāritiam sed irrītat.* (17)

281. Write. ★ ○ ○ Pecūnia nōn satiat avāritiam s__ ir_____.

A: **Pecūnia nōn satiat avāritiam sed irrītat.**

282. The first four words form an {__ __ __} kernel plus the negator ____.

A: {-s -m -t} nōn.

283. **Sed** is the part of speech called a _____.

A: connector.

284. The function of a connector is to connect *equal* things. In this sentence **sed** connects two kernels. The first kernel is **Pecūnia nōn satiat avāritiam**; the second kernel is the one word _____.

A: **irrītat**.

285. **Irrītat** is a transitive verb. To make an {-s -m -t} we must expand it with the {__} and the {__} which we find elsewhere in the sentence.

A: {-s} {-m}

286. Expand with the {-s} and the {-m}. Pecūnia nōn satiat avāritiam sed _____ irrītat _____.

A: **pecūnia avāritiam.**

Here are 12 more "by means of" expressions.

306. by means of the law = l___ ★ ○ •
VCh: lēge

307. by means of praise = l____ ★ ○ •
VCh: laude

308. by means of money = p_____ ★ ○ •
VCh: pecūniā

309. by means of wisdom = s_____ ★ ○ •
VCh: sapientiā

310. by means of a step = gr___ ★ ○ •
VCh: gradū

311. by means of an eye = oc___ ★ ○ •
VCh: oculō

312. by means of trickery = fr____ ★ ○ •
VCh: fraude

313. by means of night = n_____ ★ ○ •
VCh: nocte

10-54

8-51

287. Echo the contrasting forms for the word for "money."

★ ○ • ○ • **pecūnia**
　　　　　　 pecūniam

288. The signal for nominative case in **pecūnia** is _____.

A:　　Ø (or zero).

289. Echo the contrasting forms for the word for "greed."

★ ○ • ○ • **avāritia**
　　　　　　 avāritiam

290. If someone told you that you were going to receive a *pecuniary* reward for something, you would know that you would be getting some _____.

A: money.

291. The vice of *avarice* is the vice of _____.

A:　　　　　　　　　　　　greed.

292. In comparing Latin **avāritia** with English "avarice" you notice that final **-tia** becomes ___ in English derivatives.

A:　　　　　　　　　　　　-ce

293. *Satiat* means "satisfies." Ignore the position and pay attention to the Latin signal. **Pecūnia nōn satiat avāritiam** = _____ doesn't _____ _____.

A:　　　　　　　　　　Money doesn't satisfy greed.

---

298. by means of clothes = v_____
A: **veste**

299. by means of a shadow = um_____
A: **umbrā**

300. by means of time = d_____
A: **diē**

301. by means of a hand = m_____
A: **manū**

302. by means of an ear = au_____
A: **aure**

303. by means of a statue = ef_____
A: **effigiē**

304. by means of an oak tree = qu_____
A: **quercū**

305. by means of truth = vēr_____
A: **vēritāte**

10-53

294. Of course, here the word order is the same in Latin as in English, but it is just a coinc_____.

A: coincidence.

295. The word **irrītat** is the part of speech called a _____.

A: verb.

296. **Irrītat** looks like a common English word. Make a guess as to its meaning. **Pecūnia irrītat avāritiam** = _____ _____s _____.

A: Money irritates greed.

297. Pronounce and check. **Pecūnia nōn satiat avāritiam sed irrītat.** (17) √ ★ ○ •

298. This means, "_____ doesn't _____ _____ but m____ _____s gr____."

A: Money doesn't satisfy greed but money irritates greed.

299. We explained earlier that it is characteristic of Latin not to repeat words: they are often left out and the reader has to supply them from the rest of the sentence. In English we often do not repeat words either; however, we use such words as "he," "she," and "it," and the reader has to understand what these words mean from _____. [In your own words.]

A: the rest of the sentence.

300. Improve the English sentence "Money doesn't satisfy greed but money irritates greed" by using the word "it." Money doesn't satisfy greed but __ _____s ___.

A: it irritates it.

VCh: aure

290. by means of an ear = a____ ★ ○ •

VCh: fēlīcitāte

291. by means of prosperity = f_____ ★ ○ •

VCh: quercū

292. by means of an oak tree = qu____ ★ ○ •

VCh: effigiē

293. by means of a statue = ef_____ ★ ○ •

Now say and write the Latin for the same 12 expressions.

A: avāritiā

294. by means of greed = av_____

A: capillō

295. by means of a hair = cap_____

A: fēlīcitāte

296. by means of prosperity = fēl_____

A: morsū

297. by means of a bite = m_____

8-53

301. Now further improve the sentence by leaving out one of the two "its." Money doesn't satisfy greed but _____.

A: Money doesn't satisfy greed but irritates it.

302. Write this meaning in your Notebook along with Basic Sentence 17.

303. Our expanded Latin version was **Pecūnia nōn satiat avāritiam sed pecūnia irrītat avāritiam**. Write the original Basic Sentence. _____. [There are four long vowels: mark them.]

A: **Pecūnia nōn satiat avāritiam sed irrītat.**

304. This means that the more the greedy man gets, _____. [In your own words.]

A: the more he wants.

305. **Vestis virum reddit** is a one-kernel sentence, but **Pecūnia nōn satiat avāritiam sed irrītat** is a ___ kernel sentence.

A: two

306. Missing in the second kernel of this two-kernel sentence were both the _____ and the _____.

A: subject object.

307. Money doesn't satisfy greed but irritates it = Pecū___ nōn sat___ avārit___ sed irrī___.

A: **Pecūnia nōn satiat avāritiam sed irrītat.**

10-51

Echo the Latin for the following expressions, all of which use just the ablative to show "by means of." [If you are not using a tape recorder, then study the Visual Checks and go through the sequence twice.]

282. by means of a bite = m___ • ○ ★
VCh: **morsū**

283. by means of clothes = v___ • ○ ★
VCh: **veste**

284. by means of a hand = m___ • ○ ★
VCh: **manū**

285. by means of truth = v___ • ○ ★
VCh: **vēritāte**

286. by means of greed = av___ • ○ ★
VCh: **avāritiā**

287. by means of time = d___ • ○ ★
VCh: **diē**

288. by means of a shadow = um___ • ○ ★
VCh: **umbrā**

289. by means of a hair = c___ • ○ ★
VCh: **capillō**

8-54

308-310. Now for some questions. Give short answers of one or two words.

308. "Satiatne an irrītat pecūnia avāritiam?" "_____." √ ★ ○ •

VCh: Irrītat.

309. "Satiatne pecūnia avāritiam?" "_____." √ ★ ○ •

VCh: **Nōn satiat.**

310. "Irrītatne pecūnia avāritiam?" "_____." √ ★ ○ •

VCh: Irrītat.

311. Say and write the Basic Sentence that describes this picture.

P_____ ___ s_____ av_____ ___ ir_____.

A: **Pecūnia nōn satiat avāritiam sed irrītat.**

312. Using the same pattern, describe the following pictures.

S____ nōn dīligit l_____ sed metuit.

A: **Sīmia nōn dīligit leōnem sed metuit.**

10-50

279. Many Fourth Declension nouns are action words which have the same stem as verbs. Here is an example: **Canis morsū virum sub quercū irrītat** = The ___ is _____ing the ___ under the ___ ___ by means of a bite.

A: The dog is irritating the man under the oak tree by means of a bite.

280. The Latin verb for "bites," which is connected with the Fourth Declension noun **morsus/morsum/morsū**, is the verb _____.

A: **mordet.**

281. Describe this pathetic scene. V_____ mors___ as___ n____.

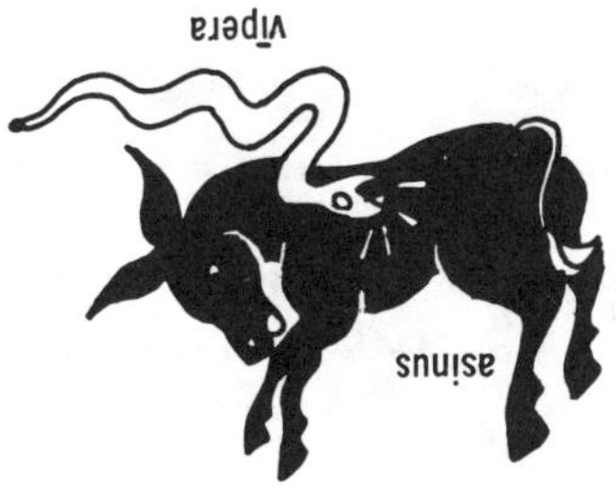

A: **Vipera morsū asinum necat.**

8-55

313. C____ nōn mordet ____ sed irrītat.

A: **Canis nōn mordet anum sed irrītat.**

314. Here is Basic Sentence 18. Echo the first kernel. ★ ○ • ○ • **Vītam regit Fortūna,**

315. There are ____ (1/2/3/4) macrons in this kernel.

A: 2

316. Write. ★ ○ ○ V____ r____ F_____,

A: **Vītam regit Fortūna,**

317. This is an {_____} type of sentence, but the order of the parts is {__} {__} {__}.

A: {-s -m -t}
   {-m} {-t} {-s}.

318. Echo the contrasting forms of the word for "life."
   ★ ○ • ○ • **vīta**
   vītam

319. Echo the contrasting forms of the word for "Fortune."
   ★ ○ • ○ • **Fortūna**
   Fortūnam

320. The signal for nominative of both **vīta** and **Fortūna** is ____.

A: Ø (or zero).

10-49

275. **Juvenis manū arcum tenet** = The ____ is h__ing a bow in his ____.

A: The young man is holding a bow in (by) his hand. [Sometimes "in" sounds better than "by."]

276. Describe the picture. J____ a____ l____ nec__.

A: **Juvenis arcū lupum necat.**

277. Ask your teacher by what means the man is holding the bow and check your question. "Quō ____ tenet?" ∧ ★ ○ •

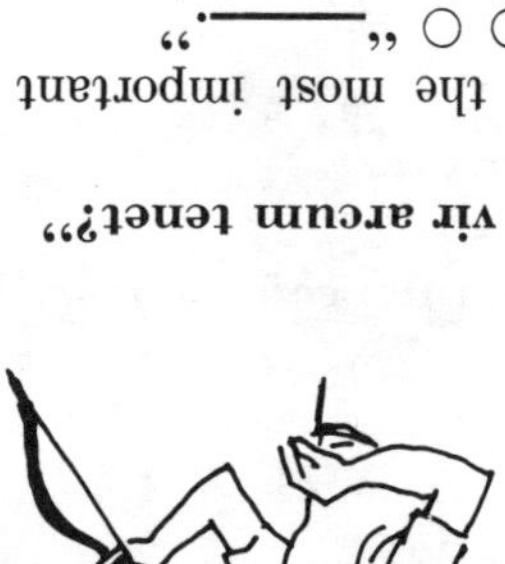

VCh: "**Quō vir arcum tenet?**"

278. Write the most important word of his answer. ★ ○ ○ "_____."

VCh: **Manū vir arcum tenet.**

A: **Manū**

8-56

321. The verb **regit** means "rules." Once again, respond to the Latin signals for {-s} and {-m} and *ignore* the position of the words in determining subject and object. Does **Vītam regit Fortūna** mean "Life rules Fortune" or "Fortune rules life?" "_____."

A: Fortune rules life.

322. Here, you see, the Latin order is the exact op_____ of the English order.

A: opposite

323. Echo the contrasting forms for the word for "Wisdom."
★ ○ • ○ •   **Sapientia**
              Sapientiam

324. Echo the entire Basic Sentence. ★ ○ • ○ • **Vītam regit Fortūna, nōn Sapientia.** (18)

325. Write. ★ ○ ○ **Vītam regit Fortūna, n__ S_____.**

A: **Vītam regit Fortūna, nōn Sapientia.** (18)

326. Sapientia is the {__} of its kernel; missing are the {__} and the {__}.

A: {-s}
    {-m}   {-t}.

327. Expand the second kernel as you have been taught. (Say the entire sentence, not just the blanks.) **Vītam regit Fortūna, _____ nōn _____ Sapientia.**

A: **Vītam regit Fortūna, vītam nōn regit Sapientia.**

328. Vītam regit Fortūna = _____.

A: Fortune rules life.

10-48

271. In this sequence the description of each picture will contain one new word, which will be italicized. It is your task to figure out what the new word (noun or verb) means. ★ ○ • ○ •

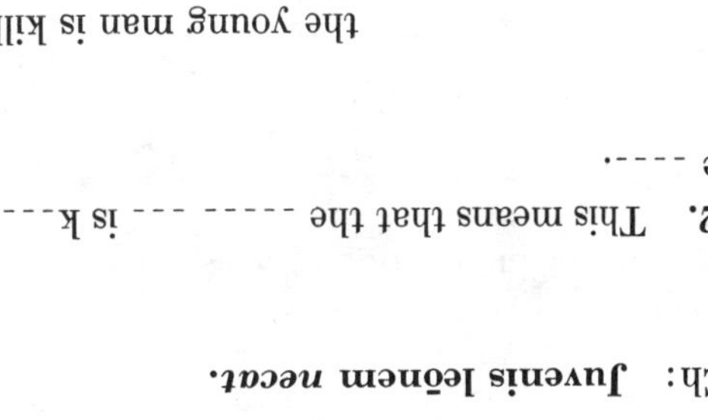

VCh: **Juvenis leōnem necat.**

272. This means that the _____ is k_____ the _____.

A: the young man is killing the lion.

273. Guess at the meaning of the new word *arcus*. **Juvenis leōnem arcū necat** = The _____ is _____ the _____ with a _____.

A: The young man is killing the lion with (by) a bow. [Sometimes "with" sounds better than "by," as a translation of the ablative.]

274. Arcus belongs to the ___ Declension.

A: 4th

8-57

329. Vītam nōn regit Sapientia = ‾‾‾‾‾‾‾.

A: Wisdom does not rule life.

330. We have spelled **Fortūna** with a capital letter to show that this refers to the Goddess of Fortune. We have spelled **Sapientia** with a capital letter in order to show that this refers to ‾‾‾‾‾‾‾‾‾‾.

A: the Goddess of Wisdom.

331. Our expanded sentence was, **Vītam regit Fortūna, vītam nōn regit Sapientia.** Say the original version of the Basic Sentence: ‾‾‾‾‾ ‾‾‾‾‾ ‾‾‾‾‾‾‾, ‾‾‾ ‾‾‾‾‾‾‾‾‾‾.

A: **Vītam regit Fortūna, nōn Sapientia.**

332. An English version of this might be, "‾‾‾‾‾‾‾, not ‾‾‾‾‾‾, r‾‾‾s our ‾‾‾‾."

A: Fortune, not Wisdom, rules our life (or, our lives).

333. Copy Basic Sentence 18 and this meaning in your Notebook.

334. This means that the author felt that our success or failure in life depends on ‾‾‾‾‾‾‾ rather than ‾‾‾‾‾‾.

A: fortune (luck, etc.) wisdom (brains, etc.)

335. Echo the author's name. ★ ○ • ○ • Cicero

VCh: "sis-sir-row"

---

264. Sub jūdice līs est was written by H‾‾‾‾‾‾.

A: Horace.

265. The question word **Quō?** by itself means "By what?" Ask your teacher **Quō leōnem vir capit?** ∨ ★ ○ •

266. Write down his answer. ★ ○ ○ "‾‾‾‾‾."

VCh: Foveā.

267. You asked your teacher in Latin, "By what is the ‾‾‾‾ing the ‾‾‾‾?"

A: By what is the man catching the lion?

268. He answered that he is catching it by a ‾‾‾‾‾‾‾.

A: pitfall.

269. To express "by" in the sense of "by means of" Latin uses the ablative case ‾‾‾‾‾‾ any preposition.

A: without

270. avāritia = ‾‾‾‾‾‾‾‾‾‾‾‾‾‾‾‾‾‾‾‾‾‾.

A: by greed (or, "by means of greed.")

10-47

8-58

336. This Basic Sentence was written by the famous Roman statesman Cicero when he was in a ____ (happy/discouraged) frame of mind.

A: discouraged

337. "Fortune, not Wisdom, rules our life" = Vīt__ reg__ Fort___, nōn Sapien____.

A: **Vītam regit Fortūna, nōn Sapientia.**

Now for some questions.

338. "Regitne vītam Sapientia an Fortūna?" "_____." √ ★ ○ •

VCh: **Fortūna.**

339. "Quis vītam regit?" "_____." √ ★ ○ •

VCh: **Fortūna.**

340. "Quis vītam nōn regit?" "_____." √ ★ ○ •

VCh: **Sapientia.**

341. "Regitne vītam Fortūna?" "_____." √ ★ ○ •

VCh: **Regit.**

342. "Regitne vītam Sapientia?" "_____." √ ★ ○ •

VCh: **Nōn regit.**

343. The sentence **Vītam regit Fortūna, nōn Sapientia** was written by C_____.

A: **Cicero.**

---

258. Write. ★ ○ ○ S_ j_____ ___ ___.

A: **Sub jūdice līs est.**

259. This is a well known saying by the poet Horace which means that a certain matter has not yet been decided. We might say in English, "The _____ is _____."

A: The lawsuit is before the judge.

260. But the real meaning of **Sub jūdice līs est** is that some matter has not been _____ed by a competent authority.

A: decided

261. **Sub jūdice līs est** is an {__ __} type of sentence.

A: {-s -t}

262. **Est** is the kind of verb we call _____tive.

A: intransitive.

263. Now answer this question on this last Basic Sentence. "**Sub quō est līs?**" _____ _____.

A: **Sub jūdice.**

10-46

8-59

344. Say and write the Basic Sentence that describes this picture. **Vī___ r____ F_____, nōn Sap_____.** [There should be three macrons.]

▼

A: **Vītam regit Fortūna, nōn Sapientia.**

345. Describe the following pictures using the pattern of **Vītam regit Fortūna, nōn Sapientia.**

Īnfantem videt ___s, nōn _____s.

▼

A: **Īnfantem videt anus, nōn medicus.**

346. This means that the ___ ____ and not the _____ ___s the _____.

▼

A: old lady and not the doctor sees the baby.

347. Mūrem capit _____s, nōn _____s.

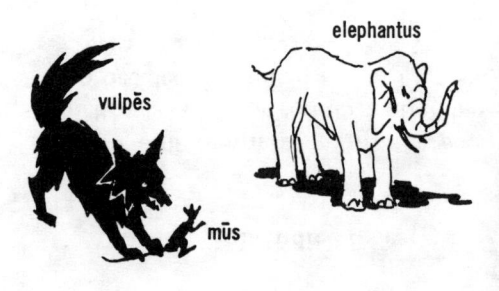

▼

A: **Mūrem capit vulpēs, nōn elephantus.**

10-45

253. Parva v_____ cum l_____ magnō l_____ habet. ✓ ★ ○ •

254. Parva f_____ el___ ___ magnō l___ h_____. ✓ ★ ○ •

VCh: **Parva fēmina cum elephantō magnō Item habet.**

255. Parva means "_____," and magnus means "_____."

A: small (little).
    large (big).

256. Because **parva** and **magnus** modify nouns they are the part of speech called a_____.

A: adjectives.

257. Echo a new Basic Sentence. ★ ○ • ○ •
Sub jūdice līs est. (20)

VCh: **Parva vulpēs cum lupō magnō Item habet.**

348. This means, "_____"

A: The fox, not the elephant, catches the mouse.

349. Now there is not much help. Study the picture carefully.

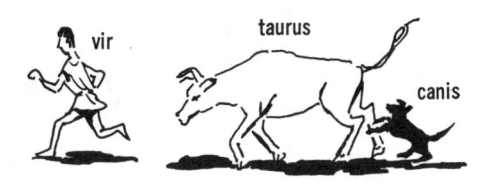

_____m metuit ___, nōn c___s.

A: **Taurum metuit vir, nōn canis.**

350. This means, "_____"

A: The man, not the dog, fears the bull.

351. El_____ lavat _____ nōn _____.

A: **Elephantum lavat sīmia, nōn fēmina.**

352. _____ dīligit _____, nōn _____.

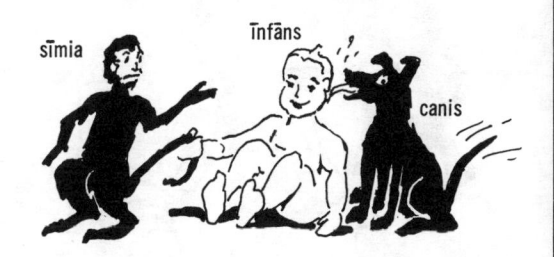

A: **Īnfantem dīligit canis, nōn sīmia.**

---

250. The adjectives **parva** and **magnus** are antonyms. When we "magnify" something we make it b__er.

A: bigger.

251. **Parva sīmia elephantum magnum irrītat** = The _____ _____ is _____ing the _____.

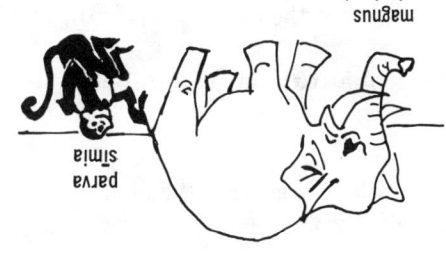

A: The small monkey is irritating (annoying) the big elephant.

252. Now the little one quarrels with the big one. Parva s_____ l_____ cum l_____ magnō l_____.

∨ ✴ ○ •

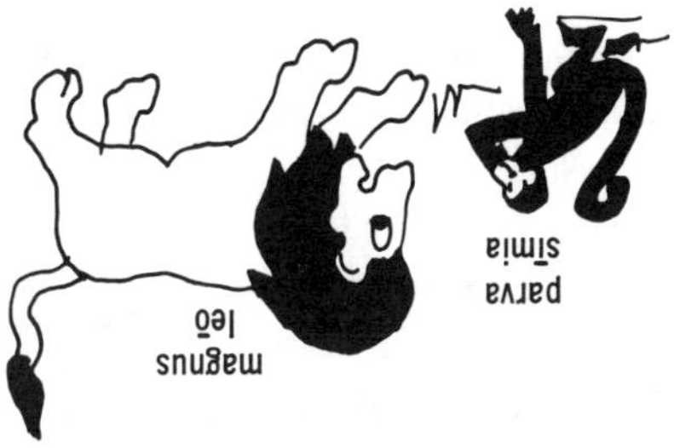

VCh: **Parva sīmia cum leōne magnō item habet.**

353. _____ cognōscit _____, nōn ____.

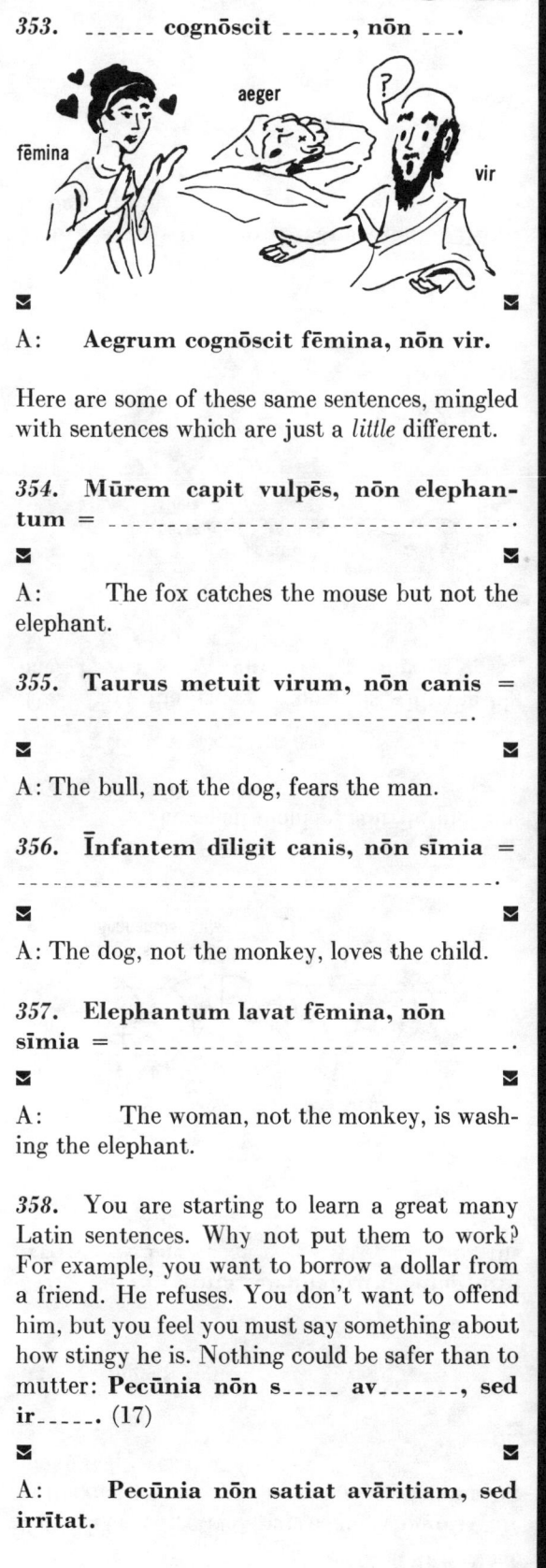

A: Aegrum cognōscit fēmina, nōn vir.

Here are some of these same sentences, mingled with sentences which are just a *little* different.

354. **Mūrem capit vulpēs, nōn elephantum** = _____.

A: The fox catches the mouse but not the elephant.

355. **Taurus metuit virum, nōn canis** = _____.

A: The bull, not the dog, fears the man.

356. **Īnfantem dīligit canis, nōn sīmia** = _____.

A: The dog, not the monkey, loves the child.

357. **Elephantum lavat fēmina, nōn sīmia** = _____.

A: The woman, not the monkey, is washing the elephant.

358. You are starting to learn a great many Latin sentences. Why not put them to work? For example, you want to borrow a dollar from a friend. He refuses. You don't want to offend him, but you feel you must say something about how stingy he is. Nothing could be safer than to mutter: **Pecūnia nōn s_____ av_____, sed ir_____.** (17)

A: **Pecūnia nōn satiat avāritiam, sed irrītat.**

246. Jūd__ c__ a____ h____ ˅____ ★ ○ •

VCh: **Jūdex cum anū ītem habet.**

247. S____ cum l____ h____ ˅____ ★ ○ •

VCh: **Sīmia cum leōne ītem habet.**

248. V____ cum l____ ˅____ ★ ○ •

VCh: **Vulpēs cum lupō ītem habet.**

249. Fēm___ cum el____ ˅____ ★ ○ •

VCh: **Fēmina cum elephantō ītem habet.**

8-62

359. Suppose your younger brother pesters you. You refuse to be drawn into an argument and say loftily: **Elephantus n__ c____ m____.** (5)

A: **Elephantus nōn capit mūrem.** (5)

360. It's the night before the big exam and you're a little nervous about it. Your friend wants you to go to the show. You refuse, saying: **Cautus m_____ f_____ l____.** (8)

A: **Cautus metuit foveam lupus.** (8)

361. You don't do as well on an exam as you had hoped. Your teacher asks you what happened. You sigh: **Vītam r____ F_____a, n__ S_____.** (18)

A: **Vītam regit Fortūna, nōn Sapientia.** (18)

SUMMARY

362. In this Unit you learned about a new type of sentence, the kind that has more than one _____.

A: kernel.

363. You learned two new words, **sed** and **an**, whose use is to join equal things. Like **et**, these words **sed** and **an** are the part of speech called a _____.

A: connector.

364. You also learned that words which are opposite to each other in meaning are called "_____s."

A: antonyms.

365. Although **lēx** and **nox** are spelled with the letter **-x**, they end in the sound ___ and therefore have the signal ___ for nominative case.

A: -s s

8-63

366. You learned six new Basic Sentences. If you forgot to enter any of them in your Reference Notebook, do it now. Write the Basic Sentence which fits the picture.

L__ v____ ī_____, ī_____ l____ n__ v____. (13)
[Seven macrons]

A: **Lēx videt īrātum, īrātus lēgem nōn videt.** (13) [Did you remember all the macrons?]

367. F____ f__ c_____ et l____ l____. (14)
[Three macrons]

A: **Fūrem fūr cognōscit et lupum lupus.** (14)

368. V_____ v___ fr_____, l____ ag___, f_____ l_____. (15) [Two macrons]

A: **Vulpēs vult fraudem, lupus agnum, fēmina laudem.** (15)

10-41

The word **līs** not only means a lawsuit but it can also mean just a quarrel. We will use it in this sense in the following sequence. Each one of the people and animals that you see in the pictures is having a quarrel with another of the same type. It is a most unpleasant sequence.

Describe and check.

240. M_____ cum med___ l____ habet. ∨ ★ ○ •

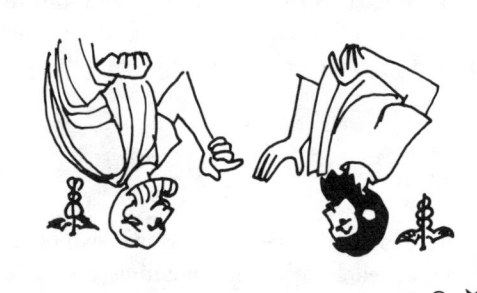

VCh: **Medicus cum medicō lītem habet.**

241. J_____ cum j_____ l___ h__ t. ∨ ★ ○ •

VCh: **Juvenis cum juvene lītem habet.**

242. S_____ ____ l___ h____ ∨ ★ ○ •

VCh: **Simia cum simiā lītem habet.**

8-64

369. D___ n__ pr____, d__ n_____. (16)
[One macron]

A: Diem nox premit, diēs noctem. (16)

370. P_____ n__ s_____ av_____ s__ ir_____. (17)

A: Pecūnia nōn satiat avāritiam sed irrītat. (17) [Did you have four macrons?]

371. V____ r____ F_____, n__ S_____. (18)

A: Vītam regit Fortūna, nōn Sapientia. (18)

---

231. ✶ ○ • jūdex
jūdicem
jūdice

232. Write the paradigm of jūdex. _____

A: jūdex
jūdicem
jūdice

233. Latin j sounds much like English "____".

A: y.
[If you do not have a tape recorder, go to frame 237.]

234. ✶ ○ • ○ • English "juvenile," Latin juvenis

235. ✶ ○ • ○ • English "just," Latin jūstus

236. ✶ ○ • ○ • English "judicial," Latin jūdice

237. "Judicial" robes are the clothes worn by a _____.

A: judge.

238. Echo this English word. ✶ ○ • ○ • litigation.

VCh: "lit-tee-gáy-shun"

239. The word "litigation" means "lawsuit." The Latin word from which "litigation" is derived is līs/lītem/līte, which means "l_____."

A: lawsuit.

10-40

8-65
VOCABULARY INVENTORY

In this Unit you learned the following nouns:

agnus		**īrātus**	
agnum	(132)	īrātum	(6)
avāritia		**laus**	
avāritiam	(289)	laudem	(157)
fēmina		**lēx**	
fēminam	(128)	lēgem	(4)
Fortūna		**nox**	
Fortūnam	(319)	noctem	(220)
fraus		**pecūnia**	
fraudem	(156)	pecūniam	(287)
fūr		**Sapientia**	
fūrem	(101)	Sapientiam	(323)
		vīta	
		vītam	(318)

You also learned the following new verbs:
    cognōscit (103)
    irrītat (296)
    premit (221)
    regit (321)
    satiat (293)
    vult (155)

You learned a new question word:
    -ne (38)

And you learned two connectors:
    an (76)
    sed (259)

If you wish to review any of these words you can refer to the frame given in parenthesis after each word.

Review your Reference Notebook if you wish.

10-39

225. This means: "The --- is ---------ing the "
    an ----- --- -----."

▲

A: The dog is irritating (annoying) the man under an oak tree.

▲

226. The new word **sub** is part of speech we call a -----------.

▲

A: preposition.

▲

227. A thief has been caught and is about to be sentenced. ✷ ○ • **Fūr jūdicem metuit.**

▲

228. = The -------- s the j----e.

▲

A: The thief fears the judge.

▲

229. In an earlier frame the word **sub** meant "under." Here it means something a little different. ✷ ○ • **Fūr sub jūdice est.**

▲

230. We would not say that the thief is "under" the judge; we would say rather that he is be---e the judge.

▲

A: before

8-66

TEST INFORMATION

In the test for Unit Eight you will be asked to perform the following tasks:

1) to write some of the six new Basic Sentences when prompted by a picture and some letters, as in frames 366-371.

2) to expand two kernel sentences with missing elements, as in frames 99, 146, etc. The sentences will be new sentences on the model of the new Basic Sentences.

3) to ask questions, as in frames 196-206.

4) to answer questions on the new Basic Sentences, as in frames 175-187.

5) to be able to produce *as usual* the review Basic Sentences. You will not be told to review the old Basic Sentences in the next Unit, since we expect that you will remember that this is *always* part of the test.

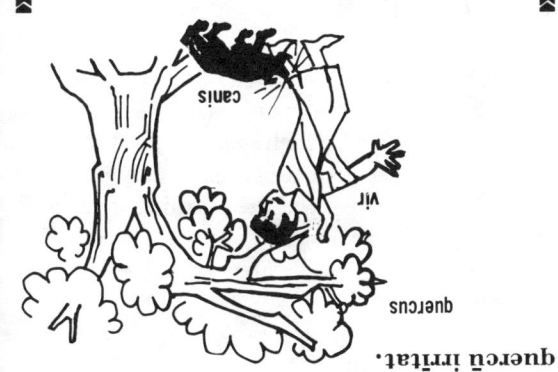

10-38

219. Here is some vocabulary for a new Basic Sentence. Something that is *subterranean* is under the earth. Something that is *submarine* is ----- the sea.

A: under

220. Echo a new technical term. • ○ • ○ ★

prefix

VCh: "preé-fix"

221. The "sub-" part of the English words "subterranean" and "submarine" is a "prefix," which is an element put on the *first* part of a word. In these two words the element "sub-" is a -------.

A: prefix.

222. The English word "subterranean" is a derivative of the Latin word *subterrāneus*, so you can see that Latin has a prefix ----.

A: sub-.

223. Prefixes are not words that stand alone but are ----s of words.

A: parts

224. Besides the Latin prefix **sub-** there is a Latin preposition **sub**. Echo this sentence in which it is used. ★ ○ • ○ • **Canis vīrum sub quercū irrītat.**

UNIT NINE

1. As you have discovered, you are learning Latin by doing a great many easy tasks. But just because you move by such small steps, it is sometimes hard to see your progress. It may help you to see just how fast you are learning if we give you here a problem which you cannot possibly solve now but *will* be able to solve in Unit Eighteen.

Echo the first line of this poem: ★ ○ • ○ •
Thāis habet nigrōs, niveōs Laecānia dentēs.
◼   ◼

2. Now echo the second line: ★ ○ • ○ • **Quae ratiō est? Ēmptōs haec habet, illa suōs.**
◼   ◼

3. The impossible problem is this: what does the poem mean? You may think that it is only the vocabulary that bothers you. This is not true. To prove it, we will give you the "dictionary meaning" of each word. You still will not be able to understand the poem.

Thāis habet nigrōs, niveōs Laecānia dentēs.
  Quae ratiō est? Ēmptōs haec habet, illa suōs.

Thāis name of a girl
habet have, hold, carry, contain, wear, be wealthy, keep, intend, cause, use, manage, treat, consider, possess, rule over, regard
nigrōs black, dark, blackening, referring to death, unlucky, wicked
niveōs of snow, snowy, white as snow
Laecānia name of a girl
dentēs tooth, mattock, fluke (of an anchor), sickle, any instrument of evil
quae which, what, what kind
est be, exist, be there, be living, be so, be such and such, happen
ratiō reckoning, account, business affair, computation, calculation, transaction, plan, scheme, system, method, order, reason, motive, ground rule, theory, doctrine, science, knowledge, the faculty of the mind which plans

ēmptōs purchase, bribe, buy
haec this, this here, this one referred to, the former, the present
illa that yonder, that well known, the latter
suōs his, her, its, their, proper, due, suitable, favorable, propitious, one's own people, property

The problem is impossible for you now. Do not spend more than a few minutes on it.

4. You may wonder why you cannot read the poem now. The answer is that although you have been given the *dictionary* meanings of all these words, you do not understand the str‗‗‗‗‗‗‗ meanings of most of them.

A: structural

5. There are many different meanings given for each word in the poem because in all languages words "mean" many things. Look for example at the following pictures, which illustrate four meanings of one English word.

He has an athletic w‗‗‗‗. He is shoveling the w‗‗‗‗.

The pitcher is giving up a w‗‗‗‗. He is having a pleasant w‗‗‗‗.

The one English word that fits all four situations is "‗‗‗‗."

A: walk.

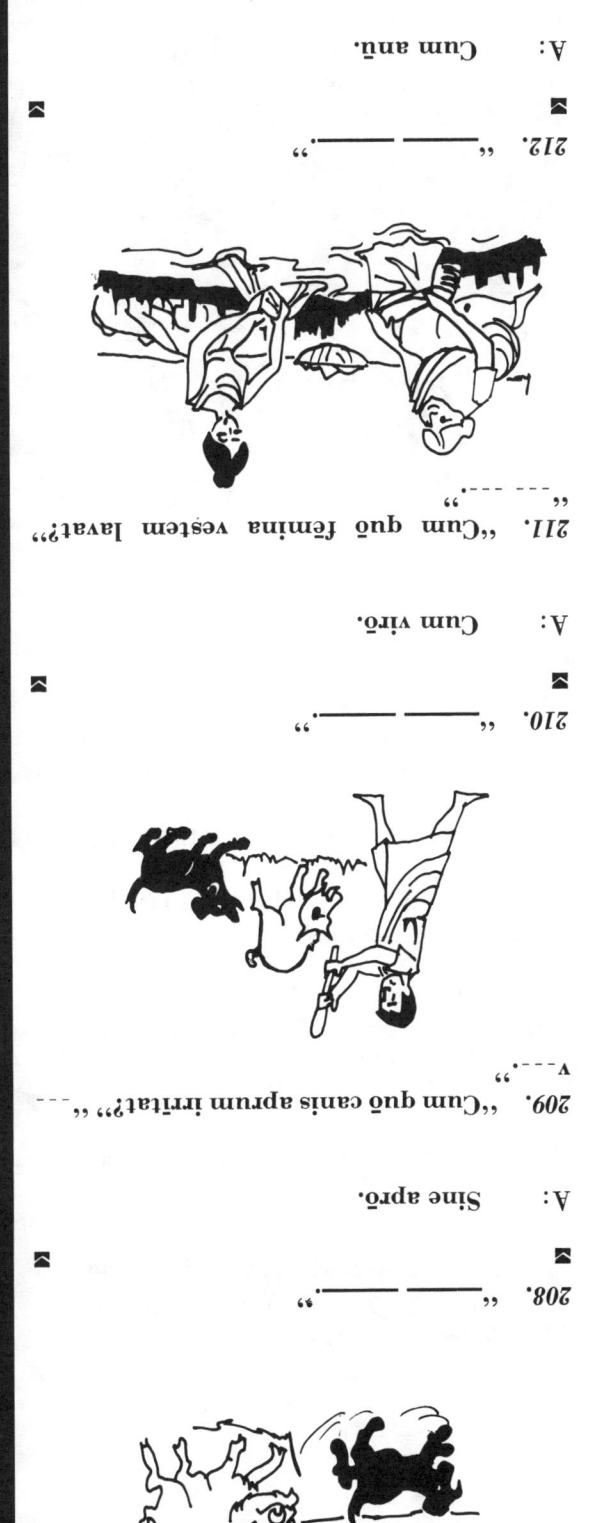

9-2

207. "Sine quō currit canis?" "‗‗‗ ‗‗‗‗."

208. "‗‗‗‗ ‗‗‗‗‗."

A: Sine aprō.

209. "Cum quō canis aprum irritat?" "‗‗‗‗ ‗‗‗‗."

210. "‗‗‗‗ ‗‗‗‗‗."

A: Cum virō.

211. "Cum quō fēmina vestem lavat?" "‗‗‗‗ ‗‗‗."

212. "‗‗‗‗ ‗‗‗‗."

A: Cum anū.

10-36

9-3

6. Would it be safe to assume that *one* Latin word would describe these four different meanings of English "walk?" ____ (Yes/No)

A: Definitely, No!

7.

He has a funny walk.   He has a funny walk.

Many times, if a sentence is quoted without the "context" of the conversation (that is, without what went right before or after it), you cannot tell what meaning is intended. "He has a funny walk" in one context may mean that the person looks strange when he moves about, but in a different context it could mean that the path to his house is unusual.

We could understand this sentence only if we could hear the rest of the conversation: that is, the meaning would be made clear by the c_____.

A: context.

8. In the frame above, the pictures made the statement intelligible in different ways by furnishing the _____s.

A: contexts.

---

201. "Quō locō est avāritia?" "... fa____."

202. "_____."

A: In faciē.

203. "Cum quō manet juvenis?" "____"

A: Cum agnō.

204. "_____."

205. "Quō locō manet aciēs?" "____"

206. "_____."

A: In plānitiē.

9. If a sentence begins with the words "The glass," we are ready to assign to "glass" any one of a number of meanings, depending on the context.

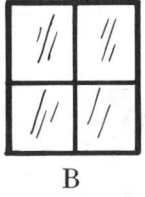

```
   A        B        C
```

It is the context which will explain whether "glass" refers to A, B, or C. If "The glass" occurs in the context, "The glass is full of milk," then we know that the word "glass" means the object labeled ____ (A/B/C).

A: A.

10. We knew that "glass" in this sentence meant something that holds a liquid because the c_____ was "is full of milk."

A: context

11. On the other hand, if you were to see the sentence, "She admired herself in the glass," you would know that the word "glass" referred to picture ____ (A/B/C).

A: C.

12. Our brain will even reject all the meanings it knows and accept a *new* one if the context requires it. This is how we learn. Most of you are probably unfamiliar with the following use of the word "glass": "The glass had been falling rapidly for several hours and we were all anxiously waiting for the storm." In this sentence a "glass" must be _____." [In your own words]

A: an instrument which is used to predict the weather. This is the old-fashioned kind pictured here.

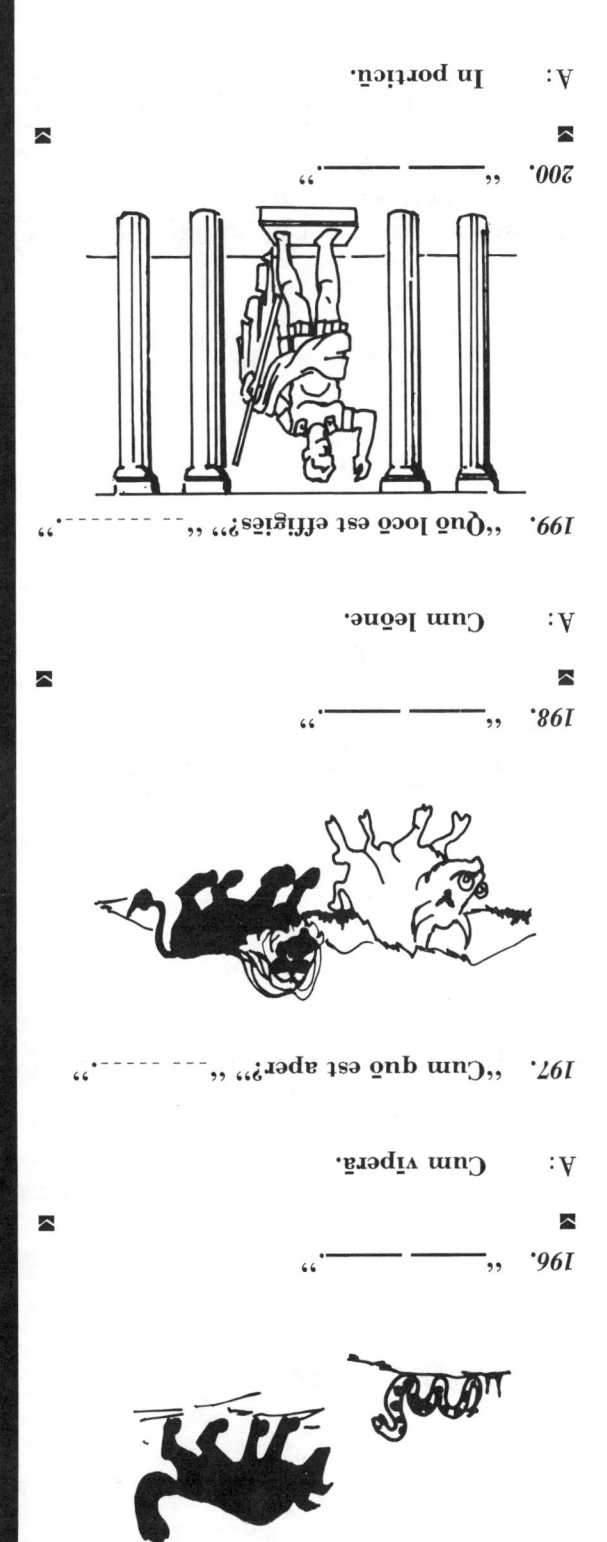

---

195. "Cum quō est vulpēs?" "_____."

196. "_____," "_____."

A: Cum vīperā.

197. "Cum quō est aper?" "_____."

198. "_____," "_____."

A: Cum leōne.

199. "Quō locō est effigiēs?" "_____."

200. "_____," "_____."

A: In porticū.

9-5

13. Let us look again at **Vestis virum reddit.**

The dictionary meanings of **vestis** are "veil, garment, clothing, blanket, awning, carpet, tapestry, skin of a snake, spider's web, beard." Some of these meanings are more common than others, but the brain of an educated Roman was prepared to accept any one of these meanings according to the c_____.

A: context.

14. The one Latin word that describes all these items is _____.

A: **vestis**.

15. The next word in the sentence is **virum,** whose dictionary meanings are: "man, male person, grown man (as opposed to a boy), husband, head animal of a flock, man of character or courage, 'he-man,' soldier (especially a foot soldier), individual."

The dictionary meanings of **reddit** are: "give back something taken away, restore, recite, represent, give back something in return, make, cause to be, give something as due or expected, pay up."

---

189. "Cum quō currit simia?" "_____."

190. "_____," "_____."

A: Cum cane.

191. "Cum quō est rāna?" "_____."

192. "_____," "_____."

A: Cum mūre.

193. "Quō locō est fūr?" "_____."

194. "_____," "_____."

A: In saccō.

10-33

So we have these combinations:

vestis	reddit	virum
veil	returns something	man
garment	taken away	male person
clothes	restores	grown man
blanket	recites	husband
awning	represents	head animal
carpet	gives back some-	hero
tapestry	thing in return	he-man
skin of a	makes	soldier
snake	causes to be	foot soldier
spider's web	gives as expected	individual
beard	pays up	

Is there just one combination of these English words that makes sense, or are there several possibilities? _____ (One/Several)

A: Several
[For example, "The tapestry represents a grown man" (that is, there is a grown man pictured on the tapestry).]

16. We can tell which meaning is intended only if we know the _____.

A: context.

17. These Basic Sentences did not occur in isolation; they have been taken from some context. The thought in **Vestis virum reddit** occurs several times in Latin literature where it is used as advice to young men who are planning to enter public life. In this context, the only meaning of **Vestis virum reddit** that makes sense is that if you wish to make a successful speech you must dress well, since people will judge you not only by how well you speak but also _____. [In your own words]

A: by how well you dress.

18. Therefore we know that **Vestis virum reddit** does not mean "A beard makes a he-man" but rather "_____."

A: Clothes make the man.

9-7

19. Today you will learn a new form of the Latin noun. First of all, echo this sentence which uses the two noun forms you already know. ★ ○ • ○ • **Vīpera rānam cognōscit.**

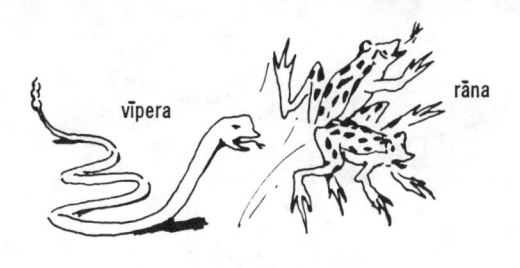

20. This means, "The ____ ____s the ____."

A: The snake recognizes the frog.

21. **Vīpera** is the _____ of the sentence; it is _____ case.

A: subject
nominative

22. The word **rānam** is _____ of the sentence, _____ c____.

A: object
accusative case.

23. Now for the new case. Echo your teacher as he says in Latin that the snake recognizes the frog IN THE PITFALL. ★ ○ • ○ • **Vīpera rānam in foveā cognōscit.**

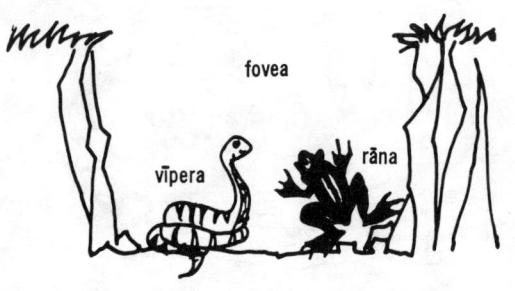

10-31

177. In this sequence, say the answer aloud and then write it. "Quō locō est elephantus?"
"_____."

178. "_____."
A: In aciē.

179. "Quō locō est pecūnia?" "_____."

180. "_____."
A: In angulō.

181. "Quō locō est musca?" "_____."

182. "_____."
A: In effigiē.

24. **Vīpera** is _____ case and **rānam** is _____ case.

A: nominative accusative

25. The Latin expression for "in the pitfall" uses a new form of the noun which ends in long -ā (with a macron).
　　　in the pitfall = _____ _____

A: **in foveā** [With the macron.]

26. ★ ○ • ○ • ablative case

VCh: "áb-luh-tive case"

27. The new form **foveā** is the ablative case. To say in Latin "in the pitfall," we use the Latin word **in** followed by the _____ case of **fovea**.

A: ablative

28. Say in Latin that the fly irritates the lion in the pitfall. M____ l____ __ f____ ir____.

A: **Musca leōnem in foveā** [with a long -ā] **irrītat**.

29. The form **foveā** (with long -ā) is the _____ case of the word **fovea**.

A: ablative

167-171. Echo the paradigms of these nouns, which represent the five declensions.

167. ★ ○ •　*168.* ★ ○ •　*169.* ★ ○ •　*170.* ★ ○ •　*171.* ★ ○ •
fortūna　**ager**　**auris**　**quercus**　**aciēs**
fortūnam　agrum　aurem　quercum　aciem
fortūnae　agrō　aure　quercū　aciē

172. Write the paradigm of these three nouns.

———— **gradus**

A:　gradus
　　gradum
　　gradū

173. **faciēs** ————

A:　faciēs
　　faciem
　　faciē

174. **plānitiēs** ————

A:　plānitiēs
　　plānitiem
　　plānitiē

175. The expression **In quō locō?** is usually abbreviated to **Quō locō?**, that is, without the ————.

A: preposition.

176. **Quō locō?** is much more common than **In quō locō?** Therefore, to ask "In what place?" or "Where?", in place of the longer **In quō locō?** we will use the shorter phrase, ————?

A: **Quō locō?**

30. Say in Latin that the wolf bites the wolf in the pitfall. L____ l____ __ ____ mordet.

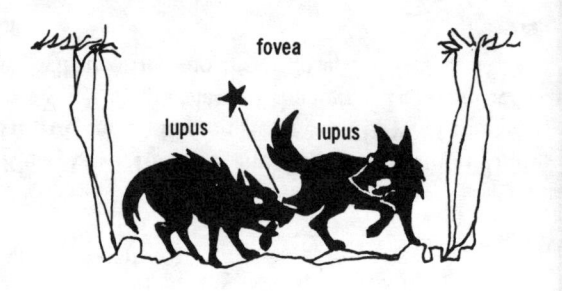

A: Lupus lupum in foveā mordet.

31. Using **fovea** as a model, say and write these three forms of **umbra**.

nominative	fovea	umbra ____
accusative	foveam	umbr__ ____
ablative	foveā	umbr_ ____

A: umbra
umbram
umbrā

32. Describe what the young man sees. V__ f____ in um___ v____.

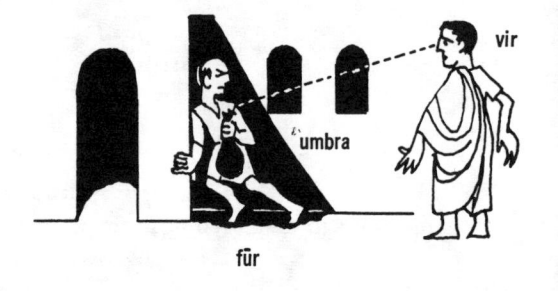

A: Vir fūrem in umbrā videt.

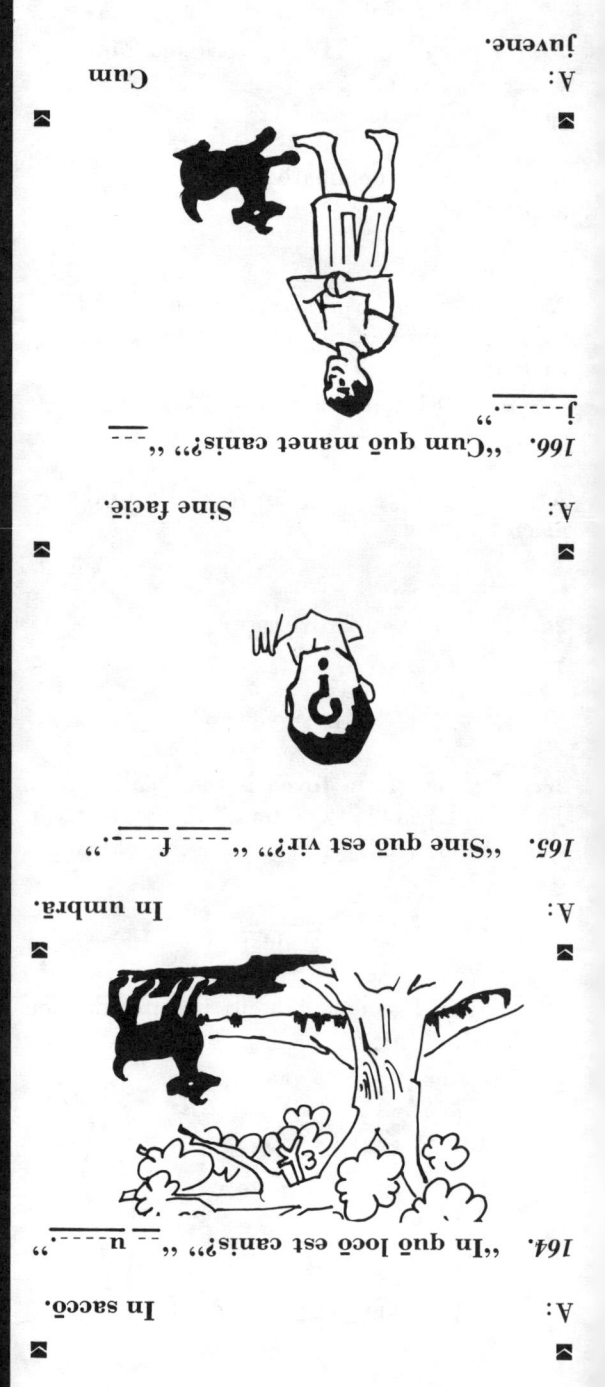

---

163. "In quō locō est vipera?" "__ s____."

A: In saccō.

164. "In quō locō est canis?" "__ u____."

A: In umbrā.

165. "Sine quō est vir?" "____ f____."

A: Sine facie.

166. "Cum quō manet canis?" "____ j____."

A: Cum juvene.

9-10

33. _____ in _____ est.

A: **Agnus in umbrā est.**

34. _____ __ _____ ___.

A: **Īnfāns in umbrā est.**

35. The word **umbrā** is _____ case.

A: ablative

36. ★ ○ • ○ • Preposition

VCh: "prep-poe-zísh-shun"

We call the word **in** a "preposition." A preposition comes before a noun and causes the noun to modify (describe) some other word in the sentence, usually the verb.

37. We say that in the sentence **Īnfāns in umbrā est**, the word **est** is modified by the phrase **in umbrā**, consisting of the _____ **in** and the _____ noun **umbrā**.

A: preposition, ablative

10-28

159. The next sequence uses all three of the Latin prepositions which you know. They are _____, _____, and _____.

A: **in, cum,** and **sine.**

Write a two word answer in the next seven frames.

160. "Cum quō est leō?" "_____ m_____."

A: **Cum mūre.**

161. "In quō locō stat vir?" "_____ p_____."

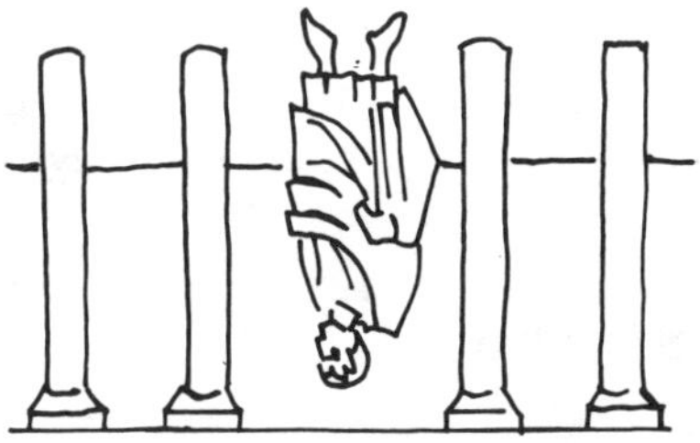

A: **In porticū.**

162. "Cum quō currit īnfāns?" "_____ c_____."

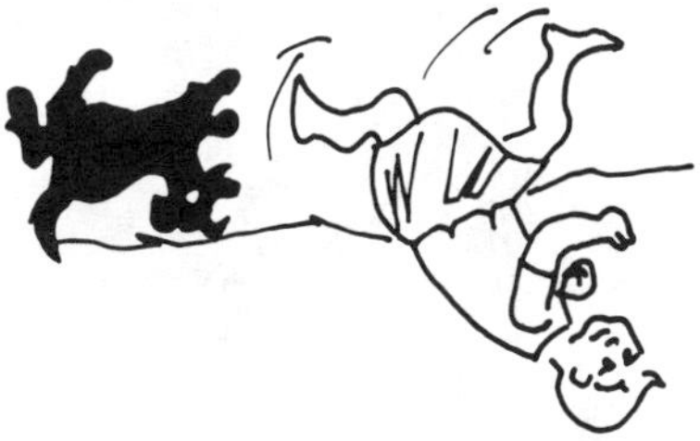

A: **Cum cane.**

38. Echo your teacher as he says in Latin, "The child is with the woman." ★ ○ • ○ •
Īnfāns cum fēminā est.

▼

39. with the woman = ____ ____

▼

A: cum fēminā [With a long -ā on fēminā.]

40. The sentence **Īnfāns cum fēminā est** ____ (has an {-m}/does not have any {-m}).

▼

A: does not have any {-m}.

41. Therefore **Īnfāns cum fēminā est** is an {__ __} sentence, but it has a modifier of the verb **est**.

▼

A: {-s -t}

42. The modifier of the verb **est** is the phrase ___ _____.

▼

A: **cum fēminā**.

43. In the phrase **cŭm fēminā**, the word **cum** is a _____ and the noun **fēminā** is in the _____ case.

▼

A: preposition
ablative

44. **Īnfāns cum fēminā est** = The ____ __ ____ the _____.

▼

A: The child is with the woman.

---

152. "In quō locō est musca?" "... f_____."

A: In faciē.

▼

153-154. Echo the paradigms of these two nouns.

153. ★ ○ •   **154.** ★ ○ •
vulpēs   effigiēs
vulpem   effigiem
vulpe   effigiē

▼

155. You can tell which declension a noun belongs to by its _____ case.

▼

A: ablative

▼

156. **Vulpēs** and **effigiēs** belong to ____ (the same declension/different declensions).

▼

A: different declensions.

▼

157. While **vulpēs** has a sh__ e in the ablative, **effigiēs** has a l____ e in the ablative.

▼

A: short
long

▼

158. **Vulpēs** belongs to the ___ Declension, and **effigiēs** belongs to the ___ Declension.

▼

A: 3d
5th

9-12

45. Chorus the description of this picture.
★ ○ ○ ◉ ◉ (If you have no tape recorder, pull mask down to visual check and read aloud several times.)

vīpera   īnfāns

VCh: **Īnfāns cum vīperā est.** [With a long -ā on **vīperā**.]

46. The preposition in this last sentence was the word ____.

A: **cum**.

47. **Īnfāns cum vīperā est** = _____.

A: The child is with the snake.

48-52. Echo your teacher as he gives the Latin for the following phrases.

48. with a snake   ★ ○ • ○ • **cum vīperā**
49. with a monkey ★ ○ • ○ • **cum sīmiā**
50. with a frog   ★ ○ • ○ • **cum rānā**
51. with a woman   ★ ○ • ○ • **cum fēminā**
52. with a fly   ★ ○ • ○ • **cum muscā**

53. These ablatives all end in the sound _____.

A: -ā. [With the macron.]

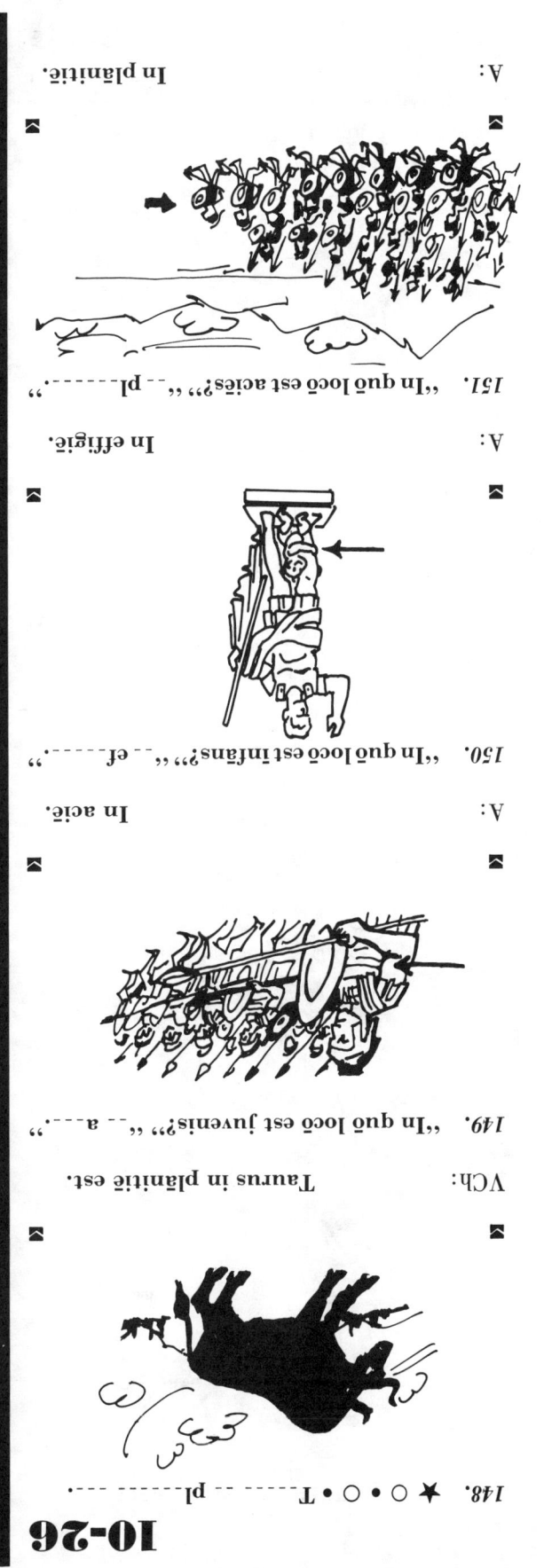

10-26

148. T ★ ○ • ○ • pl_____.

VCh: **Taurus in plānitiē est.**

149. "In quō locō est juvenis?" "_ a____."

150. "In quō locō est īnfāns?" "_ ef____."

A: **In aciē.**

A: **In effigiē.**

151. "In quō locō est aciēs?" "_ pl____."

A: **In plānitiē.**

9-13

54. Using the pattern of **Īnfāns cum vīperā est**, describe the following pictures. Remember that the word following **cum** will end in long **-ā**.

Eq___ cum s___ā est.

sīmia / *equus*

A: **Equus cum sīmiā est.**

55. This means, "The _____ __ ____ the _____."

A: The horse is with the monkey.

56. P_____ cum r___ est.

piscis / *rāna*

A: **Piscis cum rānā est.**

57. C_____ ___ f_____ est.

fēmina / *canis*

A: **Canis cum fēminā est.**

10-25

140-144. Echo the paradigms of Fifth Declension nouns.

140.	141.	142.	143.	144.
★ • ○ •	★ • ○ •	★ • ○ •	★ • ○ •	★ • ○ •
diēs	aciēs	plānitiēs	faciēs	effigiēs
diem	aciem	plānitiem	faciem	effigiem
diē	aciē	plānitiē	faciē	effigiē

[Did you repeat these nouns enough times to learn the paradigms?]

Echo your teacher's description of four pictures.

145. ★ • ○ • ○ S____ in ef_____t.

VCh: **Sīmia in effigiē est.**

146. ★ • ○ • ○ El____ in ac_____

VCh: **Elephantus in aciē est.**

147. ★ • ○ • ○ Oc____ f_____

VCh: **Oculus in faciē est.**

9-14

58. R___ ___ m____ est.

musca
rāna

A: **Rāna cum muscā est.**

59. The ablatives you have been using (**vīperā, sīmiā, rānā, fēminā,** and **muscā**) all end in a vowel which is ____ (long/short).

A: long.

60-63. Echo the contrasting forms of the following words.

	60. ★ ○ •	61. ★ ○ •
nominative	vīpera	musca
accusative	vīperam	muscam
ablative	vīperā	muscā

	62. ★ ○ •	63. ★ ○ •
nominative	Fortūna	pecūnia
accusative	Fortūnam	pecūniam
ablative	Fortūnā	pecūniā

[Repeat as often as necessary to learn them.] Notice that these words change their forms in the same way.

64. ★ ○ • ○ • declension

VCh: "dee-klén-shun"

65. Nouns which change their forms in the same way are said to belong to the same "declension." The four words you just echoed all change form in the same way and therefore they all _____.

A: belong to the same declension.

10-24

131-134. Now for some new Fifth Declension nouns. Echo your teacher as he describes these four pictures.

131.   132.   133.   134.

Plānitiēs est.   Efflgiēs est.   Aciēs est.   Faciēs est.

★ • ○ • ★ ○ • • ○ ★ • ○ • • ★ ○ • ○ •

135. It's a statue = _____ est. [Say your answer out loud.]

A: **Efflgiēs est.**

136. It's a face = ____ ____ = ____.

A: **Faciēs est.**

137. It's a plain = ____ _____ = ____.

A: **Plānitiēs est.**

138. It's a battle line = ____ ____ ____.

A: **Aciēs est.**

139. All these nouns belong to the ___ Declension.

A: Fifth

66. The words you have just practiced, whose ablatives end in long **-ā,** are said to belong to the *First* Declension. You know that **musca** belongs to the First Declension because its ablative form ends in _____.

A: -ā.

67. You know that **fovea** belongs to the First Declension because _____.

A: its ablative form ends in -ā.

68. The noun **fēmina** belongs to the First D_____.

A: Declension.

69. You can now correctly predict the ablative of *any First Declension noun in Latin.* Echo the nominative case of a First Declension noun which is completely new to you. ★ ○ • ○ • via

70. Use **fovea** as a model to write the three forms of **via.**

nominative	fovea	via	_____
accusative	foveam	____	_____
ablative	foveā	___	_____

A:
via
viam
viā

71. ★ ○ • ○ • Paradigm

VCh: "pára-dime"

---

124. _____ fovea

A: fovea
foveam
foveā

125. _____ vulpēs

A: vulpēs
vulpem
vulpe

126. _____ porticus.

A: porticus
porticum
porticū

127. _____ vir.

A: vir
virum
virō

128. _____ mūs

A: mūs
mūrem
mūre

129. Now for the Fifth Declension. The Fifth Declension has very few nouns, but it must be learned just as thoroughly as the other four. Echo the paradigm of Fifth Declension noun ★ ○ • ○ • diēs

A: diēs
diem
diē

130. The vowel **ē** is the _____ of the Fifth Declension.

A: characteristic vowel

9-16

The collected forms of a word, written like those of **rāna** below, are called the "paradigm" of that word. On the model of **rāna,** say all three forms in the paradigm of each of these First Declension nouns. Check each noun with the tape. [If you cannot do it, do not just echo; go back to frame 48.]

72. nominative **rāna** **sīmia**
    accusative **rānam** ------
    ablative **rānā** ----- ✓ ★ ○ •

VCh: **sīmia**
     sīmiam
     sīmiā

73. nominative **vīta**
    accusative -----
    ablative ---- ✓ ★ ○ •

VCh: **vīta**
     vītam
     vītā

74. nominative **Sapientia**
    accusative ----------
    ablative ---------- ✓ ★ ○ •

VCh: **Sapientia**
     Sapientiam
     Sapientiā

75. You have just given the p_____s of four First Declension nouns.

A: paradigms

76. The word **rāna** belongs to the F____ D_____.

A: First Declension.

10-22

118. Write the paradigm of the following nouns, representing all four declensions which you know so far.

First ("a" type): **umbra** ——————

A: umbra
   umbram
   umbrā

119. Second ("o" type): **elephantus** ——————

A: elephantus
   elephantum
   elephantō

120. Third ("e" or "i" type): **juvenis** ——————

A: juvenis
   juvenem
   juvene

121. Fourth ("u" type): **lacus** ——————

A: lacus
   lacum
   lacū

122. Now without being told what declension these nouns are, write the paradigm.

gradus

A: gradus
   gradum
   gradū

123. **Gradus** belongs to the --- Declension.

A: 4th

9-17

77-81. There are five different declensions of nouns. Here are examples from the five declensions for you to look at. THE DIFFERENCE BETWEEN THE DECLENSIONS SHOWS UP IN THE ABLATIVE CASE. [Don't memorize these words now; echo each one just once; you will *learn* the forms later.]

Declension:	77. First ★ ○ •	78. Second ★ ○ •	79. Third ★ ○ •
nominative	fémina	agnus	léō
accusative	féminam	agnum	leónem
ablative	féminā	agnō	leóne

Declension:	80. Fourth ★ ○ •	81. Fifth ★ ○ •
nominative	manus	diēs
accusative	manum	diem
ablative	manū	diē

82. You can see that in each declension the ablative form ends in a v_____.

A: vowel.

83. Furthermore, in every declension (except the Third) this vowel is ____ (long/short).

A: long.

84. Since **Īnfāns cum fēminā est** means "The child is with the woman," you can figure out that **Īnfāns cum vulpe est** means "The child is ____ ___ ___."

A: with the fox.

10-21

110-113. Echo the paradigm of these nouns which represent the four declensions you know so far.

110. First "a" type ★ ○ •	111. Second "o" type ★ ○ •	112. Third "e" type ★ ○ •	113. Fourth "u" type ★ ○ •
musca	asinus	laus	anus
muscam	asinum	laudem	anum
muscā	asinō	laude	anū

Now say the paradigm of these same nouns and then check.

114. First musc- ∨ ★ ○ •

-----

115. Second asin- ∨ ★ ○ •

VCh: musca
muscam
muscā

116. Third lau- ∨ ★ ○ •

VCh: asinus
asinum
asinō

VCh: laus
laudem
laude

117. Fourth an- ∨ ★ ○ •

VCh: anus
anum
anū

85-90. Now for the ablative of some Second Declension nouns. Echo the following phrases.

85. ★ ○ • ○ • **cum asinō**

86. ★ ○ • ○ • **cum agnō**

87. ★ ○ • ○ • **cum equō**

88. ★ ○ • ○ • **cum medicō**

89. ★ ○ • ○ • **cum taurō**

90. ★ ○ • ○ • **cum lupō**

91. These ablatives all end in the letter _____.

A: long **-ō**. [With the macron]

92. Because the ablative forms of **agnus (agnō)** and **taurus (taurō)** end in long **-ō**, you know that **agnus** and **taurus** belong to the ____ (First/Second) Declension.

A: Second

93. Echo as your teacher describes this picture.
★ ○ • ○ • **Sīmia cum asinō est.**

94. This means, "_____."

A: The monkey is with the donkey.

A: ablative

109. From now on we will omit the labels of nom, acc, and abl. You are to understand that the third form down in a paradigm is the _____ case.

A: 3d e i.

108. **Leō** belongs to the ___ Declension. Its characteristic vowel is ___ or ___.

A: 4th u.

107. **Anus** belongs to the ___ Declension. Its characteristic vowel is ___.

A: 1st a.

106. **Rāna** belongs to the ___ Declension. Its characteristic vowel is ___.

A: 2d o.

105. **Taurus** belongs to the ___ (1st/2d/3d/4th) Declension. Its characteristic vowel is ___.

A: **Cum taurō.**

104. "**Cum quō juvenis est?**" "_____."

A: **Juvenis.**

103. "**Quis cum taurō est?**" "J_____."

9-19

95. On the model of **Sīmia cum asinō est**, describe the following pictures. The words which follow the preposition **cum** will all end in **-ō**, because we will use all Second _____ nouns.

A: Declension

96. Ca___ cum ___ō ___.

agnus   *canis*

A: Canis cum agnō est.

97. V__ cum ____ ___.

vir   *equus*

A: Vir cum equō est.

98. _____ c_ m_____ ___.

medicus   *aeger*

A: Aeger cum medicō est.

99. The word **medicō** is the ablative of a S_____ D_____ noun.

A: Second Declension

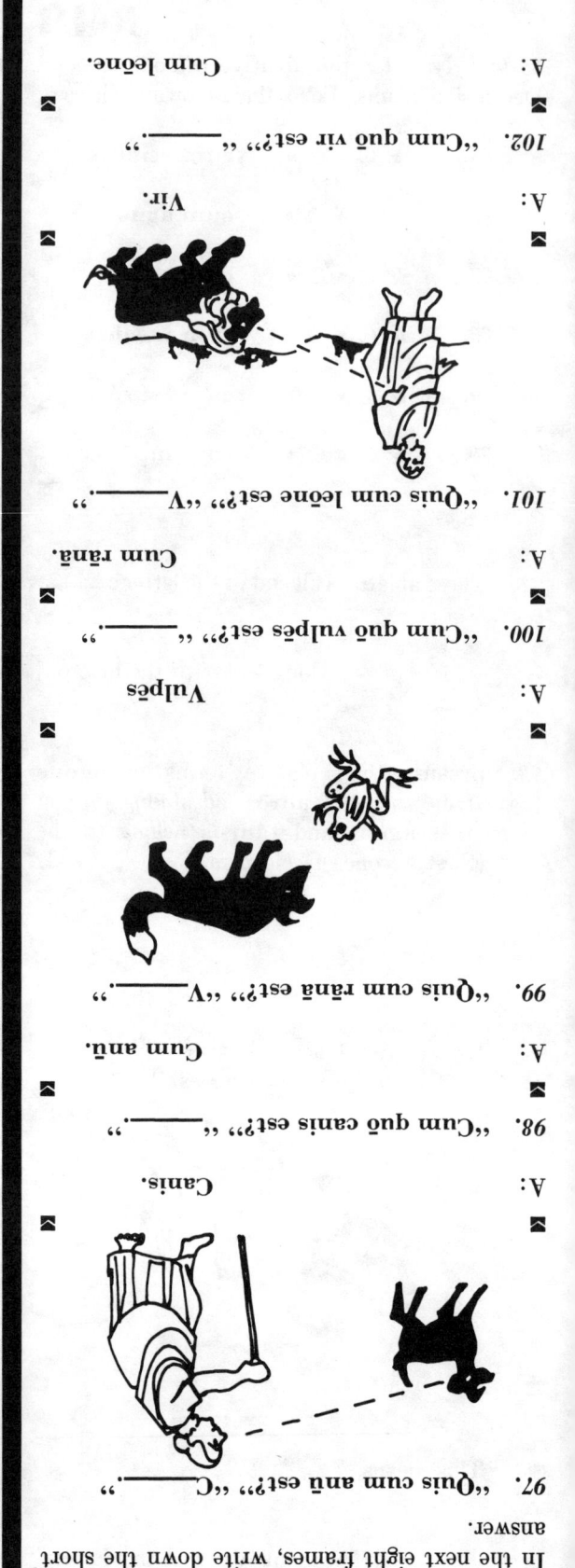

10-19

In the next eight frames, write down the short answer.

97. "Quis cum anū est?" "C____."

A: Cum anū.

98. "Cum quō canis est?" "_____."

A: Canis.

99. "Quis cum rānā est?" "V____."

Vulpēs

A: Vulpēs

100. "Cum quō vulpēs est?" "_____."

A: Cum rānā.

101. "Quis cum leōne est?" "V____."

Vir.

A: Vir.

102. "Cum quō vir est?" "_____."

A: Cum leōne.

9-20

100. A___ ___ t___ ___.

A: **Anus cum taurō est.**

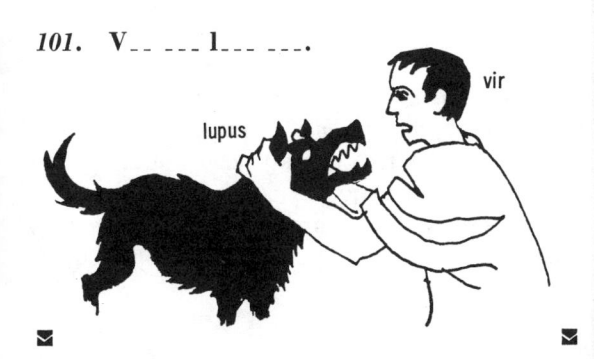

101. V__ ___ l___ ___.

A: **Vir cum lupō est.**

102. However, a word of warning. Not *all* words that end in **-ō** are ablative case of Second Declension nouns. **Leō** is Third Declension and _____ case.

A: nominative

103-108. In the second declension there are nouns with the signal **-s** and nouns with the signal zero. Echo the paradigms. (Repeat as often as necessary.)

	103. ★ ○ •	*104.* ★ ○ •	*105.* ★ ○ •
nominative	vir	equus	medicus
accusative	virum	equum	medicum
ablative	virō	equō	medicō

	106. ★ ○ •	*107.* ★ ○ •	*108.* ★ ○ •
nominative	aper	lupus	aeger
accusative	aprum	lupum	aegrum
ablative	aprō	lupō	aegrō

10-18

94. F__ in s____ est.

A: **Fūr in saccō est.**

95. V_____ in u____ est.

A: **Vulpēs in umbrā est.**

96. P_____ in o____ est.

A: **Piscis in orbe est.**

9-21

109. The Second Declension nouns in this list with the variant signal -s are _____, _____, and _____. [Look back to frames 103–108 if you wish.]

A: **equus medicus lupus**.

110. The Second Declension nouns in this list with the signal zero are: ___, ____, and _____.

A: **vir aper aeger**.

111. Now describe the next three pictures, all of which use a Second Declension ablative ending in -ō. C_____ c__ ____ est.

A: **Canis cum aprō est.**

112. M_____ ___ _____ est.

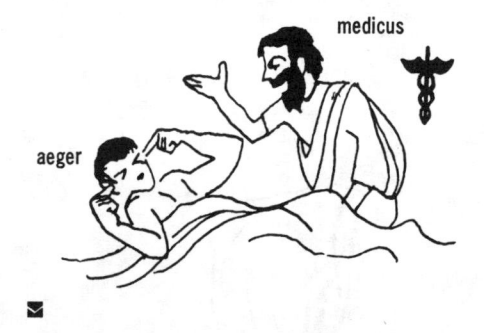

A: **Medicus cum aegrō est.**

10-17

91. "In quō locō equus est?" "_____."

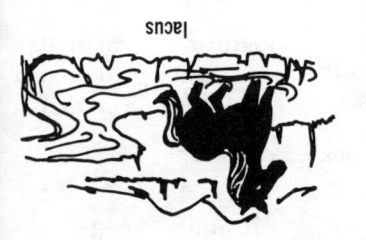

A: **In lacū equus est.**

92. "In quō locō rāna est?" "_____."

A: **In manū rāna est.**

In the following sequence you will use the ablative of nouns from each of the four declensions you know. On the model of **Elephantus in orbe est**, describe each of these four pictures. [The dashes show the number of missing letters.] Use these words: **fūr, manus, mūs, orbis, piscis, saccus, umbra, vulpēs.**

93. M___ in m___ est.

A: **Mūs in manū est.**

9-22

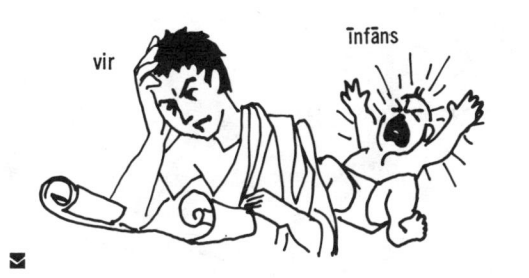

113. Īnf___ ___ ____ est.

A: Īnfāns cum virō est.

114. This is an {_ _ _} sentence with the modifier c__ v____.

A: {-s -t} cum virō.

115-117. In the following three frames you will use the words **vir**, meaning "____;" **aper**, "____;" and **aeger**, "____ _____."

A: man   boar   sick person.

118. Say and write the paradigm of the word for "man."

    nominative   v__   _____
    accusative   v____   _____
    ablative   v___   _____

A: vir
                  virum
                  virō

(If you are using the system of the 3 by 5 cards, you can now add the ablative.)

119. Say and write the paradigm of the word for "boar."

    nominative   ap__   _____
    accusative   ap___   _____
    ablative   ap__   _____

A: aper
                  aprum
                  aprō

10-16

88. "In quō locō musca est?" "_____."

A: In aure musca est.

89. "In quō locō fūr est?" "_____."

A: In orbe fūr est.

90. "In quō locō asinus est?" "_____."

A: In umbrā asinus est.

9-23

120. Say and write the paradigm of the word for "sick person."

nominative	aeg_ _	_____
accusative	aeg_ _ _	_____
ablative	aeg_ _	_____

A:
aeger
aegrum
aegrō

121-122. Let us now compare the First and Second Declensions. Echo the paradigms.

	121. First ★ ○ •	122. Second ★ ○ •
nominative	fēmina	agnus
accusative	fēminam	agnum
ablative	fēminā	agnō

123. The vowel in which the ablative ends is called the "characteristic vowel" of that declension. Whether it is long or short, it is characteristic of that declension because it occurs in the ablative and in most other forms in the paradigm. In the First Declension, **a** is the ch_ _ _ _ _ _ _ _ _ _ _ _ _ _ _ _ _.

A: characteristic vowel.

124. In the First Declension the characteristic vowel **a**, whether long or short, occurs in _ _ _ _ (just one form/two forms/all three forms).

A: all three forms.

125. The characteristic vowel of the First Declension is _____.

A: **a.**

---

85. "In quō locō vipera est?" "_____."

A: In angulō vipera est.

86. "In quō locō lupus est?" "_____."

A: In foveā lupus est.

87. "In quō locō taurus est?" "_____."

A: In saccō taurus est.

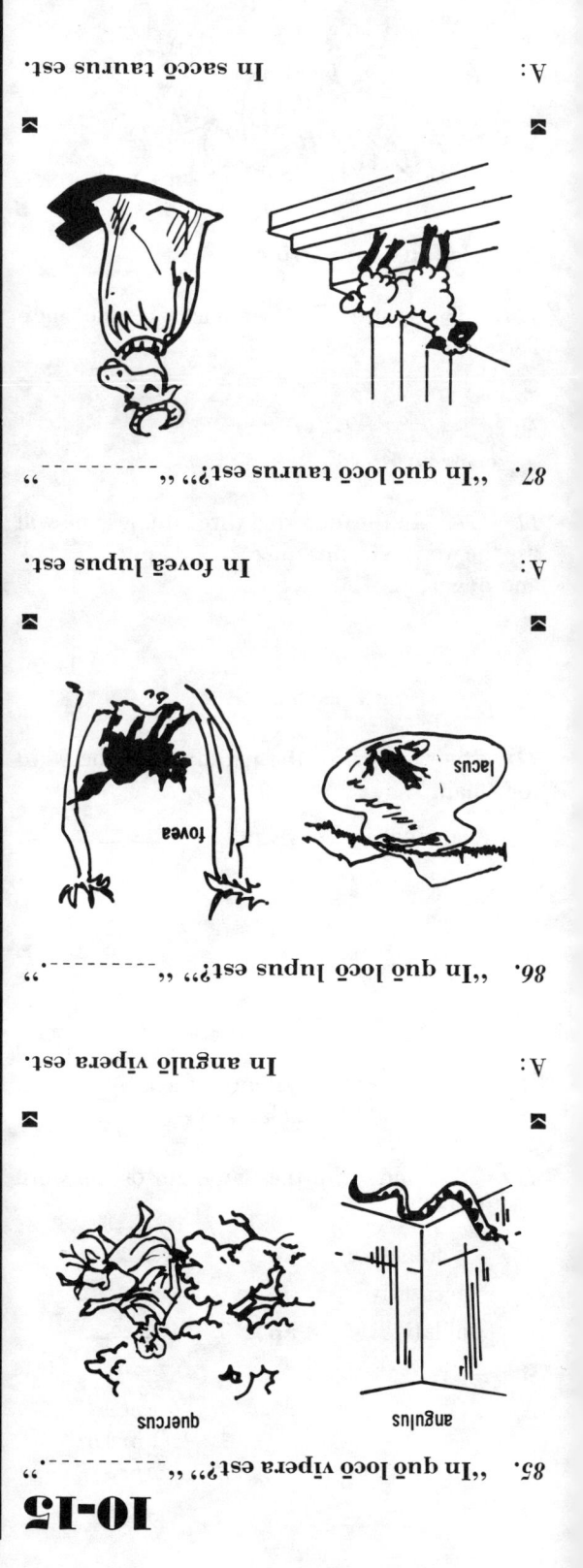

10-15

9-24

126-127. Echo these First and Second Declension paradigms.

	126. First ★ ○ •	127. Second ★ ○ •
nominative	vīpera	Deus
accusative	vīperam	Deum
ablative	vīperā	Deō

128. In the Second Declension, **o** is the ch_____ v____.

A: characteristic vowel.

129. In the Second Declension the characteristic vowel **o** occurs in ____ (just one form/two form/all three forms).

A: just one form.

130. What happens to the characteristic vowel **o** in the nominative and accusative? Here is the explanation. Look at the paradigm of **agnus**.

nominative	agnus
accusative	agnum
ablative	agnō

You notice that instead of finding **o** in the nominative and accusative cases, we find the vowel _____ instead.

A: u

131. It is one of the facts of the Latin language that short **o** does not occur before the endings **-s** and **-m**. Where we would expect short **o** we find **u** instead. Look now at the imaginary forms of the following word.

nominative	*agnos	_____
accusative	*agnom	_____
ablative	agnō	_____

Change the **o** in the imaginary forms to **u** and write the correct paradigm.

A: agnus
               agnum
               agnō

132. The characteristic vowel of the First Declension is **a,** but the characteristic vowel of the Second Declension is ____.

A: o.

133. You know that **avāritiā** is the ablative form of a _____ Declension noun, because of the ending _____.

A: First
       -ā.

134. You know that **medicō** is the ablative form of a _____ Declension noun, because of the ending _____.

A: Second
       -ō.

135. **Aper** has the ablative form _____; it belongs to the _____ Declension.

A: aprō
       Second

136. **Fovea** has the ablative form _____; it belongs to the _____ Declension.

A: foveā
       First

137. Here is a list of nouns from several declensions.

    áquila   leó   elephántus
    áquilam   leónem   elephántum
    áquilā   leóne   elephántō

    sīmia   sapiéntia   vulpēs
    sīmiam   sapiéntiam vulpem
    sīmiā   sapiéntiā   vulpe

We identify First Declension nouns by the _____ case ending, which is ___.

A: ablative   -ā.

9-26

138. The First Declension nouns in this list are _____, _____, and _____. [Look back to frame 137 if you like.]

A: **aquila, sīmia, sapientia.**

139. Here is another list of nouns from several declensions:

vḗritās	equus	vir	laus
vēritā́tem	equum	virum	laudem
vēritā́te	equō	virō	laude
fūr	aper	auris	
fūrem	aprum	aurem	
fūre	aprō	aure	

We identify Second Declension nouns by the _____ case ending, which is ___.

A: ablative   -ō.

140. The Second Declension nouns in this list are: _____, ___, and ____.

A: **equus, vir, aper.**

141. You will now practice giving the ablative of both First and Second Declension nouns. When we had the drill on the First Declension ablative, you had only to remember to use **-ā** on the end of the ablative; in the drill on the Second Declension you had only to remember to use **-ō** on the end of the ablative. Now you must remember whether to use ___ or ___ for the ablative ending.

A: -ā   -ō

---

67. ★ ○ • Saccus est.

68. ★ ○ • ○ • Angulus est.

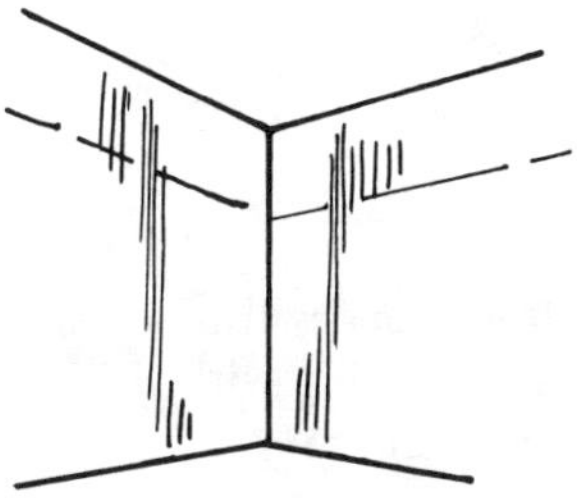

Answer questions on the following series of pictures.

69. "Quis in saccō est?"

70. "S____ in _____." ∧ ★ ○ •

VCh: Simia in saccō est.

71. "In quō locō sīmia est?" "In _____." ∧ ★ ○ •

VCh: In saccō.

142. Echo your teacher as he describes this picture, using a new verb **manet** that means "remains."

★ ○ • ○ • Canis cum sīmiā, nōn equō, manet.

143. This means that: the d__ r_____ with the _____, not with the _____.

A: the dog remains with the monkey, not with the horse.

144. Since there is no {-m}, this is an {__ __} type of sentence.

A: {-s -t}

145. Your teacher will now ask you, in Latin, "Is the dog remaining with the monkey?" Write down his question. "M_____ c____ c__ s____?" ★ ○ ○

A: Manetne canis cum sīmiā?

146. To give a "Yes" answer you merely repeat the word that had the **-ne,** leaving off the_____.

A: -ne.

For the next sequence you will need two new Second Declension nouns. Echo your teacher as he describes these two objects.

VCh: Cum juvene.

66. "Cum quō fēmina manet?" ^ " ------ ," • ○ ★ •

VCh: Fēminam.

65. " ------ ," ^ " ★ ○ •

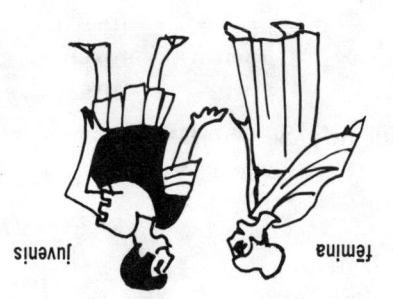

64. "Quem juvenis dīligit?"

VCh: Cum anū.

63. " ------ ," ^ " ★ ○ •

62. Here is a second question on this same picture. "Cum quō īnfāns est?"

VCh: Īnfantem.

61. " ------ ," ^ " ★ ○ •

60. "Quem anus lavat?"

10-11

9-28

147. Your teacher will ask you this same question again. ★ ○ ○

[illustration: canis, sīmia, equus]

▼

VCh: "Manetne canis cum sīmiā?" Answer him. "----------."

▼

A: Manet. (Manet canis cum sīmiā.)

▼

148. He will ask you a different question about this same picture. ★ ○ ○

▼

VCh: "Manetne canis cum equō?" Answer him. "----------."

▼

A: Nōn manet.

▼

149. Now he will ask you in Latin whether the dog is with the monkey or with the horse. Write down his question. ★ ○ ○ _____? [This sentence has three macrons.]

[illustration: canis, sīmia, equus]

▼

VCh: "Manetne canis cum sīmiā an cum equō?"

10-10

52. Say the paradigm of **gradus** and check. ∨ ★ ○ •

VCh: gradus
       graduṃ
       gradū

▼

53. From looking at the paradigm, you can see that the characteristic vowel of the Fourth Declension is ---- (a/e/i/o/u).

▼

A: u.

▼

54. In the following frames your teacher will ask you questions about pictures which will require you to use three cases of all four declensions. **Quis?** asks for a personal noun in the ---------- case.

▼

A: nominative

▼

55. **Quō?** asks for a noun in the -------- case.

▼

A: ablative

▼

56. The question **In quō locō?** is answered by the Latin preposition -- plus the ---------- case.

▼

A: in   ablative

▼

57. The question **Quem?** is answered in Latin by a -------- noun in the ---------- case.

▼

A: personal   accusative

▼

58. Your teacher will ask in Latin, "Who is the monkey standing with?" (or "With whom is the monkey standing?")

[illustration: sīmia, equus]

▼

59. "**Cum quō sīmia stat?**" Now answer him. "Cum ----." ∨ ★ ○ •

▼

VCh: Cum equō.

150. To this kind of question you reply with one of the two items on either side of the connector **an.** In other words, you say either **Cum sīmiā** or **Cum equō.** Look at the picture and then answer. ★ ○ ○ **"Manetne canis cum sīmiā an cum equō?"** "--- -----."

A: **Cum sīmiā.**

151. You will now have a series of pictures where the teacher will ask you whether a person (or animal) is remaining with A or with B. You must choose between the two phrases connected by **an.**

152. **Manetne canis cum sīmiā an cum equō?** Give a two-word answer (either **Cum sīmiā,** or **Cum equō**). "--------."

A: **Cum equō.**

153. **Manetne vulpēs cum agnō an cum rānā?** "--------."

A: **Cum rānā.**

47. **"Quis in gradū est?"** "---------------------." √ ★ ○ •

VCh: **Piscis in gradū est.**

48. **"In quō locō piscis est?"** "---------------------." √ ★ ○ •

VCh: **In gradū piscis est.**

49. **"Quis in lacū est?"** "----------------------." √ ★ ○ •

VCh: **Medicus in lacū est.**

50. **"In quō locō medicus est?"** -----------------------." √ ★ ○ •

VCh: **In lacū medicus est.**

51. Write the paradigm of **quercus.** ______

A: **quercus**
quercum
quercū

9-30

154. Manetne vir cum fēminā an cum asinō? "_____."

▼ ▼

A: Cum fēminā.

155. Manetne īnfāns cum taurō an cum aquilā? "_____."

▼ ▼

A: Cum taurō.

156. Manetne aper cum lupō an cum vīperā? "_____."

▼ ▼

A: Cum vīperā.

10-8

43. "Quis in quercū est?" "S_____ in qu_____." ∧ ★ ○ •

▼ ▼

VCh: Simia in quercū est.

▼ ▼

VCh: In quercū simia est.

44. "In quō locō simia est?" "_____." ∧ ★ ○ •

▼ ▼

VCh: "Quis in porticū est?" "_____." ∧ ★ ○ •

45. "Quis in porticū est?" "_____." ∧ ★ ○ •

▼ ▼

VCh: Aquila in porticū est.

▼ ▼

VCh: In porticū aquila est.

46. "In quō locō aquila est?" "_____." ∧ ★ ○ •

9-31

157. Manetne leō cum virō an cum aprō?
"‗‗‗‗‗‗‗."

A: **Cum aprō.**

158. The sentence **Leō cum aprō manet** is an {‗‗ ‗‗} sentence.

A: {-s -t}

159. Now for some practice in pronunciation. The letter "e" on the end of an English word is almost never pronounced. For example, the English word "cane" is a ‗‗‗‗ (one-syllable/two-syllable) word.

A: one-syllable

160. The function of the final "e" in the word "cane" is to indicate the pronunciation of the "a." As the reading teachers tell their students, "It makes the letter say its name." The vowel sound in "cane" is different from the vowel sound in "can," and this is signalled in the English spelling system by adding the letter ‗‗‗ to "can."

A: -e

---

39. But no other word in Latin changes forms exactly like **quis?** We therefore cannot set up a rule that includes **quis?** We learn **quis?** by itself, and because there is no rule to guide us we say that **quis?** is an "ir‗‗‗‗‗‗r" word.

A: irregular

40. We have felt it necessary to make this short explanation because, strange to say, we have found that since the word "irregular" in ordinary speech often means "wrong" ("His conduct was most irregular!"), students think that there is something wrong with a word like **quis?** We call **quis?** an irregular word because

[In your own words.]

A: it changes form in a way unlike most words.

41. You will be glad to know that there are only a few irregular words in Latin. The only Latin word that you know is irregular is the word ‗‗‗‗‗.

A: **quis?**

[Some of the words which you have been using are also irregular; this will be explained later.]

42. Now back to our practice on the ablative. You will now have a sequence in which you will use the phrase **In quō locō?** which means "‗‗‗‗ ‗‗‗‗?" or "‗‗‗‗‗?."

A: In what place? Where?

Your teacher will ask you two questions on each of four pictures. Answer the first question, check with the tape; then listen to the second question and answer that. [Answer in complete sentences.]

10-7

9-32

161. That is not true in Latin. In Latin, all vowels are pronounced. Here is an English word and a Latin word, spelled alike but pronounced quite differently. (Incidentally, they also mean different things.)

This is for pronunciation practice only: the Latin words are all new and you may not even know the meanings of some of the English words. Echo the Latin word.

★ ○ • ○ • English "cane," Latin **cane**

162. The English word contains ___ syllable(s), while the Latin word contains ___ syllable(s).

A: one
    two

163. Here are some other pairs which also have quite different meanings in the two languages.
★ ○ • ○ • English "rate," Latin **rate**

164. ★ ○ • ○ • English "dare," Latin **dare**

165. The following pairs of words happen to have about the same meaning, but are still different in pronunciation. ★ ○ • ○ • English "fragile," Latin **fragile**

166. ★ ○ • ○ • English "facile," Latin **facile**

167. How many syllables are there in the Latin word **fīne**? ___.

A: Two.

168. ★ ○ • ○ • English "sine," Latin **síne**

10-6

32. The fact that the ablative for **locō** has the final vowel **-ō** indicates that it belongs to the ____ (First/Second/Third/Fourth) Declension.

A: Second

33. **Quis/quem/quō** is declined like ____ (fēmina/agnus/piscis/vir/gradus/diēs/none of these).

A: none of these.

34. Echo. ★ ○ • ○ • English "regular," Latin **regula**

35. The Latin word **regula** means a "rule," and from it we get the word "regular," meaning something that follows certain r___s.

A: rules.

36. "Rules" in school are customs of behavior which have been decided upon by the authorities, and breaking the rules is punished. A "rule" in language is something quite different. In language a "rule" is a description of how the language operates. We can say that the fact that the accusative ends in **-m** is a ____ of the Latin language.

A: rule

37. All First Declension nouns change form in the same way. We therefore say that they follow the same ____.

A: rule.

38. Because they follow the same *rule* they are called "r____r" nouns.

A: regular

9-33

169. The Latin word **sine** is the antonym of **cum**. Since **cum asinō** means "with a donkey," you know that **sine asinō** means "w_____ a donkey."

A: _____ without a donkey.

170. Echo your teacher as he describes this picture. ★ ○ • ○ • **Vir sine asinō manet.**

171. Your teacher told you that the man remains w_____ the d_____.

A: without the donkey.

172. Describe the following pictures on the same pattern as **Vir sine asinō manet.** Remember that the ablative which follows **cum** may end in either **-ā** or **-ō**. **Piscis sine _____ manet.**

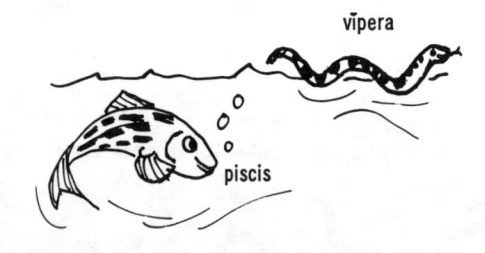

A: **Piscis sine vīperā manet.**

---

27. P _____

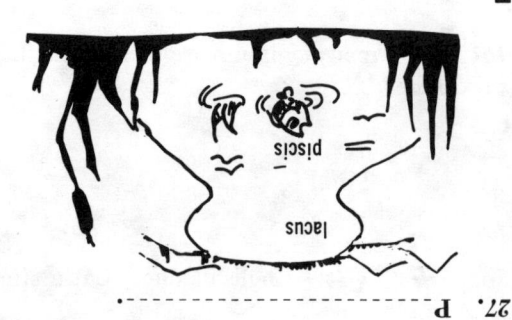

A: **Piscis in lacū est.**

28. A _____

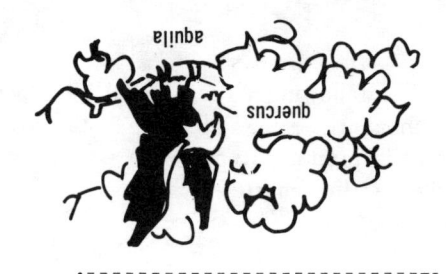

A: **Aquila in quercū est.**

29. Echo the Latin for "In what place?" or "Where?" ★ ○ • ○ •

VCh: **In quō locō?**

30. Echo your teacher as he asks WHERE the doctor is. ★ ○ • ○ •

VCh: **In quō locō medicus est?**

31. Answer the question **In quō locō medicus est?** Notice that the doctor has moved. "In _____ est."

A: **In gradū medicus est.**

9-34

173. C____ s___ a___ manet.

A: Canis sine agnō manet.

174. Ae___ s___ m_____ mane_.

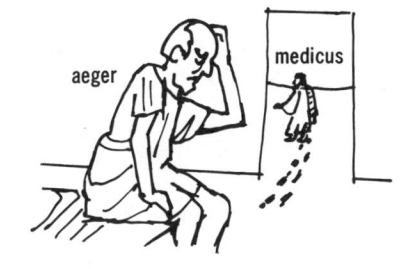

A: Aeger sine medicō manet.

175. L____ s___ a___ man___.

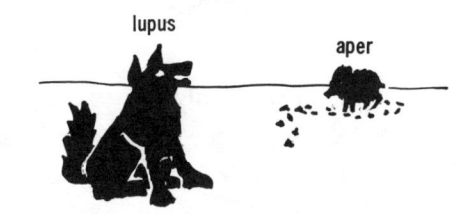

A: Lupus sine aprō manet.

176. V__ s___ f_____ ma____.

A: Vir sine fēminā manet.

10-4

19. ★ ○ ○ "Quis in lacū est?"

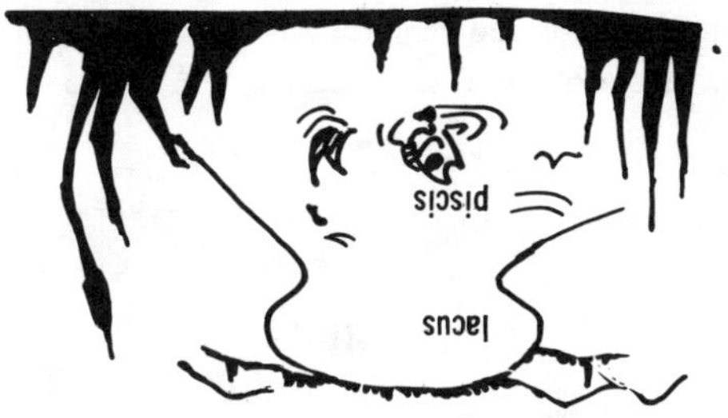

20. "____ ___ _____" ^ ★ ○ •

VCh: Piscis in lacū est.

21-24. Echo the paradigms of these four words. Repeat until learned.

21.	22.	23.	24.
oak tree	covered walk	step	lake
★ ○ •	★ ○ •	★ ○ •	★ ○ •
nom quercus	porticus	gradus	lacus
acc quercum	porticum	gradum	lacum
abl quercū	porticū	gradū	lacū

25. Describe this picture aloud. Sim__ in ____ū est.

A: Simia in gradū est.

26. M_____ __ p_____ ____.

A: Medicus in porticū est.

9-35

177. Īn____ s___ r___ m____.

A: Īnfāns sine rānā manet.

178. A___ s___ s____ ____.

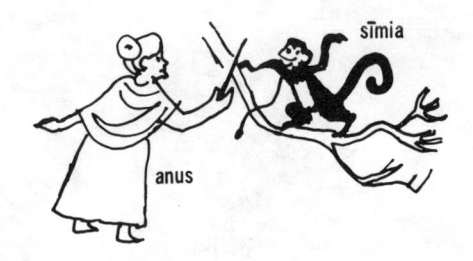

A: Anus sine sīmiā manet.

179. F____ s___ v___ ____.

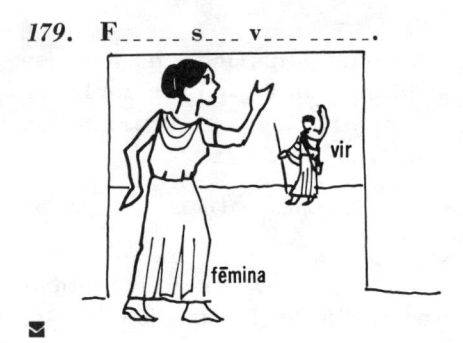

A: Fēmina sine virō manet.

180. Write the paradigms of the following six nouns. Three of them will be First Declension nouns and three Second Declension. Write the paradigm of **sīmia**. _____

A: sīmia
 sīmiam
 sīmiā

10-3

13. The Latin preposition, **in**, followed by the ablative, means either "in," or "on." In this sequence the teacher will ask you who is IN or ON each of these places. ★ ○ ○ "Quis in gradū est?"

14. "S____ in gr____ est." ∨ ★ ○ •

VCh: Sīmia in gradū est.

15. ★ ○ ○ "Quis in quercū est?"

16. "____ in ____." ∨ ★ ○ •

VCh: Aquila in quercū est.

17. ★ ○ ○ "Quis in porticū est?"

18. "____." ∨ ★ ○ •

VCh: Medicus in porticū est.

9-36

181. In a paradigm, the first form is the _____ case, the second form is the _____ case, and the third form is the _____ case.

A: nominative
accusative
ablative

182. Write the paradigm of **asinus**. _____

A: **asinus**
                        asinum
                        asinō

183. **lupus** _____

A: **lupus**
   lupum
   lupō

184. **vir** _____

A: **vir**
   virum
   virō

185. **rāna** _____

A: **rāna**
   rānam
   rānā

186. Now write the paradigm of the Second Declension noun **oculus**. This is a noun you have never seen, but its forms are like those of other Second Declension nouns. _____

A: **oculus**
                       oculum
                       oculō

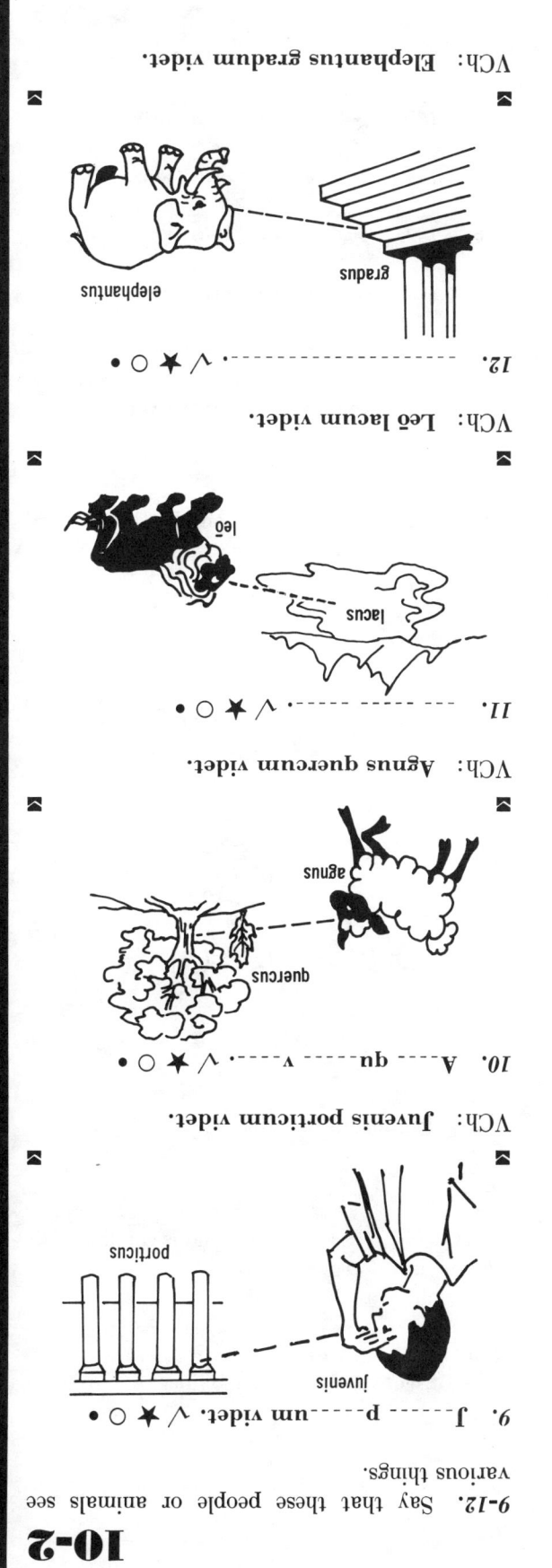

9-37

187-192. We move to the Third Declension.

187. ★ ○ • ○ • cum mūre

188. ★ ○ • ○ • cum leōne

189. ★ ○ • ○ • cum vulpe

190. ★ ○ • ○ • cum cane

191. ★ ○ • ○ • cum pisce

192. ★ ○ • ○ • cum īnfante

193. These Third Declension ablatives all end in the sound short _____.

A: -e.

194. Echo your teacher as he describes this picture. ★ ○ • ○ • Īnfāns cum mūre currit.

195. This means that the ch____ is r_____ w___ the _____.

A: the child is running with the mouse.

196. Īnfāns cum mūre currit is an {__ __} type of sentence with the modifier c__ m____.

A: {-s -t}
         cum mūre.

UNIT TEN

1-4. In the last unit you learned the ablative of the first three declensions, to which the great majority of Latin nouns belong. To drill on the Fourth Declension, we will introduce some new vocabulary. Echo your teacher as he describes each one of these four pictures.

Quercus Porticus Lacus Gradus
 est.   est.   est.   est.
★ ○ • ○ ★ ○ • ○ ★ ○ • ○ ★ ○ • ○ •

5. It's a step = ---- ----.

A: Gradus est.

6. It's an oak tree = ---- ----.

A: Quercus est.

7. It's a lake = ---- ----.

A: Lacus est.

8. It's a covered walk = ---- ----.

A: Porticus est.
(This is a kind of covered walk where people gathered to talk in ancient times.)

10-1

9-38

197. You know that **mūre** is the ablative form of a _____ Declension noun, because of the ending ___.

A: Third
   -e.

198. Cane is _____ case of a _____ Declension noun.

A: ablative   Third

199. Lupō is _____ case of a _____ Declension noun.

A: ablative   Second

200. Leō, however, is _____ case of a _____ Declension noun.

A: nominative
Third

201. Aquilā is ablative of a _____ Declension noun.

A: First

202. Here is a new word. Echo your teacher as he says that the person in the picture is a young man. ★ ○ • ○ •

juvenis

VCh: **Juvenis est.**

TEST INFORMATION

You will be asked to perform the following tasks:
1) to answer "**Cum quō**" questions, as in frames 254-267. The pictures however will be different pictures. The animals and people will not be labeled, but you will be given a list of nouns from which to choose the proper name.
2) to write the paradigm of nouns of the first three declensions, as in frames 374-378. You will be asked to write the paradigm only of the 37 nouns which you practiced in this unit.
3) when shown the picture and given the first letter of each word, to write the new Basic Sentence.

If you cannot recall the meaning of these new words, you can refer to the frame indicated, where they first occurred.

There was one new adjective in this unit:

nūlla (314)

There were these new nouns:

juvenis   oculus   poena
juvenem   oculum   poenam
juvene (202)   oculō (275)   poenā (314)

And these verbs:

manet (145)
stat (254)

9-77

9-39

203. Echo. ★ ○ • ○ • English "juvenile," Latin **juvenis**

204. Latin **j** sounds like the English sound "___."

A: y.

205. Echo your teacher as he describes the following pictures, all of which use the ablative of a Third Declension noun, ending in **-e**.
★ ○ • ○ • J_____ cum īn_____ c_____.

VCh: **Juvenis cum īnfante currit.**

206. ★ ○ • ○ • V__ ___ j_____ c_____.

VCh: **Vir cum juvene currit.**

207. ★ ○ • ○ • Eq___ ___ c___ c_____.

VCh: **Equus cum cane currit.**

9-76

391. Vulpēs belongs to the ____ (First/Second/Third) Declension.

A: Third

392. The characteristic vowel of the Third Declension is --- or ----.

A: e i.

393. In this Unit you also did some work on English _____ s of Latin words.

A: derivatives

394. You learned one new Basic Sentence, 19.
Nū__ av_____ s_____ p___ _t.

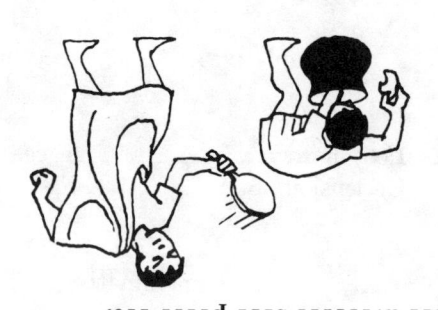

A: **Nūlla avāritia sine poenā est.**

395. This means, "_____."

A: There is no greed without punishment.

VOCABULARY INVENTORY

In this Unit you learned about a new kind of word, called a preposition, which is used with nouns to make them modify some other word. You learned these prepositions:

cum (38)
in (27)
sine (169)

9-40

208. ★ ○ • ○ • El_____ ___ _____
_____.

VCh: **Elephantus cum leōne currit.**

209. ★ ○ • ○ • C_____.

VCh: **Canis cum vulpe currit.**

210. Say the same descriptions of the same pictures. E____ ___ c___ **currit.**

A: **Equus cum cane currit.**

---

384. The collected forms of a noun are called a par-_____.

A: paradigm.

385. Nouns that change their form in the same way are said to belong to the same d-_____.

A: declension.

386. The characteristic vowel is the one that shows up in the _____ case.

A: ablative

387. **Lupus** belongs to the ---- (First/Second/Third) declension.

A: Second

388. The characteristic vowel of the Second Declension is ----.

A: **o**.

389. **Fovea** belongs to the ---- (First/Second/Third) Declension.

A: First

390. The characteristic vowel of the First Declension is ----.

A: **a**.

9-75

9-41

211. El_____ l____ c_____.

A: Elephantus cum leōne currit.

212. V__ ___ j_____ c_____.

A: Vir cum juvene currit.

213. J_____ ___ in___t_ c_____.

A: Juvenis cum īnfante currit.

214. C_____ ___ v____ c_____.

A: Canis cum vulpe currit.

9-74

378. As an example of the Third Declension with the nominative in -s, write the forms of piscis.

nom   piscis
acc   piscem
abl   pisce

379. Now let's hope that you will *never* have to use your notebook. But we have discovered that in learning, when more and more information accumulates, there may come a time when you seem to have forgotten everything. This happens to different people at different times. You know that you have to master these Latin forms; you also know that if a time ever comes when you get mixed up you can -----------------------------.

A: look in your Reference Note-book.

SUMMARY

380. In this Unit you learned a new case called the _____ case.

A: ablative

381. The only use of this case which you have seen so far has been to m_____ verbs.

A: modify

382. To show "in the company of," we use the ablative with the preposition ----.

A: cum.

383. To show "by means of," as in the expression "by means of money," we use the ablative ---- (with/without) a preposition.

A: without

Echo the paradigms of these Third Declension nouns. [Repeat until you have learned them.]

	215. ★ ○ •	216. ★ ○ •	217. ★ ○ •
nominative	laus	dátor	fraus
accusative	laudem	datórem	fraudem
ablative	laude	datóre	fraude

	218. ★ ○ •	219. ★ ○ •
nominative	fūr	piscis
accusative	fūrem	piscem
ablative	fūre	pisce

220. Now see if you can predict the ablative of the Third Declension noun **vestis**.

nom	vestis
acc	vestem
abl	_____

A: **veste**

221. Fraude is the _____ case of a _____ Declension noun.

A: ablative   Third

222. In all the Third Declension nouns which you have practiced, the characteristic vowel that occurs in the ablative is the vowel ___.

A: **e**.

223. The characteristic vowel of the Third Declension, however, is either **e** or **i**. At this point you have seen the **i** only in the nominative of some words. The characteristic vowel in the nominative form **vulpēs** is **e**, but the characteristic vowel in the nominative form **vestis** is ___.

A: **i**.

---

372. A current of water that is ___ing.

A: running.

373. If you liked working with these derivatives, _____, you will have a chance to do more of them later on.

A: deriva-tives

374. All the First Declension nouns which you will meet this year are declined alike. Write in your Reference Notebook under "Forms," "First Declension." Check carefully to make sure that three forms of **fēmina** and label them "First Declension." [Of course your Reference Notebook is accurate. You may write these forms on your 3 by 5 cards if you prefer.]

nom	fēmina
acc	fēminam
abl	fēminā

375. Now write in your Notebook the forms of **agnus** and label them "Second Declension."

nom	agnus
acc	agnum
abl	agnō

376. There is a small class of Second Declension nouns which have the signal zero for the nominative. These nouns all end in the sound /r/. Write **vir** as a sample of this type.

nom	vir
acc	virum
abl	virō

377. Write in your Notebook the forms of **fūr** and label "Third Declension."

nom	fūr
acc	fūrem
abl	fūre

224. And in some form of some words, the characteristic vowel is zero. The characteristic vowel before the signal -s in the Third Declension noun **vēritās** is ____ (e/i/Ø)

A: Ø.

225. We mention such things as "characteristic vowels," because we want you to understand that each language has its own system. We want you to learn something about the _____ of Latin and English.

A: system

226. This talk *about* the system helps some people to learn to operate the system. Our main interest, however, is to teach you how to operate the system, that is, to learn how to r___ L____.

A: read Latin.

227. Let us now go back to practice on the ablative. In this sequence you will be given two nominatives, as in the expression **Aper et sīmia**, which means, "The ____ and the _____."

A: boar   monkey.

228. You are to change the second noun (which we will put in italics) to the ablative with **cum**, like this: **Aper et *sīmia*** becomes **Aper cum sīmiā. Aper cum sīmiā** means, "_____ _____."

A: The boar with the monkey.

---

366. A *laudatory* message is one which s_____ someone.

A: praises

367. You may not believe it, but there is such a word as *agnification*. It means representing people as looking or acting like ____s.

A: lambs.

368. *Manual* labor is labor that is done by _____.

A: hand.

369. If you heard that some one had made a *mordant* remark, you would know that this was a ___ing remark.

A: biting

370. *Nocturnal* animals are those that are active chiefly at _____.

A: night.

371. You would go to an *oculist* if you had trouble with your ___s.

A: eyes.

229. Now make the change yourself: **Aper *et sīmia*** → A___ c__ s___ā. ✓ ★ ○ •

VCh: **Aper cum sīmiā.**

Do the same in the next 2 frames.

230. **Vulpēs *et lupus*** → **Vulpēs cum** l__ō.
✓ ★ ○ •

VCh: **Vulpēs cum lupō**

231. **Juvenis *et mūs*** → J_____ **cum** m__e
✓ ★ ○ •

VCh: **Juvenis cum mūre**

[Just a reminder here. Are you proceeding properly by giving your answer *before* you check? Or are you doing it the "easy" way and merely echoing? If you find the sequence too hard, then you should *go back* to a place in the program where you feel secure and start again.]

232. **Musca *et agnus*** → M____ c__ a__ō
✓ ★ ○ •

VCh: **Musca cum agnō**

233. **Dator *et rāna*** → D____ c__ r__ā
✓ ★ ○ •

VCh: **Dator cum rānā**

234. **Asinus *et aeger*** → As____ ___ ___ō
✓ ★ ○ •

VCh: **Asinus cum aegrō**

A: shadow

365. If you were to read that a certain event adumbrated the future, you would know that it gave a faint ------ of what was to come.

A: monkey.

364. If someone said that your features were *simian*, you would know that he thought you looked like a -------

A: dog.

363. The *canine* teeth in a human are the four pointed teeth on either side of the jaw. They are so called from their resemblance to the teeth of a ----

A: ears

362. If you had been told that this course required a lot of *aural* work, you would know that you would have to use your ----s a great deal.

235. **Anus** *et aquila* → An__ c__ a____ā
✓ ★ ○ •

VCh: **Anus cum aquilā**

236. **Rāna** *et vir* → R___ c__ v__ō

VCh: **Rāna cum virō**

237. **Elephantus** *et equus* →
El_____ c__ e__ō ✓ ★ ○ •

VCh: **Elephantus cum equō**

238. **Medicus** *et vulpēs* →
M_____ c__ v__e ✓ ★ ○ •

VCh: **Medicus cum vulpe**

239. **Aeger** *et juvenis* → A____ c__ j____e
✓ ★ ○ •

VCh: **Aeger cum juvene**

240. **Leō** *et aper* → L__ c__ a__ō ✓ ★ ○ •

VCh: **Leō cum aprō**

241. **Fūr** *et asinus* → F__ c__ a___ō
✓ ★ ○ •

VCh: **Fūr cum asinō**

---

358. Shakespeare says, "Basons and ewers to *lave* her dainty hands." Because of Latin, you know that "to lave" means "to ____."

A: wash.

359. Many proper names come from Latin. The name *Hilary* means "____ful."

A: cheerful.

360. This child is ____ (well/poorly) named.

"Hilary"

A: poorly

361. If we were to describe this person as *asinine*, we would mean that he acts like a _____

A: donkey.

9-46

242. Īrātus et musca → Ī____ c__ m___ā
√ ★ ○ •

VCh: Īrātus cum muscā

243. Canis et vīpera → C____ c__ v___ā
√ ★ ○ •

VCh: Canis cum vīperā

244. Taurus et fēmina →
T_____ c__ f_____ √ ★ ○ •

VCh: Taurus cum fēminā

245. Lupus et fūr → L____ c__ f__e
√ ★ ○ •

VCh: Lupus cum fūre

246. Īnfāns et leō → Ī____ c__ l__e
√ ★ ○ •

VCh: Īnfāns cum leōne

247. Piscis et elephantus →
P____ c__ e_____ √ ★ ○ •

VCh: Piscis cum elephantō

248. Aquila et piscis → A_____ c__ p____
√ ★ ○ •

VCh: Aquila cum pisce

---

353. In the previous frame you may have wondered why Latin **vēritās** is "verity," in English. **-tās** regularly changes to "ty" in English. For example, the English derivative of the word **pūritās** is "pur___."

A: purity.

354. Let's continue. Something which is per-*manent* is something which is going to r_____ forever.

A: remain

355. The "per-" in "permanent" is a "prefix" (syllable put at the start of a word). The prefix "per-" makes the verb stronger and gives it the meaning "remains a long time." The "-nt" part is a form used to change a verb into adjective. But right now all we wish you to do is to see that the word "permanent" is derived from the Latin verb _____.

A: manet.

356. A person who acts in a *furtive* manner acts like a _____.

A: thief.

357. An *umbrageous* location would be one that had a lot of _____s.

A: shadows.

9-47

249. Fēlīcitās *et* īnfāns →
F_____ c__ ī_____ ✓ ★ ○ •

VCh: **Fēlīcitās cum īnfante**

250. Sapientia *et* medicus →
S_____ c__ m_____ ✓ ★ ○ •

VCh: **Sapientia cum medicō**

251. Equus *et* canis → E____ c__ c___
✓ ★ ○ •

VCh: **Equus cum cane**

252. Sapientia *et* Fortūna →
S_____ c__ F_____ ✓ ★ ○ •

VCh: **Sapientia cum Fortūnā**

253. Echo your teacher as he uses a new verb that means "stands" to say that the woman is standing with the man. ★ ○ • ○ • **Fēmina cum virō stat.**

Fēmina   vir

9-68

348. Even if you have never seen or heard the English word "taurine" before, you can probably guess that it means "l___ a _____."

A: like a bull.

349. The ending -**culus** on a Latin noun means that this noun is a little one of its kind. For example, the word **rāniculus** (rān- plus -iculus) means a _____ _____.

A: little frog.

350. The Latin word **mūsculus** (mūs plus -culus) means "a _____ m_____."

A: a little mouse.

351. A *muscle* gets its name from the fact that people once thought a muscle looked like a little _____ running under the skin.

A: mouse.

352. If you read that a writer deals with an eternal "verity," you know that he discusses an eternal _____.

A: truth.

254. Using this pattern of **Fēmina cum virō stat**, describe the following pictures. Use some of the nouns of the last sequence. You have to choose between the endings -ā, ō, and -e.
M_____ cum ____ stat. √ ★ ○ •

medicus   vir

VCh: **Medicus cum virō stat.**

255. J_____ c__ _____ sta__.

fēmina   juvenis

VCh: **Juvenis cum fēminā stat.**

256. Īn____ cum ____ st___. √ ★ ○ •

īnfāns   canis

VCh: **Īnfāns cum cane stat.**

9-49

257. L__ c__ e_____ ____. ✓ ★ ○ •

leō   elephantus

VCh: **Leō cum elephantō stat.**

258. V_____ ___ t____ ____. ✓ ★ ○ •

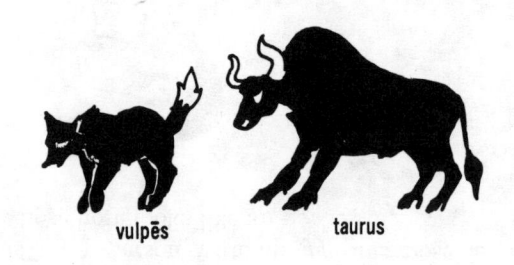

vulpēs   taurus

VCh: **Vulpēs cum taurō stat.**

259. F__ ___ s____ stat. ✓ ★ ○ •

fur   sīmia

VCh: **Fūr cum sīmiā stat.**

9-66

343. If someone said this to you, you would not be so alarmed, because you would know that it was only a ---- in the pond.

"I just saw a rāna catooboiana!"

A: frog

344. Words with Latin origins are common in literature, and your knowledge of Latin will enable you to read much faster, because many new words will be instantly recognized since you know the Latin word from which the English word was -----ed.

A: derived.

345. **Equīnus** is a Latin adjective formed from the stem of the word for "horse," and the ending **-īnus** that means "like." There are numerous English words ending in "-ine" that refer to animals. For example, if someone said you had an *equine* laugh, it would mean that your laugh sounded like a ------.

A: horse.

260. The sentence **Fūr cum sīmiā stat** is an {-- --} sentence with the verb's modifier c-- s----.

A: {-s -t}
cum sīmiā.

261. Therefore you know that **stat** is ---- (a transitive verb/an intransitive verb).

A: an intransitive verb.

262. We will run through the same set of pictures again, but instead of saying that the thief is standing with the monkey, we will let the monkey play the starring role and say that the monkey is standing with the thief. Remember to say your answers aloud. S---- c--- f--- st--.

A: Sīmiā cum fūre stat.

263. F---- c-- j----- ----.

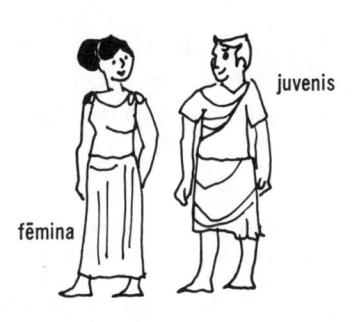

A: Fēmina cum juvene stat.

---

339. Scientific terms are almost always constructed from either Greek or Latin words. We will give you some illustrations. We wish you to figure out from your knowledge of Latin, italics part of the word whose meaning we wish Don't worry about how to pronounce these new English words.

A capillary tube is one with a hole in it the size of a ----.

A: hair.

340. When biologists speak of *foveated* bones, they refer to bones that have small ----s in them.

A: pits

341. If an animal is *piscivorous*, you know that he eats ----.

A: fish.

342. There is an order of insects that has a single pair of membranous wings, called the *muscidae* family. You know that in this family belongs the insect that we call the ----.

A: fly.

9-51

264. T_____ ___ v____ ____.

vulpēs *taurus*

A: Taurus cum vulpe stat.

265. E_____ ___ l_____ ____.

leō *elephantus*

A: Elephantus cum leōne stat.

266. C_____ ___ īn_____.

juvenis *canis*

A: Canis cum īnfante stat.

9-64

334. You may have noticed how often we relate Latin words to English. For example, the English word "juvenile" is derived from Latin j-----is.

A: juvenis.

335. Therefore when people speak of "juvenile delinquency" they are talking about the problems raised by ----- people.

A: young

336. Often we have not bothered to point out the relationship because it was so obvious. We didn't want to insult your intelligence by pointing out that the Latin word **īnfāns/īnfantem** was the source of the English word "------."

A: infant. (Or was that so obvious?)

337. The problem of learning vocabulary is greatly simplified in Latin because there are so many English der--------s.

A: derivatives.

338. There is another side to the coin. Knowing Latin will be of the greatest assistance to you in figuring out the meaning of unknown words in English. We will show you how this works by giving you a number of sentences that contain words which we are quite sure very few of you know. But you will be able to figure out the unknown words because you know the ----- words from which they are derived.

A: Latin

9-52

267. V__ ___ m_____ _____.

A: **Vir cum medicō stat.**

268-269. Echo the paradigms of these Third Declension nouns.

	268. ★ ○ •	269. ★ ○ •
nom	mūs	leō
acc	mūrem	leōnem
abl	mūre	leōne

270. Now with these as a model, write the paradigm of **īnfāns**. _____ [Only the nominative has the macron over ā.]

A: īnfāns
īnfantem
īnfante

271. Now write the paradigm of **leō**. _____

A: leō
leōnem
leōne

---

328. "Quis vītam regit?" "_____."

A: Fortūna.

329. "Quis vītam nōn regit?" "_____."

A: Sapientia.

330. Nū__ av____ s___ p___ e___. (19)

A: **Nūlla avāritia sine poenā est.** (19)

331. Echo the paradigm of the question word.

★ ○ •
nom Quis?
acc Quem?
abl Quō?

332. Sine quō? means, "_____ whom?" or "_____ what?"

A: Sine quō? Without whom?
Without what?

333. "Sine quō est nūlla avāritia?" "_____."

A: Sine poenā.

9-53

272. Echo your teacher as he describes this picture. J_____ oc____ h____. ★ ○ • ○ •

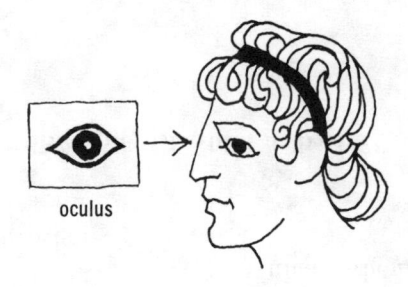

VCh: **Juvenis oculum habet.**

273. Using the question word **quis?**, ask your teacher in Latin who has a cruel eye: "Q___ oc____ crūdēlem ha____?" √ ★ ○ •

VCh: "**Quis oculum crūdēlem habet?**"

274. Write down his answer ★ ○ ○ "_____."

A: _____ **Juvenis.**

275. Echo the paradigm of this new word.

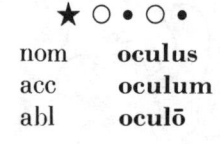

★ ○ • ○ •

    nom   **oculus**
    acc   **oculum**
    abl   **oculō**

276. Echo your teacher's description of this picture. ★ ○ • ○ •

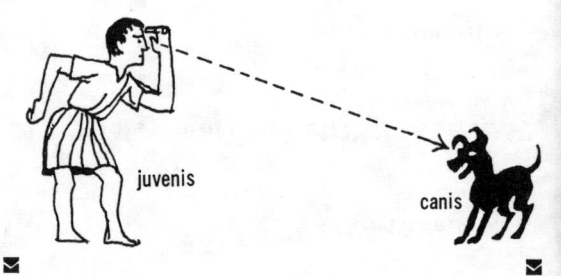

VCh: **Juvenis canem videt.**

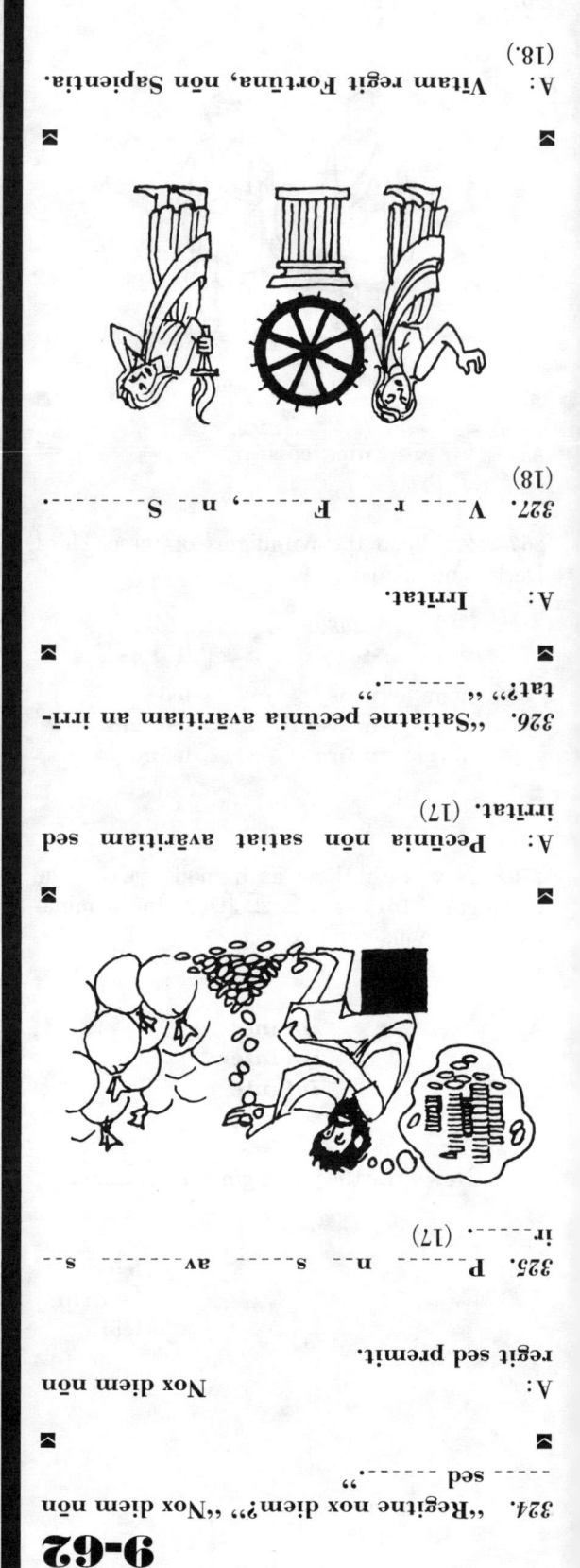

9-62

324. "Regitne nox diem?" "Nox diem nōn _____ sed _____."

A: **Nox diem nōn regit sed premit.**

325. P____ n____ s____ av____ s____ ir____. (17)

A: **Pecūnia nōn satiat avāritiam sed irrītat.** (17)

326. "Satiatne pecūnia avāritiam an irrītat?" "_____."

A: **Irrītat.**

327. V____ r____ F____ n____ S____. (18)

A: **Vītam regit Fortūna, nōn Sapientia.** (18)

277. This is an {-- -- --} type of sentence.

A: {-s -m -t}

278. The nominative noun **juvenis** is the _____ of the sentence, and the accusative noun **canem** is the _____.

A: subject   object.

279. Sometimes an ablative noun is used without any preposition to modify the verb and tell HOW something happens. Your teacher will repeat the last Latin sentence, but he will add a word in the ablative case to say HOW the young man sees the dog, and tell you that he sees him BY MEANS OF HIS EYE. Chorus. ★○○◉◉

VCh: **Juvenis canem OCULŌ videt.**

280. In this sentence the ablative noun **oculō** is used to m_____ the verb and tell ___ the young man sees the dog.

A: modify   how

281. In the sentence **Juvenis canem oculō videt**, the word **oculō** means "by m___s of his eye."

A: by means of

282. The ablative form **fraude** means "_____ of tr_____."

A: by means of trickery.

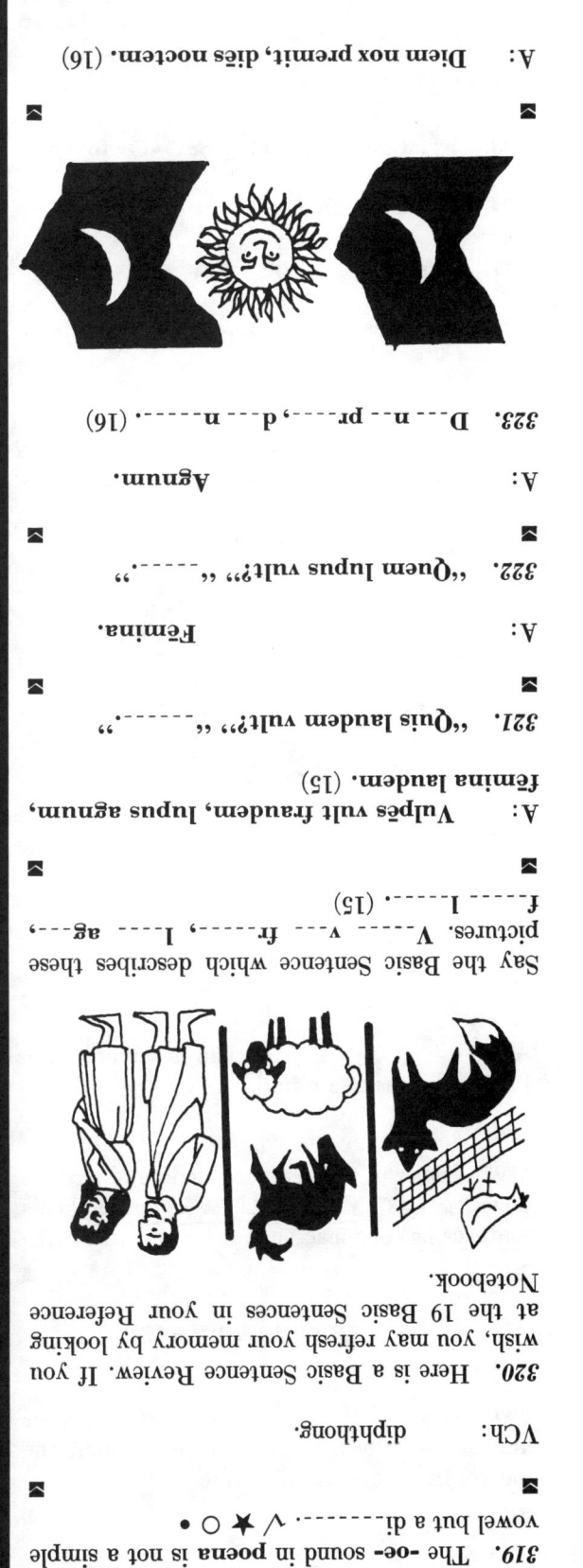

---

319. The -oe- sound in **poena** is not a simple vowel but a di------. ∧ ★ ○ •

VCh: diphthong.

320. Here is a Basic Sentence Review. If you wish, you may refresh your memory by looking at the 19 Basic Sentences in your Reference Notebook.

Say the Basic Sentence which describes these pictures. V----, v--- fr------, l---- ag---, f----- l------. (15)

A: **Vulpēs vult fraudem, lupus agnum, fēmina laudem.** (15)

321. "Quis laudem vult?" "------."

A: **Fēmina.**

322. "Quem lupus vult?" "------."

A: **Agnum.**

323. D---n- pr----d---n------. (16)

A: **Diem nox premit, diēs noctem.** (16)

283-286. Echo your teacher as he gives the Latin for the following phrases:

283. by means of a pitfall ★○•○• **foveā**

284. by means of money ★○•○• **pecūniā**

285. by means of greed ★○•○• **avāritiā**

286. by means of the shadow ★○•○• **umbrā**

287. Echo your teacher as he describes this picture and tells HOW the man is catching the boar.

★ ○ • ○ • **Vir aprum foveā capit.**

288. This means that the ___ is _____ a ____ by _____ __ a _____.

A: the man is catching a boar by means of a pitfall.

289. Listen to this sentence again and write it down. ★ ○ ○ V__ ap___ f____ c_____. [This sentence has one macron.]

A: **Vir aprum foveā capit.**

290. If you left the macron off **foveā** your answer was *wrong*, because **fovea** (without the macron) is the _____ case.

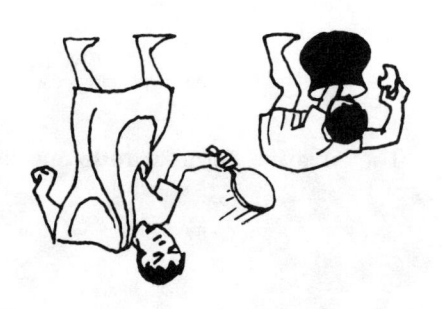

A: nominative

314. Pronounce and check. **Nūlla avāritia sine poenā est.** (19) ∨ ★ ○ •

315. This means that ----------------------.

A: there is no greed without punishment.

316. This means that people who are greedy are always eventually -------ed.

A: punished.

317. There is no greed without punishment =
N--- av------ s--- p---- e---.

318. Copy Basic Sentence 19 and its meaning in your Reference Notebook.

A: **Nūlla avāritia sine poenā est.** (19)

9-56

291. Echo your teacher as he describes this picture. ★ ○ • ○ • **Vir fēminam pecūniā satiat.**

292. Listen to this sentence again and write it down. ★ ○ ○ <u>V__</u> <u>fēm___</u> <u>p_____</u> <u>sat___</u>. [This sentence has three macrons.]

A: **Vir fēminam pecūniā satiat.** (If you don't have a tape recorder, copy the sentence.)

293. This means that the ___ is _____ the _____ __ _____ __ _____.

A: the man is satisfying the woman by means of money.

294. The woman in the last picture was not greedy; this one unfortunately is, and it annoys her friend. Echo your teacher as he describes this picture. ★ ○ • ○ • **Fēmina virum avāritiā irrītat.**

9-59

307. Write. ★ ○ ○ <u>N____</u> <u>a_____</u>

A: **Nūlla avāritia**

308. Echo the complete sentence. ★ ○ • ○ • **Nūlla avāritia sine poenā est.** (19)

309. Write. ★ ○ ○ <u>Nūlla</u> <u>avāritia</u> <u>s___</u> <u>p__ __t</u>.

A: **Nūlla avāritia sine poenā est.** (19)

310. This is an {__ __} sentence.

A: {-s -t}

311. So you know that est is ____ (a transitive verb/an intransitive verb).

A: an intransitive verb.

312. **Nūlla** is an adjective that means "no." The verb **est** in this sentence means "There is." **Nūlla avāritia est** = There -- gr----.

A: There is no greed.

313. Echo the paradigm of the word for "punishment."

★ ○ • ○ •
nom **poena**
acc **poenam**
abl **poenā**

295. This means that _____.

A: _____ the woman is irritating the man by means of her greed.

296. The boy is irritated because the elephant is interfering with his sunbath. Describe the picture in Latin. El_____ j_____ um___ irr_____.

A: Elephantus juvenem umbrā irrītat.

297. The sentence **Elephantus juvenem irrītat** is an {__ __ __} sentence.

A: {-s -m -t}

298. The sentence **Elephantus juvenem umbrā irrītat** is still an {-s -m -t} type of sentence, but it is expanded with a _____ of the {-t}.

A: _____ modifier

299. Elephantus juvenem umbrā irrītat = _____.

A: The elephant is irritating the young man by means of his shadow.

Say and write the Latin for the following expressions.

300. by means of money = pec___ _____

A: pecūniā

301. By means of (his) ear = au___ _____

A: aure

302. By means of a hair = capi___ _____

A: capillō

303. By means of praise = lau___ _____

A: laude

304. By means of a law = lē___ _____

A: lēge

305. Where English uses the phrase "by means of," Latin uses the _____ case without a preposition.

A: ablative

306. Now for Basic Sentence 19. Echo the first part. ✱ ○ • ○ • **Nūlla avāritia**

To continue the program, turn your book around and begin work on column 9-58.